Fundamentals of Marketing

Fundamentals of Marketing

SECOND EDITION

Paul **Baines**

Sophie **Whitehouse**

Paolo **Antonetti**

Sara **Rosengren**

Great Clarendon Street, Oxford, OX2 6DP,
United Kingdom

Oxford University Press is a department of the University of Oxford.
It furthers the University's objective of excellence in research, scholarship,
and education by publishing worldwide. Oxford is a registered trade mark of
Oxford University Press in the UK and in certain other countries

© Oxford University Press 2021

The moral rights of the authors have been asserted

First edition 2017
Second edition 2021

Impression: 1

All rights reserved. No part of this publication may be reproduced, stored in a retrieval system, or transmitted, in any form or by any means, without the prior permission in writing of Oxford University Press, or as expressly permitted by law, by licence or under terms agreed with the appropriate reprographics rights organization. Enquiries concerning reproduction outside the scope of the above should be sent to the Rights Department, Oxford University Press, at the address above

You must not circulate this work in any other form
and you must impose this same condition on any acquirer

Published in the United States of America by Oxford University Press
198 Madison Avenue, New York, NY 10016, United States of America

British Library Cataloguing in Publication Data
Data available

Library of Congress Control Number: 2020947517

ISBN 978–0–19–882925–6

Printed in Great Britain by
Bell & Bain Ltd., Glasgow

Links to third party websites are provided by Oxford in good faith and for information only. Oxford disclaims any responsibility for the materials contained in any third party website referenced in this work.

To Ning, for making life interesting.
Paul Baines

To Mum, my greatest teacher.
Sophie Whitehouse

To Qianni and Alice, for making everything better.
Paolo Antonetti

To Olof, Alma, and Moa—my own dream team.
Sara Rosengren

Brief Contents

Detailed Contents

Case Insights

Case Insight 1.1 Aldoraq Water

Established in 1994 by Khaled A. Almaimani, Aldoraq Water Bottling Plant was one of the first water bottling factories in Madinah, Saudi Arabia. We speak to Abdurahman Almaimani, general manager, to find out more about how the company seeks to compete with well-known international brands.

Case Insight 2.1 Aircall

Aircall is the cloud-based phone system of choice for modern brands, with over 300 employees across its Paris and New York offices. It is a trusted provider around the world. We speak to Carly Dell, director, demand generation at Aircall, to find out how the company shifted its customers from buying a monthly service subscription to buying an annual one.

Case Insight 3.1 CLiKD

CLiKD is an award-winning dating app based in London that gives people a creative way to meet new people. We speak to Emin Can Turan, head of marketing, to find out how this SME competes with much bigger rivals in the online dating world by leveraging marketing analytics data.

Case Insight 4.1 3scale

Through its staff and offices in Barcelona and San Francisco, 3scale helps organizations open, manage, and use application programming interfaces (APIs). We speak to Manfred Bortenschlager, API market development director, to find out how the company competes in its marketplace.

Case Insight 5.1 Lanson International

Founded in 1760, Champagne Lanson is one of the oldest existing Champagne Houses in France, making some of the world's finest champagnes. We speak to Paul Beavis, MD, Lanson International, to find out more about how the company looks to further develop its presence in international markets, including the UK.

Case Insight 6.1 Micro-Fresh

We speak to Jigna Varu, the chief commercial officer, to find out how Micro-Fresh® has helped to maintain distribution of its product with the Away from Home Channel throughout the Covid-19 crisis.

Case Insight 7.1 Ammon Zeus

Ammon Zeus is a leading luxury hotel in Halkidiki, the popular tourist destination, in northern Greece. We speak to Efrosini Psychopoulou, its vice president, to find out more about how the company sought to develop its value proposition.

Case Insight 8.1 *The Guardian*

How could an organization realize its objective not only to shift audience perceptions but also to change behaviours? We speak to Agathe Guerrier, strategy director at the advertising agency Bartle Bogle Hegarty, to find out more about the work it undertook for its client *The Guardian*.

Case Insight 9.1 Pepsi Cola Colombia

Pepsi Cola Colombia Ltd has sold PepsiCo beverages in Colombia through Postobon SA since 1947, when PepsiCo Colombia signed an exclusive bottler agreement for a lifetime, the only such agreement at PepsiCo in the world. We speak to Catalina Dixon, a customer management senior analyst, to find out how Pepsico Colombia has helped maintain distribution of its product with the Away from Home Channel throughout the Covid-19 crisis.

Case Insight 10.1 Spotify

What role do social media play and how should organizations incorporate them into their communication campaigns? We talk to Chug Abramowitz, VP global customer service and social media at Spotify, to find out more.

Case Insight 11.1 Novartis

Employing approximately 108,000 people across the globe, Novartis's treatments reach more than 750 million people and are available in approximately 155 countries. We speak to Mark Chakravarty, global head, communications & patient advocacy, Novartis Pharmaceuticals, to find out how this Swiss multinational communicates about its offerings in such a tightly regulated market.

Case Insight 12.1 Tarkett

With a history stretching back more than 140 years, Tarkett is a world leader in innovative flooring and sports surface solutions. We speak to Fabrice Barthélemy, CEO of Tarkett, to find out how this multinational flooring company, with headquarters based in France, innovates in a rapidly changing and increasingly sustainability-centric marketplace.

List of Figures

List of Tables

New to this Edition

In writing the second edition, we were mindful that we wanted to retain those features of the first edition that adopters and readers found interesting and helpful but also renew the text with new and exciting features that pique readers' curiosity about marketing. For this edition, we've included the following features:

- A new chapter on marketing, society, and sustainability and ethics; as well as updated coverage on digital and social media marketing, emphasizes the balance between traditional marketing theory and leading trends.
- One-third of the case insights have been updated and replaced to feature both established companies and successful start-ups such as Novartis (Switzerland), Aircall (France–USA), and PepsiCo (Colombia); including a case on marketing during the Covid-19 pandemic.
- Half of all market insights are new for this edition and constitute a broader range of European, digital, and ethics-focused examples to illustrate the reality of marketing in today's business world. New market insights include the Greek trading company STEROPAL's survival of the Greek economic crisis; how Dutch chocolatier Tony's Chocolonely raises awareness of slavery in the cocoa industry; and how the Danish consumer review website Trustpilot fights fake online reviews.

Author Profiles

Paul Baines is Professor of Political Marketing and Associate Dean (Business & Civic Engagement) at University of Leicester School of Business. He is author/co-author of over a hundred published journal articles, book chapters, and books. Over the last twenty years, Paul's research has particularly focused on political marketing, marketing, and propaganda and has been published in, inter alia, *Journal of the American Statistical Association*, *European Journal of Marketing*, *Journal of Business Research*, and *Psychology & Marketing*. He is a Fellow of the Market Research Society and the Institute of Directors and a member of the Academy of Marketing. Paul's consultancy work includes extensive experience working with various UK and overseas government departments on strategic communication research projects as well as many small, medium, and large private enterprises including Saint Gobain Glassolutions, IBM, 3M, and many more. Paul is a non-executive director of the Business Continuity Institute and Director of Baines Associates Limited.

Sophie Whitehouse is member of the teaching staff at the University of Leicester with a particular focus on marketing in the creative industries. An Associate Fellow of the Higher Education Academy, Sophie has over six years of experience in leading and delivering undergraduate and postgraduate marketing education and has earned university honours for excellence in teaching. Sophie holds a PhD in marketing, a master's degree in English language and linguistics, and a bachelor's degree in management with marketing.

Paolo Antonetti is Professor of Marketing and Academic Director of the Global Executive MBA at NEOMA Business School (France). His research interests lie in the area of consumer emotions and especially the role of emotions in sustainability, corporate social responsibility, corporate social irresponsibility, and consumer ethics. His research has appeared in leading international publications including the *Journal of Service Research*, *Journal of Business Ethics*, *British Journal of Management*, *Journal of Business Research*, *European Journal of Marketing*, and *International Journal of Management Reviews*. Paolo is also an associate editor of the *Journal of Marketing Management*.

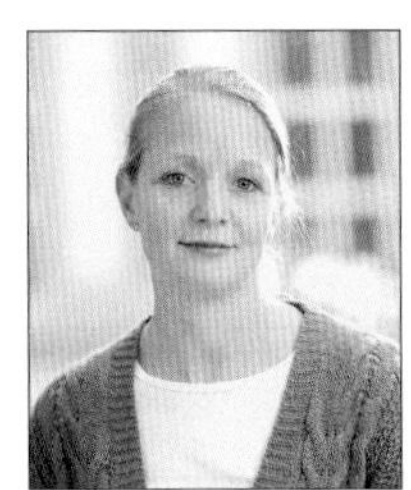

Sara Rosengren is Professor of Business Administration (Marketing) and holder of the ICA Retailers' Chair in Business Administration, especially Retailing at the Stockholm School of Economics where she also heads the school's Center for Retailing. Her research deals with consumer behaviour, marketing communications, and retailing and has been published in leading academic journals such as the *Journal of Marketing*, *Journal of Advertising*, *Journal of Business Research*, and *Journal of Advertising Research*. Sara is passionate about bridging the gap between marketing academy and practice. She is frequently invited to speak at academic institutions, industry seminars, and company get-togethers, and has received several awards for both her research and her teaching.

Acknowledgements

Course textbooks are substantial writing and research projects, resulting from the sweat and toil of many people in the design, development, and production of the text, and in the associated sales, marketing, and distribution tasks. Some of the people involved are outlined below, other contributors chose to remain anonymous, but their contributions deserve to be acknowledged nonetheless.

We would like to thank our colleagues at University of Leicester School of Business, the Stockholm School of Economics and NEOMA Business School for their support and discussions, all of which have made it into the book in some way. We would like to thank Ms. Yanjun Gao at Cranfield University for her excellent contributions to the Ancillary Resource Centre.

This work is the result of a co-production between the authors and Oxford University Press editors and staff. Consequently, we would like to thank Nicola Hartley, our commissioning editor, for her role in commissioning the work; Elena Chiu, our publishing editor, for her help in improving the content and format of the book, and incorporating the many comments of reviewers. We would like to thank Mrs Sumintra Gaur at SPI-Global and our production editor at OUP, Mairi Patterson, for their roles in shaping the final design of the book and bringing it out on schedule. We would also like to thank our friends at Oxford Digital Media for their superb work on video production for the Ancillary Resource Centre, including James Tomalin (for steadying the ship); and Matt Greetham and Fred Davis (for support with filming).

Unless our customers, students, and lecturers seek to use this book, there's little point writing and producing it, so we also recognize the efforts of the marketing team, Marianne Lightowler, head of marketing, and Robyn Hewett, OUP's marketing manager for natural and social sciences, for their help in devising and implementing the sales and marketing plans for the book. Thanks must also go to members of OUP's fantastic sales team, who are too numerous to mention, but who do a fantastic job of not just selling the book, but supporting the authors in finding case study organizations and interviewees, and who are always helpful when interfacing with our adopters.

The authors and publishers would like to thank the following people for their comments and reviews throughout the process of developing the text and the Ancillary Resource Centre:

Professor Norman Peng, University of Westminster, UK
Mr Joe Liddiatt, University of the West of England, UK
Professor Anne Odile Peschel, Aarhus University, Denmark
Dr Marilena Antoniadou, Manchester Metropolitan University, UK
Dr Nick Yip, University of East Anglia, UK
Ms Lianne van den Berg-Weitzel, Utrecht University of Applied Sciences, the Netherlands
Ms Monalisa Haque, University of Portsmouth, UK
Mr Stuart Carnell, Nottingham Trent University, UK
Dr Arooj Rashid, Nottingham Trent University, UK
Ms Birger Opstad, University of South-Eastern Norway, Norway

Professor Lina Fogt Jacobsen, Aarhus University, Denmark
Dr Lucill Curtis, University of East Anglia, UK
Ms Cheryl Greyson, Anglia Ruskin University, UK
Mr David Lane, Leeds Beckett University, UK
Mr George Szanto, Fontys University of Applied Sciences, the Netherlands
Dr Catherine Groves, Swansea University, Wales, UK
Dr Diliara Mingazova, University of East London, UK
Dr Jayne Heaford, King's College London, UK

We would particularly like to thank the following lecturers, students, and practitioners who have contributed market insights to the second edition:

Dr Ning Baines, De Montfort University, UK
Ms Marie O'Dwyer, Waterford Institute of Technology, Republic of Ireland
Mr Orlando Wood, Chief Innovation Officer, System1 Group, UK
Mr Ashwien Bisnajak, Market Intelligence Manager, Hunkemöller
Dr Rajiv Maher, Post-Doctoral Researcher at the Pontifical Catholic University of Chile
Dr Mona Sinha, Kennesaw State University, Georgia, USA
Mr Chris Liassides, University of Sheffield, International Faculty, CITY College, UK
Dr Niki Glaveli, Aristotle University of Thessaloniki, Greece
Dr Georgios Patsiaouras, School of Business, University of Leicester, UK
Dr Jonas Gunnarsson, Market and Consumer Research Manager at ICA AB, Sweden
Ms Jenny Li, Adjunct Lecturer in Marketing, NEOMA Business School, France
Ms Caitlin Sear, Master's Student, University of Bath, UK
Mr Karl Wikström, Planner, TBWA Stockholm, Sweden
Dr Erik Modig, Stockholm School of Economics, Sweden
Prof Iain Black, University of Stirling, Scotland, UK
Dr Frauke Mattison Thompson, Universiteit van Amsterdam, the Netherlands

We've also incorporated a series of practitioner marketing 'problems' within the text. This requires considerable commitment from practitioners to develop a marketing 'problem' with the authors and film the 'solution' to that problem. Consequently, we would like to thank the following practitioners for their time, effort, and commitment to this project:

Mr Abdurahman Almaimani, General Manager, Aldoraq Water Bottling Plant, Saudi Arabia
Ms Carly Dell, Director, Demand Generation, Aircall, France–USA
Mr Emin Can Turan, Head of Marketing, CLiKD, UK
Mr Manfred Bortenschlager, API Market Development Director, 3scale.net, Spain
Mr Paul Beavis, Managing Director, Champagne Lanson UK/International Markets, UK
Ms Jigna Varu, Chief Commercial Officer, Micro-Fresh®, UK
Ms Efrosini Psychopoulou, Vice President, Ammon Zeus, Greece
Mr Lubos Jahoda, Advertising Agency Account Director, Budweiser Budvar, Czech Republic
Ms Catalina Dixon, Customer Management Senior Analyst, Pepsico Colombia, Colombia

Mr Chug Abramowitz, VP Global Customer Service and Social Media, Spotify, Sweden–USA
Mr Mark Chakravarty, Global Pharma Head of Communication & Advocacy, Novartis, Switzerland
Mr Fabrice Barthélemy, CEO of Tarkett, Tarkett, France

A number of reviewers have chosen to remain anonymous even though they contributed considerably to the final proposition. We would like to thank them for taking their time to pour over various draft chapters of the book and provide us with invaluable feedback. The publishers would be pleased to clear permission with any copyright holders that we have inadvertently failed, or been unable, to contact.

Preface

Welcome to the second edition of *Fundamentals of Marketing*. The aim of this book is to provide an engaging and comprehensive text that covers all of the fundamental areas of marketing knowledge in a concise manner. Our research suggests that students need:

- a rigorous textbook (offering contemporary marketing insights) that is suitable for courses running over a single semester;
- an inspirational book, able to pique curiosity and inspire the next generation of marketers to excel in this exciting and fast-moving discipline;
- to be able to link marketing theory to marketing practice better—and, accordingly, the textbook offers several student-friendly 'market insight' vignettes in each chapter;
- a book that recognizes the need to go beyond the conventional '4Ps', and to offer extended insights on services, digital and social media marketing; to recognize the importance of ethical issues in marketing—an area given special attention in this text, with the introduction of one market insight in each chapter to deal with matters of ethics, corporate social responsibility, or sustainable marketing; and
- coverage of marketing in context, particularly from a European perspective.

Fundamentals of Marketing starts with a look at classical marketing perspectives, and contrasts these with contemporary perspectives from the services and societal schools of marketing, helping you to develop your knowledge and understanding of marketing. To recognize the importance of the service-dominant logic perspective now so prevalent in marketing, we have integrated content on services marketing into one chapter, although there remain a large number of case and market insights throughout the book which make use of services examples.

On the Ancillary Resource Centre, we also provide you with web-based research activities, abstracts from seminal papers, study guidelines, multiple-choice questions, and a flashcard glossary to help you to broaden and reinforce your own learning. We aim to provide powerful learning insights into marketing theory and practice through a series of 'insight' features—that is, case, market, and research insights.

Who Should Use this Book?

The main audiences for this book are as follows.

- Undergraduate students in universities and colleges of higher and further education, who are taught in English, around the world—The case material and the examples within the text are global and international in scale, so that international students can benefit from the text.

- Postgraduate students on MBA and MSc/MA courses with a strong marketing component—It is hoped that such readers will find this text useful for pre-course and background reading, particularly because of the real-life case studies presented at the beginning of each chapter, accompanied by audiovisual material presenting the solution(s) available at the Ancillary Resource Centre.
- Professional students studying for marketing qualifications through the Chartered Institute of Marketing, the Direct Marketing Association, and other professional training organizations and trade bodies—The extensive use of examples of marketing practice from around the world make this text relevant for those working in a marketing or commercial environment.

How to Use this Textbook

We have tried to make your learning fun and meaningful by including a multitude of real-life cases. If there is a seminal article associated with a particular concept, try to get hold of the article through your university's online library resources and read it. Reflect on your own experience, if possible, around the concepts you are studying. Above all, recognize that you are not on your own in your learning: you have your tutor, your classmates, and us to help you to learn more about marketing.

This textbook includes not only explanatory material and examples of the nature of marketing concepts, but also a holistic learning system designed to aid you, as part of your university or professional course, to develop your understanding through reading the text and working with the materials available in the Ancillary Resource Centre described in the following pages. Work through the examples in the text and the review questions; read the seminal articles that have defined a particular subdiscipline in marketing; use the learning material on the website. This textbook aims to be reader-focused, designed to help you to learn marketing for yourself.

To help your learning experience, we strongly suggest that you complete the exercises, visit the web links, and conduct the Internet activities and worksheets at the end of each chapter, and other activities available at the Ancillary Resource Centre, to improve your understanding and your course performance.

Learning such an exciting discipline as marketing should be both fun and challenging. We hope that this textbook and its online resources bring the discipline to life for you and pique your curiosity about how the marketing world works (and doesn't work).

Good luck with your learning and in your career!

Guide to the Book

This book comes equipped with a range of carefully designed learning features to help you get to grips with marketing and develop the essential knowledge and skills you'll need for your future career.

IDENTIFY & REVIEW *through* Learning Outcomes

Introducing you to every chapter, Learning Outcomes outline the main concepts and themes that will be covered to clearly identify what you can expect to learn. These bullet-pointed lists can also be used to review your learning and effectively plan your revision.

> **Learning Outcomes**
>
> **After reading this chapter, you will be able to:**
> - define the marketing concept;
> - explain how marketing developed over the twentieth and into the twenty-first centuries;
> - understand the exchange and marketing mix concepts in marketing;

LEARN & EVALUATE *through* Case Insights

Learn from the professionals with real-life case studies from leading marketers at organizations including Micro-Fresh, PepsiCo, and Novartis. Discover what their businesses aim to do, what their jobs involve, and what kind of challenges they face, before evaluating your own response to tackling their marketing problem. On the Ancillary Resource Centre you can find bespoke video interviews with all these professionals, and gain an insight into how they ultimately resolved their marketing dilemmas.

Case Insight 1.1 **Aldoraq Water**

Established in 1994 by Khaled
Water Bottling Plant was one o
factories in Madinah, Saudi Ara
Abdurahman Almaimani (pictu
find out more about how the c
with well-known international

ANALYSE & APPLY *through* Market Insights

Contemporary and varied examples from the business world illustrate the concepts discussed in the chapter, prompting you to analyse the marketing practices and apply the marketing theory to practical examples from a huge range of companies, with accompanying questions reinforcing your learning.

Market Insight 1.1 **Customer Obsessio**

As of 2019, customer-centric companies are often ranked as the most successful as they manage to attract new customers while maintaining strong relationships with existing ones. It is no longer only marketing departments that are focused on customers but the wider organization, often illustrated by the employee culture within it. The characteristics of such companies include their ability to provide personalized services and

RESEARCH & PROGRESS *through* Research Insights

Take your learning further with the key books and journal articles highlighted in Research Insights, to aid your research and progress your understanding of key topics.

Research Insight 1.1

To take your learning further, you might wish to read this in

Borden, N. H. (1964). 'The concept of the marketing mix'. ***Journ***

This easy-to-read, early article explains how marketing managers a

RECAP & CONSOLIDATE *through* Chapter Summaries

Recap the core themes and ideas of the chapter to consolidate and review your learning in these handy chapter summaries.

Chapter Summary

To consolidate your learning, the key points from this chapter are sum

- **Define the marketing concept.**

  Marketing is the process by which organizations anticipate and sa parties' benefit. It involves mutual exchange. Over the last twenty-fi

REVIEW & REVISE *through* Review Questions

Stimulating questions at the end of every chapter will review your knowledge and highlight any areas that need further revision ahead of the exam.

Review Questions

1. **How do we define the 'marketing' concept?**
2. **How do the AMA and the CIM definitions of marketing differ?**
3. **What is the difference between customers and consumers?**
4. **How has marketing developed historically?**

PRACTISE & UNDERSTAND *through* Worksheet Summaries

These useful summaries signpost to Worksheets available for each chapter on the Ancillary Resource Centre. Visit the Worksheets to put your new marketing knowledge into practice and reinforce your understanding.

Worksheet Summary

To apply the knowledge you have gained from this chapter and to **online resources** and complete Worksheet 1.1.

CHALLENGE & REFLECT *through* Discussion Questions

Develop your analytical and reasoning skills by challenging the theory and reflecting on key issues with these stimulating discussion questions designed to create lively debate.

Discussion Questions

1. Having read Case Insight 1.1 at the beginning of this chapter, how attempts to differentiate itself from national and international bra
2. Read the section 'The Marketing Mix and the 4Ps' and draw up ma organizations and their target customers.

LOOK UP & CHECK *through* Key Terms and Glossaries

Key terms are highlighted in blue when they first appear and are collated into Glossaries at the end of each chapter, designed for you to look up terms and check your understanding of essential definitions.

Glossary

advertising a form of non-personal communication, by an identified sponsor, transmitted through the use of paid-for media.

American Marketing Association (AMA) a

market orient whole-orga collection, a intelligence

Guide to the Online Resources

https://learninglink.oup.com/signin

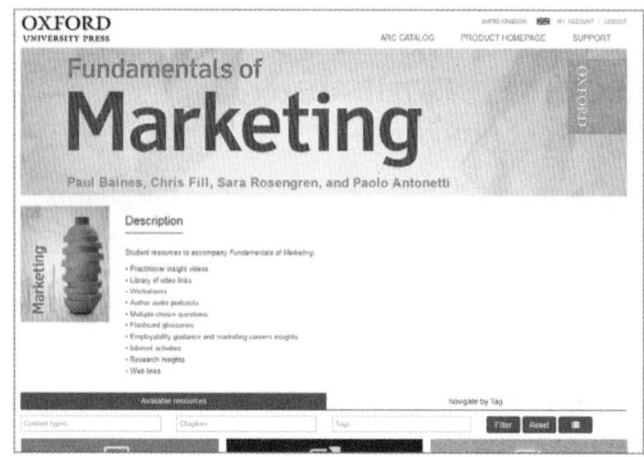

The Ancillary Resource Centre is signposted throughout the chapters and provides you with access to a superior selection of fully integrated online resources for both students and lecturers.

Understanding Customers

Part 1	Understanding Customers
Part 2	Designing and Delivering the Market Strategy
Part 3	Implementing the Marketing Mix
Part 4	Managing Marketing Relationships

1. Marketing Principles and Society
2. Understanding Customer Behaviour
3. Market Research and Customer Insight

Chapter 1
Marketing Principles and Society

Learning Outcomes

After reading this chapter, you will be able to:

- define the marketing concept;
- explain how marketing developed over the twentieth and into the twenty-first centuries;
- understand the exchange and marketing mix concepts in marketing;
- understand the role of the marketing department within the organization; and
- understand the positive contribution that marketing makes to society.

Case Insight 1.1
Aldoraq Water

Market Insight 1.1
Customer Obsession at First Direct

Market Insight 1.2
Servitization at Rolls-Royce

Market Insight 1.3
Google: World-Changing Innovations

Case Insight 1.1 **Aldoraq Water**

Established in 1994 by Khaled A. Almaimani, Aldoraq Water Bottling Plant was one of the first water bottling factories in Madinah, Saudi Arabia. We speak to Abdurahman Almaimani (pictured), general manager, to find out more about how the company seeks to compete with well-known international brands.

Aldoraq, headquartered in Madinah, Saudi Arabia, distributes its natural mineral water **products** throughout the Kingdom, and particularly in Madinah, Makkah, and Yanbu. It is one of the biggest factories in the Middle East, and a member of one of the oldest and largest family-owned businesses in Saudi Arabia. The company produces purified drinking water in different bottle sizes and capacities (from 250 ml to 5 gallon containers) and was the first water company in Saudi Arabia to join the International Bottled Water Association. The water produced by Aldoraq contains a good percentage of fluoride, is derived from natural water borewells, and is purified by ozone. In 2015, sales of the company's 250 ml, 375 ml, and 600 ml products were increasing strongly on 2014 sales, but falling slightly in the 2 litre, 1 gallon, 5 litre, and 5 gallon bottle categories. The 5 gallon refill category, however, saw a slight gain.

The future looks bright for bottled water in the Kingdom, with population growth expected at 20 per cent per year until 2019, growing retail infrastructure, and an increasing number of *baqalah* (small independent stores). Aldoraq's **customers** are mostly hypermarkets, supermarkets, and medium and small stores that distribute or sell bottled waters to **consumers** (restaurants, fast-food stores, canteens, hospitals, households, etc.). Other customers include catering companies, hotels, airport retail outlets, and corporate offices. Often, such customers are looking for **price** discounts, longer terms of payment, and even coolers in which to store the water. Distributors decide to buy bottled drinking water from the factory based on which products are available in time and can steadily be supplied to customers' volume requirements, and the terms of deals and consignments, including beneficial payment terms. Of particular importance to customers is their ability to buy all of the products they need from one location. Because there are more than thirty water distributors in Medinah, many customers base their decision on the price they pay.

To promote awareness of the brand, Aldoraq recommends that customers display the product prominently in their stores, in potential customers' line of sight, and Aldoraq offers volume discounts to its largest distributors accordingly. In addition, it supports the community by giving free water to charities, and discounted water to mosques and other religious places. Nevertheless, more recently, some large hotels and stores have started to purchase only premium water from companies selling international brands, such as Evian, Nestlé, and Aquafina, making it hard for Aldoraq to compete with them. These big brands are competing by trying to dominate the supply chain system. For example, Aquafina, owned by PepsiCo, is pushing its water product alongside other products such as Pepsi Cola. When Aquafina first entered the market, PepsiCo gave away free samples of water with the Pepsi product and then pushed customers to buy the Aquafina water brand from them at the same time as buying Pepsi. Coca-Cola also competed in this way with Arwa, its water product.

How should Aldoraq seek to differentiate itself, and thereby compete against both local and international brands?

Introduction

How have companies marketed their offerings to you in the past? Consider the last smartphone you bought, the music you stream, and the airlines on which you have flown. Why did you decide to purchase these offerings? Each one has been marketed to you to cater for a particular need that you have. Consider how the offering was distributed. What physical and service-based components is it made of? What societal contributions, if any, positive or negative, do these offerings make? Are other versions of these offerings available that meet your needs and the needs of society better? These are some of the questions that marketers should ask themselves when designing, developing, and delivering offerings to the customer.

This chapter develops our understanding of marketing principles and marketing's impact on society by defining 'marketing'. We consider the origins and development of marketing throughout the twentieth and into the twenty-first centuries. The core principles of marketing, incorporating the **marketing mix**, the principle of marketing exchange, **market orientation**, **relationship marketing**, and **service-dominant logic**, are all considered. We then discuss the role of marketing with organizations. Finally, we review the positive and negative impacts that marketing has on society.

What is Marketing?

There are numerous definitions of 'marketing', but we present three for easy reference in Table 1.1.

The Chartered Institute of Marketing (CIM) and American Marketing Association (AMA) definitions recognize marketing as a 'management process' and an 'activity', although many firms organize marketing as a discrete department, rather than as a service across departments (Sheth and Sisodia, 2005). Nike, for example, uses a regional matrix organizational structure, enabling marketing to operate within and across departments, such as apparel and footwear (Brenner, 2013).

What all of these definitions display is how the concept of marketing has changed over the years, from including only transactional concepts such as pricing, **promotion**, and distribution, to encompassing relationship concepts as well, such as the importance of customer trust, risk, commitment, and co-creation.

In addition, the nature of the relationships between an organization and its customers, in its offerings and its mission, are different in not-for-profit and for-profit organizations. Nevertheless, the broad principles of how marketing is used remain the same. All definitions recognize this widened concept of the wider societal applicability of marketing.

Visit the **online resources** and complete Internet Activity 1.1 to learn more about professional marketing associations around the world.

What's the Difference between Customers and Consumers?

What is the difference between a 'customer' and a 'consumer'? The difference is subtle, but real. A customer is a buyer, a purchaser, a patron, a client, or a shopper, and therefore someone who buys from a shop, a website, a business, or, in the sharing economy, another customer

Table 1.1 Definitions of marketing

Defining institution/author	Definition
CIM	The management process responsible for identifying, anticipating, and satisfying customer requirements profitably. (Chartered Institute of Marketing, 2015: 2)
AMA	Marketing is the activity, set of institutions, and processes for creating communicating, delivering, and exchanging offerings that have value for customers, clients, partners, and society at large. (American Marketing Association, 2017)
A French perspective	Le marketing est la stratégie d'adaptation des organisations à des marchés concurrentiels, pour influencer en leur faveur le comportement des publics dont elles dépendent, par une offre dont la valeur perçue est durablement supérieure à celle des concurrents. Dans le secteur marchand, le rôle du marketing est de créer de la valeur économique pour l'entreprise en créant de la valeur perçue par les clients. (Lendrevie and Lévy, 2014: 5) [Broadly translated:] Marketing is the adaptation strategy of organizations to competitive markets so that they can influence the behaviour of the customer segments on which they depend, through an offering whose perceived value is durably superior to that of competitors. In the commercial sector, the role of marketing is to create economic value for the company by creating value as perceived by customers.

(e.g. via Airbnb or eBay). The consumer is someone who uses the offering (or eats it, in the case of food).

To illustrate, consider Mondelez International's Dairylea Dunkers, dairy food designed to be a good source of calcium, with each pack contributing at least 26 per cent of the daily reference intake of calcium. In this case, the customer is the chief shopper, the parent or guardian, and the consumer is the child. Sometimes, the customer and consumer can be the same person, for example a woman buying cinema tickets for herself and a friend online.

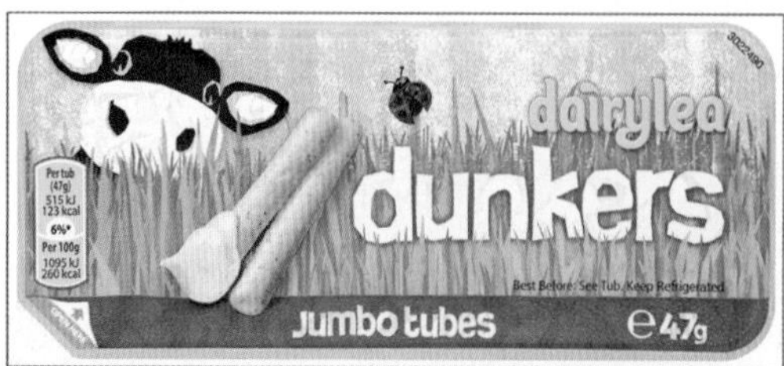

Dairylea Dunkers, the 'moo-vellous' snack for children.
Source: Reproduced with kind permission of Mondelez International.

Market Orientation

The concept of market orientation (Kohli and Jaworski, 1990) lies at the heart of marketing. Developing a market orientation makes organizations more profitable in both the long and short runs (Kumar et al., 2011). In a meta-analysis of market orientation studies, Kirca et al. (2005) conclude that market orientation may be imperative for survival in service firms and the source of competitive advantage in manufacturing firms.

But developing a market orientation is not the same as developing a market*ing* orientation. So what is the difference? A company with a marketing orientation would be a company that recognizes the importance of marketing within the organization, for example by appointing a marketing person as chief executive officer (CEO), or to chair its board of directors (or trustees in the case of a charity), or to the executive team more generally in a limited company or partnership.

Developing a market orientation refers to 'the organization-wide generation of market intelligence pertaining to current and future customer needs, dissemination of the intelligence across the departments, and organization-wide responsiveness to it' (Kohli and Jaworski, 1990: 3). So a market orientation not only involves marketing, but also requires a focus on:

- *customer orientation*, which is concerned with creating superior **value** by continuously developing and redeveloping offerings to meet customer needs (see Market Insight 1.1);
- *competitor orientation*, which requires an organization to develop an understanding of its competitors' short-term strengths and weaknesses, and its own long-term capabilities and strategies (Slater and Narver, 1994); and
- *interfunctional coordination*, which requires all functions of an organization to work together for long-term profit growth.

A Brief History of Marketing

Marketing developed in a four-stage sequence, as follows.

1. *Production period, 1890s–1920s*—The period was characterized by a focus in the firm on physical production and supply, where demand exceeded supply, there was little competition, and the range of products was limited. This phase came after the Industrial Revolution.
2. *Sales period, 1920s–50s*—The second period was characterized by a focus in the firm on personal selling supported by market research and **advertising**. This phase took place after the First World War.
3. *Marketing period, 1950s–80s*—Next came a more advanced focus in the firm on the customer's needs. This phase came after the Second World War.
4. *Societal marketing period, 1980s–present day*—Marketing then came to be characterized by a stronger focus on social and ethical concerns in marketing in the firm and recognition that not-for-profits could also undertake marketing. This phase took place during the 'information revolution' of the late twentieth century (Enright, 2002).

In the last twenty years, marketing practice has quickly evolved thanks to its increasing importance for boards of executives and the dramatic development of new technologies. Marketers have been able to focus on individual customers and gain further insights based on short feedback loops. More recently, marketing teams have become one of the key functions in many companies and have learned how to integrate with other business departments. In the meantime, the development of new digital media (see Chapter 10) has created novel opportunities for marketers to learn about and interact with existing and new customers (Kumar, 2015). Marketing, as a discipline, has developed

Market Insight 1.1 **Customer Obsession at First Direct**

As of 2019, customer-centric companies are often ranked as the most successful as they manage to attract new customers while maintaining strong relationships with existing ones. It is no longer only marketing departments that are focused on customers but the wider organization, often illustrated by the employee culture within it. The characteristics of such companies include their ability to provide personalized services and understand their customers' high expectations. Through their structure, customer-centric companies are also able to respond quickly to queries and solve the issues of unsatisfied customers in a timely manner. They also demonstrate empathy, the ability to understand customers' situations, and react accordingly. Finally, these companies develop integrity and a strong sense of purpose to generate trust from their customers. This last point is particularly helpful to attract younger customers who are keen to pay more for stronger brands.

This is the case at UK bank First Direct which excels at providing financial services. In 2019, the company was ranked first (among more than 300 brands) in terms of customer experience by KPMG's Customer Experience Excellence report. This is especially remarkable given that the bank does not have any physical branches and only interacts with its customers online and over the phone. The company has also been praised for its ability to solve customers' queries quickly while demonstrating empathy. To achieve such results, First Direct has successfully adapted to recent changes in how customers manage their accounts while maintaining a consistent service quality. In particular, the firm has managed to keep up with digital innovation and trends in the financial technology sector (fintech).

UK bank First Direct only operates online and over the phone.

Source: Mtaylor848/WikiMedia Commons (CC BY-SA 4.0).

For example, First Direct has closely worked with smaller companies to develop Open Banking solutions to allow third-party applications secure access to customers' accounts. First Direct also recently developed its co-creation platform 'fdesign' to gather customers' feedback on some of their new ideas.

1. **How can the integrity and trustworthiness of a brand help win the loyalty of existing and new customers?**
2. **With the rise of new digital banks such as Monzo and Starling, how can First Direct adapt its strategy to maintain its reputation as a top customer-oriented firm?**
3. **What other companies can you think of that would benefit from being more customer-oriented?**

Sources: KPMG Nunwood (2019); https://www1.firstdirect.com/.

as a result of the influence of its practitioners, as well as developments in related disciplines, including the areas of industrial economics, psychology, sociology, and anthropology, as follows.

- *Industrial economics influences*—Our knowledge of the matching of supply and demand, within industries, owes much to the development of microeconomics. For instance, the economic concepts of 'perfect competition' and the 'matching of supply and demand' underlie the marketing concept, particularly in relation to the concepts of the price at which offerings are sold and the quantity distributed (see Chapter 7). Theories of income distribution, scale of operation, monopoly, competition, and finance all derive from economics (Bartels, 1951), although the influence of economics over marketing is declining (Howard et al., 1991).

- *Psychological influences*—Our knowledge of consumer behaviour derives principally from psychology, especially in the early days, motivation research (see Chapter 2) in relation to consumer attitudes, perceptions, motivations, and information processing (Holden and Holden, 1998), and our understanding of persuasion, consumer personality, and customer satisfaction (Bartels, 1951).
- *Sociological influences*—Knowledge of how groups of people behave derives from sociology, with insights into areas such as how people from similar gender and age groups behave (demographics), how people in different social positions within society behave (class), why we do things in the way that we do (motivation), general ways that groups behave (customs), and culture (Bartels, 1951, 1959). Our understanding of what society thinks as a whole (i.e. public opinion), how communications pass through opinion leaders (Katz, 1957), and how we influence people in the way that they think and to adopt our perspective (e.g. propaganda research—see Lee, 1945; Doob, 1948) have all informed marketing practice.
- *Anthropological influences*—Our debt to **social anthropology** increases as we use qualitative approaches such as **ethnography**, **netnography**, and **observation** in researching consumer behaviour (see Chapter 3), particularly the behaviour of subgroups and cultures (such as **tweenagers**, **haul girls**).

The Principal Principles of Marketing

Marketing involves a series of highly complex interactions between individuals, organizations, society, and government. Consequently, it is difficult to develop general principles that apply to all contexts. However, we can make at least some law-like generalizations. According to Leone and Shultz (1980), these include the following generalizations:

- *1*—Advertising has a direct and positive influence on total industry (market) sales: all advertising done at industry level serves to increase sales within that industry.
- *2*—Selective advertising has a direct and positive influence on individual company (brand) sales: advertising undertaken by a company tends to increase the sales of the particular brand for which it was spent.
- *3*—The **elasticity** of selective advertising on company (brand) sales is low (inelastic): for frequently purchased goods, advertising has only a very limited effect in raising sales.
- *4*—Increasing store shelf space (display) has a positive impact on sales of **non-staple** grocery items, such as products bought on impulse (e.g. ice cream, chocolate bars) rather than those that are planned purchases, which are less important, but perhaps more luxurious, types of good (e.g. desserts, certain types of cooking sauces). For impulse goods, the more shelf space you give an item, the more likely you are to sell it.
- *5*—Distribution, defined by the number of outlets, has a positive influence on company sales (market share): setting up more retail locations has a positive influence on sales.

Marketing as Exchange

Marketing is a two-way exchange process. It is not solely about the marketing organization doing the work; the customer also inputs—sometimes extensively. Customers specify how we might satisfy their needs, because marketers cannot read their minds. Customers must then pay for the offering. In the mid-1970s, there was an increasing belief that marketing centred on the exchange process between buyers and sellers, and associated supply chain intermediaries (see Chapter 9). Exchange relationships were seen to be economic (e.g. a consumer buying groceries) and social (e.g. the service provided by the police on behalf of society paid for by government) (Bagozzi, 1975). There are numerous types of buyer–seller exchange in marketing. Figure 1.1 illustrates some examples of two-way (**dyadic**) exchanges and the resources exchanged in these interactions. By understanding how exchanges take place between members of the supply chain, we can determine where to add value to the customer experience.

The Marketing Mix and the 4Ps

Neil Borden originally developed the concept of the 'marketing mix' in his teaching at Harvard University in the 1950s. His idea was that marketing managers were 'mixers of ingredients'—that is, chefs who concoct a unique marketing recipe to fit the requirements of customers' needs at any

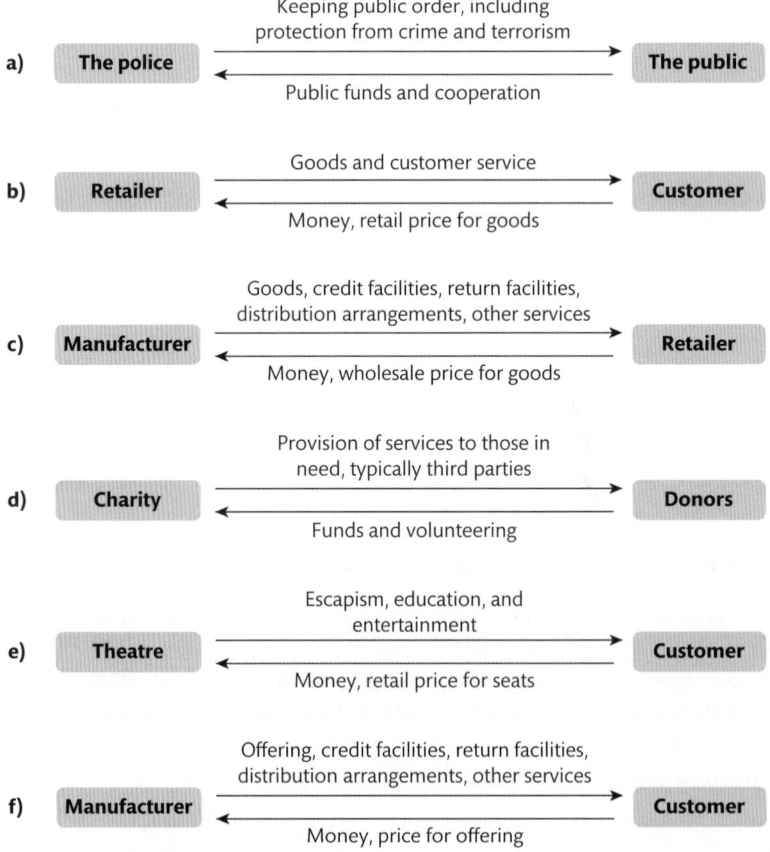

Figure 1.1 Examples of marketing exchange processes

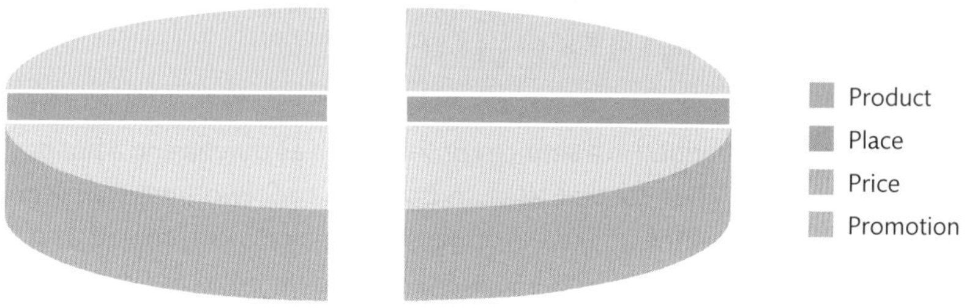

Figure 1.2 The 4Ps of the marketing mix

particular time. He composed a twelve-item list of elements that the manufacturer should consider when developing marketing mix policies and procedures (Borden, 1964). This list was simplified and amended by Eugene McCarthy (1960) to become the more memorable, but rigid, '4Ps' (see Figure 1.2)—that is:

- *Product*—for example the offering and how it meets customers' needs, its packaging, and its labelling (see Chapter 6);
- *Place (distribution)*—for example the way in which the offering meets customers' needs (see Chapter 9);
- *Price*—for example the cost to the customer and the cost plus profit to the seller (see Chapter 7); and
- *Promotion*—for example how the offering's benefits and features are conveyed to the potential buyer (see Chapter 8).

The intention was to create a simpler framework around which managers could develop their planning. Although there was recognition that all of these elements might be interlinked (e.g. promotion based on the price paid by the consumer), such interplay between these mix components was not taken into account by McCarthy's framework.

Research Insight 1.1

To take your learning further, you might wish to read this influential paper:

Borden, N. H. (1964). 'The concept of the marketing mix'. *Journal of Advertising Research*, 4, 2–7.

This easy-to-read, early article explains how marketing managers act as 'mixers of ingredients' when developing marketing programmes. The marketing mix, popularized as the '4Ps', remains popular today, although the advent of relationship marketing challenged the impersonal notion of marketers as manipulators of marketing policies and focused more on the need to develop long-term interpersonal relationships with customers.

 **Visit the online resources to read the abstract and access the full paper.**

The Extended Marketing Mix

It might seem that what is exchanged in a service context (such as purchasing a holiday) is different from what is exchanged in a goods context (such as buying a car). Two American scholars (Booms and Bitner, 1981) suggested an extension to the original model and incorporated a further three 'Ps' into the marketing mix to reflect the need to market services differently, as follows (see Figure 1.3).

- *Physical evidence*—The aim here is to emphasize that the tangible components of services are strategically important: potential university students, for example, might assess whether or not they want to attend a university and a particular course by requesting a copy of brochures or by visiting the campus to assess the **servicescape** for themselves.
- *Process*—This aims to emphasize the importance of the service delivery. When processes are standardized, it is easier to manage customer expectations: DHL International GmbH, the German international express, transport, and air freight company, is a master at producing a standardized menu of service options, such as track-and-trace delivery services, which are remarkably consistent around the world.
- *People*—This emphasizes the importance of customer service personnel, sometimes experts and often professionals interacting with the customer. How they interact with customers, and how satisfied customers are as a result of their experiences, is of strategic importance. For example, McKinsey & Company prides itself on the quality of its more than 9,000 consultants, and its 2,000 research and information specialists as an integral part of its offering (McKinsey & Co., 2016).

Table 1.2 applies the marketing mix for the airline industry.

Relationship Marketing, Service-Dominant Logic, and Co-creation

If marketing is about exchange, should marketing not also be concerned with relationships between those parties that are exchanging value? This was the principal idea behind the development of 'relationship marketing' in the 1990s. The concept spawned further evolution of marketing's conceptual foundations. There was a shift from the need to engage in transactions towards the need to develop long-term customer relationships, including relationships with other stakeholders (Christopher et al., 2002), including:

- suppliers;
- potential employees;

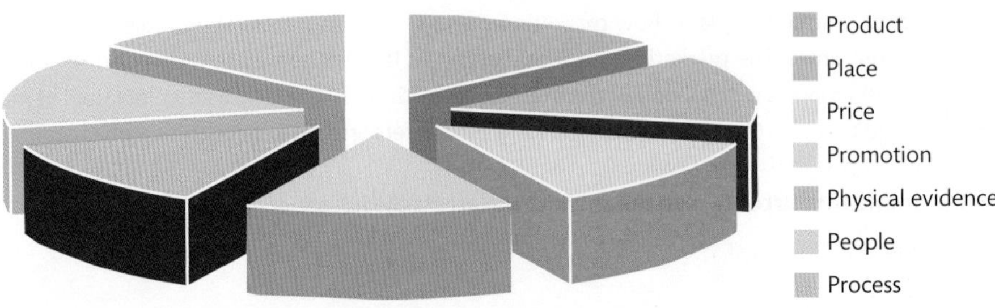

Figure 1.3 The amended marketing mix for services: the 7Ps

Table 1.2 The marketing mix: the airline industry

Marketing aspect	Airline industry
Basic customer need	Safe long- and short-haul transportation, domestic and international
Target market	Mass consumer market (economy class), the discerning traveller (economy plus), business people (business class), and high-net-worth individuals (HNWIs) (first class)
Offering	Typically, differentiated based on class of passenger, with seat size increasing, check-in and boarding times reducing, quality of food increasing, and levels of ancillary services (e.g. limousine service) increasing as we move from economy through business to first class Some carriers focus on 'no-frills' basic services (e.g. EasyJet, Ryanair, Air Asia)
Price	Substantial difference depending on class of service, type of carrier, and purchasing approach (e.g. cheaper via Internet)
Principal promotional tools	(1) the Internet; (2) press, magazine, and radio advertising; (3) billboards
Distribution	Increasingly purchased via mobile apps and the Internet, including third-party brokerages such as Expedia, as well as (to a lesser degree in many countries) through physical travel agents
Process	Self-service via mobile phone or Internet, or aided by travel agent in retail location Travel options increasingly customized to the customer's needs, including size of baggage allowance, class of travel, and increasing availability of alternative and multi-centre locations Customer and organizational use of social media to air and resolve problems now very important
Physical evidence	Airline loyalty cards and souvenirs, in-flight magazines, in-flight entertainment services, food and snack meals, grooming and toiletry products provided On some flights, depending on class purchased, suites, bars, and shower facilities offered
People	Combination of check-in staff, customer service personnel, baggage handlers, and cabin crew/pilot teams, all of whom interface with the customer or their belongings at different points in the experience

- recruiters;
- referral markets—where they exist, for example retail banks partly relying on professional services organizations, including estate agents, for mortgage referrals;
- influence markets—such as regulatory authorities, politicians, and civil servants (see also Viney and Baines, 2012); and
- internal markets, for example existing employees.

Companies employing a relationship marketing approach stressed customer retention over customer acquisition. Customer retention is an important activity in marketing, with research demonstrating that when a company retains loyal customers, it is more likely to be profitable compared with competitors who do not, because loyal customers:

- will increase their purchases over time;
- are cheaper targets for promotion;
- who are happy with their relationship with a company are happy to refer it to others; and
- are often prepared to pay a (small) price premium (Reichheld and Sasser, 1990).

More recently, there has been a realization that marketing needed to shift beyond a goods-based paradigm towards a service-dominant logic (Vargo and Lusch, 2004). This new marketing paradigm sees service as *the* fundamental basis of exchange (see Research Insight 1.2). In that sense, for physical goods offerings, the good is simply the distribution mechanism (see also Market Insight 1.2).

To understand this concept better, consider the difference between purchasing a music CD from a shop (such as HMV) versus streaming a music file from Spotify's subscription service. The knowledge and technologies embedded in the offering by the company to meet customers' needs are the source of competitive advantage. Because offerings are inherently service-based, customers become co-creators of the service experience. Therefore, in the end, the ultimate value-in-use of the offering is specified by the customer, often after the sale has taken place.

According to Prahalad and Ramaswamy (2004a, 2004b), organizations should use co-creation to differentiate their offerings, given that value is tied up inside the customer's experience with the organization. The co-creation experience is about *joint* creation of value, in which customers take part in an active dialogue and co-construct personalized experiences. Therefore organizations wishing to enhance customer input to co-creation should map supplier and customer processes to identify how to design their services accordingly (Payne et al., 2008). The process of co-creation therefore potentially shifts value creation from value-in-exchange, at the point of purchase, to value-in-use, after purchase (Grönroos and Voima, 2013). For example, airplane manufacturer Boeing incorporated feedback from both airline companies and passengers into its Dreamliner plane design before final production.

Research Insight 1.2

To take your learning further, you might wish to read this influential paper:

Vargo, S. L., and Lusch, R. F. (2008) 'Service-dominant logic: Continuing the evolution', *Journal of the Academy of Marketing Science*, 36(1), 1–10.

This article builds on, and updates, the authors' original ground-breaking article (Vargo and Lusch, 2004), which redefined how marketers should think about offerings, arguing that it was necessary to move beyond the idea of tangible versus intangible goods, embedded value and transactions, and other outmoded concepts derived from economics towards the notion of intangible resources and the co-creation of value and relationships. The article asserts that service is the fundamental basis of all exchanges in marketing and that value is always determined by the beneficiary.

 **Visit the online resources to read the abstract and access the full paper.**

Market Insight 1.2 **Servitization at Rolls-Royce**

Rolls-Royce is a global provider of integrated power systems and services to the civil and defence aerospace, marine, nuclear, and power systems markets. However, Rolls-Royce plc (which no longer owns the Rolls-Royce motor car brand) has completely redefined itself since the early 1970s, when it was nationalized by the then Conservative government after running into financial problems. In 2018, it had underlying revenues of £15.1 bn, up 10 per cent on 2017, with an order book of £63.1 bn. Product–service revenue ratios in 2014 were 42:58 in civil aerospace, 46:54 in defence, and 67:33 in power systems. By comparison, after-market sales, as they were then known, were only 20 per cent of the civil aerospace division's revenues in 1981.

Since then, Rolls-Royce has transformed its business model from selling engines and aftercare (to ensure that the engines work properly and are maintained) to selling its customers 'power by the hour', recognizing that it is not in the engine manufacturing business; rather, it is in the power-generation integrated solutions business. In the civil aerospace sector, Rolls-Royce sells its engines with TotalCare®. With TotalCare®, a customer enters into an overall agreement with Rolls-Royce that provides visibility of cost and a guarantee of product reliability. It was first introduced in the 1990s and charges airline customers based on the total number of hours flown. By collecting data from aircraft engines in flight worldwide on a continuous basis, Rolls-Royce maintains those engines better, predicts engine failures, optimizes engine maintenance programmes, and improves future engine design.

Rolls-Royce wins contract to supply IAG with Trent XWB engines and long-term TotalCare® service support.

Source: © Airbus S.A.S. 2011. Photo by exm company/H. Goussé.

1. **Why do you think Rolls-Royce has been so successful in selling the service concept?**
2. **Check out the websites of Rolls-Royce's competitors, GE and Safran. How do their service offerings in their civil aerospace divisions compare with that of Rolls-Royce?**
3. **Can all manufacturers' products be servitized, do you think?**

Sources: Rolls-Royce (2018); Ryals and Rackham (2015); https://www.rolls-royce.com/about.aspx.

What Do Marketers Do?

The marketing department within organizations has become increasingly important as customers' buying behaviours are fast-changing and their expectations have skyrocketed (IBM Watson Marketing, 2018). Today, most firms embrace a customer-oriented approach and no longer only focus on selling their products and services. Instead, they aim to build trust and long-term relationships with new and existing customers. This trend has led marketers to exert a growing influence on other functions within the organization as they sit at the interface with customers.

Measuring the impact of the marketing activities on a firm's financial performance is crucial to assess their importance. However, it can be difficult to quantify it as marketers do not necessarily generate short-term profit—unlike sales and operations teams (Feng et al., 2015). For example, strengthening brand image via sponsorship may not result in immediate profit in the short term, but may positively impact the company in the long term (see Chapter 8). Nonetheless, studies have demonstrated the importance of the marketing department on the financial performance of the company (e.g. Homburg et al., 2015).

Within organizations, two opposed internal structures are considered:

- *Functional marketing organization*—in which a dedicated group of experts are in charge of all marketing activities; and
- *Marketing process organization*—in which the marketing activities are shared between all functions (Moorman and Rust, 1999).

In practice, marketing organizations are structured somewhere between these two approaches: a dedicated team is usually in charge of the marketing-related activities but collaborates extensively with other departments. The marketing team should maintain clear ownership of the customer activities so that market knowledge is not thinly dispersed between too many departments (Verhoef and Leeflang, 2009).

The UK's CIM developed a framework of marketing abilities to guide the skills and behaviours of professional marketers at different levels of proficiency and seniority (CIM, 2019) (see Figure 1.4).

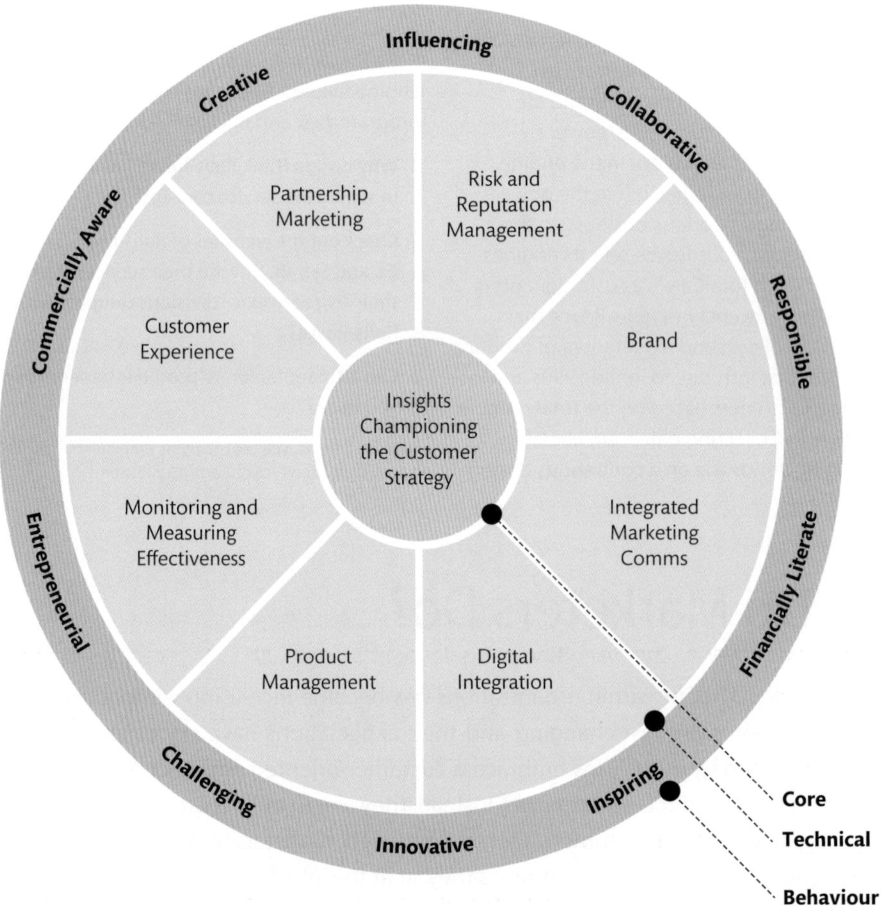

Figure 1.4 A functional map for professional marketing competencies

Source: © Chartered Institute of Marketing 2019. Reproduced with kind permission.

It is important to stress that marketing is present in all aspects of an organization, since all departments have some role to play with respect to creating, delivering, and satisfying customers. For example, members of the **procurement** department buying components for a new product or service must purchase those components of a specific quality and at a certain cost that will meet customer needs. In fact, we can go through all departments of a company and find that, in each department, there is a marketing role to be played to some extent. In other words, marketing is distributed throughout the organization and all employees can be considered to be part-time marketers (Gummesson, 1990).

Interface with Customers

In an increasing customer-centric context, the marketing function ensures three connections between the firm and its customers:

- *customer–product*—this connection is about informing customers about a product or service;
- *customer–service delivery*—this connection guarantees that customer are satisfied with the services delivered by the firm, measuring their satisfaction, and adapting future delivery accordingly; and
- *customer–financial accountability*—this is about measuring the impact of customer satisfaction and the firm's revenues (Moorman and Rust, 1999).

Recent technological development has also contributed to the timely and continuous measuring of customer satisfaction that can be acted on quickly and effectively. This process, referred to as **marketing agility**, enables firms to adapt their offering to customer feedback and reduce delivery time (IBM Watson Marketing, 2018).

Influence within the Firm

The marketing department advocates the customer orientation to the rest of the firm, focusing on long-term strategic goals rather than short-term priorities. It is also in charge of communicating market information within the firm and orchestrating the actions that can impact customers across all other functions (Verhoef and Leeflang, 2009).

In large organizations, the **CMO (chief marketing officer)** is responsible for all marketing activities and promotes them to the board of executives. The CMO's impact on the performance of a firm can be as high as 15 per cent (Germann et al., 2015). To provide a consistent message to customers, the CMO also ensures alignment of the mission statement and values between the different functions of the firm, from the executives to the marketing and sales teams (Ellett, 2015). In recent years, some companies have replaced their CMO with the **CCO (chief customer officer)** to emphasize their customer-centric approach. Even if this new role is often not clearly outlined, the CCO is in charge of the interface between the firm and its customers, defining a customer strategy and executing it (Rust et al., 2009).

Innovation and Marketing

The marketing department plays a crucial role in the development of new propositions. By collaborating with employees in the research and development (R&D) department, marketers generate innovations and provide their market and customer knowledge to shape new offerings and ensure

Research Insight 1.3

To take your learning further, you might wish to read this influential paper:

De Luca, L. M., and Atuahene-Gima, K. (2007) 'Market knowledge dimensions and cross-functional collaboration: Examining the different routes to product innovation performance', *Journal of Marketing*, 71(1), 95–112.

In this seminal article, the authors describe the factors that affect product innovation from a marketing perspective. They list market knowledge, cross-functional collaboration, and knowledge integration mechanisms as the three predictors of the performance of new offerings. From a sample of 750 Chinese technology companies, they conclude that market knowledge breadth is the most important factor for predicting successful innovations.

 **Visit the online resources to read the abstract and access the full paper.**

that they meet customer demand. The role of marketers is especially important since the effectiveness of product innovation is shaped by three main factors:

- *market knowledge*—the information on customers and competitors. Both breadth (the diversity of information) and depth (the complexity of information) should be considered;
- *cross-functional collaboration*—the collaboration between different functions, especially marketing and R&D, to generate new offerings; and
- *knowledge integration mechanisms*—the process of collecting and analysing market insights and sharing it across multiple functions (De Luca and Atuahene-Gima, 2007).

Marketing's Positive Impact on Society

Marketing impacts both positively and negatively on society. Wilkie and Moore (1999) describe the complexities of what they call the 'aggregate marketing system'. The distributive capacity of the aggregate marketing system is amazing, especially when we consider that there were around 517 million people in the European Union in 2018, each of whom is brought his or her own unique mixture of breakfast offerings each morning (CIA, 2019). Broadly, the aggregate marketing system in most countries works well. We are not all starving and we do not have to ration our food to preserve the amount we eat. There are parts of certain countries in Africa, North Korea, and parts of China where people are dying of hunger, but these countries often experience imperfections in supply and demand because of political (such as war, dictatorship, famine) and environmental circumstances (such as drought). Thus marketing plays an important role in developing and transforming society (see also Market Insight 1.3).

Some of the world's most important inventions have come to us through the aggregate marketing system. Consider how some of the offerings outlined in Table 1.3 have affected your own life. What would we do without these inventions today? We enjoy them because innovative individuals and companies made them available to us.

Table 1.3 Some modern consumer products and their dates of invention

Consumer product	Product attribute	Consumer need	Inventors/ pioneers*	Year of invention
Breakfast cereals	Cereals that, when added to milk, can provide a healthy meal	Quick and easy-to-prepare foodstuff that was rapidly adopted as a breakfast meal	W. K. Kellogg Foundation, United States	1906
Television	Transmission of moving images	Information, entertainment, and education	Baird Television Development Company, UK/ Telefunken, Germany	1929/1932
Carton	Cardboard liquid storage device	Allows liquid foodstuffs to be stored, packaged, and distributed in an environmentally friendly way	Tetra Pak, Sweden	1951
Artificial sweeteners	Xylitol (as the sweetener is known) used to sweeten food products such as sugar-free chewing gum and toothpastes	Sweetens food products without damaging teeth	Cultor, Finland	1969
Mobile phone	Hand-held device for making telephone calls while in motion	Ability to stay in telephone contact with others regardless of location	NTT, Japan	1979
Personal computer	Machine allowing users to play electronic games, perform calculations, and write word-processed documents and other applications	Time-saving device, simplifying complex writing/arithmetic tasks, offering recreational possibilities (e.g. game-playing)	IBM, United States	1980

*The named companies are not always the inventors per se; they often acquired the patents from the inventor, and so were licensed to produce and distribute the invention.

Sources: Various, including http://www.inventors.about.com and manufacturers' websites

The aggregate marketing system also impedes offerings that do not meet consumer needs. Hence it provides a number of benefits to society, including the following (Wilkie and Moore, 1999):

- the promotion and delivery of desired offerings;
- the provision of a forum for market learning (i.e. we can see what does and what does not get through the system);

Market Insight 1.3 **Google: World-Changing Innovations**

In 1996, Google began life as a research project developing what became its acclaimed search engine and PageRank algorithm. Since those heady early days, Google has completely transformed society—by changing the way in which we acquire information. Many of Google's other innovations have become part of peoples' daily lives—for example Google Books, which has digitized millions of books so that people can preview a snippet of a book's contents prior to making purchase decisions, or Google Maps, which allows people to plan and pursue their travel routes on foot, or by car, bicycle, or public transport, wherever they have a mobile Internet connection.

So what is the company's secret to achieving innovation success? Part of the answer is that Google has been renowned for its policy of allowing its engineers and developers to spend 20 per cent of their time on independent projects; '20 per cent time' projects have included Gmail, Google News, and AdSense. Its corporate principle for innovation is referred to as the '8 Pillars of Innovation'. These highlight important ideas for building innovation capacity, such as having a mission, thinking big, but starting small, striving for continual innovation, and being willing to fail. But Google's innovation success does not derive only from corporate policy; it is generated from an understanding of what customers and users are thinking. Google champions and capitalizes on ideas gained from customer insight. Customers or users are deemed as an open source for creativity and inspiration on the basis of which Google can create something novel.

Google[x], a semi-secret R&D facility, manifests Google's innovation practices. Google[x]'s mandate is to invent new technologies or ways of fixing anything that presents a significant problem for humankind. Since its inception in 2010, Google[x] has been home to many avant-garde innovations, including the self-driving car initiative and Internet-connected spectacles, known as Google Glass, among other incredible projects.

The origin of world-changing innovations: the quirky Googleplex in California.

Source: © Uladzik Kryhin/Shutterstock.

1. **Why are the innovations created by companies such as Google so important to local communities and society in general?**
2. **Do futuristic innovations, such as Google Glass and the self-driving car, really help society or do they simply generate profit for the developers?**
3. **What other companies are you aware of that have had a big impact on society? With what offerings?**

Sources: Bort (2014); D'Onfro (2015); George (2015); McDonnell (2015); Scott (2015); Tait (2015).

This market insight was kindly contributed by Dr Ning Baines, De Montfort University, UK.

- the stimulation of market demand;
- the provision of a wide scope of choice of offerings by providing a close or customized fit with consumer needs;
- the facilitation of purchases (or acquisitions generally, for example if no payment is made directly, as in the case of public services);

- time savings and the promotion of efficiency in customer requirement matching;
- new offerings, and improvements, to meet latent and unserved needs; and
- the pursuit of customer satisfaction for repeat purchases.

Visit the **online resources** and complete Internet Activity 1.2 to learn more about how marketing innovation impacts upon society.

Chapter Summary

To consolidate your learning, the key points from this chapter are summarized below.

- **Define the marketing concept.**

  Marketing is the process by which organizations anticipate and satisfy their customers' needs to both parties' benefit. It involves mutual exchange. Over the last twenty-five years, the marketing concept has changed to recognize the importance of long-term customer relationships to organizations.

- **Explain how marketing has developed over the twentieth and into the twenty-first centuries.**

  There have been four main phases in the history of marketing: the production era; the sales era; the marketing era; and the societal marketing era.

- **Understand the exchange and marketing mix concepts in marketing.**

  The concept of exchange is important: empathizing with customers to understand what they want and determining how sellers seek to provide what buyers want is a central concept in marketing. The marketing mix comprises *product* (the offering), *place* (the distribution mechanism), *price* (the value placed on the offering), and *promotion* (how the company communicates that value). For services marketing, because of the intangible nature of the service, marketers consider an extra 3Ps, including *physical evidence* (how cues are developed for customers to recognize quality), *process* (how the experience is designed to meet customers' needs), and *people* (the training and development of those delivering the customer experience).

- **Understand the role of the marketing department within the organization.**

  The marketing department within the firm is in charge of the interface with customers and advocates a customer-oriented approach to other functions. Marketing activities are not limited to the marketing department and are also undertaken by other functions. It is crucial that marketing teams collaborate with other parts of the organization, particularly for generating new offerings.

- **Understand the positive contribution that marketing makes to society.**

  The aggregate marketing system delivers to us a wide array of offerings, either directly or indirectly through business markets, to serve our wants and needs. There is much that is positive about the aggregate marketing system and it has served to improve the standard of living for many people around the world.

Review Questions

1 **How do we define the 'marketing' concept?**
2 **How do the AMA and the CIM definitions of marketing differ?**
3 **What is the difference between customers and consumers?**
4 **How has marketing developed historically?**
5 **What is the marketing mix?**
6 **What are the responsibilities of the marketing department?**
7 **What are the roles of the CMO?**
8 **What is marketing agility?**
9 **How can marketing teams contribute to innovation?**
10 **What positive contributions does marketing make to society?**

Worksheet Summary

To apply the knowledge you have gained from this chapter and to test your understanding, visit the **online resources** and complete Worksheet 1.1.

Discussion Questions

1 Having read Case Insight 1.1 at the beginning of this chapter, how would you advise Aldoraq as it attempts to differentiate itself from national and international brands?

2 Read the section 'The Marketing Mix and the 4Ps' and draw up marketing mixes for the following organizations and their target customers.

- A Streaming video company Netflix and its audiences
- B A luxury hotel group and its wealthy clientele
- C Pharmacies (such as Boots UK Ltd, Sweden's Apoteket AB, Holland's Etos BV) and their consumers
- D A company supplying glass to construction companies

3 Select a company that transitioned to a service-dominant strategy. Why do you think it was successful?

4 Research the CMO of a large company (e.g. Unilever or Apple). What values of the brands that it represents does it communicate online?

Visit the **online resources** and complete the multiple-choice questions to assess your knowledge of this chapter.

Glossary

advertising a form of non-personal communication, by an identified sponsor, transmitted through the use of paid-for media.

American Marketing Association (AMA) a professional body for marketing professionals and marketing educators based in the United States, operating principally there and in Canada.

Chartered Institute of Marketing (CIM) a professional body for marketing professionals based in the UK, with study centres and members around the world.

CCO (chief customer officer) executive in charge of all customer-related activities within an organization.

CMO (chief marketing officer) executive in charge of all marketing activities within an organization.

consumer the user of a product, service, or other form of offering.

customer the person who purchases and pays for (or initially requests and specifies, in the case of a non-financial transaction) a product, service, or other form of offering from a company or organization.

dyadic essentially meaning 'two-way'; a dyadic commercial relationship is an exchange between two people—typically, a buyer and a seller.

elasticity an economic concept associated with the extent to which changes in one variable are related to changes in another, for example if a price increase in a good causes a decline in volume of sales of that good, we say the good is 'price elastic' and specify by how much; if it causes no change or very little change, we say it is 'price inelastic'.

ethnography a subdiscipline derived from cultural anthropology as an approach to research, which emphasizes the collection of data through participant observation of members of a specific subcultural grouping and observation of participation of members of a specific subcultural grouping.

haul girls women who go shopping for clothes or beauty products, then make a YouTube video showing viewers what they have bought, item by item.

market orientation refers to the development of a whole-organization approach to the generation, collection, and dissemination of market intelligence across different departments, and the organization's responsiveness to that intelligence.

marketing agility refers to the ability to quickly deliver products and change priorities through short iterations.

marketing mix the list of items that a marketing manager should consider when devising plans for marketing products, including product decisions, place (distribution) decisions, pricing decisions, and promotion decisions; later extended to include physical evidence, process, and people decisions, to account for the lack of physical nature in service products.

netnography the branch of ethnography that seeks to analyse Internet users' behaviour.

non-staple in the grocery context, grocery products that are not a main or important food.

observation a research method that requires a researcher to watch, and record, how consumers or employees behave, typically in relation to either purchasing or selling activities.

place (distribution) essentially about how you can place the optimum amount of goods and/or services before the maximum number of members of your target market, at times and locations that optimize the marketing outcome—that is, sales.

price the amount that the customer has to pay to receive a good or service.

procurement the purchasing (buying) process in a firm or organization.

product anything that is capable of satisfying customer needs.

promotion the use of communications to persuade individuals, groups, or organizations to purchase products and services.

relationship marketing the development and management of long-term relationships with customers, influencers, referrers, suppliers, recruiters, and employees.

service-dominant logic asserts that organizations, markets, and society are concerned fundamentally with exchange of service, based on the application of knowledge and skills; rejects the notion of dualism between goods and services marketing by arguing that all offerings provide a service.

servicescape the physical environment in which a service takes place, such as a stadium for a football game.

social anthropology the scientific discipline of observing and recording the way in which humans behave in their different social groupings.

tweenagers pre-adolescent children, typically taken to be between the ages of 9 and 12, who are hence about to enter their teenage years.

value the regard that something is held to be worth, typically, although not always, in financial terms.

References

AMA (2017) 'Definition of Marketing'. Retrieve from: https://www.ama.org/the-definition-of-marketing-what-is-marketing/ (accessed 30 October 2020).

Bagozzi, R. P. (1975) 'Marketing as exchange', *Journal of Marketing*, 3(4), 32–39.

Bartels, R. D. W. (1951) 'Can marketing be a science?, *Journal of Marketing*, 15(3), 319–28.

Bartels, R. D. W. (1959) 'Sociologists and marketologists', *Journal of Marketing*, 24(2), 37–40.

Booms, B. H., and Bitner, M. J. (1981) 'Marketing strategies and organisation structures for service firms', in J. H. Donnelly and W. R. George (eds), *Marketing of Services*, Chicago, IL: AMA, 47–52.

Borden, N. H. (1964) 'The concept of the marketing mix', *Journal of Advertising Research*, 4, 2–7.

Bort, J. (2014) 'A rare look inside Google's secret labs where they invent amazing new things', *Business Insider*, 20 April. Retrieve from: https://www.businessinsider.com.au/inside-googles-secret-google-x-labs-2014-4 (accessed 30 October 2020).

Brenner, B. (2013) 'Inside the NIKE Matrix'. *Wirtschafts Universität Wien Case Series No. 0001/2013*. Retrieve from http://epub.wu.ac.at/3791/1/Nike__WUCaseSeries.pdf (accessed 30 October 2020).

Central Intelligence Agency (CIA) (2019) *The World Factbook: European Union*. Retrieve from: https://www.cia.gov/library/publications/the-world-factbook/geos/ee.html (accessed 30 October 2020).

Chartered Institute of Marketing (CIM) (2015) *Marketing and the 7Ps. Retrieve* from: https://www.thensmc.com/sites/default/files/CIM%207Ps%20Resource.PDF (accessed 30 October 2020).

Chartered Institute of Marketing (CIM) (2019) *ProfessionalMarketing Competencies. Retrieve* from: https://www.cim.co.uk/membership/professional-marketing-competencies/ (accessed 30 October 2020).

De Luca, L. M., and Atuahene-Gima, K. (2007) 'Market knowledge dimensions and cross-functional collaboration: Examining the different routes to product innovation performance', *Journal of Marketing*, 71(January), 95–112.

D'Onfro, J. (2015) 'The truth about Google's famous "20% time" policy', *Business Insider UK*, 17 April. Retrieve from: https://www.businessinsider.com/google-20-percent-time-policy-2015-4?r=US&IR=T (accessed 20 October 2020).

Doob, L.W. (1948) *Public Opinion and Propaganda*, Oxford: Henry Holt.

Ellett, J. (2015) 'The CMO solution guide for building a modern marketing organization'. Retrieve from: http://thecmoclub.com/wp-content/uploads/2015/10/FINALCMO-Solution-Guide_ModernMarketing_October2015.pdf (accessed 30 October 2020).

Enright, M. (2002) 'Marketing and conflicting dates for its emergence: Hotchkiss, Bartels and the fifties school of alternative accounts', *Journal of Marketing Management*, 18(5–6), 445–61.

Feng, H., Morgan, N. A., and Rego, L. L. (2015) 'Marketing department power and firm performance', *Journal of Marketing*, 79(September), 1–20.

George, B. (2015) 'The world's most innovative company', *Huffington Post*, 28 October. Retrieve from: https://www.huffingtonpost.com/bill-george/the-worldsmostinnovativ_b_8406556.html (accessed 30 October 2020).

Germann, F., Ebbes, P., and Grewal, R. (2015) 'The chief marketing officer matters!', *Journal of Marketing*, 79(May), 1–22.

Grönroos, C., and Voima, P. (2013) 'Critical service logic: Making sense of value creation and co-creation', *Journal of the Academy of Marketing Science*. 41(2), 133–50.

Gummesson, E. (1990) 'Marketing orientation revisited: The crucial role of the part-time marketer', *European Journal of Marketing*, 25(2), 60–75.

Holden, A. C., and Holden, L. (1998) 'Marketing history: Illuminating marketing's clandestine subdiscipline', *Psychology and Marketing*, 15(2), 117–23.

Homburg, C., Vomberg, A., Enke, M., and Grimm, P. H. (2015) 'The loss of the marketing department's influence: Is it really happening? And why worry?', *Journal of Academic Marketing Science*, 43(1), 1–13.

Howard, D. G., Savins, D. M., Howell, W., and Ryans, J. K., Jr (1991) 'The evolution of marketing theory in the United States and Europe', *European Journal of Marketing*, 25(2), 7–16.

IBM Watson Marketing (2018) '2019 marketing trends: Nine factors reshaping marketing and how you can stay ahead of them'. Retrieve from: https://downloads.digitalmarketingdepot.com/IBM_1901_2019MarkTr_landingpage_gdpr.html (accessed 30 November 2019).

Katz, E. (1957) 'The two-step flow of communication: An up-to-date report on an hypothesis', *Public Opinion Quarterly*, 21(1), 61–78.

Kirca, A. H., Jayachandran, S., and Bearden, W. O. (2005) 'Market orientation: A meta-analytic review and assessment of its antecedents and impact on performance', *Journal of Marketing*, 69(2), 24–41.

Kohli, A. K., and Jaworski, B. J. (1990) 'Market orientation: The construct, research propositions and managerial implications', *Journal of Marketing*, 54(2), 1–18.

KPMG Nunwood (2019) *Power to the People: 2019 UK Customer Experience Excellence Analysis*. Retrieve from: https://home.kpmg/uk/en/home/insights/2019/06/power-to-the-people-uk-customer-experience-excellence-report.html (accessed 30 October 2020).

Kumar, V. (2015) 'Evolution of marketing as a discipline: What has happened and what to look out for', *Journal of Marketing*, 79, 1–9.

Kumar, V., Jones, E., Venkatesan, R., and Leone, R. P. (2011) 'Is market orientation a source of sustainable competitive advantage or simply the cost of competing?', *Journal of Marketing*, 75(1), 16–30.

Lee, A. M. (1945) 'The analysis of propaganda: A clinical summary', *American Journal of Sociology*, 51(2), 126–35.

Lendrevie, J., and Lévy, J. (2014) *Mercator: Tout le marketing à l'ère numérique* (11th edn), Paris: Dunod.

Leone, R. P., and Shultz, R. L. (1980) 'A study of marketing generalisations', *Journal of Marketing*, 44(Winter), 10–18.

McCarthy, E. J. (1960) *Basic Marketing*, Homewood, IL: Irwin.

McDonnell, F. (2015) 'New PwC and Google innovation lab will be located in Belfast', *The Irish Times*, 24 November. Retrieve from: https://www.irishtimes.com/business/new-pwc-and-google-innovation-lab-will-be-located-in-belfast-1.2442406 (accessed 30 October 2020).

McKinsey & Co. (2016) 'About us'. Retrieve from https://www.mckinsey.com/about-us/overview (accessed 30 October 2020).

Moorman, C., and Rust, R. T. (1999) 'The role of marketing', *Journal of Marketing*, 63, 180–97.

Payne, A., Storbacka, K., and Frow, P. (2008) 'Managing the co-creation of value', *Journal of the Academy of Marketing Science*, 36(1), 83–96.

Prahalad, C. K., and Ramaswamy, V. (2004a) 'Co-creation experiences: The next practice in value creation', *Journal of Interactive Marketing*, 18(3), 5–14.

Prahalad, C. K., and Ramaswamy, V. (2004b) 'Co-creating unique value with customers', *Strategy and Leadership*, 32(3), 4–9.

Reichheld, F. F., and Sasser, W. E., Jr (1990) 'Zero defections: Quality comes to services', *Harvard Business Review*, 68(5), 105–11.

Rolls-Royce (2018) *Rolls-Royce Holdings plc Annual Report 2018*. Retrieve from: https://www.rolls-royce.com/~/media/Files/R/Rolls-Royce/documents/annual-report/2018/2018-full-annual-report.pdf (accessed 30 October 2020).

Rust, R. T., Moorman, C., and Bhalla, G. (2010) 'Rethinking marketing', *Harvard Business Review*, 88(1/2), 94–101.

Ryals L., Rackham N. (2015) 'The impact of servitization on selling.' In: Deeter-Schmelz D. (Eds.) Proceedings of the 2010 Academy of Marketing Science (AMS) Annual Conference. Developments in Marketing Science: Proceedings of the Academy of Marketing Science. Springer, Cham. Retrieve from: https://doi.org/10.1007/978-3-319-11797-3_144 (accessed 30 October 2020).

Scott, A. (2015) 'Google-backed lab brings robotics and other technologies to RAK and Northern Emirates', *The National*, 9 April. Retrieve from: https://www.thenationalnews.com/business/google-backed-lab-brings-robotics-and-other-technologies-to-rak-and-northern-emirates-1.5766 (accessed 30 October 2020).

Sheth, J. N., and Sisodia, R. J. (2005) 'A dangerous divergence: Marketing and society', *Journal of Public Policy and Marketing*, 24(1), 160–2.

Slater, S. F., and Narver, J. C. (1994) 'Market orientation, customer value and superior performance', *Business Horizons*, 37(2), 22–8.

Tait, S. (2015) 'Interview with Google's head of marketing innovation APAC', *Marketing*, 24 September. Retrieve from: https://www.marketingmag.com.au/hubs-c/interview-googles-head-marketing-innovation-apac/ (accessed 30 October 2020).

Vargo, S. L., and Lusch, R. F. (2004) 'Evolving to a new service-dominant logic for marketing', *Journal of Marketing*, 68(1), 1–17.

Vargo, S. L., and Lusch, R. F. (2008) 'Service-dominant logic: Continuing the evolution', *Journal of the Academy of Marketing Science*, 36(1), 1–10.

Verhoef, P. C., and Leeflang, S. H. (2009) 'Understanding the marketing department's influence within the firm', *Journal of Marketing*, 73, 14–37.

Viney, H., and Baines, P. (2012) 'Engaging government: Why it's necessary and how to do it', *European Business Review*, Sept–Oct, 9–13.

Wilkie, W. L., and Moore, E. S. (1999) 'Marketing's contributions to society', *Journal of Marketing*, 63(3–4): 198–218.

Chapter 2
Understanding Customer Behaviour

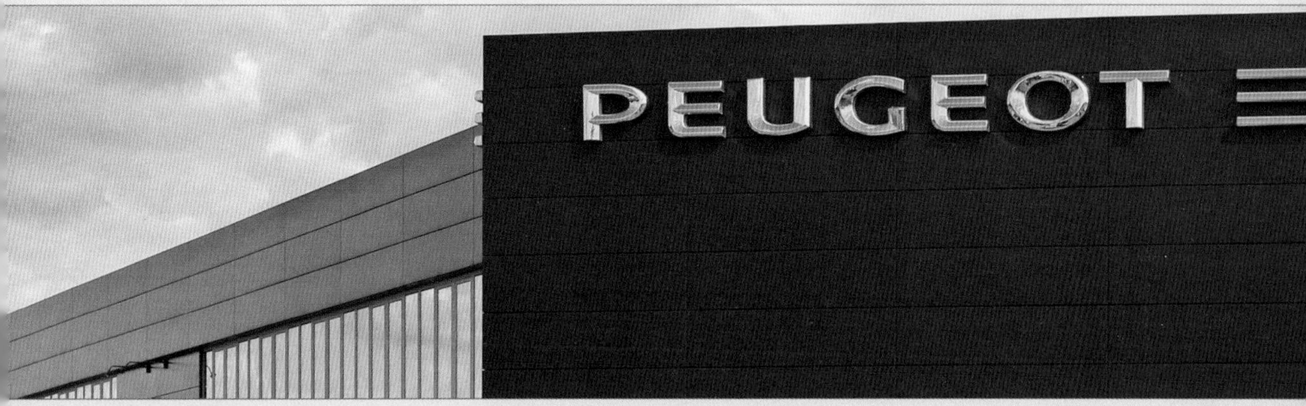

Learning Outcomes

After studying this chapter, you will be able to:

- explain the consumer product acquisition process;
- explain the processes involved in human perception, learning, and memory in relation to consumer choice;
- understand the importance of personality and motivation in consumer behaviour; and
- set out the main processes and stages associated with organizational buying and purchasing.

Case Insight 2.1
Aircall

Market Insight 2.1
Easy Purchasing at Peugeot

Market Insight 2.2
Guilt Appeals: How Do They Change Behaviour?

Market Insight 2.3
Making an Airbus

Case Insight 2.1 **Aircall**

Aircall is the cloud-based phone system of choice for modern brands, with over 300 employees across its Paris and New York offices. It is a trusted provider around the world. We speak to Carly Dell, director, demand generation at Aircall to find out how it shifted its customers from buying a monthly service subscription to buying an annual one.

Founded in 2014, Aircall has raised US$41 million from Efounders, Balderton and NextWorld Capital, Draper Esprit, and Newfund. Modern small to medium-sized enterprises (**SMEs**) choose Aircall to provide exceptional customer experiences by bringing value to voice. These companies believe voice is a powerful way to communicate with customers, prospects, candidates, and colleagues, and enables their teams to make genuine connections to drive business and deliver memorable brand experiences. A few of the reasons they select Aircall as a provider include its ease of use and flexibility, powerful integrations (e.g. with Salesforce, HubSpot, Zendesk, Slack, Intercom), and proven quality.

Operating a Software as a Service (**SaaS**) business model, our pricing (see https://aircall.io/pricing/) is subscription-based. Customers pay per user on a regular basis for continued use of our product. We offer two billing options—monthly and annual; monthly prices are typically up to 40 per cent higher than annual prices. The majority of our new customers were signing up for Aircall on a monthly subscription because it was a much smaller upfront cost, and gave them more flexibility and control over commitments to regular expenses—something very important to SMEs. However, for our own business, monthly pricing meant there was less predictability on the amount of net growth we were going to see in any given month because of unpredictable churn, making forecasting difficult.

Because of this, we wanted to move as many current and new customers over to annual pricing as possible to enable more predictable growth and stronger, longer-term revenue streams. Plus, as a high-growth company, it's always better to have cash up front to invest in growth. In order to accomplish this, we needed to change how we marketed our pricing structure to our prospects and customers. We wanted to increase the percentage of our customer base using an annual pricing subscription by at least four times. In addition, we needed to educate our prospects and customers on the benefits of being on an annual pricing plan, including: up to a 40 per cent discount on services, billing being less of a hassle, and only having to go through procurement processes once per year.

The question for Aircall was how could it increase the proportion of new customers to sign up for annual contracts, and how could it persuade existing customers to shift from monthly to annual contracts when renewing their contracts?

Introduction

What process did you go through when deciding which university course to study? After reading this chapter, you will understand why consumers think and behave as they do. You will also understand how organizations make purchasing decisions, and that there are differences between consumer behaviour and business-to-business (B2B) buying behaviour. We start with the former, considering **cognition** (thoughts), **perception** (how we see things), and learning (how we memorize techniques and knowledge). These are processes that are fundamental in explaining how consumers think and learn about offerings.

We also discuss **personality** and motivation to illustrate how these psychological concepts affect how we buy. Because marketing comes alive when it is woven into the fabric of our social lives, we consider how **social class**, life cycles, and lifestyles influence consumer behaviour. We then examine the characteristics of organization buyer behaviour, focusing on the processes that allow companies to purchase the products they need to operate successfully.

Consumer Proposition Acquisition

The consumer proposition acquisition process consists of six distinct stages (see Figure 2.1). The process model is useful, because it highlights the importance and distinctiveness of proposition selection and re-evaluation phases in the process. In Figure 2.1, the buying process is iterative—that is, each stage can lead back to previous stages or move forward to the next.

Motive Development

The process begins when we decide that we wish to obtain an offering. This involves the initial recognition that a problem needs solving. To solve the problem, we must first become aware of it. A consumer may decide that she needs to buy a new jacket to wear to work, for example; perhaps

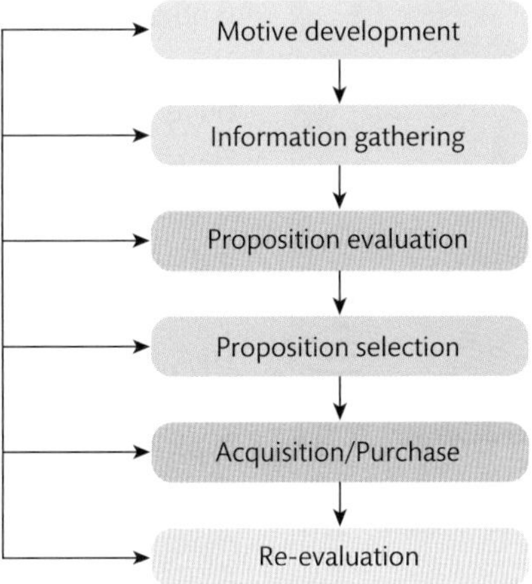

Figure 2.1 The consumer proposition acquisition process

she has grown tired of the old one, or she thinks it is out of fashion, or decides to cheer herself up, or wants to buy for a particular occasion (such as a job interview or presentation), or wants to buy it for a whole host of other reasons.

Information Gathering

In the next stage, we seek alternative ways of solving our problems. Our jacket buyer might ask herself where she bought her last jacket, how much jackets typically cost, what different retail outlets stock jackets, and where those retailers are located. She might ask herself where she normally buys work clothing (online or in-store), what kinds of jackets are in fashion, perhaps which retailers have sales on, which store staff treat her well if she shops in-store, and what the returns policies are of various online and high-street retailers. Our search for a solution may be active, an **overt search**, or passive. In other words, we are open to ways of solving our problem, but we are not actively looking for information to help us (Howard and Sheth, 1969). The search for information may be internal—that is, we may consider what we already know about the problem and the offerings that we might buy to solve our problem. Alternatively, it might be external—that is, when we do not know enough about our problem and so we seek advice or supplementary information. At this stage, we build our awareness by increasing our knowledge both of an offering and of the competitors making that offering available. For example, someone interested in buying make-up may seek information by watching a tutorial or a product review from Dutch make-up artist and vlogger NikkieTutorials who has over twelve million YouTube subscribers.

Proposition Evaluation

Once we have all of the information necessary to make a decision, we evaluate alternative propositions. But, first, we must determine the criteria used to rank the various offerings. These might be rational (e.g. based on cost) or irrational (e.g. based on desire or intuition). The jacket buyer might ask herself which website or retail outlet is the best **value** for money and which is the most fashionable. Consumers are said to have an **evoked set** of products in mind when they come to evaluate which particular product, brand, or service they want to solve a particular problem. An evoked set for the jacket buyer might include Zara, H&M, Mango (known as MNG in some countries), ASOS, or Net-a-Porter, for instance. The more affluent buyer might visit a department store (such as Harrods or Selfridges in the UK), or the websites of DKNY or Gucci, for example. This stage might also be termed the 'consideration' stage.

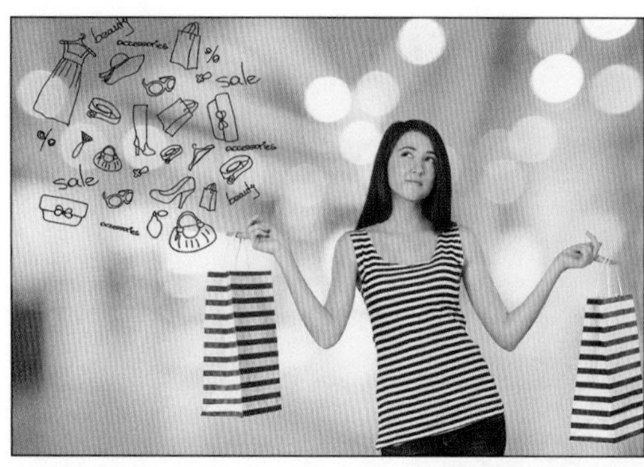

Shopping is influenced by a myriad of personal and social variables: it might be a much more complex process than you ever imagined.
Source: © Billion Photos/Shutterstock.

Proposition Selection

Typically, the offering that we eventually select is that which we evaluate as fitting our needs more closely. However, we might select a particular offering at some distance from where we actually buy or acquire it. For example, the jacket buyer may have checked online to make her selection (intending to go to the shop to try it on), but turns up at the retailer only to find that the jacket she wants is not available, so decides on an alternative on impulse at the point of purchase. Proposition selection is therefore a separate stage in the proposition acquisition process, distinct from proposition evaluation, because there are times when we must re-evaluate what we buy or acquire because what we want is not available, for example buying a cinema ticket for one film because the seats for another are sold out.

Acquisition/Purchase

Once selection has taken place, different approaches to purchasing might exist. For example, our jacket buyer may make a routine purchase: a pair of sports socks. A routine purchase is a purchase made regularly. Because the purchase is regular, we do not get too involved in the decision-making process; we simply buy the offering that we bought previously unless new circumstances arise. The purchase may be specialized, conducted on a one-off or infrequent basis, for example an evening gown for a ball or a formal work event. In this case, we may become much more involved in the decision-making process to ensure that we understand what we are buying and that we are happy it will satisfy our needs (to look classy, perhaps, and not cheap). For routine purchases, we might use debit cards or cash; for infrequent purchases, we might use a credit or store card. With infrequent purchases, the marketer might ease the pain of payment by offering credit or generous warranties. Our jacket buyer might be intending to purchase the jacket, but the store's policy on returns (i.e. whether it allows this or not over what period of time) may have an impact on whether or not she actually buys a jacket from that particular shop.

Re-evaluation

The theory of **cognitive dissonance** (Festinger, 1957) suggests that we are motivated to re-evaluate our beliefs, **attitudes**, **opinions**, or values if the position we hold on them at one time is not the same as the position we held at an earlier period owing to some intervening event, circumstance, or action. This difference in evaluations, termed 'cognitive dissonance', is psychologically uncomfortable (i.e. it causes anxiety). For example, we may feel foolish or regretful about a purchasing decision (perhaps we spent too much on a night out or on a meal at a slightly too fancy restaurant). Therefore we are motivated to reduce our anxiety by redefining our beliefs, attitudes, opinions, or values to make them consistent with our circumstances (by not going to that particular bar as often or to that particular restaurant again). We will also actively avoid situations that might increase our feeling of dissonance.

To reduce dissonance, we might try to neutralize it by:

- selectively forgetting information;
- minimizing the importance of an issue, decision, or act;
- selectively exposing ourselves only to new information consonant with our existing view (rather than information that is not); and/or
- reversing a purchase decision, for instance by taking an offering back or selling it for what it was worth.

Market Insight 2.1 **Easy Purchasing at Peugeot**

Car manufacturer Peugeot, with operational headquarters in Sochaux, France, sold 81,043 new cars in the UK in 2018, taking a 3.4 per cent share of the market, significantly behind more popular brands in the UK such as Ford, Volkswagen, Vauxhall, Mercedes-Benz, BMW, Audi, and Nissan. Market share was down 1.4 per cent on the previous year. Worldwide, PSA Peugeot Citroën, the brand's owner, saw sales increase 6.8 per cent in 2018. In Europe, group sales rose 30.6 per cent to 3,106,160 units. However, PSA saw a decline in other overseas markets, including China and South East Asia (down 34.2 per cent to 262,583 units), the Middle East and Africa (down 52.8 per cent to 291,998 units), Latin America (down 15 per cent), while sales increased in India-Pacific 1.6 per cent to 26,479 units.

Given relatively sluggish economic growth and the low rates of wage inflation in many countries, vehicle manufacturers and dealership sales personnel understand the psychological anxiety that car buyers feel when purchasing new cars, especially after the purchase. The buyer's key consideration is value for money and the feeling that they have spent their money wisely. The problem is particularly acute when customers buy new cars, because new cars are considerably more expensive than second-hand cars.

Given that cars lose 15–35 per cent of their value in depreciation the moment they leave the showroom and up to 50 per cent by the third year, we can see why new car buyers feel vulnerable. Of course, there are benefits: new cars look better, incorporate the latest design features, and have reduced maintenance costs.

Car dealers work hard to reinforce the purchase decisions made by buyers of new cars by sending customers newsletters and offering efficient (or free three-year warranty) after-sales service to ensure that there are no, or few, maintenance problems. In many cases, new vehicles are sold with free insurance, 0 per cent finance deals, or 'buy now, pay later' schemes, all designed to reduce the post-purchase cognitive dissonance car buyers naturally feel after their purchase.

The Peugeot 308: even more attractive when it comes interest-free with free insurance and deposit contribution.
Source: © Dong liu/Shutterstock.

In the UK, Peugeot sweetens the sales of selected models with its Just Add Fuel® deal, by offering a time-limited offer of a fixed monthly payment over thirty-seven months, three years' free insurance, and three years' servicing (including warranty, car tax, and roadside assistance), for eligible customers.

But, Skoda, Seat, Nissan, Mazda, Jeep, and Hyundai also offer finance deals on selected models. The question for Peugeot, therefore, is whether their promotion will help to turn the tide of negative sales growth in the UK and result in an increase in market share for Peugeot.

1 **What else could Peugeot do to reduce the cognitive dissonance felt by its customers?**
2 **Do you think that cognitive dissonance would increase or decrease during an economic downturn?**
3 **Consider a time when you purchased something that left you feeling anxious afterwards. What were you purchasing and why did it make you feel anxious?**

Sources: Groupe PSA (2019); SMMT News (2019).

The concept of cognitive dissonance has significant application in marketing. Industrial or consumer purchasers are likely to feel cognitive dissonance if their expectations of proposition performance are not met in reality. This feeling of dissonance may be particularly acute in a high-**involvement** purchase, such as a car, house, holiday, or high-value investment product. (See Market Insight 2.1 on Peugeot's time-limited, fixed monthly payment scheme, aiming to minimize customer cognitive dissonance.) We are also likely to search out information to reinforce our choice of offering.

On the other hand, if we are happy with our purchase, we might decide to repurchase it, thereby displaying some degree of behavioural loyalty to a particular brand. This stage is termed the 'loyalty stage'. If we really like our purchase, we might also encourage others to buy the brand—the so-called advocacy stage. Such advocacy is common in the user-generated content (UGC) developed online.

In Figure 2.1, the buying process is iterative (i.e. it occurs in steps), particularly at the re-evaluation phase of the acquisition process. This is because the re-evaluation of the offering leads us back to any, or all, of the previous phases in the proposition acquisition process as a result of experiencing cognitive dissonance. For example, we may have bought a games console (Xbox Series X), but not be completely happy with it (perhaps we think it has poor picture quality or sound). If it were covered under warranty, this would lead us to the acquisition phase, where a new perfect product should be provided by the retailer. If the product were delivered in perfect working order, but we simply did not enjoy using it, we might revisit the original alternatives we selected (e.g. a next-generation PlayStation or a Nintendo Switch) and pick one of the other alternatives (perhaps one that might offer a larger variety of games). If we were really not sure about which games console to buy after this initial purchase, we might re-evaluate the alternatives we originally selected and then decide. If we were to really dislike our original purchase and if this were to shake our belief in what we thought was important in selecting a games console, we might go back to the information-gathering phase to get more of an idea about the offerings available. Finally, if we were extremely disappointed, we might decide that our original motive—the need to play, to relax, and to have fun—can best be solved by purchasing something other than a games console, which will still meet the same need, such as membership of a sports club.

Perceptions, Learning, and Memory

Often, consumers do not understand the messages that marketers convey, either because they have not received, comprehended, or remembered those messages, or because the messages were unclear. Consumer understanding depends on how effectively the message is transmitted and perceived. Consumers receive thousands of messages every day. Human perception, learning, and memory processes must be used to attend to, filter, and store so many messages.

Perceptions

Harris (2009) defines 'perception' as:

> the process of acquiring, interpreting, selecting, and organizing sensory information into a meaningful picture of the world. A fundamental aspect of perception is that it represents the perceiver's effort to organize stimuli into meaningful structures and understandings of their environment.

As consumers, we are interested in certain types of offering that are relevant to us when we receive marketing messages. So, men would not usually be interested in adverts or promotional messages about female sanitary products such as tampons unless they were to want to buy them on behalf of a woman in their lives. We avoid exposure to certain messages and actively seek out others. We may also expose ourselves selectively to particular messages through the media we choose to read (such as certain newspapers, magazines, ezines, Facebook pages, Twitter feeds) or watch (e.g. certain terrestrial, cable, satellite, or Internet television channels). It is therefore important to determine which media channels customers use.

Advertisers label this concept of representing the personal importance that a person attaches to a given communication message as 'involvement'. This is important because it explains a person's receptivity to communications, and people can therefore be segmented into high, medium, and low involvement groups (Michaelidou and Dibb, 2008). We are interested in consumers' receptivity because we are interested in changing or altering their perceptions of particular offerings.

An interesting way of displaying how people think about particular offerings uses perceptual mapping, a technique dating back to at least the early 1960s (Mindak, 1961). People view champagne brands differently in the UK, for example, using (brand) personality keywords 'zesty' vs 'mellow' and 'fresh fruit' vs 'baked fruit'. Lanson is associated with zesty and fresh fruit; Moët et Chandon is associated with mellow and baked fruit. Organizations deliberately seek to position themselves in the minds of specific target audience groups. To do this properly, they must understand the nature of the group's subculture.

Learning and Memory

How do consumers continually learn about new offerings, their relative performance, and new trends? The answer is by learning. Learning is the process by which we acquire new knowledge and skills, attitudes and values, through study, experience, or modelling others' behaviour. Theories of human learning include **classical conditioning**, **operant conditioning**, and **social learning**.

- *Classical conditioning* occurs when the unconditioned stimulus becomes associated with the conditioned stimulus. In other words, we learn by associating one thing with another. This approach to learning is frequently used in marketing. For example, perfume and aftershave manufacturers (such as L'Oréal) place free samples of products in sachets in magazines so that, when readers see an advert for a particular brand of perfume or aftershave, they associate the image they see with the smell and so are more likely to purchase the product when they see its image in the future.

- *Operant conditioning* is learning through behavioural reinforcement. Skinner (1954) termed this 'reinforcement', because the behaviour would occur more readily in connection with a particular stimulus if the required resulting behaviour had been reinforced through punishment or reward. In marketing, consider the typical in-store sales promotion, perhaps of a new yoghurt brand offered in a supermarket. If we do not normally eat this brand and we are curious, we might try it, because there are no costs in terms of time, effort, or money in having a taste. The sales promotion provides the stimulus, the trial behaviour occurs, and if the consumer likes the yoghurt and is rewarded with a money-off coupon, the behaviour of purchasing that particular yoghurt brand is reinforced. Supermarkets reinforce our loyalty by providing reward cards and points for purchasing particular items, for example the Nectar card in the UK or the stamps system used by the retailer 7-Eleven in its convenience stores worldwide.
- *Social learning* was proposed by the psychologist Albert Bandura (1977), who argued that humans can delay gratification and dispense their own rewards or punishment. As a result, we have more choice over how to react to stimuli; we can reflect on our own actions and change future behaviour. This led to the idea that humans learn not only from how they respond to situations, but also from how other humans respond to situations. Bandura (1977) called this 'modelling'. In social learning, we learn by observing others' behaviour. The implications for marketers are profound. For adolescents, role models include parents, athletes, and entertainers, but parents are the most influential (Martin and Bush, 2000). Parents socialize their children into purchasing and consuming the same brands that they buy, actively teaching them consumer skills—materialistic values and consumption attitudes—in their teenage years. Interaction with peers also makes adolescents more aware of different offerings (Moschis and Churchill, 1978). Companies have long recognized the power of peers, particularly in the social media world, encouraging purchasers to leave reviews of products that they have previously bought, 'like' their Facebook pages, and retweet their messages. Research indicates that product reviews from third-party websites have a greater impact on online sales compared to product reviews on seller websites. Likewise, expert reviews appear to be valued more highly than those left by ordinary consumers (Floyd et al., 2014).

But what happens once consumers have learned information? How do they retain it—that is, what stops them from forgetting such information? Knowledge develops with familiarity, repetition of marketing messages, and a consumer's acquisition of product or service information. Marketing messages need to be repeated often, because people forget them over time—particularly the specific arguments or message presented. The general substance or conclusion of the message is marginally more likely to be remembered (Bettinghaus and Cody, 1994).

We enhance memorization through the use of symbols, such as corporate identity logos, badges, and signs. Shapes, creatures, and people carry significant meanings, as seen in badges, trademarks, and logos. Airlines around the world have adopted symbols, such as the kangaroo of Australian airline Qantas. Well-recognized symbols worldwide include the KFC 'Colonel' symbol, Intel's symbol, Apple's bitten apple logo, Coca-Cola's ubiquitous script logo, and Google's multicoloured script symbol.

Our memories—as a system for storing perceptions, experience, and knowledge—are highly complex (Bettman, 1979). A variety of memorization processes affect consumer choice, including the following (see also Market Insight 2.2).

- *Factors affecting* **recognition** and **recall**—Less frequently used words in advertising are recognized more and recalled less.

- *The importance of context*—Memorization is strongly associated with the context of the stimulus, so information available in memory will be inaccessible in the wrong context.
- *The form of object coding and storage*—We store information in the form it is presented to us, either by object (brand) or dimension (offering attribute), but there is no evidence that one form is organized into memory more quickly, or more accurately than the other (Johnson and Russo, 1978).

Five of the world's most iconic logos.
Sources: Wikimedia Commons.

- *Load processing effects*—We find it more difficult to process information into our short-term and long-term memories when we are presented with a great deal of information at once.
- *Input mode effects*—Short-term recall of sound input is stronger than short-term recall of visual input where the two compete for attention, for example in television and YouTube advertising.
- *Repetition effects*—Recall and recognition of marketing messages or information increase the more a consumer is exposed to them, although later exposures add less and less to memory performance.

Market Insight 2.2 **Guilt Appeals: How Do They Change Behaviour?**

Marketers often use messages based on guilt to influence consumer behaviour. Whether it is a charity asking for donations or a gym promoting a new exercise plan, messages aimed at eliciting guilt to change behaviour are very common. How do these messages work and are they really effective? Let us consider each question in turn.

Guilt is often used in persuasive messages to trigger consumer responses.
Source: Courtesy of Greenpeace.

Marketers used to think that the learning from guilt appeals was based mostly on motivation and the negative feeling that consumers experience. Because feeling guilty about one's lack of exercise is unpleasant, consumers would decide to exercise

Market Insight 2.2 (continued)

more to feel better about themselves. In most cases, however, this view is flawed, because when we see an advert, we do not change our behaviour straight away; the idea is that the message will influence our decision at a later point in time. Recent research suggests that guilt does not work simply by making people feel bad, but influences consumers because it engages them more deeply with the message (what researchers call 'transportation'). Feelings of guilt favour persuasion because they make us pay much more attention to the message and make us feel that the message is really relevant to us. Through this process, people internalize the information communicated more effectively.

Some remain sceptical about the effectiveness of guilt and other negative messages. So what is the evidence? The reality is that guilt and other negative emotions can be effective when used appropriately. However, guilt messages can also backfire, because consumers can resent advertisers who try to manipulate them through the use of negative emotions. To avoid such negative reactions, marketers need to make sure that (a) their target audience will be predisposed to accept a message based on guilt, and (b) the message is not too explicit and assertive. The most effective campaigns use mild messages to elicit guilt.

1 **What are the implications for advertisers of the findings discussed?**

2 **Find an advertisement containing a guilt appeal (i.e. a message based on guilt) and evaluate its effectiveness based on the information noted here.**

3 **What product categories might be promoted effectively using guilt appeals? Why would these product categories be suitable for this form of communication?**

Sources: Antonetti, Baines and Jain (2018); research funded by the British Academy Small Research Grant SG142942.

Personality, Motivation, and Social Groups

How and what we buy is also based on our personalities. Personality is that aspect of our psyche that determines how we respond to our environment in a relatively stable way over time. There are various theories of personality. One popular approach categorizes people into different personality types or so-called traits. Researchers characterize personalities using bipolar scales, including the following traits:

- sociable–timid;
- action-oriented–reflection-oriented;
- stable–nervous;
- serious–frivolous;
- tolerant–suspicious;
- dominant–submissive;
- friendly–hostile;
- hard–sensitive;
- quick–slow; and/or
- masculine–feminine.

Researchers frequently talk about the 'big five' personality dimensions (McRae and Costa, 1987):

- extraversion (sociable, fun-loving, affectionate, friendly, and talkative);
- openness (original, imaginative, creative, and daring);
- conscientiousness (careful, reliable, well organized, and hard-working);
- neuroticism (worrying, nervous, highly strung, self-conscious, and vulnerable); and
- agreeableness (soft-hearted, sympathetic, forgiving, and acquiescent).

Certain types of personality prefer certain brands, for example 'conscientious' people prefer 'trusted' brands, while extroverts prefer 'sociable' brands. There are also gender differences, for example neurotic males and conscientious females prefer 'trusted brands' (Mulyanegara et al., 2009). An understanding of personality types therefore helps marketers to segment customer groups using personality dimensions.

Various companies use personality as a segmentation criterion, for example car manufacturers link personality to particular car attributes (such as safety features, aesthetics, handling). Makers of running shoes and mobile phones are interested in two personality traits in particular, extraversion and openness to experience, because these traits link to attitudinal and purchase loyalty displayed towards those brands (Matzler et al., 2006).

Visit the **online resources** and complete Internet Activity 2.1 to learn more about your own personality across a number of key personality traits.

Motivation

Abraham Maslow (1943) suggested a hierarchical order of human needs, as outlined in Figure 2.2. According to Maslow, we satisfy lower-order physiological needs first, before safety needs, then belongingness needs and esteem needs, before finally addressing the need for self-actualization.

Figure 2.2 Maslow's hierarchy of needs

Source: Adapted from Maslow (1943). This content is in the public domain.

There is little research evidence to confirm Maslow's hierarchy, but the concept possesses logical simplicity, making it a useful tool for understanding how we prioritize our own needs and therefore why we might buy what we buy.

Theory of Planned Behaviour

Theories of motivation in marketing help us to understand why people behave as they do. The theory of planned behaviour explains that behaviour is brought about by our **intention** to act in a certain way. This intention to act is affected by the attitude that a subject has towards a particular behaviour, encompassing the degree to which the subject has favourable or unfavourable evaluations or appraisals of the behaviour in question. Intention to act is also affected by the subjective norm, which is perceived social pressure to perform or not perform a particular behaviour. Finally, intention to act is affected by perceived behavioural control, referring to the perceived ease or difficulty of performing the behaviour, based on a reflection on past experience and future obstacles. Figure 2.3 provides a graphical illustration.

For example, if we consider cigarette use, we might have different attitudes towards smoking based on our geographical location, for example whether we live in France or Greece versus the UK or Sweden. We might think we cannot give up smoking because we need a cigarette to calm our nerves (perhaps we have a stressful job). Equally, we might also consider the opinions that significant others (our spouses, our children, or our friends) have towards smoking cigarettes. If we place ourselves in the mind of government (de)marketers, the key elements of the theory of planned behaviour (i.e. attitudes, subjective norms, and perceived behavioural control) can help us to understand how to discourage smoking. For example, we could try to (a) alter subjects' attitudes towards smoking, (b) change their views on how others see them as smokers, or (c) change their perceptions of how they perceive their own ability to give up. An advertising campaign called 'smokefree' from Public Health England, running in late 2015, actively discouraged smoking by showing 'disgusting' images of 'rotting' entrails in roll-up cigarettes. The idea is to make people realize that smoking roll-ups is just as dangerous as smoking manufactured cigarettes (Raven, 2014).

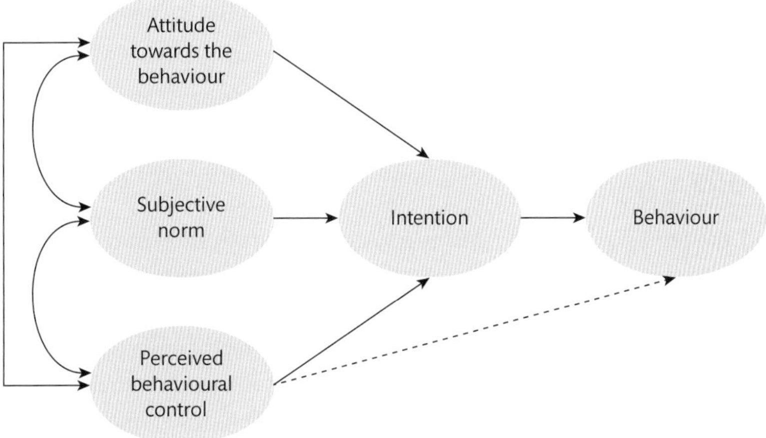

Figure 2.3 Theory of planned behaviour

Source: Ajzen (1991).

Public Health England uses a 'disgust' appeal to discourage 'roll-up' smoking.
Source: Image courtesy of DARE and Public Health England. Photography by Nick Georghiou.

Research Insight 2.1

To take your learning further, you might wish to read this influential article.

Ajzen, I. (1991) 'The theory of planned behaviour', *Organisational Behaviour and Human Decision Processes*, 50(2), 179–211.

In this highly cited seminal article, the author outlines how behaviour and behavioural intention to act in a certain way are affected by the attitude the subject has towards a particular behaviour, the subjective norm, and perceived behavioural control. The author developed our understanding of the fact that how humans intend to act may not be how they end up acting in a given situation. Intention, perception of behavioural control, attitude toward the behaviour, and subjective norm all reveal different aspects of the target behaviour and serve as possible directions for attack in attempts to alter particular behaviours, making this a powerful motivational theory in marketing.

 **Visit the online resources to read the abstract and access the full paper.**

Social Grade

In marketing, the term **social grade** refers to a system of classification of consumers based on their socio-economic grouping. NRS Ltd—the successor to the Joint Industry Committee for National Readership Surveys (JICNARS)—provides social grade population estimates, not only for the National Readership Survey, but also for a number of other major industry surveys (see Table 2.1). There is a widely held belief that consumers make purchases based on their socio-economic position within society, and that different social classes have different self-images, social horizons, and consumption goals (Coleman, 1983).

Table 2.1 Social grading scale

Social grade	Social status	Occupational status	Population estimate, UK, age 15+ (Jan 2018–Dec 2018) (%)	Population estimate, UK, age 15+ (July 1984–June 1985) (%)
A	Upper middle class	Higher managerial, administrative, and professional	4	3
B	Middle class	Intermediate, managerial, administrative, and professional	22	14
C1	Lower middle class	Supervisory, clerical, and junior managerial, administrative, and professional	29	22
C2	Skilled working class	Skilled manual workers	21	29
D	Working class	Semi-skilled and unskilled manual workers	15	18
E	Those at lowest levels of subsistence	State pensioners; casual and lowest grade workers; unemployed with state benefits only	9	14

Source: Reproduced with the kind permission of the National Readership Survey.

Lifestyle

Marketers increasingly target consumers on the basis of their lifestyles. Harris (2009) defines 'lifestyle' as 'the way a person (or group) lives. This includes patterns of social relations, consumption, entertainment and address. A lifestyle typically also reflects an individual's attitudes, values or worldview. Having a specific "lifestyle" implies a conscious or unconscious choice of one set of behaviours over others. In business, lifestyles provide a means of targeting consumers as advertisers and marketers endeavour to match consumer aspirations with products.' For example, a segmentation of the global sportswear market reveals the following lifestyle types (Ko et al., 2012).

- *Fashion leaders* (15.7 per cent of the population)—Consumers who are highly concerned with appearance, fashion, and brands. They are more likely to be trendsetters in comparison to other types of consumers, and are also less price sensitive.
- *Conspicuous fashion consumers* (27.4 per cent of the population)—Unlike fashion leaders, this group are relatively price sensitive. They are driven by status and a desire to show off to others.

- *Sensational seekers* (24.8 per cent of the population)—These consumers seek high-quality, functional clothing. They are likely to purchase less frequently than other segments, but are willing to spend money when they do decide to buy.
- *Sociable followers* (32.1 per cent of the population)—The most sociable consumers, this group are more balanced in their approach to price, brands, showing off to others, and trends. They value good-quality, fashionable items, but would not be inclined to splash out on something exciting or adventurous like sensational seekers.

Life Stage

Marketers frequently hypothesize that people at certain stages of life purchase and consume similar kinds of offerings. Most market research agencies routinely measure attitudes and purchasing patterns based on life stage to determine differences among groups. Table 2.2 indicates that there is a difference in the types of offering purchased as a result, with solitary survivors far more likely to purchase funeral plans, nursing home care, and cruise holidays, and bachelors more likely to spend their income on package and long-haul holidays and educational service products, for instance.

Visit the **online resources** and complete Internet Activity 2.2 to learn more about how Volkswagen uses the family life cycle to communicate its brand values to its target audience.

Ethnic Groups

In a globalized society, marketers are increasingly interested in how to market offerings to ethnic groups within particular populations. For example, in the United States, the Hispanic population—often immigrants from Mexico—and the black population together represent a sizeable proportion of the total population. France and the UK both have large Muslim populations. In Sweden, there are large groups of Finns, former Yugoslavs, Iraqis, and Iranians. Multicultural consumers spent about US$3.9 trillion in the United States in 2017 and, importantly, ethnic groups behave differently (Humphreys, 2017). Cui (1997) proposes that in any country in which there are ethnic marketing opportunities, a company has four main strategic options, as follows.

Have a break, have a green tea KitKat!
Source: © Paul Baines.

1. *Total standardization*—Use the existing marketing mix without modification to the ethnic market. This is very difficult to do. Even Coca-Cola, well known for its ardent approach to standardization, adapts its cola around the world (e.g. by adding pineapple in Indonesia to cater for local tastes).
2. *Product adaptation*—Use the existing marketing mix, but adapt the product to the ethnic market in question (e.g. Nestlé selling green-tea-flavoured KitKats in Thailand).

Table 2.2 The life stage concept

Bachelor (young, single person not living with parents/guardians)	Newly married or long-term cohabiting (young, no children)	Full nest I (youngest children under age of 6)	Full nest II (youngest children aged 6 or over)	Full nest III (older, married couples, with dependent children)	Empty nest I (older, married couples, no children living at home, chief income earner or both in work)	Empty nest II (older, married couples, no children living at home, chief income earner or both retired)	Solitary survivor, in work	Solitary survivor, retired
Few financial burdens Fashion opinion leaders Recreation-oriented Buy: basic kitchen equipment; basic furniture; cars; package and long-haul holidays; education	Better off financially, because of dual wages High purchase rate of consumer durables Buy: cars; refrigerators; package holidays	Home purchasing at peak Low level of savings Buy: washer-dryers; TV; baby food and related products; vitamins; toys	Financial position better Sometimes both parents in work Buy: larger-sized family food packages; cleaning materials; pianos; child-minding services	Financial position better still Both parents more likely to be in work Some children will have part-time jobs High average purchase of consumer durables Buy: better homeware and furniture products; magazines; non-essential home appliances	Home ownership at peak Most satisfied with savings and financial position Interested in travel, recreation, self-education More likely to give gifts and make charitable contributions Less interested in new products Buy: luxurious holidays; meals out; home improvements	Drastic cut in household income More likely to stay at home Buy: medical appliances and private health care; sleep aids; digestive aids	Medical needs depend on age Buy: financial, healthcare, and retirement plans; meals for one	Same medical needs as other retired group Drastic cut in income Buy: household staples; cruise holidays; nursing home services; funeral plans

Source: Adapted from Wells and Gubar (1966). Published by the American Marketing Association.

3 *Advertising adaptation*—Use the current marketing mix, but adapt the advertising, particularly the use of foreign languages, to the target ethnic market by promoting the product using different associations that are more resonant with ethnic audiences (e.g. stores in some parts of Finland advertising in Swedish and Finnish to cater for the minority Swedish population, and in the United States, in Spanish).

4 *Ethnic marketing*—Use a totally new marketing mix (e.g. Bollywood films aimed at audiences in the Indian subcontinent and in diaspora around the world using strong love and ethical themes, and a musical format).

Organizational Buyer Behaviour

Organizational buying behaviour (OBB) concerns fulfilling the needs of an organization rather than the needs of individuals (Parkinson and Baker, 1994). This therefore requires marketers to adopt processes that take into account the needs of different people, not a single individual.

The buying processes undertaken by organizations differ in a number of ways from those used by consumers. These differences are a reflection of the potential high financial value associated with these transactions, the product complexity, the relatively large value of individual orders, and the nature of the risk and uncertainty. As a result, organizations have developed particular processes and procedures that often involve a large number of people. What is central, however, is that the group of people involved in organizational purchasing processes are referred to as a **decision-making unit** (DMU), that the types of purchase they make are classified as **buyclasses**, all of which are made in various **buyphases**.

Characteristics of the DMU

The group of people tasked with buying decisions is referred to as either the 'decision-making unit' (DMU) or the **buying centre**. In many circumstances, these are informal groupings of people who come together in varying ways to contribute to the decision-making process. Certain projects, usually of major significance or value, require a group of people to be formally constituted with the responsibility for overseeing and completing the purchase of a stipulated item or products and services relating to a specific project.

DMUs vary in composition and size according to the nature of each individual purchasing task. Webster and Wind (1972) identified a number of people who undertake different roles within buying centres, and these are set out in Figure 2.4.

- **Initiators** start the whole process by requesting the purchase of an item. They may also assume other roles within the DMU or wider organization.
- **Users** literally use the product once it has been acquired and they will also evaluate its performance. Users may not only initiate the purchase process, but also sometimes be involved in the specification process. Their role is continuous, although it may vary from the highly involved to the peripheral.
- **Influencers** very often help to set the technical specifications for the proposed purchase and assist the evaluation of alternative offerings by potential suppliers. These may be consultants hired

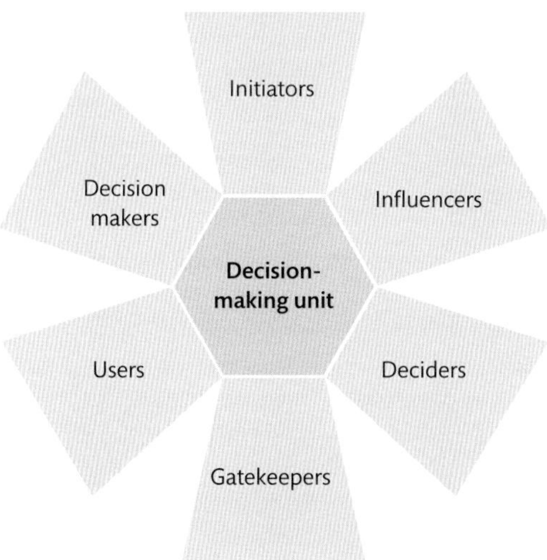

Figure 2.4 Membership of the DMU

Source: Fill and McKee (2012). Reproduced with the kind permission of Goodfellow Publishers.

to complete a particular project. An office furniture manufacturer, for example, will regard office managers as key decision makers, but understand that specifiers, such as office designers and architects, influence the office manager's decision about furniture.

- **Deciders** are those who make purchasing decisions and they are the most difficult to identify. This is because they may not have formal authority to make a purchase decision, yet are sufficiently influential internally that their decision carries the most weight. In repeat-buying activities, the buyer (see the next section) may also be the decider. However, it is normal practice for a senior manager to authorize expenditure decisions involving sums over a certain financial limit.
- **Buyers** or *purchasing managers* select suppliers and manage the process whereby the required products are procured. Buyers may not decide which product is to be purchased, but they influence the framework within which the decision is made. They will formally undertake the process whereby products and services are purchased once a decision has been made to procure them. They may be formal buyers, for example, and kick-start the purchase of a type of lubricant because the stock figures have fallen to a threshold level that indicates that current supplies will be exhausted within three weeks. They will therefore assume the role of both an initiator and a buyer.
- **Gatekeepers** have the potential to control the type and flow of information to the organization and the members of the DMU. These gatekeepers may be assistants, technical personnel, secretaries, or telephone switchboard operators.

Processes of the DMU

There are three main types of buying situation. Referred to by Robinson et al. (1967) as 'buyclasses', these are: **new task**; **modified rebuy**; and **straight rebuy**. These are summarized in Table 2.3.

Table 2.3	Main characteristics of the buyclasses		
Buyclass	**Degree of familiarity with the problem**	**Information requirements**	**Alternative solutions**
New buy	Problem fresh to decision makers	Great deal of information required	Alternative solutions unknown; all considered new
Modified rebuy	Requirement not new, but different from previous situations	More information required, but past experience of use	Buying decision needs new solutions
Rebuy	Problem identical to previous experiences	Little or no information required	Alternative solutions not sought or required

Source: Fill and Turnbull (2016). Reproduced with the kind permission of Pearson Education Ltd.

Buyclasses

New Task

As the name implies, the 'new task' buyclass sees the organization faced with a first-time buying situation. Risk is inevitably large at this point, because there is little collective experience of the product or service or of the relevant suppliers. As a result of these factors, there are normally a large number of decision participants. Each participant requires a lot of information, and a relatively long period of time is needed for the information to be assimilated and a decision to be made.

Modified Rebuy

Having purchased a product, uncertainty is reduced, but not eliminated, so the organization may request through its buyer(s) that certain modifications be made to future purchases, such as adjustments to the specification of the product, further negotiation on price levels, or perhaps an arrangement for alternative delivery patterns. Fewer people are involved in the 'modified rebuy' decision-making process than in the new task situation.

Straight Rebuy

In the 'straight rebuy' situation, the purchasing department reorders on a routine basis, very often working from an approved list of suppliers. These may be products that an organization consumes to keep operating (e.g. office stationery), or may be low-value materials used within the operational, value-added part of the organization (e.g. the manufacturing processes). No other people are involved with the exercise until different suppliers attempt to change the environment in which the decision is made. For example, a new supplier may interrupt the procedure with a potentially better offer. This may stimulate the emergence of a modified rebuy situation.

Straight rebuy presents classic conditions for the use of automatic reordering systems. Costs can be reduced, managerial time redirected to other projects, and the relationship between buyer and seller embedded within a stronger framework. One possible difficulty is that both parties perceive the system to be a significant exit barrier should conditions change and this may deter flexibility or restrict opportunities to develop the same or other relationships.

Buyphases

OBB consists of a series of sequential activities through which organizations proceed when making purchasing decisions. Robinson et al. (1967) referred to these as 'buying stages' or 'buyphases'. The following sequence of buyphases is particular to the new task situation just described. Many of these buyphases can be ignored or compressed according to the complexity of the offering and when either a modified rebuy or straight rebuy situation is encountered.

Need/Problem Recognition

The need/problem recognition phase is about the identification of a gap between the benefits an organization is experiencing now and the benefits it would like to experience. For example, when a new product is to be produced, there is an obvious gap between having the necessary materials and components and being out of stock and unable to build. The first decision is therefore about how to close this gap and there are two broad options: outsourcing the whole or parts of the production process; or building or making the objects in-house. Thus the need has been recognized and the gap identified.

The rest of this section is based on a build decision being taken.

Product Specification

As a result of identifying a problem and the size of the gap, influencers and users can determine the desired characteristics of the product needed to resolve the problem. This may take the form of either a general functional description or a much more detailed analysis and the creation of a detailed technical specification for a particular product. What sort of photocopier is required? What is it expected to achieve? How many documents should it copy per minute? Is a collator or tray required? This is an important part of the process, because if it is executed properly, it will narrow the supplier search and save on the costs associated with evaluation prior to a final decision. The results of the functional and detailed specifications are often combined within a purchase order specification.

Supplier and Product Search

At the supplier and product search stage, the buyer actively seeks suppliers who can supply the necessary product(s). There are two main issues at this point: first, will the product match the specification and the required performance standards; and second, will the potential supplier meet the other organizational requirements such as experience, reputation, accreditation, and credit rating?

In most circumstances, organizations review the market and their internal sources of information, then arrive at a decision that is based on rational criteria.

Evaluation of Proposals

Depending on the complexity and value of the potential order(s), the proposal is a vital part of the process and should be prepared professionally. The proposals from the shortlisted organizations are reviewed in the context of two main criteria: the purchase order specification; and the evaluation of the supplying organization. If the potential supplier is already a part of the network, little search and review time is needed. If the proposed supplier is not part of the network, a review may be necessary to establish whether it will be appropriate (in terms of price, delivery, and service) and whether there is the potential for a long-term relationship or whether this is a single purchase that is unlikely to be repeated.

Supplier Selection

The DMU will normally undertake a supplier analysis and use a variety of decision criteria, according to the particular type of item sought. A further useful perspective is to view supplier organizations as a continuum, from reliance on a single source through to the use of a wide variety of suppliers for the same product. Some companies maintain a range of multiple sources (a practice of many government departments). The major disadvantage is that this approach fails to drive cost as low as possible, because the discounts derived from volume sales are not achieved. The advantage to the buying centre is that a relatively small investment is required and little risk is entailed in following such a strategy. At the other end of the continuum are organizations that use only a single-source supplier. All purchases are made from the single source until circumstances change to such a degree that the buyer's needs are no longer being satisfied. An increasing number of organizations are choosing to enter alliances with a limited number of, or even single-source, suppliers (see Market Insight 2.3). The objective is to build a long-term relationship, to work together to build quality, and for each to help the other to achieve its goals. Outsourcing manufacturing activities for non-core activities has increased considerably.

Evaluation

The order is written for the selected supplier, which is then monitored and evaluated against such diverse criteria as responsiveness to enquiries, modifications to the specification, and timing of delivery. When the product is delivered, it may reach the stated specification, but fail to satisfy the original need. In this case, the specification needs to be rewritten before any future orders are placed. Developments in the environment can impact on organizational buyers, changing both the nature of decisions and the way in which they are made. The decision to purchase new plant and machinery, for example, requires consideration of the future cash flows generated by the capital item. Many people will be involved in the decision and the time necessary for consultation may mean that other parts of the decision-making process are completed simultaneously.

Visit the **online resources** and complete Internet Activity 2.3. This will help you to learn about the seven buying phases through which organizations go when purchasing industrial goods and services.

Market Insight 2.3 **Making an Airbus**

Airbus is a European aerospace corporation that designs and manufactures commercial aircrafts, helicopters, satellites, as well as other products and services in the defence sector. In 2018, Airbus delivered 800 commercial aircrafts and 356 helicopters, generating revenues of €63.7 billion. While Airbus has a global workforce, the company's main production facilities are based in Western Europe in France, Germany, Spain, and the UK. For example, one of their market leading products, the commercial aircraft A330neo, was first assembled in the French city of Toulouse in 2016.

Large-scale technological solutions can often take years to be designed and manufactured before they can be delivered. Airbus sources about 80 per cent of its activity to more than 12,000 external companies. Moreover, due to the stringent certifications required to fly a commercial aircraft or launch a satellite into orbit, Airbus is very selective when it comes to choosing whom the company works with. Its suppliers must therefore adhere to a detailed code of conduct, ensuring they can demonstrate ethical business practice such as showing concern for the environment and employee rights.

Competing suppliers that wish to offer their services to Airbus can contact the company via their dedicated online platform. They can view the precise requirements set by Airbus, and submit their proposals for the Airbus procurement team to review.

The A330neo is one of Airbus's latest commercial aircraft.

Source: © Skycolors/Shutterstock.

1. **What are the advantages of a company like Airbus assembling the final product itself, rather than outsourcing this to a supplier?**
2. **What advantages does outsourcing other parts of the production process offer Airbus?**
3. **Why do you think it is important for suppliers to adhere to a code of ethics consistent with those of Airbus?**

Sources: Airbus (2018); https://www.airbus.com/be-an-airbus-supplier.html.

Research Insight 2.2

To take your learning further, you might wish to read this influential paper.

Johnston, W. J., and Lewin, J. E. (1996) 'Organizational buying behavior: Toward an integrative framework', *Journal of Business Research*, 35(1), 1–15.

Although written in 1996, this paper is important because it includes critical contributions by the leading researchers, including the work of Robinson et al. (1967), Webster and Wind (1972), and Sheth (1973). The paper concludes by developing a model of buying behaviour drawing on a number of constructs developed since these three leading models were published.

 **Visit the online resources to read the abstract and access the full paper.**

Purchasing in Organizations

All organizations have to buy a variety of products and services to operate normally and achieve their performance targets. What we have set out so far are the general principles, types, and categories associated with organizational buying. The way in which organizations buy products and services, however, varies considerably and does not always fit neatly with the categories presented here. Professional purchasing is not only an important (if not critical) feature, but also, for many organizations, an integral part of their overall operations and strategic orientation (Ryals and Rogers, 2006; Pressey et al., 2007).

A common approach is to reduce the number of suppliers, sometimes to only one, and to use **strategic procurement** (as it is often termed) to negotiate with suppliers on a cooperative basis, to help to build long-term relationships. Purchasing has become an integral and strategic part of an organization's operations, and managing a smaller number of suppliers can improve performance considerably.

There are several strategic issues related to the purchasing activities undertaken by organizations. First, there is the 'make or buy' decision. Should organizations make and/or assemble products for resale, or outsource or buy in particular products, parts, services, or sub-assemblies, and concentrate on what is referred to as 'core' activities or competencies? Second, the benefits that arise through closer cooperation with suppliers and the increasing influence of buyer–seller relationships and 'joint value creation' have inevitably led to a tighter, more professional, and integrated purchasing function. The third strategy-related issue concerns the degree to which the purchasing function is integrated into the organization. New information technology (IT) systems have raised the level of possible integration of purchasing and operations to the extent that the competitive strength of the organization is enhanced (Hemsworth et al., 2008). As though to highlight the variation in approaches to purchasing behaviour, Svahn and Westerlund (2009) identify six principal purchasing strategies used by organizations, as follows.

- The *price minimizer* purchasing strategy refers to a buyer's efficiency orientation whereby the main purchasing goal is to seek the lowest price for the offering. To help to achieve this, the buyer actively promotes competition among several potential suppliers.
- The *bargainer* purchasing strategy focuses on a dyadic buyer–seller relationship. Here, the buyer's strategy is to achieve operational efficiency through long-term collaboration with a selected supplier (Håkansson and Snehota, 1995).
- The *clockwiser* purchasing strategy refers to network relationships that function predictably and precisely, just as a clock works. Again, the goal is strict efficiency, achieved through the vigilant integration of production-based integrated control systems and IT, and the careful coordination of the value activities performed by each supply network partner (Glenn and Wheeler, 2004).
- The *adaptator* purchasing strategy focuses on adapting the manufacturing processes between the exchange parties. This can arise during the purchase of one major product or service when the seller is required to accommodate its offering to the particular needs of the buyer.
- The *projector* purchasing strategy occurs between buyers and sellers who are development partners. This can occur during projects when partners develop their offerings in close collaboration, after which the joint-development project is completed and the parties continue the development work independently. As an example of this strategy, we could explore

the collaboration between Nokia and Skype. These major players in the information and communication technology (ICT) industry joined their development efforts to develop a radically novel type of mobile phone that utilizes the Voice-over-Internet Protocol (VoIP) service (the free call system created by Skype).

- The *updater* purchasing strategy is based on collaboration in research and development. Here, collaboration between partners is continuous and the nature of the relationship is not a dyad, but a supply network. This collaboration is intentional, as demonstrated by Intel and various personal computer (PC) manufacturers, which produce updated versions of PCs based on constant co-development.

Chapter Summary

To consolidate your learning, the key points from this chapter are summarized here.

- **Explain the consumer product acquisition process.**

  The consumer product acquisition model has six key stages: motive development; information gathering; product evaluation; product selection; acquisition; and re-evaluation.

- **Explain the processes involved in human perception, learning, and memory in relation to consumer choice.**

  The human perception, learning, and memory processes involved in consumer decision-making are complex. When designing advertising, developing distribution strategies, designing new offerings, and implementing other marketing tactics, marketers should (repeatedly) explain the information associated with these actions to consumers. Such an approach is necessary to encourage consumers to engage with, remember, and learn about different offerings, which in turn influences consumers' buying decisions.

- **Understand the importance of personality and motivation in consumer behaviour.**

  Consumers are motivated differently in their purchasing behaviours depending on their personalities and social identities, and, to some extent, how they feel their personality or social identity fits with particular offerings. Maslow's (1943) seminal work on human needs helps us to understand how we are motivated to satisfy five key human desires. From the theory of planned behaviour (Ajzen, 1991), we know that how we intend to behave is not always how we actually behave, because this is affected by our attitudes towards the behaviour in question, subjective norms (how we think others perceive that behaviour), and our own perceptions of how we can control our behaviour.

- **Set out the main processes and stages associated with organizational buying and purchasing.**

  Organizational buying behaviour can be understood to be a group buying activity in which a number of people with differing roles make purchasing decisions that affect the organization and the achievement of its objectives. Buying decisions can be understood in terms of different types of decision (buyclasses) and different stages (buyphases).

Review Questions

1. What is the process through which consumers go when buying offerings?
2. How are the psychological concepts of perception, learning, and memory relevant to understanding consumer choice?
3. How are concepts of personality relevant to understanding consumer behaviour?
4. How are concepts of motivation relevant to understanding consumer behaviour?
5. What is the theory of planned behaviour?
6. What are opinions, attitudes, and values, and how do they relate to consumer behaviour?
7. How does lifestyle and ethnicity influence how we buy?
8. Name four of the different types of person that make up a DMU.
9. Distinguish clearly between buyphases and buyclasses.
10. What are the main purchasing strategies adopted by organizations?

Worksheet Summary

To apply the knowledge you have gained from this chapter and to test your understanding, visit the **online resources** and complete Worksheet 2.1.

Discussion Questions

1. Having read Case Insight 2.1 at the beginning of this chapter, how could Aircall persuade existing customers to shift from monthly to annual contracts?

2. Describe the purchasing process that you would use in the following instances using the consumer product acquisition model shown in Figure 2.1.
   - **A** A chocolate bar, for example a Snickers or Cadbury's Dairy Milk in the UK, Plopp in Sweden, or Droste in the Netherlands
   - **B** A flight to the Caribbean from your home country
   - **C** A tablet computer to help you to write essays and complete group work for your marketing course
   - **D** Selecting a hosting service for your new personal website
   - **E** Refuse collection services from the local council (paid for indirectly through local taxes)

3. As the manager of the DMU of a tech company, describe the purchasing process that you would use in the following instances:
   - **A** A 3D printer for the new innovation team
   - **B** New PC monitors for the whole company after many employees complained about their poor resolution and brightness
   - **C** A new order of sticky notes prompted by low stock levels in the stationery cupboard

Visit the **online resources** and complete the multiple-choice questions to assess your knowledge of this chapter.

Glossary

attitudes refers to the mental states of individuals that underlie the structuring of perceptions and guide behavioural response.

buyclasses the different types of buying situation faced by organizations.

buyers also known as 'purchasing managers', these people select suppliers and manage the process whereby the required products are procured.

buying centre *see* **decision-making unit**

buyphases the series of sequential activities or stages through which organizations proceed when making purchasing decisions.

classical conditioning a theory of learning propounded by Russian physiologist Ivan Pavlov, who carried out a series of experiments with his dogs. He realized that if he were to ring a bell before serving food, the dogs would automatically associate the sound of the bell (the conditioned stimulus) with the presentation of the food (the unconditioned stimulus), and begin salivating. Classical conditioning occurs when the unconditioned stimulus becomes associated with the conditioned stimulus.

cognition a psychological term relating to the action of thinking about something. Our opinions are cognitive—that is, mental structures formed about something in our minds.

cognitive dissonance a psychological theory proposed by Leon Festinger in 1957, which states that we are motivated to re-evaluate our beliefs, attitudes, opinions, or values if the position we hold on them at one point in time does not concur with the position held at an earlier period owing to some intervening event, circumstance, or action.

deciders people who make organizational purchasing decisions; often very difficult to identify.

decision-making unit a group of people who make purchasing decisions on behalf of an organization.

evoked set a group of goods, brands, or services for a specific item brought to mind in a particular purchasing situation and from which a person makes a decision as to which product, brand, or service to buy.

gatekeepers people who control the type and flow of information into an organization, and in particular to members of the DMU.

influencers people who help to set the technical specifications for a proposed purchase and assist the evaluation of alternative offerings by potential suppliers.

initiators people who start the organizational buying decision process.

intention in the consumer context, linked to whether or not we are motivated to purchase a good or service.

involvement the greater the personal importance people attach to a given communication message, the more involvement they are said to have with that communication.

media facilities used by companies to convey or deliver messages to target audiences; plural of medium.

modified rebuy the organizational processes associated with the infrequent purchase of products and services.

new task the organizational processes associated with buying a product or service for the first time.

operant conditioning a learning theory developed by B. F. Skinner, which suggests that when a subject acts on a stimulus from the environment (antecedents), this is more likely to result in a particular behaviour (behaviour) if that behaviour is reinforced (consequence) through reward or punishment.

opinions refers to observable verbal responses given by individuals to an issue or question; easily affected by current affairs and discussions with significant others.

organizational buyer behaviour the characteristics, issues, and processes associated with the behaviour of producers, resellers, government units, and institutions when purchasing goods and services.

overt search the point in the buying process at which a consumer seeks further information in relation to a product or buying situation, according to the Howard–Sheth model of buyer behaviour.

perception a mental picture based on existing attitudes, beliefs, needs, stimulus factors, and factors specific to our situation, which governs our attitudes and behaviour towards objects, events, or people in the world about us.

personality that aspect of our psyche which determines the way in which we respond to our environment in a relatively stable way over time.

recall a measure of advertising effectiveness based on what an individual is able to remember about an advert.

recognition refers to the process whereby new images and words are compared with existing images and words in memory and a match is found.

SaaS a method of software distribution in which users pay for a subscription to access hosted software.

SME a small to medium company in terms of headcount and revenues.

social class a system of classification of consumers or citizens, based on the socio-economic status of the chief income earner in a household, typically into various subgroupings of middle class and working class.

social grade a system of classification of people based on their socio-economic group, usually based on the household's chief income earner.

social learning a theory, advocated by Albert Bandura, which suggests that we can learn from observing the experiences of others, and that, in contrast with operant conditioning, we can delay gratification and even administer our own rewards or punishment.

straight rebuy the organizational processes associated with the routine reordering of good and services, often undertaken from an approved list of suppliers.

strategic procurement an approach used to negotiate with suppliers on a cooperative basis, to help to build long-term relationships.

users people or groups who use business products and services once they have been acquired, and who then evaluate the performance of the products or services.

value the regard in which something is held, typically, although not always, expressed in financial terms.

References

Airbus (2018) 'Annual Report 2018'. Retrieve from: https://www.airbus.com/investors/financial-results-and-annual-reports.html#annualreports (accessed 30 October 2020).

Ajzen, I. (1991) 'The theory of planned behavior', *Organizational Behavior and Human Decision Processes*, 50(2), 179–211.

Antonetti, P., Baines, P., and Jain, S. (2018) 'The persuasiveness of guilt appeals over time: Pathways to delayed compliance', *Journal of Business Research*, 90, 14–25.

Bandura, A. (1977) *Social Learning Theory*, Englewood Cliffs, NJ: Prentice-Hall.

Bettinghaus, E. P., and Cody, M. J. (1994) *Persuasive Communication* (5th edn), London: Harcourt Brace.

Bettman, J. R. (1979) 'Memory factors in consumer choice: A review', *Journal of Marketing*, 43(2), 37–53.

Coleman, R. P. (1983) 'The continuing significance of social class to marketing', *Journal of Consumer Research*, 10(3), 265–80.

Cui, G. (1997) 'Marketing strategies in a multi-ethnic environment', *Journal of Marketing Theory and Practice*, 5(1), 122–35.

Festinger, L. (1957) *A Theory of Cognitive Dissonance*. Palo Alto, CA: Stanford University Press.

Fill, C., and McKee, S. (2012) *Business Marketing*. Oxford: Goodfellow.

Fill, C., and Turnbull, S. (2016) *Marketing* Communications (7th edn), London: Pearson.

Floyd, K., Freling, R., Alhoqail, S., Cho, H. Y., and Freling, T. (2014) 'How online product reviews affect retail sales: A meta-analysis', *Journal of Retailing*, 90(2), 217–32.

Glenn, R. R., and Wheeler, A. R. (2004) 'A new framework for supply chain manager selection: Three hurdles to competitive advantage', *Journal of Marketing Channels*, 11(4), 89–103.

Groupe PSA (2019) 'A new record set in 2018 at 3.9M units with worldwide sales up 6.8%', 15 January. Retrieve from: https://media.groupe-psa.com/en/new-record-set-2018-39m-units-worldwide-sales-68 (accessed 30 October 2020).

Håkansson, H., and Snehota, I. (1995) *Developing Relationships in Business Networks*, London: Routledge.

Harris, P. (2009). *Penguin Dictionary of Marketing*. London: Penguin.

Hemsworth, D., Sánchez-Rodríguez, C., and Bidgood, B. (2008) 'A structural model of the impact of quality management practices and purchasing-related information systems on purchasing performance: A TQM perspective', *Total Quality Management & Business Excellence*. 19(1–2), 151–64.

Howard, J. A., and Sheth, J. N. (1969) *The Theory of Buyer Behavior*. New York: Wiley.

Humphreys, J. M. (2017) *The Multicultural Economy 2017*, Selig Center for Economic Growth, Terry College of Business, University of Georgia.

Johnson, E. J., and Russo, J. E. (1978) 'The organisation of product information in memory identified by recall times', in K. Hunt (ed.), *Advances in Consumer Research, Vol. V*. Chicago, IL: Association for Consumer Research, 79–86.

Johnston, W. J., and Lewin, J. E. (1996) 'Organizational buying behavior: Toward an integrative framework', *Journal of Business Research*, 35(1), 1–15.

Ko, E., Taylor, C. R., Sung, H., et al. (2012) 'Global marketing segmentation usefulness in the sportswear industry', *Journal of Business Research*, 65(11), 1565–75.

McRae, R. R., and Costa, P. T. (1987) 'Validation of the five-factor model of personality across instruments and observers', *Journal of Personality and Social Psychology*, 52(1), 81–90.

Martin, C. A., and Bush, A. J. (2000) 'Do role models influence teenagers' purchase intentions and behavior?', *Journal of Consumer Marketing*, 17(5), 441–54.

Maslow, A. H. (1943) 'A theory of motivation', *Psychological Review*, 50(4), 370–96.

Matzler, K., Bidmon, S., and Grabner-Kräuter, S. (2006) 'Individual determinants of brand affect: The role of the personality traits of extraversion and openness to experience', *Journal of Product and Brand Management*, 15(7), 427–34.

Michaelidou, N., and Dibb, S. (2008) 'Consumer involvement: A new perspective', *Marketing Review*, 8(1), 83–99.

Mindak, W. A. (1961) 'Fitting the semantic differential to the marketing problem', *Journal of Marketing*, 25(4), 29–33.

Moschis, G. P., and Churchill, G. A., Jr (1978) 'Consumer socialisation: A theoretical and empirical analysis', *Journal of Marketing Research*, 15(4), 599–609.

Mulyanegara, R. C., Tsarenko, Y., and Anderson, A. (2009) 'The big five and brand personality: Investigating the impact of consumer personality on preferences towards particular brand personality', *Journal of Brand Management*, 16(4), 234–47.

Parkinson, S. T., and Baker, M. J. (1994) *Organizational Buying Behaviour: Purchasing and Marketing Management Implications*, London: Macmillan.

Pressey, A., Tzokas, N., and Winklhofer, H. (2007) 'Strategic purchasing and the evaluation of "problem" key supply relationships: What do key suppliers need to know?', *Journal of Business & Industrial Marketing*, 22(5), 282–94.

Raven, D. (2014) 'Watch graphic anti-smoking advert which shows father rolling rotting flesh to shock smokers into kicking habit', *The Mirror*, 29 December. Retrieve from: https://www.mirror.co.uk/news/uk-news/watch-graphic-anti-smoking-advert-shows-4886649 (accessed 30 October 2020).

Robinson, P. J., Faris, C. W., and Wind, Y. (1967) *Industrial Buying and Creative Marketing*, Boston, MA: Allyn & Bacon.

Ryals, L. J., and Rogers, B. (2006) 'Holding up the mirror: The impact of strategic procurement practices on account management', *Business Horizons*, 49(1), 41–50.

Sheth, J. N. (1973) 'A model of industrial buyer behavior', *Journal of Marketing*, 37(4), 50–6.

Skinner, B. F. (1954) 'The science of learning and the art of teaching', *Harvard Educational Review*, 24(2), 88–97.

SMMT News. (2019) 'Fall in new car market wake up call to policy makers as environmental goals at risk', Society of Motor Manufacturers and Traders, 7 January. Retrieve from: https://www.smmt.co.uk/2019/01/fall-in-new-car-market-wake-up-call-to-policy-makers-as-environmental-goals-at-risk/ (accessed 10 December 2019).

Svahn, S., and Westerlund, M. (2009) 'Purchasing strategies in supply relationships', *Journal of Business & Industrial Marketing*, 24(3–4), 173–81.

Webster, F. E., and Wind, Y. (1972) *Organizational Buying Behaviour*, Englewood Cliffs, NJ: Prentice Hall.

Wells, W. D., and Gubar, G. (1966) 'Life cycle concept in marketing research', *Journal of Marketing Research*, 3(4), 355–63.

Chapter 3
Market Research and Customer Insight

Learning Outcomes

After studying this chapter, you will be able to:

- define the terms 'market research', 'marketing research', and 'customer insight';
- describe the customer insight process and the role of marketing research within it;
- explain the role of marketing research and list the range of possible research approaches;
- define the term 'big data' and describe its role in marketing;
- discuss the importance of ethics and the adoption of a code of conduct in marketing research; and
- understand the concept of 'equivalence' in relation to obtaining comparable data.

Case Insight 3.1
CLiKD

Market Insight 3.1
Bord Bia's Appetite for Insight

Market Insight 3.2
How Scent Sells Lingerie at Hunkemöller

Market Insight 3.3
M&S Spies Data Opportunity

Case Insight 3.1 CLiKD

CLiKD is an award-winning dating app based in London that gives people a creative way to meet new people. We speak to Emin Can Turan, head of marketing, to find out how this SME competes with much bigger rivals in the online dating world by leveraging marketing analytics data.

CLiKD, the dating application, was first founded in March 2016 and launched as a **minimum viable product (MVP)** in June 2017. Its mission is to provide meaningful connections and quality dates in the digital era. It achieves that with its **unique selling point/proposition (USP)**, using creativity and individuality, via user-rated photographs, in a highly engaging way to determine matches between dates. In a seemingly crowded market, CLiKD has successfully differentiated itself and played into newly developing societal trends.

Our app provides the user with the ability to custom-create, or to choose, a three-question personality test as the qualification mechanism for the matching process. These questions are posed using binary 'which picture do I prefer?' options. When both parties pass two out of three questions by answering the questions in the same way, they are matched and are able to talk to each other. These questions are themed around values, interests, and beliefs, ranging from 'Jesus Christ—is he a swear word or your saviour?', to 'Football player or rugby lad?', to 'Gryffindor or Slytherin'—the latter a reference to the world of Harry Potter. The matching experience is fun and highly gamified, placing personality first in the matching process, not simply how someone looks. For these reasons, CLiKD has become one of the few dating apps to appeal to **Gen Z**,who grew up with digital technology.

We target Gen Z and **millennials**. In the digital dating world, Tinder paved the way with convenience, because people could achieve many more matches and dates within a short time frame by famously swiping left (dislike) or right (like) on each photograph of a prospective date. The problem with this approach however is that it is rather superficial, based on looks alone, and lacks personality, and has resulted in a surge of bad dates. In fact, the news is plastered with horror stories of Tinder dates gone wrong. Consumers are now experiencing swipe fatigue and a genuine hunger for more meaningful connections in a fast-paced, highly digitalized world.

Match.com attempted to solve this matching problem by using complex tests and long questionnaires. However, both Gen Z and millennials have turned their back on this approach as well, finding it too time-consuming, tedious, and intrusive. CLiKD has sought to solve this problem by allowing consumers to use the three-question method, which combines the speed and simplicity of Tinder's approach with the insights gleaned from Match.com's success with its own questions. The unique quiz element allows users to define what is important to them in relationships and matches them accordingly with people on their wavelength.

Having a great matching process is one thing but getting noticed in a crowded market on a small budget is another, very difficult problem. We realized we needed to be much cleverer in how we should use our marketing budget when competing in a crowded market against incumbent companies with significantly larger budgets. To stand out, and gain app downloads, we knew we had to be smarter than our competitors.

Currently the industry cost per acquisition (CPA) is between £2.55 and £5 per customer. For example, top professional digital acquisition companies claim to have an average CPA of £2.55, using their own proprietary techniques. Industry incumbents—such

Case Insight 3.1 (continued)

as Match.com—our competitor intelligence informs us, pay their affiliates around £5 for a referral.

The problem is that while acquiring customers in the traditional way is too expensive for us, our marketing budget is also completely dwarfed by our competitors' marketing budgets. Consequently, going head-to-head with them by paying £2–£5 CPA was not plausible. We had to come up with a different way. We figured one way of doing this was by making use of marketing analytics to come up with better customer insight data.

The question for us was: how could we lower our CPA and what role would marketing analytics play in the process?

Introduction

How do companies develop their successful offerings? More often than not, companies develop propositions using research programmes designed to identify customers' changing needs.

Contemporary **marketing research** is very much affected by technology. Digitization has led to a proliferation of information and data being available to marketers. This shift in availability, often referred to as 'big data', is currently transforming the market research industry. Traditional market research companies, such as A.C. Nielsen and Mintel Group, are under pressure from large tech firms, such as IBM and Adobe, as well as fast-growing analytic companies, such as System1 Group (formerly BrainJuicer) and Qualtrics, offering a wide range of tools with which to track customer behaviours in real time (GreenBook, 2016; Market Research Society, 2017).

We begin this chapter by defining the difference between 'marketing research' and 'market research'. Whereas market research is conducted to understand markets—customers, competitors, and industries—marketing research also determines the impact of marketing strategies and tactics. Marketing research thus subsumes market research. 'Customer insight' refers to actionable knowledge about customers gained through research. We then introduce the different steps through which marketers need to go when conducting research. We also introduce big data, which is increasingly being used to generate insights that lead to strategic marketing decisions. Finally, we consider the challenges of conducting international marketing research.

The Customer Insight Process

In Chapter 2, we examined the fundamentals of customer behaviour. The customer insight process allows organizations to generate knowledge about consumers that is relevant to their specific circumstances. Market research is work undertaken to determine the structural characteristics of the industry of concern (e.g. demand, market share, market volumes, customer characteristics, and segmentation), whereas marketing research is work undertaken to understand how to make specific marketing strategy decisions (e.g. for pricing, sales forecasting, proposition testing, and promotion research). Marketing research is further characterized by being systematic, meaning that the procedures followed in each step of the research process are methodologically sound, well documented, and, as far as possible, planned in advance (Malhotra, 2019).

In contrast, customer insights are generated based on the knowledge gained by different research activities. Information requires transformation to generate insight. Customer insights are thus distinct from customer information: they are an acquired, deeper understanding of customers (see Market Insight 3.1). 'Marketing analytics' refers to the mathematical and statistical analytical procedures used to distil insights out of high-volume, high-velocity, and/or high-variety information, typically denoted as 'big data'. We will discuss this further in the section 'Big Data and Marketing Analytics', but before doing so we will look at different steps in the insight generation and market research processes, respectively.

A customer insight is of value if it is rare, difficult to imitate, and of potential use to formulate management decisions (Said et al., 2015). Cowan (2008) suggests that if organizations are to genuinely make use of insights:

- chief executive officers (CEOs) and/or chief marketing officers (CMOs) should recognize the importance of supporting the insight process, ask 'helicopter' (i.e. wide-ranging) questions, not try to guess the answers to strategic problems, demand evidence-based answers, and provide the necessary resources;
- researchers should view themselves as problem-solvers, not reporters, focus on trying to gain a causal understanding, not only describing attitudes, and focus on changing the marketing situation; and
- insight managers should challenge the strategy assumptions that the organization is making, challenge the 'obvious' solution, since it is often wrong, analyse and combine all existing relevant data, and devote greater resources to extracting insight.

Market Insight 3.1 **Bord Bia's Appetite for Insight**

Bord Bia (the Irish Food Board) is a state agency and marketing business which partners with Irish food, drink, and horticulture suppliers to help grow their brands internationally. It acts as a link between these suppliers and existing and potential customers throughout the world. Irish food, drink, and horticulture exports are hugely valuable to the Irish economy and were valued at €12.1 billion in 2018.

In March 2016, Bord Bia opened a state-of-the-art Customer Insights Centre at its headquarters in Dublin as part of its growing investment in market and consumer research. This 'Thinking House' is a creative space that includes a 'Trends Zone' to highlight the latest food and drink innovations from around the world, and a packaging and branding gallery to promote best class design and showcase Bord Bia's recent work with Irish food and drink brands. It also includes a 'Living Room' and an adjacent viewing room that allows Bord Bia and the industry to conduct qualitative focus and discussion groups. A library provides invaluable access to a wide range of databases and reports that previously would have been financially prohibitive for many small and medium-sized companies in the industry. Finally, an innovative working space, with room for up to seventy people, is available for the industry to use for workshops, meetings, and presentations.

Market Insight 3.1 (continued)

Bord Bia's Customer Insights team currently works with over one hundred brands a year across all sectors, ranging from small start-ups to large multinationals, to help better prepare their products for international sale. Bord Bia has set itself the ambitious target of doubling its exports to reach a target of €19 billion by 2025. According to Helen King, Director of Customer Insights at Bord Bia, 'Insights gives us a deep understanding of our markets and end users, so that our industry can make better informed decisions based on what consumers and customers want and need. Ultimately, this will lead to commercial success'.

1 **Why are customer insights so important for Irish food, drink, and horticulture exporters?**

2 **Is there ever a danger in having too much customer insight?**

3 **Visit the Bord Bia website (www.bordbia.ie). Highlight how the Customer Insights Centre is helping Irish exporters better prepare for the political uncertainty and currency fluctuations surrounding Brexit.**

Sources: Bord Bia (2016, 2019); Hubert (2016); RTE (2016).

This case is kindly contributed by Marie O'Dwyer at Waterford Institute of Technology, Republic of Ireland

Research Insight 3.1

To take your learning further, you might wish to read this influential paper:

Lemon, K. N., and Verhoef, P. C. (2016) 'Understanding customer experience throughout the customer journey', *Journal of Marketing*, 80(6), 69–96.

In this article, the authors emphasize the complexity of the 'customer journey', i.e. the multiple ways customers engage with businesses through various channels and media. Customer experience is considered a blend of multiple dimensions (e.g. cognitive, emotional, sensorial) in the lead up to, during and after a purchase is made. The authors explain why customer experience has become a priority for modern business by reviewing a broad range of literature from different areas of marketing. Moreover, they explore what firms do to understand their customers' experience, including how customers interact with 'touch points', and the variety of paths that a customer can take to complete their purchase. They also discuss how customer experience can be measured by firms and suggest managerial implications and further research avenues.

 **Visit the online resources to read the abstract and access the full paper.**

Commissioning Market Research

Much market research is not conducted in-house by marketers. When commissioning research, a client determines whether or not it wants to commission an agency, a consultant, a field and tabulation (tab) agency, or a data preparation and analysis agency. Typically, a consultant might do a job that does not require extensive fieldwork; a field and tab agency is used when the organization can design its own research, but not undertake the data collection; a data preparation and analysis agency, when it can both design and collect the data, but does not have the expertise to analyse it; and a **full-service agency**, when it does not have the expertise to design the research and collect or analyse the data.

Agencies are shortlisted according to criteria and asked to make a presentation of their services. Visits are made to their premises to check the quality of agency staff and facilities, and previous reports are considered to assess the quality of the agency's work. Permission to interview or obtain references from an agency's clients is usually requested. Each agency is evaluated based on its ability to undertake work of an acceptable quality at an appropriate price. The criteria used to evaluate an agency's suitability (after proposal submission) includes:

- the agency's reputation;
- the agency's perceived expertise;
- whether the study offers value for money;
- the time taken to complete the study; and
- the likelihood that the research design will provide insights into the **management problem**.

Shortlisted agencies are given a preliminary outline of the client's needs in a **research brief**, and asked to provide proposals on research methodology, timing, and costs. After this, an agency is selected to undertake the work required. In the long term, clients are most satisfied with flexible agencies that avoid rigid research solutions and demonstrate professional knowledge of the industry, an ability to focus on the management problem, and provide solutions, and consistent service quality (Cater and Zabkar, 2009).

The Marketing Research Process

There are numerous basic stages that guide a marketing research project (see Figure 3.1). The first, most crucial, stage involves problem definition and setting the information needs of the decision-makers. The client organization explains the basis of the problem(s) it faces to the market researcher. This might be the need to understand market volumes in a potential new market or the reason for an unexpected sudden increase in uptake of an offering. Problem definition does not always imply that threats face the organization. The initial stage allows the organization to assess its current position, define its information needs, and make informed decisions about its future.

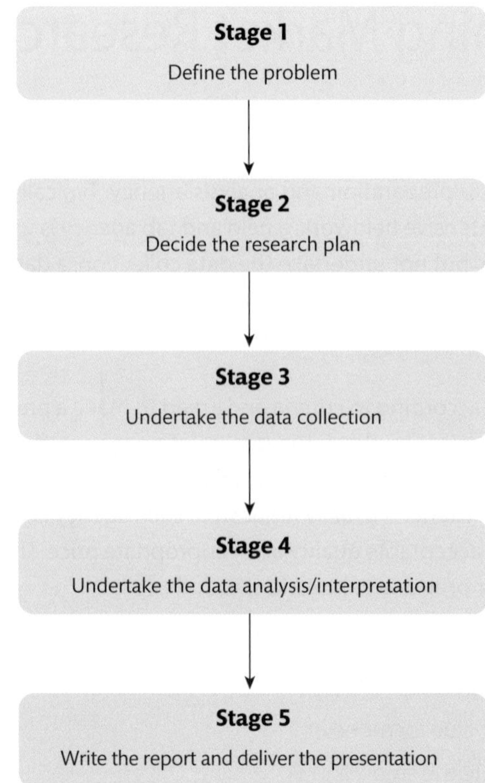

Figure 3.1 The marketing research process

Source: Baines and Chansarkar (2002). © John Wiley & Sons. Reproduced with permission.

Stage 1: Problem Definition

The first step in a market research project is defining the management problem and writing the research brief. It is important that these are not expressed in vague terms, because organizations are not always sure what information they require. An example might be Carrefour, the supermarket chain, explaining that sales are not as strong as expected in its Spanish stores and wondering whether or not this is a result of the emergence of a competitor supermarket in the region of Madrid (see Figure 3.2).

Management problem

Sales at the new store have not met management expectations, possibly owing to the emergence of a new competitor

Figure 3.2 Example of a management problem

Marketing research question

Why are sales levels not meeting management expectations?

1. Sub-question: has customer disposable income in the area declined over the last six months?
2. Sub-question: is a new competitor, Tesco, taking away customers?
3. Sub-question: are customers tired/bored of the current product range in the existing supermarket?
4. Sub-question: are customers conducting more of their shopping online?
5. Sub-question: were management expectations set too high and/or market potential overestimated?

Figure 3.3 Example of a marketing research question

The problem description provides the researcher with relatively little depth of understanding of the situation in which the supermarket finds itself, so the researcher needs to discuss the problem with the staff commissioning the study to investigate further. This allows the researcher to translate the management problem into a marketing research question. Typically, this question may include a number of sub-questions for further exploration. An example of a marketing research question and a number of more specific sub-questions is shown in Figure 3.3.

Carrefour, the French supermarket chain, operates globally.
Source: © PhotoStock10/Shutterstock.

The marketing research question transforms the management problem into a question while trying to remove any assumptions made by the organization's management. The more clearly the commissioning organization defines the management problem, the easier it is for the agency to design the research to solve that problem. Once the agency discusses the brief with the client, the agency provides a detailed outline of how it will investigate the problem. This document is called the **research proposal**. Figure 3.4 briefly outlines a typical marketing research proposal.

Stage 2: Decide the Research Plan

Once the marketing research question(s) have been decided, it is time to develop a research plan. At this stage, the framework for conducting the project is developed. In developing this framework, marketing researchers need to consider what type of research is needed. The market research need can be specified based on objective (exploratory, descriptive, or causal research), as well as source (primary vs secondary data) and methodology (qualitative vs quantitative). The research need will have implications for the design of the research plan.

The basic structure and contents of a typical research proposal should include the following.

- **Executive Summary**–A brief summary of the research project including the major outcomes and findings. Rarely more than one page in length, it allows the reader to obtain a summary of the main points of the project without having to read the full report.
- **Background to the Research**–An outline of the problem or situation and the issues surrounding this problem. This section demonstrates the researcher's understanding of the management problem.
- **Research Objectives**–An outline of the objectives of the research project, including the data to be generated and how they will be used to address the management problem.
- **Research Design**–A clear, non-technical description of the research type adopted and the specific techniques to be used to gather the required information. This will include details of data-collection instruments, sampling procedures, and analytical techniques.
- **Personnel Specification**–The details of the people involved in the collection and analysis of the data, providing a named liaison person and outlining the company's credibility in undertaking the work.
- **Time Schedule**–An outline of the time requirements with dates for the various stages to completion and presentation of results.
- **Costs**–A detailed analysis of the costs involved in the project is usually included for large projects or simply a total cost for the project.
- **References**–Typically, three references are outlined, so that a client can be sure that an agency has the requisite capability to do the job in hand.

Figure 3.4 A marketing research proposal outline

Type of Market Research Based on Objectives

There are three types of research depending on the management problem that the research should solve. These include the following:

1. **Exploratory research** is used when little is known about a particular management problem and it needs to be explored further. Exploratory designs enable the development of hypotheses or help in developing new concepts.
2. **Descriptive research** focuses on accurately describing the variables being considered, such as market characteristics or spending patterns in key customer groups. Examples are consumer profile studies, usage studies, attitude surveys, and media research.
3. **Causal research** is used to determine whether or not one variable causes an effect in another variable. To determine causality, experimental or longitudinal studies are needed. Experimental studies are characterized by the marketing researchers manipulating a specific variable (cause) thought to influence important outcomes (effect), thereby allowing them to carefully test causation. Longitudinal studies, on the other hand, track the effect of a certain variable (cause) over time. Examples of causal research are studies of customer satisfaction and advertising effectiveness, which typically set out to understand what factors of an offer or an advert impact on consumer evaluations.

Type of Market Research Based on Source

When conducting market research, we can either use what is already known or devise research that creates new knowledge. **Primary research** is research conducted for the first time, involving the collection of data for the purpose of a particular project. Secondary data are second-hand data, collected for someone else's purposes. **Secondary research** (also known as **desk research**) involves gaining access to the results of previous research projects. This method can be a cheaper and more efficient process of data collection. Common sources of secondary data include:

- government sources, such as export databases, government statistics, social trend databases, and other resources;
- the Internet, including sources identified using search engines, blogs and microblogs, and discussion groups;
- company internal records, including information housed in a marketing information or customer relationship management (CRM) system such as Salesforce, or published in reports;
- professional bodies and trade associations, which frequently have databases available online for research purposes, and may also publish industry magazine articles and research reports; and
- market research companies, which frequently undertake research into industry sectors or specific product groups and can be highly specialized, for example Mintel, Euromonitor, ICC Keynote, and Google.

In practice, most research projects involve both secondary and primary research, with desk research occurring initially to ensure that a company does not waste money. Once this initial insight is gleaned, the decision is made on whether or not it is necessary to commission a primary data study. Assuming that primary research needs to be undertaken, researchers usually design their research by considering what type of research to employ. Marketing directors should understand what types of study can be conducted, because this impacts on the type of information collected and hence the data that they receive to solve the management problem.

Euromonitor is well known for its in-depth industry reports, which can provide useful secondary data to inform marketing decision-making.
Source: Courtesy of Euromonitor.

Type of Market Research Based on Methodology

At the outset of a research project, we might consider whether to use **qualitative research** or **quantitative research**, or a combination of both.

- *Qualitative* research denotes research methodologies relying on small samples, using open and probing questions that set out to uncover underlying motives and feelings. The data gathered are then interpreted focusing on meanings and are typically quite hard to replicate. Typically, qualitative research is intended to provide insights and understanding of the problem setting, and thus it is frequently used in exploratory market research. The main methods for collecting qualitative data are individual interviews, focus groups, and observations.

- *Quantitative* research methods are used to elicit responses to predetermined standardized questions from many respondents. This involves collecting information, quantifying the responses as frequencies or percentages and descriptive statistics, and analysing them statistically. Quantitative research is thus commonly used in descriptive and causal marketing research, and replication is a highly desirable trait of the outcome of such research. Thus quantitative data collection methods are much more structured than qualitative data collection methods. Common methods include different types of surveys (online, offline), face-to-face or telephone interviews, and longitudinal studies.

Table 3.1 summarizes the key differences between qualitative and quantitative research methods. In many cases, qualitative and quantitative methods can be combined to generate insights from different perspectives.

The client (or in-house research client) may also have specific budget constraints or know which particular approach it intends to adopt. However, the choice primarily depends on the circumstances of the research project and its objectives. If there is little advance understanding of the management problem, it would be better to explore the problem using qualitative research to gather insights. In the UK in 2015, 83 per cent of the market research budget was being spent on

Table 3.1 Qualitative and quantitative research methods compared

Characteristic	Qualitative	Quantitative
Purpose	Oriented towards discovery and exploration	Oriented towards cause and effect
Procedure	Emergent design; merges data collection and analysis	Predetermined design; separates data collection and analysis
Emphasis	Meaning and interpretation	What can be measured
Role of researcher	Involved; used as a 'research instrument'	Detached; uses standardized research instruments
Unit of analysis	Analyses a holistic system	Analyses specific variables
Size of sample	Involves a small number of respondents, typically fewer than 30	Involves a large number of respondents, more than 30
Sampling approach	Uses purposively selected samples	Tends to use **probability sampling** techniques

quantitative research, as opposed to only 13 per cent for qualitative research (MRS, 2017). Industry surveys also indicate that marketers combine both qualitative and quantitative methods, although recent declines in revenue have been attributed to poor fit between the research problem and the most appropriate research method (Murphy, 2019).

Designing the Research Project

Once we know what type of research to conduct, we should consider:

- whom to question and how (the sampling plan and procedures to be used);
- what methods to use (e.g. discussion groups or an experiment);
- which types of question are required (open questions for qualitative research or closed questions for a survey); and
- how the data should be analysed and interpreted (e.g. what approach to data analysis should be undertaken).

Research methods describe the techniques and procedures used to obtain the necessary information (see Market Insight 3.2). We might use a survey or a series of in-depth interviews. We might use observation to see how consumers purchase goods online or how employees greet consumers when they enter a particular shop (i.e. mystery shopping). We could use consumer panels whereby respondents record their weekly purchases or their television viewing habits over a specified time period. Nielsen Homescan is a service whereby consumers use specially developed barcode readers to record their supermarket purchases in return for points, which are redeemed for household goods. Nowadays, companies increasingly use online methods. According to a 2019 survey of CMOs, many marketers use AI to generate customer insights using predictive analytics, with budget spent on marketing analytics expected to grow significantly. Marketers also report using experiments one-third of the time to understand the impact of their marketing on customers (Moorman, 2019).

Market Insight 3.2 **How Scent Sells Lingerie at Hunkemöller**

Behavioural economics explores why people sometimes make irrational decisions and why their behaviour does not follow traditional economic models. It has produced hundreds of fascinating academic case studies, but many businesses find it hard to apply it in a way that produces real business advantage.

One exceptional example was when System1 Group and lingerie retailer Hunkemöller worked to create and test interventions, based around behavioural economics designs, in Hunkemöller stores in the Netherlands. Why did Hunkemöller want to use behavioural economics? There is a growing body of evidence of the immense importance of context to decision-making. This means that small interventions in the environment can have a small, but significant, impact on customer behaviour and sales. For instance, in a related study for a separate System1 Group client, introducing a brand logo at the point of sale was associated with a 4 per cent increase in purchases for that brand. Context—for example music, scent, and emotion—plays a

Market Insight 3.2 (continued)

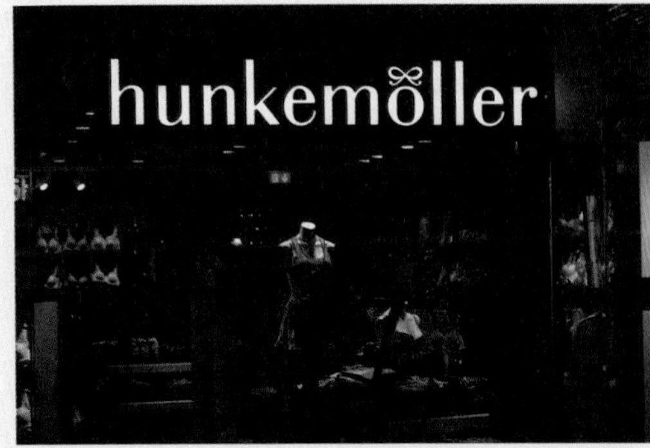

Hunkemöller uses behavioural economics to create and test interventions in its stores.
Source: © 360b/Shutterstock.

huge part in shopper decisions, but shoppers hardly notice some of the most important factors, so researching it can be very difficult. The study explained how using scent in Hunkemöller stores led to a striking gain in average customer value.

System1 Group began by undertaking a behavioural audit of the retail environments of Hunkemöller stores, and consumers' behaviour within them, to design appropriate in-store interventions designed to increase sales. The experiment was designed using an alternating experimental and control store run over six weeks, alternating week on week, to measure the effect of using scent in stores as a 'prime'—that is, to make customers feel happy and romantic before buying Hunkemöller's lingerie. Store sales data were used for effectiveness data. This work was supplemented with a short questionnaire when customers exited the store, which was designed to uncover the extent to which they had enjoyed their visit and noticed the intervention (the scent prime).

The experiments showed that in-store scent increased average customer basket value for Hunkemöller by 20 per cent. Hunkemöller would later roll out scent in all new and refurbished stores. The research also helped the company to develop protocols for undertaking behavioural economic research—running audits, creating interventions, and working with a research agency to make the interventions happen, and to understand how to prime customer emotion and satisfaction. The results of the research offered a strong argument for continuing the experimental, hands-on research approach rooted in behavioural science, backed up with traditional data. It is a method pointing to the future of research—away from what customers say and towards what they do.

1 **Why do you think it was necessary to use a behavioural experimental approach?**

2 **Why is it necessary to use a control group in an experiment?**

3 **What other decision-making scenarios can you think of that might use the experimental approach?**

Sources: Goyal (2013); Leach and Bisnajak (2013); http://www.brainjuicer.com/html/stream/labs; http://www.Hunkemöller.com/en/about-us/corporate-info.html.

This market insight was kindly contributed by Orlando Wood, System1 Group, and Ashwien Bisnajak, Market Intelligence Manager, Hunkemöller.

Figure 3.5 indicates the key considerations when designing qualitative and quantitative research projects. The design of marketing research projects involves determining how each of these components interrelates with the others. The components comprise:

- research objectives;
- the sampling method;
- the interviewing method to be used;
- the research type and methods undertaken;

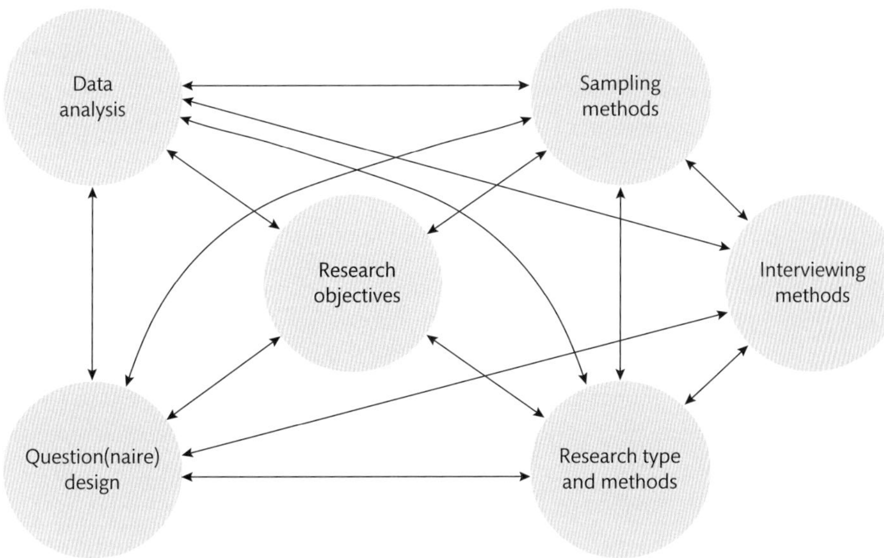

Figure 3.5 The major components of research design

Source: Baines and Chansarkar (2002). © John Wiley & Sons Ltd. Reproduced with permission.

- question and questionnaire design; and
- data analysis.

When designing research projects, we must first determine the type of approach to use for a given management problem (e.g. exploratory, descriptive, or causal). We then determine which techniques are most capable of producing the desired data at the least cost and in the minimum time period.

Generally, certain types of research (exploratory, descriptive, causal) use certain methods or techniques. Exploratory research studies, for example, use qualitative research methods, non-probability sampling methods, and non-statistical data analysis methods. Descriptive research projects often adopt survey interviews using quota or random sampling methods and statistical analysis techniques. Causal researchers use experimental research designs using convenience or probability sampling methods and statistical data analysis procedures.

Stage 3: Data Collection and Sampling

The third stage involves the conduct of fieldwork and the collection of data. At this stage, we send out questionnaires, or run the online focus group sessions, or conduct a netnographic study, depending on the decisions taken in the first design stage of the fieldwork. The procedures undertaken when conducting the fieldwork might relate to how to ask the questions of the respondents—whether this involves using the Internet, telephone, (e)mail, or in person—and how to select an appropriate sample, how to **pre-code** the answers to a questionnaire (quantitative research), or how to code the answers arising out of open-ended questions (particularly with qualitative research).

The market research manager might be concerned about whether or not to conduct the research in-company or to commission a field and tab agency. Other issues concern how to ensure high data quality. When market research companies undertake shopping mall intercept interviews, they usually re-contact a proportion of the respondents to check their answers to ensure that the interviews have been conducted properly.

In qualitative research, samples are often selected on a convenience or judgemental basis. In quantitative research, we might use either probability or non-probability methods, including:

- *simple random sampling*, whereby the population elements are accorded a number and a sample is selected by generating random numbers that correspond to the individual population elements;
- *systematic random sampling*, whereby population elements are known and the first sample unit is selected using random number generation, but after that each of the succeeding sample units is selected systematically on the basis of an *n*th number, where *n* is determined by dividing the population size by the sample size; or
- *stratified random sampling*, whereby a specific characteristic(s) is used (such as gender, age) to design homogeneous subgroups from which a representative random sample is drawn.

Non-random methods include:

- *quota sampling*, whereby criteria such as gender, ethnicity, or some other customer characteristics are used to restrict the sample, but the selection of the sample unit is left to the researcher's discretion;
- *convenience sampling*, whereby no such restrictions are placed on the selection of the respondents and anybody can be selected;
- *snowball sampling*, whereby respondents are selected from rare populations (such as buyers of high-performance cars), perhaps from among responses to newspaper adverts, and then further respondents are identified using referrals from the initial respondents, thereby 'snowballing' the sample.

With the growth of online market research, the reliance on Internet panels has become increasingly common. Two types of panel are used in online research (Miles, 2004).

- *Access panels*, which provide samples for survey-style information, are made up of targets especially invited by email to take part, with a link to a web survey.
- *Proprietary panels*, set up or commissioned by a client firm, are usually made up of that company's customers.

To encourage survey participation, the researchers use incentives (e.g. a prize draw).

Visit the **online resources** and complete Internet Activity 3.1 to learn more about Market Research World, a useful source of online research resources.

Stage 4: Data Analysis and Interpretation

The fourth stage comprises data input, analysis, and interpretation. Data input depends on the type of data collected. Increasingly, computer software applications are used for analysis of both qualitative and quantitative data (e.g. NVivo and **SPSS**, respectively). With online questionnaires,

Research Insight 3.2

To take your learning further, you might wish to read the following influential paper.

Evans, J. R., and Mathur, A. (2005) 'The value of online surveys', *Internet Research*, 15(2), 195–219.

This highly cited paper outlines the strengths and weaknesses of undertaking online research. The article also compares online survey approaches with other survey formats, making it a particularly useful paper for those undertaking online research.

 **Visit the online resources to read the abstract and access the full paper.**

the data are automatically entered into a database, saving time and ensuring a higher level of data quality. If **computer-assisted personal interviewing (CAPI)** or **computer-assisted telephone interviewing (CATI)** methods are used, analysis can also occur instantaneously as the interviews are undertaken. **Computer-assisted web interviewing (CAWI)** techniques allow the researcher to read the questions from a computer screen and directly enter the responses of the respondents. Using the Internet, CAWI techniques can also allow the playback of video and audio files.

Market research methods are used to aid managerial decision-making. Information obtained needs to be valid and reliable, because company resources are deployed on the basis of the information gleaned. **Validity** and **reliability** are important concepts, particularly in quantitative market research. They aid researchers in understanding the extent to which the data obtained from the study represent reality and 'truth'. Quantitative research methods rely on the degree to which the data elicited might be reproduced in a later study (i.e. reliability) and the extent to which the data generated are bias-free (i.e. valid).

'Validity' is defined as 'a criterion for evaluating measurement scales; it represents the extent to which a scale is a true reflection of the underlying variable or construct it is attempting to measure' (Parasuraman, 1991: 441). One way of measuring validity is for researchers to use their subjective judgement to ascertain whether an instrument is measuring what it is supposed to measure (content validity): a question asked about job satisfaction, for instance, does not necessarily infer loyalty to the organization.

'Reliability' is defined as 'a criterion for evaluating measurement scales; it represents how consistent or stable the ratings generated by a scale are' (Parasuraman, 1991: 443). Reliability is affected by the concepts of time, analytical bias, and questioning error. We can also distinguish between two types of reliability—that is, internal and external reliability (Bryman, 1989). To determine how reliable the data are, we conduct the study again over two or more time periods to evaluate the consistency of the data. This is known as the 'test–retest method' and measures external reliability. Another method used involves dividing the responses into two random sets and testing both sets independently, using ***t*-tests** or ***z*-tests**. This would illustrate internal reliability. The two different sets of results are then correlated. This method is known as 'split-half reliability testing'. These methods are more suited to testing the reliability of rating scales than data generated from qualitative research procedures. The results of a quantitative marketing research project are reliable if we conduct a similar research project within a short time period and the same or similar results are obtained in the second study. For example, if the marketing department of a travel agency chain were to interview 500 of its customers and discover that 25 per cent were in favour of a particular resort (perhaps a particular Greek island), and then repeat the study the following year and discover that only 10 per cent of the sample were interested in the same resort, the results of the first study could be said to be unreliable and chain's procurement department should not base its purchase of package holidays purely on the previous year's finding.

In qualitative research, concepts of validity and reliability are generally less important, because the data are not used to imply representativeness. Qualitative data are used more for the generation of ideas and the formulation of hypotheses. Validity can be assured by sending out transcripts to respondents and/or clients for checking, to ensure that what they have said in in-depth interviews or focus groups was properly reproduced for analysis. When analysts read the data from a critical perspective to determine whether or not they fit with their expectations, this constitutes what is termed a '**face validity** test'. Reliability is often achieved by checking that similar statements are made by the range of respondents both across and within the interview transcripts. Interviewees' transcripts are checked to assess whether or not the same respondent, or other respondents, have made the discussion point.

Stage 5: Report Preparation and Presentation

The final stage of a research project involves reporting the results and the presentation of the findings of the study to the external or in-house client. The results should be presented free from bias. Marketing research data are of little use unless translated into a format that is meaningful to the manager or client who initially demanded the data. Senior people within the commissioning organization who may or may not have been involved in commissioning the work often attend presentations. Usually, agencies and consultants prepare their reports using a basic pre-written template.

Market and Advertisement Testing

Marketing research reveals attitudes to a campaign, brand, or some other aspect of the exchange process, whereas market testing, by comparison, measures actual behaviour. Market testing studies use **test markets** to carry out controlled experiments in specific country regions, where specific adverts can be shown before exposing the 'new feature' (offering, campaign, distribution, etc.) to a full national, or even international, launch. Another region or the rest of the market may act as the control group against which results can be measured. As an example, films are often test-screened before release because of the substantial cost of producing the film in the first place.

Marketing research is used to test advertisements, whether these are in print, online, or broadcast via radio or television. Research company Kantar is renowned for this type of research. A variety of methods are used to test adverts. Typically, quantitative research is undertaken to test customer attitudes before and after exposure to see whether the advert has had a positive impact or not. In addition, research occurring after exposure to the advert tests the extent to which audiences can recognize a particular advert (e.g. by showing customers a copy of a still from a television advert, a print advert, or a photo online) or recall an advert without being shown a picture (i.e. unaided recall). Qualitative research identifies and tests specific themes that might be used in the adverts, and tests **storyboards** and **cuts** of adverts (before they are properly produced). Advances in technology have allowed us to evaluate visual imagery more objectively, without relying on respondents' opinions: technology company 3M, for example, offers a service named '3M VAS' (standing for 'Visual Attention Service'), which allows users to test communications material to see whether specific sections of the communication will be noticed and in what order, using algorithms based on sophisticated eye-tracking research. Another approach to proposition and marketing communication testing uses facial coding analysis.

Big Data and Marketing Analytics

The term 'big data' refers to a more comprehensive set of data than that traditionally used to provide marketing information and customer insights. More specifically, 'big data' refers to the volume, velocity, and variety of data used (McAfee et al., 2012; Erevelles et al., 2016).

- *Volume* denotes the sheer amount of information used. As an illustration, Wal-Mart collects more than 2.5 petabytes of data every hour. A petabyte is 1 quadrillion bytes—or the equivalent of about 20 million filing cabinets' worth of text.
- *Velocity* refers to the fact that data are recorded in real time. For example, using location data from mobile phones, Google is able to offer up-to-date information about travelling time adjusted for traffic.
- *Variety* denotes that big data analytics combines data from several different sources. For example, combining customer databases with social media and mobile data can give a more comprehensive understanding of shopper behaviours than was possible before.

With increasing digitization of business and consumers in everyday life, the availability of such varied information is growing rapidly (see Market Insight 3.3). The different sources employed in big data analysis can be divided into five categories: public data; private data; data exhaust; community data; and self-quantification data (George et al., 2014).

- *Public data* refers to information held by governments or local communities, for example with regards to incomes, transportation, or energy use, which is accessed under certain restrictions, to guard individual privacy.
- *Private data* refers to data held by private organizations or individuals that cannot readily be imputed from public sources. Examples are customer database information and browsing behaviours online.

Research Insight 3.3

To take your learning further, you might wish to read the following influential paper.

Erevelles, S., Fukawa, N., and Swayne, L. (2016) 'Big data consumer analytics and the transformation of marketing', *Journal of Business Research*, 69(2), 897–904.

This paper introduces a theoretical framework for when and how big data can lead to sustainable competitive advantage. More specifically, it discusses how three resources—physical, human, and organizational capital—moderate the processes of (a) collecting and storing evidence of consumer activity as big data, (b) extracting consumer insight from big data, and (c) utilizing consumer insight to enhance dynamic or adaptive capabilities.

 **Visit the online resources to read the abstract and access the full paper.**

Market Insight 3.3 **M&S Spies Data Opportunity**

In 2018, the London-based multinational retailer Marks & Spencer (M&S) announced a partnership with Microsoft to trial machine learning and **computer vision technologies** in its stores. The objectives of this collaboration are to improve the design of M&S stores and the placement and promotion of its products, to enhance the experience of its customers, and to optimize its supply chain. To achieve this, Microsoft offers the expertise of its engineers and provides easy access to cloud-based services for image and speech recognition as well as for detecting in-store mishaps (e.g. a milk spillage).

This set of functionalities ('Azure Cognitive Services') allows the M&S Retail Labs team, who do not have expertise in these domains, to leverage modern technologies and quickly develop responsive applications to process large amounts of varied data. These services can be used, for example, to monitor the crowdedness of a specific aisle and inform the decision to move a product to a different section of the store.

The multiplication of sensors, including cameras and screens in M&S stores, generates increasingly large amounts of data that can be processed and acted upon in real time by the Microsoft cloud. This initiative followed M&S's five-year Technology Transformation Programme to create value for customers by integrating technology into its front and back office (i.e. both the in-store experience and non-customer-facing processes).

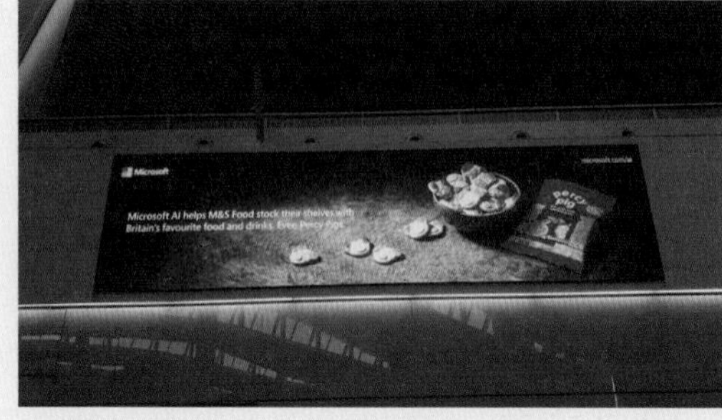

Microsoft billboard at Heathrow Airport promoting the M&S and Microsoft partnership.
Source: © Sophie Whitehouse.

1. **Other than stock levels and in-store hazards (such as the milk spillage), what other data might be useful for M&S to collect? How might they use such data?**
2. **What are the ethical implications of M&S tracking customers in its stores?**
3. **Do you think other retailers will follow in the footsteps of M&S? If so, how do you think this would benefit customers?**

Sources: Marks & Spencer (2018), Microsoft (2019).

- *Data exhaust* refers to data that are passively collected—that is, non-core data with limited or zero value to the original data-collection partner. When individuals adopt and use new technologies (such as mobile phones), they generate ambient data as a by-product of their everyday activities. These data can be recombined with other data sources to create new insights. Another source of data exhaust is information-seeking behaviour, such as online search and call centre calls, which can be used to infer people's needs, desires, or intentions.
- *Community data* refers to distilled, unstructured data, such as consumer reviews on products or 'liking' pages on social media, which are combined into dynamic networks that capture social trends.
- Individuals using technology to quantify their own personal actions and behaviours reveal *self-quantification data*, for example through the fitness bands worn on users' wrists that monitor their exercise and movement.

Marketing Research and Ethics

Marketing research should be carried out in an objective, unobtrusive, and honest manner. Researchers are also concerned about the public's increasing unwillingness to participate in marketing research and the problem of recruiting suitable interviewers. The apathy among interviewees is probably associated with the amount of research conducted, particularly through intrusive telephone interviewing, which is increasing, and door-to-door survey interviewing, which is declining. Marketing research is increasingly conducted online, creating its own set of ethical concerns. How can we verify that someone online is who they say they are? Is it acceptable to observe and analyse customer blogs and conversations on social networking sites? In social media research, ethical problems include the need to be open and transparent when conducting research within communities, and anonymizing and paraphrasing comments (since verbatim comments can often be tracked back to a particular user). Clear ethical codes for conducting social media research are, however, still in development. Consequently, key organizations such as ESOMAR and the MRS are devising clear policies on the topic.

Marketing research neither attempts to induce sales nor attempts to influence customer attitudes, intentions, or behaviours. The MRS (2019: 3) requires that its members:

1. Ensure that their professional activities can be understood in a transparent manner.
2. Be straightforward and honest in all professional and business relationships.
3. Be transparent as to the subject and purpose of data collection.
4. Ensure that their professional activities are not used to unfairly influence views and opinions of participants.
5. Respect the confidentiality of information collected in their professional activities.
6. Respect the rights and well-being of all individuals.
7. Ensure that individuals are not harmed or adversely affected by their professional activities.
8. Balance the needs of individuals, clients, and their professional activities.
9. Exercise independent professional judgement in the design, conduct, and reporting of their professional activities.

10. Ensure that their professional activities are conducted by persons with appropriate training, qualifications, and experience.
11. Protect the reputation and integrity of the profession.
12. Take responsibility for promoting and reinforcing the principles and rules of the MRS Code of Conduct.

The MRS Code of Conduct, based on the ESOMAR Code, is binding on all members of the MRS. Members of the general public are entitled to assurances that no information collected in a research survey will be used to identify them, or be disclosed to a third party, without their consent. Data in European countries are also subject to the General Data Protection Regulation (GDPR), implemented in the UK as the Data Protection Act 2018. For example, German regulators stopped social media giant Facebook collecting users' data by default in 2019 (Singer, 2019). Respondents must be informed of the purpose of the research and the length of time for which they will be involved in it. Research findings must also be reported accurately and not used to mislead. In conducting marketing research, researchers have responsibility for themselves, their clients, and their respondents or participants.

The results of research studies should remain confidential unless otherwise agreed by the client and agency, and the agency should provide detailed accounts of the methods employed to carry out the research project, where their clients request this.

Visit the **online resources** and complete Internet Activity 3.2 to learn more about ESOMAR's Marketing Research Code of Practice.

International Marketing Research

Often, marketers wish to promote their offerings internationally and to develop global brands (see Chapter 6). Marketing researchers, however, find it challenging to understand how culture operates in international markets and how it affects research design. Complexity in the international business environment makes international marketing research more complex, because it affects the research process and design. Key decisions include whether to customize the research to each of the separate countries in a study using differing scales, sampling methods, and sizes, or to try to use a single method for all countries, adopting an international **sampling frame**.

International researchers try to ensure that comparable data are collected despite differences in sampling frames, technological developments, availability of interviewers, and the acceptability of public questioning. Western approaches to marketing research, data collection, and culture might be inappropriate in some research environments because of variations in economic development and consumption patterns. How comparable are the data related to the consumption of Burger King's offerings collected through personal interviews in the United Arab Emirates (UAE), telephone interviews in France, and shopping mall intercept questionnaires in Sweden? Might an online panel be used instead across all countries? Ensuring comparability of data in research studies of multiple markets is not simple: concepts could be regarded differently; the same offerings could have different functions; language may be used differently, even within a country; offerings might be measured differently; the sample frames might be different; and the data collection methods adopted might differ because of variations in infrastructure.

Table 3.2 outlines three types of equivalence: **conceptual equivalence**; **functional equivalence**; and **translation equivalence**. All three types of equivalence impact on the semantics (i.e. the meaning) of words used in different countries, for example in developing the wording for questionnaires or in focus groups. Getting the language right is important because it affects how respondents perceive the questions and structure their answers.

When designing international research programmes, we need to consider how the meaning of words is different and how the data should be collected. Different cultures have different ways of measuring concepts. They also live their lives differently, meaning that it may be necessary to collect the same or similar data in a different way. Table 3.3 outlines how measurement, sampling, and data collection equivalence impacts on international research.

As we can see from Table 3.3, achieving comparability of data when conducting international surveys is difficult. Usually, the more countries that are included in an international study, the more

Table 3.2 Types of semantic equivalence in international marketing research

Type of equivalence	Explanation	Example
Conceptual equivalence	When interpretation of behaviour, or objects, is similar across countries, conceptual equivalence exists.	Conceptual equivalence should be considered when defining the research problem, in wording the questionnaire, and determining the sample unit, e.g. there would be less need to investigate 'brand loyalty' in a country where competition is restricted and product choice limited.
Functional equivalence	Functional equivalence relates to whether a concept has a similar function in different countries.	Purchasing a bicycle in India, perhaps for transport to and from work, or France, perhaps for shopping, is a different concept from purchasing a bike in Norway, perhaps for mountain biking. Functional differences can be determined using focus groups before finalizing the research design by ensuring that the constructs used in the research measure what they are supposed to measure.
Translation equivalence	Translation equivalence is an important aspect of the international research process. Words in some languages have no real equivalent in other languages.	The meaning associated with different words is important in questionnaire design, since words can connote a different meaning from that intended when directly translated into another language. To avoid translation errors of these kinds, the researcher can adopt one of the following two methods. • *Back translation*—A translator fluent in the language into which the questionnaire is to be translated is used, then another translator whose native language is the original language translates it back again. Differences in wording can thus be identified and resolved. • *Parallel translation*—A questionnaire is translated using different translators fluent in the languages which the questionnaire is to be translated into, as well as from, until a final version is agreed upon.

likely it is that errors will be introduced, and that the results and findings will be inaccurate and liable to misinterpretation. International research requires local and international input; therefore the extent to which one can internationalize certain operations of the research process depends on the objectives of the research.

Table 3.3 Types of measurement and data collection equivalence

Type of equivalence	Explanation	Example
Measurement equivalence	The extent to which measurement scales are comparable across countries	Surveys are conducted in the United States using imperial systems of measurement, while the metric system is used in Europe. Clothing sizes adopt different measurement systems in Europe, North America, and South East Asia. Multi-item scales present challenges for international researchers, because dissatisfaction might not be expressed in the same way in one country compared with another. Some cultures are more open in expressing opinions or describing their behaviour than others.
Sampling equivalence	Determining the appropriate sample to question may provide difficulties when conducting international marketing research projects.	The respondent profile for the same survey could vary from country to country, e.g. different classification systems are in existence for censorship of films by age shown at the cinema in France compared with the UK.
Data collection equivalence	When conducting research studies in different countries, it may be appropriate to adopt different data collection strategies.	Typically, data collection methods include (e)mail, telephone or CATI, or personal or CAPI. • *(E)Mail*—Used more where literacy or Internet access is high and where the (e)mail system operates efficiently. Sampling frames can be compiled from electoral registers, although it is now illegal in some countries to use these lists. European survey respondents can be targeted efficiently and accurately because international sampling frames do exist. • *Telephone/CATI*—In many countries, telephone penetration may be limited and CATI software, using random digit dialling, more limited still. • *Personal interviews/CAPI*—Used most widely in European countries favouring the door-to-door and shopping mall intercept variants. Shopping mall intercept interviews are not appropriate in Arab countries in which women must not be approached in the street; here, comparability is achieved using door-to-door interviews. In countries in which it is rude to openly disagree with someone (e.g. China), it is best to use in-depth interviews.

With international projects, the key decision is to determine to what extent to centralize and to what extent to delegate work to local agencies. There is, throughout this process, ample opportunity for misunderstanding, errors, and lack of cultural sensitivity. To proceed effectively, the central agency should identify a number of trusted local market research providers on a variety of continents. Typically, an international agency will have a network of trusted affiliates, whom it will monitor on a continual basis.

Chapter Summary

To consolidate your learning, the key points from this chapter are summarized below.

- **Define the terms 'market research', 'marketing research', and 'customer insight'.**

  'Market research' is research undertaken about markets (e.g. customers, channels, and competitors), while 'marketing research' is research undertaken to understand the efficacy of marketing activities (e.g. pricing, supply chain management policies). 'Customer insight' derives from knowledge about customers, which can be turned into an organizational strength.

- **Describe the customer insight process and the role of marketing research within it.**

  Understanding customers is at the core of the marketing concept and the basic idea with these systems is that marketing information should be used for timely, continuous information to support decision-making. Customer insight is typically derived from fusing knowledge generated from a range of sources, including industry reports, sales force data, competitive intelligence, CRM data, employee feedback, social media analysis data, and managerial intuition. A customer insight is of value if it is rare, difficult to imitate, and of potential use in formulating management decisions.

- **Explain the role of marketing research and list the range of possible research approaches.**

  Marketing research plays an important role in the decision-making process and contributes through ad hoc studies, as well as continuous data collection, through industry reports and from secondary data sources, as well as through competitive intelligence either commissioned through agencies or conducted internally, with data gathered informally through sales forces, customers, and suppliers. What methodologies are used depends on the type of research problem (exploratory, descriptive, causal) and the availability of data (primary or secondary sources), as well as the type of insights sought (qualitative or quantitative).

- **Define the term 'big data' and describe its role in marketing.**

  'Big data' can be defined as the systematic gathering and interpretation of high-volume, high-velocity, and/or high-variety information using cost-effective, innovative forms of information processing to enable enhanced insight, decision-making, and process automation. 'Big data' thus refers to a more comprehensive set of data than that traditionally used to provide marketing information and customer insights.

- **Discuss the importance of ethics and the adoption of a code of conduct in marketing research.**

  Ethics is an important consideration in marketing research because consumers and customers either provide personal information about themselves or personal information is collected from them. Their privacy needs to be protected through observance of a professional code of conduct and the relevant laws in the country in which the research is conducted.

- **Understand the concept of 'equivalence' in relation to obtaining comparable data.**

  International market research is complex because of the differences in language, culture, infrastructure, and other factors that intervene in the data collection process, meaning that obtaining comparable equivalent data is more difficult.

Review Questions

1. **How do we define 'market research'?**
2. **How do we define 'marketing research'?**
3. **How do we define 'customer insight'?**
4. **What is 'big data'?**
5. **What are the different types of research that can be conducted in marketing research?**
6. **What are the main differences between qualitative and quantitative marketing research?**
7. **Why is a marketing research code of conduct important?**
8. **What is a marketing information system and how is it used in the customer insight process?**
9. **What is the concept of 'equivalence' in relation to obtaining comparable data from different countries?**
10. **How are the different aspects of the research process affected by differences in equivalence between countries?**

Worksheet Summary

To apply the knowledge you have gained from this chapter, and to test your understanding of marketing research and customer insight, visit the **online resources** and complete Worksheet 3.1.

Discussion Questions

1. Having read Case Insight 3.1, how would you advise CLiKD to lower its customer acquisition costs using marketing analytics data? Use the outline proposal in Figure 3.4 to help you to design the research.
2. KPN, the Dutch telecoms company, wants to conduct a market research study aimed particularly at discovering what market segments exist across Europe, and how customers and potential customers view the KPN brand.
   - **A** Draft a market research question and a number of sub-questions for the study.
   - **B** How would you go about selecting the particular countries in which to conduct the fieldwork?
   - **C** What process would you use when conducting the fieldwork for this multi-country study?

3 What type of research (descriptive, exploratory, or causal) should be commissioned in each the following contexts? Why?

- **A** The management of UAE airline Etihad wants to measure passenger satisfaction with the flight experience.
- **B** Nintendo wants new ideas for new online games for a youth audience.
- **C** Spanish fashion retailer Zara wants to know what levels of customer service are offered at its flagship stores.
- **D** Procter & Gamble (P&G), makers of Ariel detergent, wants to test a new packaging design for six months to see if it is more effective than the existing version. Fifty supermarkets have been selected from one key P&G account: the new design is used in one half (twenty-five) of the supermarkets and the existing version in the other.

4 You are carrying out big data analysis on behalf of one of the largest supermarket chains in Europe (e.g. Kaufland in Germany and Poland) to generate new insights into its customers' behaviour. The supermarket gathers data about its millions of customers via a loyalty scheme which tracks their spending and rewards them with points and discounts on future purchases.

- **A** What type of data source(s) are you dealing with?
- **B** How important are the volume, velocity and variety of the data gathered?
- **C** There is growing concern among customers about personal data privacy. What do you suggest could be done to reassure them?

Visit the **online resources** and complete the multiple-choice questions to assess your knowledge of the chapter.

Glossary

behavioural economics the study of the psychology of consumer decision-making, particularly seeking to explain irrational decision-making and behaviour.

brand health the overall condition of a brand relative to the context in which it operates.

causal research a technique used to investigate the relational link between two or more variables by manipulating the independent variable(s) to see the effect on the dependent variable(s) and comparing effects with a control group within which no such manipulation takes place.

competitive intelligence the organized, professional, systematic collection of information, typically through informal mechanisms, used for the achievement of strategic and tactical organizational goals.

computer-assisted personal interviewing (CAPI) an approach to personal interviewing using a handheld computer or laptop to display questions and record the respondents' answers.

computer-assisted telephone interviewing (CATI) an approach to telephone interviewing using a laptop or desktop computer to display the questions to the interviewer, who reads them out and records the respondent's answers.

computer-assisted web interviewing (CAWI) an approach to online interviewing whereby the respondent uses a laptop or desktop computer to access questions in a set location, with questions automatically set based on the respondent's answers.

computer vision technologies use artificial intelligence techniques to interpret the visual world using images from cameras and videos.

conceptual equivalence the degree to which interpretation of behaviour, or objects, is similar across countries.

control group a sample group used in causal research, which is not subjected to manipulation of some sort.

CPA (cost per acquisition) a marketing metric used to determine efficiency in the use of the marketing budget in relation to winning each new customer.

cuts adverts initially produced in cartoon format, complete with dialogue, before they are produced, filmed, and edited.

descriptive research a research technique used to test, and confirm, hypotheses developed from a management problem.

desk research *see* **secondary research**

exploratory research a research technique used to generate ideas to develop hypotheses based around a management problem.

face validity the use of the researcher's or an expert's subjective judgement to determine whether an instrument is measuring what it is designed to measure.

full-service agency an advertising agency that provides its clients with a full range of services, including strategy and planning, designing the advertisements, and buying the media.

functional equivalence relates to whether or not a concept has the same function in different countries.

Gen Z (Generation Z) a demographic and generation group of consumers born between 1997 and 2012.

management problem a statement that outlines a situation faced by an organization, requiring further investigation and subsequent organizational action.

market mix modelling a research process that uses multiple-regression analysis based on customer survey data to ascertain the relative contributions of different promotional techniques on a customer-based dependent variable (such as awareness, intention to buy).

marketing research the design, collection, analysis, and interpretation of data collected for the purpose of aiding marketing decision-making.

millennials a demographic and generation group of consumers born between 1981 and 1996.

minimum viable product a product launched into the marketplace with sufficient characteristics to satisfy initial customers and from which the firm can develop an understanding to build a better product which can be rolled out to a wider customer base.

pre-code the assignation, in surveys, of a unique code (e.g. male = 1, female = 2) to answers to questions, to speed up data processing and to aid data analysis.

primary research a technique used to collect, for the first time, data which have been specifically collected and assembled for the current research problem.

probability sampling a sampling method used where the probability of selection of the sample elements from the population is known. Typical examples include simple random, stratified random, and cluster sampling methods.

qualitative research a type of exploratory research using small samples and unstructured data collection procedures, designed to identify hypotheses, possibly for later testing in quantitative research. The most popular examples include in-depth interviews, focus groups, and projective techniques.

quantitative research one that is designed to provide responses to predetermined, standardized questions from a large number of respondents, involving the statistical analysis of the responses.

reliability the degree to which the data elicited in a study are replicated in a repeat study.

research brief a formal document prepared by the client organization and submitted to either an external market research provider (such as a market research agency or consultant) or an internal research provider (such as in-house research department) outlining a statement of the management problem and the perceived research needs of the organization.

research proposal a formal document prepared by an agency, consultant, or in-house research manager and submitted to the client to outline what procedures will be used to collect the necessary information, including timescales and costs.

sampling frame a list of population members from which a sample is generated (e.g. a telephone directory or membership list).

secondary research also known as 'desk research', a technique used to collect data that have previously been collected for a purpose other than the current research situation.

SPSS short for Statistical Package for the Social Sciences, a software package used for statistical analysis marketed by SPSS, a company owned by IBM.

storyboards an outline of the story that an advertisement will follow prepared before its production, showing its key themes, characters, and messages.

***t*-test** a statistical test of difference used for small randomly selected samples with a size of fewer than thirty.

test market region within a country used to test the effects of the launch of a new product or service, typically using regional advertising to promote the service and pre- and post-advertising market research to measure promotional effectiveness.

touchpoint an occasion on which a consumer engages with a brand, including those occasions not directly associated with advertising activities.

translation equivalence the degree to which the meaning of one language is represented in another after translation.

unique selling point/proposition (USP) an attribute in your offering that other competitors do not possess which provides a reason for your customers to buy from you.

validity the ability of a measurement instrument to measure exactly the construct that it is attempting to measure.

***z*-test** a statistical test of difference used for large randomly selected samples with a size of thirty or more.

References

Baines, P., and Chansarkar, B. (2002) *Introducing Marketing Research*, Chichester: Wiley.

Bord Bia (2016) 'Bord Bia launches state-of-the-art Consumer Research Centre'. 27 September. Retrieve from: https://www.bordbia.ie/industry/news/press-releases/bord-bia-launches-state-of-the-art-consumer-research-centre/?_t_id=1B2M2Y8AsgTpgAmY7PhCfg%3d%3d&_t_q=state+of+the+art+consumer+research+centre&_t_tags=language%3aen%2csiteid%3a677072d0-3104-436a-a391-330e88570c33&_t_ip=95.149.147.162&_t_hit.id=BordBia_Web_Models_Pages_PressReleasePage/_a16a1248-6d13-45ce-957d-5828b87a2f9c_en&_t_hit.pos=1 (accessed 30 October 2020).

Bord Bia (2019) 'Resilient performance by Irish Food & Drink exports in 2018–2019', 9 January. Retrieve from: https://www.bordbia.ie/industry/news/press-releases/resilient-performance-by-irish-food--drink-exports-in-2018--creed/?_t_id=1B2M2Y8AsgTpgAmY7PhCfg%3d%3d&_t_q=Resilient+performance+by+Irish+Food+%26+Drink+exports+in+2018%e2%80%932019&_t_tags=language%3aen%2csiteid%3a677072d0-3104-436a-a391-330e88570c33&_t_ip=95.149.147.162&_t_hit.id=BordBia_Web_Models_Pages_PressReleasePage/_bc24915c-0feb-486a-8028-1b58341d3640_en&_t_hit.pos=6/ (accessed 14 December 2019).

Bryman, A. (1989) *Research Methods and Organization Studies*, London: Unwin Hyman.

Cater, B., and Zabkar, V. (2009) 'Antecedents and consequences of commitment in marketing research services: The client's perspective', *Industrial Marketing Management*, 38(7), 785–97.

Cowan, D. (2008) 'Forum: Creating customer insight', *International Journal of Market Research*, 50(6), 719–29.

Erevelles, S., Fukawa, N., and Swayne, L. (2016) 'Big data consumer analytics and the transformation of marketing', *Journal of Business Research*, 69(2), 897–04.

ESOMAR. (2015) 'Global market research report 2015: An industry report'. Retrieve from: https://www.esomar.org/knowledge-center/library/Global-Market-Research-2015-pub2701 (accessed 30 October 2020).

Evans, J. R., and Mathur, A. (2005) 'The value of online surveys', *Internet Research*, 15(2), 195–19.

George, G., Haas, M., and Pentland, A. (2014) 'Big data and management', *Academy of Management Journal*, 57(2), 321–26.

Goyal, M. (2013) 'UK-based BrainJuicer finds out how chocolates can boost lingerie sales', *Economic Times of India*, 14 April. Retrieve from: https://economictimes.indiatimes.com/news/company/corporate-trends/uk-based-brainjuicer-finds-out-how-chocolates-can-boost-lingerie-sales/articleshow/19533869.cms (accessed 30 October 2020).

GreenBook (2016) *GreenBook Research Industry Trends Report* (19th edn), New York: AMA Communication Services.

Hubert, T. (2016) 'Bord Bia to open Consumer Insights Centre', *Irish Farmers Journal*. 16 January. Retrieve from: https://www.farmersjournal.ie/bord-bia-to-open-consumer-insights-centre-198176 (accessed 14 December 2019).

Leach, W., and Bisnajak, A. (2013) 'How scent sells lingerie'. Paper presented at the ESOMAR Congress, Istanbul, Turkey, 22–25 September.

Lemon, K. N., and Verhoef, P. C. (2016) 'Understanding customer experience throughout the customer journey', *Journal of Marketing*, 80(6), 69–96.

McAfee, A., Brynjulfson, E. Davenport, T. H., Patil, D. J., and Barton, D. (2012) 'Big data: The management revolution', *Harvard Business Review*, 90(10), 60–8.

Malhotra, N. K. (2019) *Marketing Research: An Applied Orientation* (7th edn), Upper Saddle River, NJ: Pearson.

Market Research Society (MRS) (2017) *The Research Live Industry Report 2017*. Retrieve from: https://www.mrs.org.uk/pdf/MRS_RESEARCH_LIVE_REPORT_2017.pdf (accessed 30 October 2020).

Market Research Society (MRS) (2019) *Code of Conduct*. Retrieve from: https://www.mrs.org.uk/pdf/MRS-Codeof-Conduct-2019.pdf (accessed 30 October 2020).

Marks & Spencer (2018) 'Microsoft and M&S launch strategic partnership aimed at transforming the retail experience using the power of AI', 21 June. Retrieve from: https://corporate.marksandspencer.com/media/press-releases/2018/microsoft-and-m-and-s-launch-strategic-partnership-aimed-at-transforming-the-retail-experience-using-the-power-of-ai (accessed 30 October 2020).

Microsoft (2019) 'M&S is building the future of retail together with Microsoft', 28 May. Retrieve from: https://customers.microsoft.com/en-us/story/marks-and-spencer-microsoft (accessed 14 December 2019).

Miles, L. (2004) 'Online, on tap', *Marketing*, 16 June, 39–40.

Moorman, C. (2019) *CMO Survey Report: Highlights and Insights*. Retrieve from: https://cmosurvey.org/wp-content/uploads/2019/02/The_CMO_Survey-Highlights-and_Insights_Report-Feb-2019-1.pdf (accessed 30 October 2020).

Murphy, L. F. (2019) *The Greenbook Research Industry Trends (GRIT) Report*. Retrieve from: https://www.greenbook.org/mr/grit/ (accessed 30 October 2020).

Parasuraman, A. (1991) *Marketing Research* (2nd edn), Wokingham: Addison-Wesley.

RTE (2016) 'Bord Bia launches new Consumer Research Centre', *RTE*, 28 September. Retrieve from: https://www.rte.ie/news/business/2016/0928/819795-bord-bia/ (accessed 14 December 2019).

Said, E., Macdonald, E. K., Wilson, H. N., and Marcos, J. (2015) 'How organisations generate and use customer insight', *Journal of Marketing Management*, 31(9–10), 1158–79.

Singer, N. (2019) 'Germany restricts Facebook's data gathering', *New York* Times, 7 February. Retrieve from: https://www.nytimes.com/2019/02/07/technology/germany-facebook-data.html (accessed 30 October 2020).

Part 2

Designing and Delivering the Market Strategy

Part 1	Understanding Customers	
Part 2	Designing and Delivering the Market Strategy	**4** Marketing Environment and Strategy **5** Market Segmentation and Positioning
Part 3	Implementing the Marketing Mix	
Part 4	Managing Marketing Relationships	

Chapter 4
Marketing Environment and Strategy

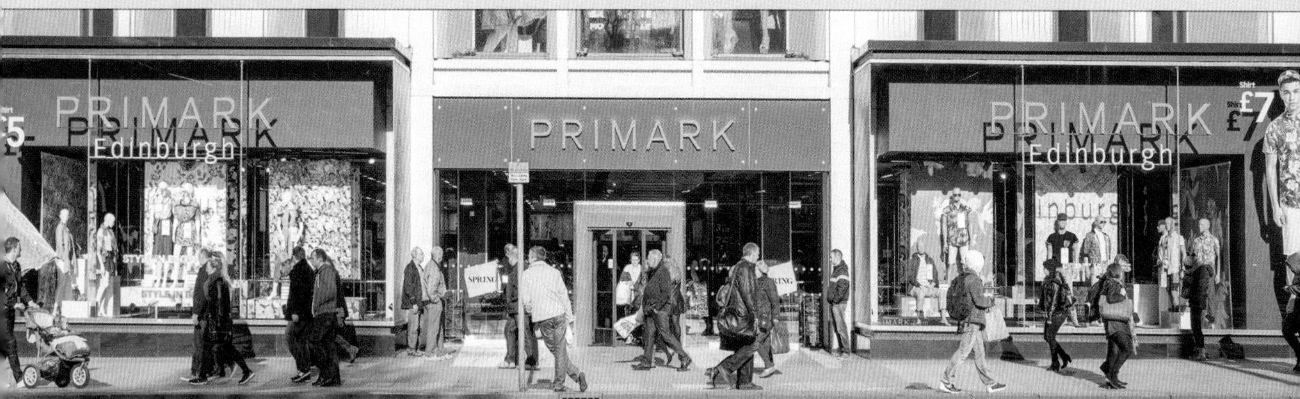

Learning Outcomes

After studying this chapter, you will be able to:

- describe the key characteristics associated with the marketing environment;
- explain the environmental scanning process and show how PESTLE analysis can be used to understand the external environment;
- analyse the performance environment using the Porter's five forces industry analysis model;
- analyse an organization's product/service portfolio to aid resource planning;
- analyse current conditions and formulate marketing strategies; and
- explain the different types of strategic marketing goal and associated growth strategies.

Case Insight 4.1
3scale

Market Insight 4.1
Negotiating a Social Licence to Operate

Market Insight 4.2
A Passage to (a Cashless) India?

Market Insight 4.3
Surviving the Greek Crisis

Market Insight 4.4
Primark: Low-Cost Leadership in the Face of Brexit?

Case Insight 4.1 **3scale**

Through its staff and offices in Barcelona and San Francisco, 3scale helps organizations to open, manage, and use application programming interfaces (APIs). We speak to Manfred Bortenschlager (pictured), API market development director, to find out how the company competes in its marketplace.

Steven Willmott and Martin Tantow founded 3scale in 2007, convinced that the world would become web-enabled, with APIs a critical digital infrastructure requirement. The initial 3scale product focused on an API marketplace, providing a matchmaking service between API providers and API consumers. The company quickly shifted to a more powerful business model: providing management capabilities for API providers. Now, 3scale sells an API management product based on monthly subscriptions with different price plans, starting with a free plan in its basic form: the Freemium, also known as the Software-as-a-Service (SaaS), model. This model is successful because it perfectly serves the customers' needs for flexibility and scale. Today, 3scale powers the APIs for close to 700 organizations.

Application programming interfaces are a software technology that provides organizations with a novel and effective way of distributing and leveraging digital assets. Application programming interfaces represent gateways to an organization's data or services (i.e. digital assets), which can be programmed and accessed by software increasing automation, scalability, and efficiency. As an analogy, APIs can be seen as an automatic door to a building with a security mechanism (like a pass code or a chip card). Digital transformation and digital strategies are based on APIs. The 3scale API management product provides the essential security, visibility, and control that allows organizations to define and measure their strategies when using APIs. In terms of value chain and customer requirements, the 3scale service follows a business-to-business-to-customer (B2B2C) model: the API provider (owning and providing digital assets) serves a developer (developing and distributing web or mobile apps), who serves the end user (the final consumer of the apps and APIs).

The most important customer requirements from the developer's perspective are, first, the value of the data or service to which the API provides access (the more unique, the higher the value) and, second, the simplicity of access to the API. The most important customer requirement from an end consumer's perspective is added value to an application via additional functionality. This is often achieved via so-called API mashups, whereby a developer combines the APIs of various API providers to create something new for the end consumer. Other requirements include 'user experience', which includes ease of use, clarity, consistency, and speed, for example.

3scale operates in a very fast-moving industry. To be successful, customer focus is essential. 3scale needs constantly to adapt its offering in terms of product features and the pricing model. To achieve that, it needs to integrate engineering, marketing, and sales processes, and to be able to react to change more quickly than can its competitors. 3scale differentiates between 'self-service' and 'enterprise' customers. Self-service customers adopt the 3scale offer almost without any human interaction, whereas customers on enterprise plans get phone support 24 hours a day, seven days a week (24/7) and/or higher guaranteed product reliability.

Case Insight 4.1 (continued)

3scale has three main competitive differentiators, as follows.

1 The 3scale product is modular and uses cloud technologies in a unique way. Based on customers' requirements, they can choose to host some of the product modules in 'the cloud' and some on their own IT infrastructure. This gives unmatched availability, scalability, and flexibility.
2 3scale offers the shortest time-to-value in the market, achieved via a comprehensive self-service model and detailed documentation. Customers can adopt 3scale very quickly and leverage the benefits of APIs instantly.
3 The Freemium subscription model is fair and transparent, with very competitive pricing. Customers appreciate the low barrier of entry and the subscription model is easy to understand, with no surprises.

One complex problem was that Amazon Web Services (AWS)—based around cloud technologies—launched the Amazon API Gateway product. This was perceived by many observers in the API management market to be a potential threat. With its size and financial resources, the expectation was that Amazon's offering could substantially impact existing players in the market. The question was: what strategy should 3scale develop to circumvent this competitive threat?

Introduction

How do companies keep up with the many changes that occur in politics, markets, and economics? What processes do they use to try to anticipate changes in technologies? How do they set their competitive positions and strategic marketing objectives? We consider these and other questions in this chapter.

The *external* environment, for example, comprises political, social, and technological factors, and organizations often have very limited, if any, control of these. The **performance environment** consists of competitors, suppliers, and indirect service providers, who shape the way and extent to which organizations achieve their objectives. Here, organizations have a much stronger level of influence. The *internal* environment concerns the resources, processes, and policies with which an organization achieves its goals, which factors it can influence directly. We also discuss how companies assess their competitive positions using strengths–weaknesses–opportunities–threats (SWOT) analysis, and how they set their intended strategic goals and actions and write associated marketing plans.

First, we turn to the concept of analysing the marketing environment (see Figure 4.1).

Understanding the External Environment

To make sense of the external environment, we use the well-known acronym **PESTLE**. The acronym derives from the political, economic, sociocultural, technological, legal, and ecological factors (see Figure 4.2) that comprise the most popular framework for examining the external environment.

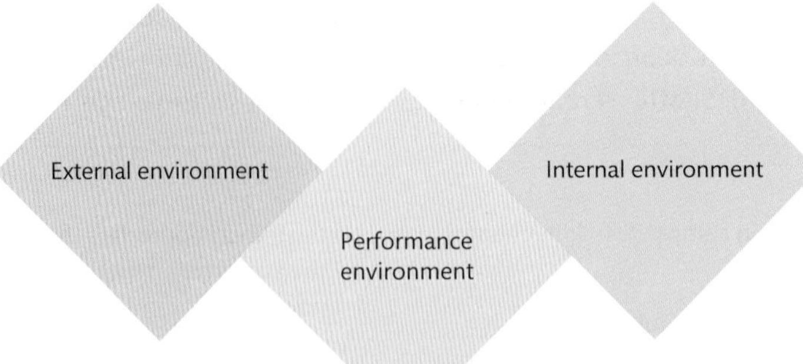

Figure 4.1 The three marketing environments

The Political Environment

The political factors in the external environment relate to the interaction between business, **society**, and **government**. An understanding of the political factors embraces the conditions that exist before laws are enacted, when they are still being formed, or when they are in dispute. Political environmental analysis is important because companies can detect signals concerning potential legal and regulatory changes in their industries, and have a chance to impede, influence, and alter that legislation.

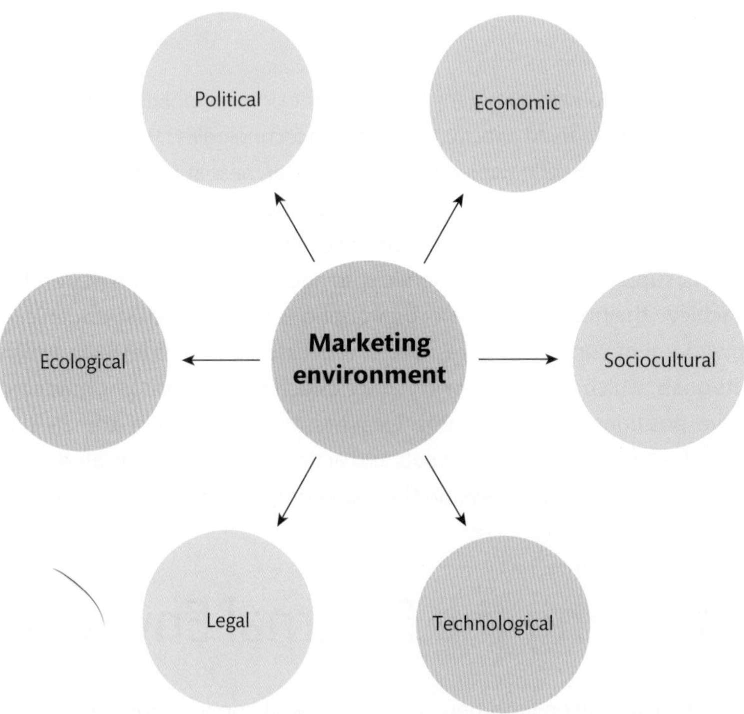

Figure 4.2 The external marketing environment

Although the **political environment** is in many ways uncontrollable, there are circumstances in which an organization, or an industry coalition, can affect legislation in its own favour. An organization can outperform other organizations over time if it can manage its relationships with government and regulatory bodies better than its competitors (Hillman et al., 2004; Lawton and Rajwani, 2011).

Generally, there are several ways in which marketers might conduct business–government relations in various countries, as follows.

- Lobbyist firms, with key industry knowledge, can be engaged either permanently or as needed.
- **Public relations (PR)** consultancies, such as Weber Shandwick, can be commissioned for their political services, often having Members of Parliament (MPs) or others with a high degree of political influence serving as directors and/or advisers, in jurisdictions where this is legal.
- A politician may be paid a fee to give political advice on matters of importance to an organization, where this is legal within that particular jurisdiction and where that politician is not serving directly within the government in question on the same portfolio as that on which he or she is advising.
- An in-house PR manager might handle government relations directly.
- An industry association might be contacted to lobby on behalf of members (e.g., in the European financial services industry, the Banking Federation of the European Union).
- A politician may be invited to join the board of directors, board of trustees, or board of advisers of an organization, where this is legal, to aid the company in developing its business–government relations.

Organizations often collaborate to influence governments. This can be achieved by means of industry or trade bodies, or by working with other large companies in their industry. For example, EuropaBio is made up of three main segments of the European biotechnology industry: healthcare (Red Biotech), industrial (White Biotech), and agri-food (Green Biotech). Experts from member companies actively participate in working groups and taskforces that cover a wide range of issues and concerns particular to their industry in an attempt to influence key **stakeholders**, including national governments and the European legislature.

In industries with significant social and environmental impact (e.g. oil and gas, transport infrastructures, telecommunications), analysis and management of the political environment is particularly important to allow a company to operate successfully. Read Market Insight 4.1 to learn about the case of a company trying to manage relationships with relevant local stakeholders.

The Economic Environment

Companies and organizations must develop an understanding of the economic factors within the external environment because a country's economic circumstances have an impact on what economists term 'factor prices' within a particular industry for a particular organization.

The economic environment of a firm is affected by the following factors.

- *Wage inflation*—Annual wage increases in a particular sector will depend on the supply of labour in that sector. Where there is scarcity of supply, wages usually increase (doctors being an example).

Market Insight 4.1 **Negotiating a Social Licence to Operate**

In 2014, after more than fourteen years of local community protests opposing its Pascua Lama gold-mining project in northern Chile, Canadian mining corporation Barrick Gold (the world's largest miner of gold) celebrated signing an agreement with the local indigenous Diaguita community. The company had obtained signatures from fifteen of the twenty-two local communities. 'We believe this Agreement will form the basis of a new relationship with Diaguita communities, one based on transparency, openness and trust', said Eduardo Flores, Barrick's executive director in Chile.

The Huasco Valley is a green and fertile valley located in the Atacama Desert, the driest in the world. The valley is home to the Diaguita people, whose main form of livelihood has been grape farming. The community opposition to the Pascua Lama gold mine (designed to be the second largest in South America) was based mainly on the negative impacts that the mining activity would have on local water supplies.

Despite the resistance to the mine, Barrick invested heavily in the local community to obtain a 'social licence to operate'. This term refers to local legitimacy—that is, to being accepted by the local community. A social licence to operate is a matter of great importance for companies extracting natural resources to show a match between their corporate social responsibility (CSR) aspirations and how local communities actually perceive them. In pursuit of this end, by 2007 Barrick claimed to have spent US$16 million on local purchasing, to have paid the Water Vigilance Board (a group of local wealthy farmers) US$60 million compensation for its water supplies, to have offered training courses for farmers, and also in Diaguita pottery and handcraft, and, controversially, to have offered to pay legal fees for those in the local community wishing to obtain official indigenous status from the Chilean state.

Once Barrick Gold reached an agreement with 15 of the 22 communities, it communicated the news on its corporate website. The agreement was said to be centred on how best to mitigate environmental and human rights, and also allows for discussion around potential benefit sharing of mining profits between Barrick and the local community. However, since the signing of the agreement in May 2014 there have continued to be numerous street marches and protests against the Pascua Lama project. For those groups still opposed, the only acceptable solution is no mine and, as such, talk of mitigating impacts and/or compensation is futile.

In a further development, OLCA and MiningWatch Canada, a national and international non-governmental organization (NGO), published a study denouncing the steps taken to obtain the fifteen signatures, claiming that the process was illegitimate. Certain local community leaders have also contested the agreement in the Chilean courts. It would therefore appear that there is still much work required if Barrick Gold is to gain a social licence to operate in the region.

1. **Why do you think it is so important for mining companies to gain a social licence to operate?**
2. **What could be the implications for mining companies if they were to fail to secure a social licence to operate?**
3. **Can you think of any flaws with the concept of a social licence to operate?**

Sources: Prno and Slocombe (2012); Younglai (2014); Wiebe (2015).

The case has been kindly contributed by Dr Rajiv Maher, postdoctoral researcher at the Pontifical Catholic University of Chile.

- *Price inflation*—How much consumers pay for goods and services depends on the rate of supply of those goods and services. If supply is scarce, there is usually an increase in the price of that consumer good or service (as in the case of petrol).

- ***Gross domestic product (GDP)*** *per capita*—The combined output of goods and services in a particular nation is a useful measure for determining relative wealth between countries when comparisons are calculated per member of the population—that is, as GDP per capita at **purchasing power parity (PPP)**.
- *Income, sales, and corporation taxes*—These taxes, typically operating in all countries around the world, sometimes at different levels, affect substantially how we market different offerings.
- *Exchange rates*—The relative value of a currency vis-à-vis another currency is an important calculation for those businesses operating in foreign markets or holding financial reserves in other currencies.
- *Export quota controls and duties*—There are often restrictions placed on the amounts (quotas) of goods and services that any particular firm or industry can import into a country, depending on to which trading bloc or country a company or firm is exporting. In addition, countries sometimes charge a form of tax on particular items to discourage or encourage imports and to protect their own economies.

Organizations usually have little impact on the wider economic environment, because they have little control over the macroeconomic variables. For example, firms have no control over oil prices, which might affect their business in different ways. The challenge when examining the macroeconomic environment is to foresee changes in the environment and how they might affect the firm's activities.

If **inflation** drives consumer prices higher in a particular country, the price of goods might become more expensive, triggering a fall in sales. Typically, during a **recession**, consumers tend to purchase fewer goods and increase their savings, and prices fall further as producers try to stimulate demand. Economic indicators are frequently available from government central banks.

Visit the **online resources** and complete Internet Activity 4.1 to learn more about how the contribution of service industries to the UK's national economy has changed over the last ten years.

The Sociocultural Environment

Lifestyles are constantly changing and, over time, consumers' preferences shift. Companies that fail to recognize changes in the sociocultural environment and to adapt or change their offerings often fail. For example, the growing demand for plant-based food has incited supermarkets to create their own vegetarian and vegan brands. In the UK, the leading market in Europe for meat substitutes, the rise of health-conscious consumers has led big names such as Tesco and Sainsbury's to release their own meat and dairy-free products. Innovation in the meat substitute market has been identified as the main enabler for growth and significant investments have already been secured by start-ups

Supermarkets need to respond to changing consumer preferences and provide products which are free from animal products if they wish to remain relevant.
Source: Wikimedia Commons.

Research Insight 4.1

To take your learning further, you might wish to read this highly influential paper.

Danciu, V. (2013) 'The future of marketing: An appropriate response to the environment changes', *Theoretical and Applied Economics*, 20(5), 33–52.

This paper looks at trends within different aspects of the marketing environment. It provides a helpful insight into the complexity and diversity of the various environments within which organizations operate.

 **Visit the online resources to read the abstract and access the full paper.**

in the US and Europe (Deloitte, 2019). Additionally, Western consumers have been increasingly exposed to Eastern food, leading to a widespread change in culinary taste and sparking popular products to offer spicy variants, such as Captain Morgan's Spiced Rum and Tanqueray Malacca Spiced Gin (Forsyth, 2013).

The sociocultural factors that companies need to consider comprise the changing nature of households, demographics, lifestyles, and family structures, and the changing **values** prevalent in society.

Demographics and Lifestyles

Changes in lifestyle impact on an organization's marketing activity. In the UK (and other European countries), the rise of single households has led to increasing provision of ready meals aimed at solo eaters rather than couples and families. This has also led to additional changes in how people eat. For instance, there is a trend among some younger, health-conscious consumers towards 'meal prepping', an Instagram hashtag which people use to share their meal ideas for batch cooking with like-minded others (Fleming, 2019).

In addition, there will also be shifts in the proportions of age groups within different populations. Some countries have a relatively large proportion of people in the 'aged 65 or over' age bracket—that is, the 'silver' or 'grey' market, so-called because of the colour of older people's hair. Some countries and regions, such as many African and Middle Eastern countries, have a comparatively high proportion of younger citizens. These shifts in population and the relative differences in age structure in different countries give rise to different-sized markets for brand propositions.

The Technological Environment

The emergence of new technologies has affected most businesses. Examples include technologies that impact productivity and business efficiency, such as changes in energy, transportation, and information and communication technologies (ICT). New technology also changes the way in which companies go to market. Companies are now compelled to use a variety of channels.

For example, one unusual app enables shoppers to test whether a melon is ripe: the user rests the microphone of a smartphone on a melon, presses a button, and taps the melon; the app uses an algorithm to determine from the sound whether the melon is ready to eat.

When scanning the technological environment, attention has to be given to research and development (R&D) trends and to competitors' R&D efforts. Strategies to ascertain these involve regular searches of patent registration, trademarks, and copyright assignations, as well as maintaining a

Market Insight 4.2 **A Passage to (a Cashless) India?**

In November 2016, the Prime Minister of India declared the top two currency notes by denomination invalid (i.e. Rs. 500, Rs. 1,000). By taking 86 per cent of India's legal tender out of circulation, he aimed to curb rampant tax evasion and counterfeiting and sought to move Indians from cash to digital transactions. Over 70 per cent of India's 1.2 billion people live in villages and over 95 per cent of transactions are in cash. Bank accounts and credit/debit cards have very low usage in India. However, there are around 650 million mobile phones in usage, of which 300 million are smart phones, making it the second largest mobile phone market in the world.

Mobile payments make use of mobile minutes to make payments, deposits, withdrawals, and transfers and can act like a bank account by storing 'money' in the form of mobile minutes. First launched in Kenya, as M-Pesa by Vodafone and Safaricom, using the mobile as a payment mechanism was hugely successful with 70 per cent of the population adopting the approach, 50 per cent of whom were poor, unbanked, and rural. However, mobile payment has not fared well since being launched in India. Multiple providers rushed in to persuade Indians to use their mobile phones for making payments digitally instead of using cash. However, most people who signed up initially to overcome the cash shortage have not continued to use the service. They have maintained low to no balances and frequently switched providers. This has resulted in a highly fragmented and unstable market. Although, education and income levels have been rising in India, financial literacy levels are still low. Plus, tax evaders found the anonymity of cash attractive.

The use of mobile payments for small transactions has become increasingly popular in developed countries.
Source: HLundgaard/Wikimedia Commons (CC BY-SA 3.0).

In a country where 'cash is king' can mobile payments succeed?

1. **What factors impact the adoption of new technologies, such as mobile payment systems, and how do these factors differ between developed countries (e.g. the UK or Sweden) and an emerging market like India?**
2. **In your view, can India as a society move from cash to mobile payments? Provide a rationale for your answer.**
3. **How might mobile payment providers increase consumer adoption of mobile payment systems in India? (Hint: consider the 4 Ps—product, price, place, promotion; see also Chapter 1.)**

Sources: Tiwari and Deepti (2013); Amberber (2014); Sen (2014); Anand and Kumar (2016); Kalavalapalli and Nair (2016); Iyengar (2017); Wade (2017).

The case was kindly contributed by Dr Mona Sinha, Kennesaw State University, Georgia, USA.

general interest in technological and scientific advances. Companies often develop new products based on modifications of patents registered by their competitors. This process, referred to as **reverse engineering**, is often the result of a firm's inability to turn its own technological advances into a **sustainable competitive advantage** (Rao, 2005). As soon as a new offering variant is introduced, it is quickly copied. To overcome this, firms attempt to introduce a consistent stream of new propositions and stay as close to the consumer as possible. Read Market Insight 4.2 to learn about how India is transitioning to a cashless society.

The Legal Environment

The legal factors in the external environment span every aspect of an organization's business. Laws and regulation are enacted in most countries, relating to issues ranging from transparency of pricing, through product safety, the promotion of good practice in packaging and labelling, the prevention of restrictive trade practices, and the abuse of a dominant market position, to codes of practice in advertising, to take only a small selection.

In the European Union, for example, product safety is covered under the 2001 General Product Safety Directive which aims to protect consumer health and safety both for EU member states and for importers from third-party countries to the European Union or their EU agents. Where products pose serious risks to consumer health, the European Commission can take action, imposing fines and/or criminal sentences for those contravening the Directive. The General Product Safety Directive does not cover food safety; this is subject to another EU directive, under which are established a European Food Safety Authority and a set of regulations covering food safety. Companies operating in these sectors need to keep up with changes in legislation, because failure to do so might jeopardize the business.

The Ecological Environment

The concept of 'marketing sustainability' is now well established and increasing numbers of consumers express concern about the impact that companies are having on ecological environments.

Sustainability issues embrace the sourcing of products from countries with poor and coercive labour policies. Both Nike and Apple have actively changed parts of their supply chain following investigations. Consumers are also keen to ensure that companies and their products are not damaging the environment or causing harm to consumers. This has been accompanied by a rise in the popularity of Fairtrade products.

Fairtrade products aim to guarantee better prices and better working conditions for farmers in developing countries.
Source: © Tracing Tea/Shutterstock.

How should an organization embrace the changing trend in sustainability? To answer this question, Orsato (2006) suggests four alternative green marketing strategies, as follows.

- *Eco-efficiency*—This strategy involves developing lower costs through organizational processes such as the promotion of resource productivity (e.g. energy efficiency) and better utilization of by-products. This approach should be adopted by firms that need to focus on reducing the costs and environmental impact of their organizational processes. Supermarket chains in Norway and other Scandinavian countries have long encouraged recycling, for example.
- *Beyond compliance leadership*—This approach involves the adoption of a **differentiation** strategy through organizational processes such as certified schemes to demonstrate ecological credentials and environmental excellence, for example the adoption of the principles outlined in the United Nations Global Compact or other environmental management system (EMS) schemes and codes. This approach should be adopted by firms that supply industrial markets, such as car manufacturers.
- *Eco-branding*—A firm might differentiate its products or services to promote environmental responsibility. Examples include the British Prince of Wales' food brand Duchy Originals, the late Thai King Bhumipol's Golden Place brand, and the Toyota Prius.
- *Environmental cost leadership*—This strategy is achieved by means of offerings that provide greater environmental benefits at a lower price and particularly suits firms operating in price-sensitive, ecologically sensitive markets, such as the packaging and chemical industries.

Whatever the company and industry, ecological trends in marketing look set to stay, and to develop further, as the sustainability debate rages on and companies use it to develop their own competitive strategies.

Environmental Scanning

Organizations need to monitor all PESTLE elements, but for some industries certain factors are more important than others. Pharmaceutical organizations such as GlaxoSmithKline and Novartis (see Case Insight 11.1) must take special care to monitor legal and regulatory developments (e.g. in relation to labelling, patents, and testing); the Environment Agency will monitor political and ecological changes (including such issues as flood plains for housing developments); road haulage companies should watch for changes that impact on transport development (e.g. congestion charging, diesel duty, toll roads); music distributors should monitor changes in technology and associated sociocultural developments (e.g. streaming trends or the revival of physical music formats such as vinyl records).

To understand changes in their external environment, organizations need to put in place methods and processes to inform them of developments. This process of gathering information about a company's external events and relationships, to assist top management in its decision-making, and the development of its course of action is referred to as **environmental scanning** (Aguilar, 1967). It is the internal communication of external information about issues that may potentially influence an organization's decision-making process, focusing on the identification of emerging issues, situations, and potential threats in the external environment (Albright, 2004).

We can gather information in environmental scanning exercises using company reports, newspapers, industry reports and magazines, government reports, and marketing intelligence reports (e.g. those published by Datamonitor, Euromonitor, and Mintel).

Research Insight 4.2

To take your learning further, you might wish to read this highly influential paper.

Levitt, T. (1960) 'Marketing myopia', *Harvard Business Review*, 38(4), 45–56.

This is perhaps the most famous and celebrated article ever written on marketing. It won the author the McKinsey Award and has been reprinted twice in the *Harvard Business Review*. The central thesis of the article—as true today as it was in 1960—is that companies must monitor change in the external environment and keep abreast of their customers' needs or else risk decline.

 **Visit the online resources to read the abstract and access the full paper.**

'Soft' personal sources of information obtained through networking, such as contacts at trade fairs, particularly for competitive and legal or regulatory information, are also important. Such verbal, personal sources of information can be critical in fast-changing environments (May et al., 2000), when reports from government, industry, or specific businesses have yet to be written and disseminated.

 Visit the **online resources** and complete Internet Activity 4.2 to learn more about a number of sources that can be useful when conducting a scan of the marketing environment.

Understanding the Performance Environment

The performance environment, often called the 'microenvironment', consists of those organizations that either directly or indirectly influence an organization's operational performance. There are three main types:

- those companies that compete against the organization in the pursuit of its objectives;
- those companies that supply raw materials, goods, and services and those that act as distributors, dealers, and retailers, further down the marketing channel, all of which have the potential to directly influence the performance of an organization by adding value through production, assembly, and distribution of products prior to reaching the end user; and
- those companies that have the potential to *indirectly* influence the performance of the organization in the pursuit of its objectives, which often supply services such as consultancy, financial services, and marketing research or communication agencies.

Analysing Industries

An industry is composed of various organizations that market similar offerings. According to Porter (1979), we should review the 'competitive' environment within an industry to identify the major competitive forces, because this helps us to assess their impact on an organization's present and future competitive positions.

Think of industries such as shipbuilding, car manufacture, coal, and steel, in which levels of profitability have been weak and unattractive to prospective new entrants. Now think of industries such as technology, fashion, airlines, and banking, in which levels of profitability have traditionally been high. The competitive pressures in all of these markets vary quite considerably, but there are enough similarities to establish an analytical framework within which to gauge the nature and intensity of competition.

Porter suggests that competition in an industry is a composite of five main competitive forces: the level of threat that new competitors will enter the market, the threat posed by substitute products, and the bargaining power of both buyers and suppliers, which in turn affect the intensity of rivalry between the current competitors. Porter called these variables the 'five forces of competitive industry analysis' (see Figure 4.3).

As a general rule, the more intense the rivalry between the industry players, the lower their overall performance. On the other hand, the lower the rivalry, the greater will be the performance of the industry players.

New Entrants

Industries are seldom static: companies and brands enter and exit industries all of the time. Consider the UK beverage industry, which has witnessed the entrance of energy-drink manufacturers such as Red Bull. This company has been competing head-on with industry stalwarts PepsiCo, Coca-Cola, and GlaxoSmithKline's Lucozade, the original energy drink in the UK beverage market.

New entrants may be restricted through government and regulatory policy or they may be frozen out of an industry because of the capital requirements necessary to set up business. In the oil and gas industry, for example, huge sums of capital are required not only to fund exploration activities, but also to fund the extraction and refining operations.

Companies may otherwise be locked out because companies within a market are using proprietary offerings or technologies. A good example of this is the pharmaceutical industry, in which patents protect companies' investments in new medicines. The cost of developing a new medicine has been estimated at US$2.87 billion (DiMasi et al., 2016). Few companies can afford to compete in a market in which the set-up and ongoing R&D costs are so large.

Substitutes

In any industry, there are usually substitute offerings that perform the same function or meet similar customer needs. Levitt (1960) warned that many companies fail to recognize the competitive threat from newly developing offerings, citing as an example the American railroad industry's refusal to see the competitive threat arising from the development of the automobile and airline industries in the transport sector.

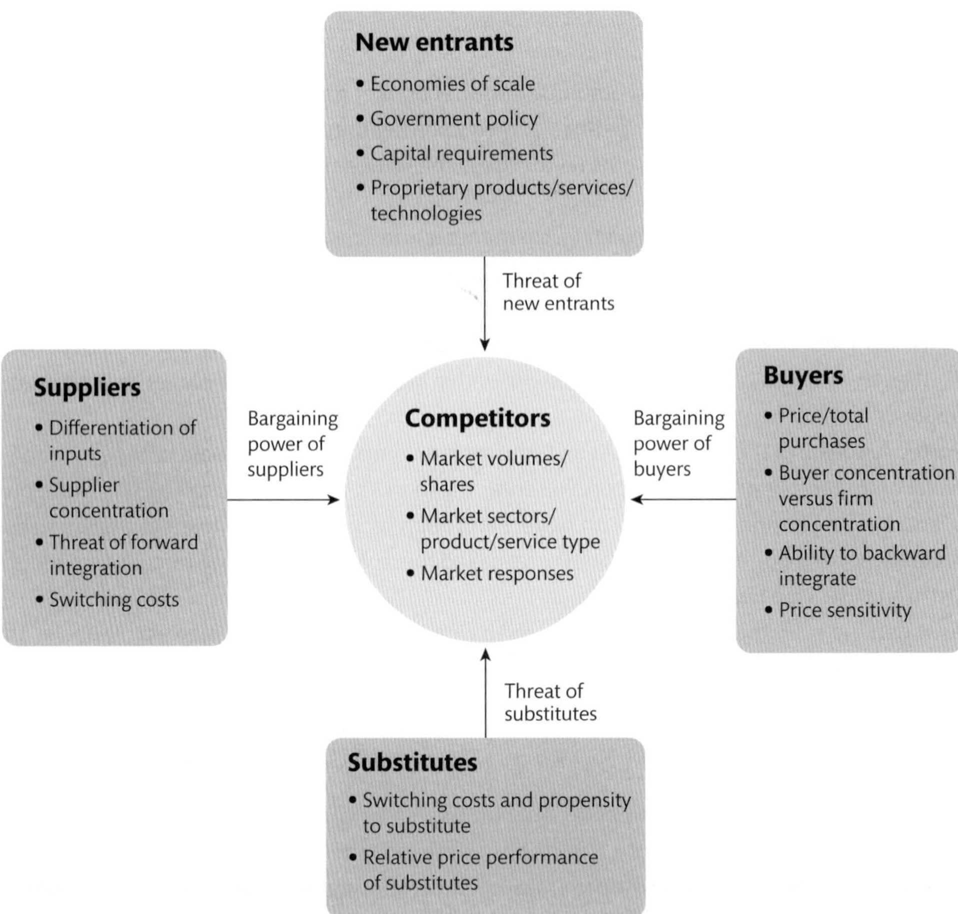

Figure 4.3 Industry analysis: Porter's five forces

Source: Adapted from Porter (1979). Reproduced with the kind permission of Harvard Business School Publishing

Consumers consider the **switching costs** associated with a purchase decision, which, in turn, affect their propensity to substitute the offering for another. If we were to wish to travel from Amsterdam to Paris, we could fly from Schiphol airport to Charles de Gaulle airport, take the train, or drive. We would consider the **relative price** differences (the flight is likely to be the most expensive, but not necessarily so), and we would also factor into this decision how comfortable and convenient these different journeys are likely to be before we finally make our choice. In analysing our place within an industry, we should similarly consider what alternative offerings exist in the marketplace that also meet—to a greater or lesser extent—our customers' needs.

Buyers

Companies should ask themselves what percentage of their sales a single buyer represents. This is an important question because if one buying company purchases a large volume of offerings from the supplying company, as car manufacturers do from steel suppliers, it is likely to be able to demand price concessions (price per total purchase) when there are lots of competing suppliers in the marketplace relative to the proportion of buyers (buyer concentration versus firm concentration).

A factor impacting on a buyer's bargaining power is how price sensitive a particular company is. Depending on their trading circumstances, some companies might be more price-sensitive than others. If such companies are more price-sensitive and yet there are lots of competing suppliers for their business, they are likely to switch suppliers rather than be loyal to one. Most companies try to enhance other factors associated with an offering, such as after-sales service or product/service customization, to try to reduce a client company's **price sensitivity**. When analysing an industry, we should understand the bargaining power that buyers have with their suppliers, because this can impact on the price charged and the volumes sold or total revenue earned.

Suppliers

Any industry analysis should determine how suppliers operate and the extent of their bargaining power. For example, the aircraft manufacture market consists of a small number of major suppliers, such as Boeing and Airbus, and a large number of customers—namely, national airlines and low-cost airline companies; hence the suppliers have the stronger bargaining advantage. Conversely, in the computer gaming industry, there is a large number of suppliers, such as game production companies and gaming console component manufacturers; the few customers, Sony, Nintendo, and Microsoft, hold the bargaining advantage. We should also consider whether or not the suppliers are providing unique components, products, or services that may enhance their bargaining situation.

Competitors

To analyse an industry, we must also understand how the companies within that particular market operate (see, for example, Market Insight 4.3). In the UK cosmetics sector, for example, the market leading cosmetic manufacturers include Avon European Holdings Ltd, Estée Lauder Cosmetics Ltd, L'Oréal (UK) Ltd, Procter & Gamble Ltd, and the Unilever Group, along with large retailers such as Boots Group plc UK Ltd, The Body Shop International plc, and Superdrug Stores plc. In undertaking a competitor analysis, we should outline each company's structure (e.g. details of the main holding company, the individual business unit, any changes in ownership), current and future developments (which can often be gleaned from reading company prospectuses, websites, and industry reports), and the company's latest financial results. We would be interested in calculating the market volumes and shares for each competitor, because market share is a key indication of company profitability and return on investment (Buzzell et al., 1975).

Competitors provide offerings that attempt to meet the same market need as does our own. There are several ways in which a need might be met, but essentially firms need to be aware of both their direct and indirect competitors. *Direct* competitors provide the same target market with similar offerings, for example EasyJet, Wizz Air, and Ryanair. Direct competitors may also offer a product in the same category, but target different segments. For example, in addition to major global mechanical watch manufacturers such as Omega and TAG Heuer, smartwatch manufacturers such as Apple and Samsung are now also competing for different target markets, namely younger, tech savvy consumers (Hotten, 2019). *Indirect* competitors are those who address the same target market, but provide a different offering to satisfy the market need, for example Spotify, Sony, and Apple's iPod.

Market Insight 4.3 **Surviving the Greek Crisis**

STEROPAL is a pioneering, family-owned, Greek trading company, founded by A. Papadopoulos in 1985, which imports and distributes furniture materials, industrial wood, and kitchen equipment. Starting as a small, 110 square metre retail store, it has evolved over the years, primarily due to the vision of Kyriakos Papadopoulos, the current owner and managing director. Since then, it has morphed into a B2B company with over €6 million revenues in 2018, and premises exceeding an area of 6,000 square metres including a processing section with machinery for cutting and welding. Its operations involve sales of components for integrated kitchen cabinets, wardrobes, desks, and other furniture and fittings.

Surprisingly, the main expansion of the company took place during the years of the Greek economic crisis. From 2009 to date, the company managed to expand its business more than twenty times, despite unfavourable market conditions, at the same time as other companies in the industry were folding due to insufficient funds, the high cost of capital, and a lack of clients. STEROPAL's market is directly affected by the construction industry, which in Greece had an average annual negative growth of −2.4 per cent between 2013 to 2017. STEROPAL, however, devised a strategy to take advantage of the very economic circumstances that had led other competitors to bankruptcy and managed an average annual growth in net profit of 3.7 per cent, despite the high corporation tax rate (31 per cent).

The company's marketing strategy was to expand by taking over the clients of those companies that had closed down. Considering both the macro- and the micro-environment, the marketing and sales plan of the company revolved around a sector-by-sector invasion plan, manoeuvring to gain market share in small towns and provinces in northern Greece first, then taking Athens by storm after. After growing its market share fast in northern Greece, STEROPAL's branding strategy was focused on increasing brand awareness, through domestic and international trade fairs, turning the firm into a wholesale brand name. Having scanned the business environment, STEROPAL formulated a strategy to expand when much of the rest of the industry was dying.

1 **What environmental factors contributed to the company's decision to expand rather than adopt a simple survival strategy?**

2 **From a strategic marketing perspective, do you think that an expansion strategy was risky or not?**

3 **Do you think that such strategies work better in B2B settings or could they be equally feasible in B2C markets?**

Sources: Anon. (2017); Epipleon Magazine (2019); GTP (2019); https://www.steropal.gr/en/.

This market insight was kindly contributed by Chris Liassides, University of Sheffield, International Faculty, CITY College, and Niki Glaveli, Aristotle University of Thessaloniki.

Suppliers and Distributors

Porter (1979) also realized that suppliers can influence competition and hence built these into his five forces model. Transport and delivery services also constitute an important part of the value offered to customers.

It is common to find high levels of integration between a manufacturer and its distributors, dealers, and retailers. Account needs to be taken of the strength of these relationships and consideration given to how market performance might be strengthened or weakened by the capabilities of the channel intermediary. Suppliers and distributors have become central to a firm's ability to develop specific **competitive advantage**. Analysis of the performance environment should therefore incorporate a review of key suppliers and distributors to the firm.

Understanding the Internal Environment

An analysis of the internal environment of an organization is concerned with understanding and evaluating the capabilities and potential of the products, systems, and human, marketing, and financial resources. Attention here is given to two main elements: products and finance, by means of **portfolio analysis**.

Portfolio Analysis

When managing a collection, or 'portfolio', of offerings, we should appreciate that the performance of an individual offering can often fail to give useful insight. What is really important is an understanding of the relative performance of the offerings.

In 1977, the Boston Consulting Group (BCG) developed the original idea of a matrix—the **Boston box**, shown in Figure 4.4—based on two key variables: market growth and relative market share. Market share is measured as a percentage of the share of the product's largest competitor, expressed as a fraction; thus a relative share of 0.8 means that the product achieves 80 per cent of the sales of the market leader's sales volume (or value, depending on which measure is used). This would not be the strongest competitive position, but neither is it a weak position. A relative market share of 1 means that the company shares market leadership with a competitor with an equal share. In Figure 4.4, the size of the circles represents the sales revenue generated by the product.

When analysed in terms of the Boston box, an offering falls into one of four categories, as follows.

- *Question marks* are offerings that exist in growing markets, but have low market share. As a result, there is negative cash flow and they are unprofitable.
- *Stars* are most probably market leaders, but their growth has to be financed through fairly heavy levels of investment.

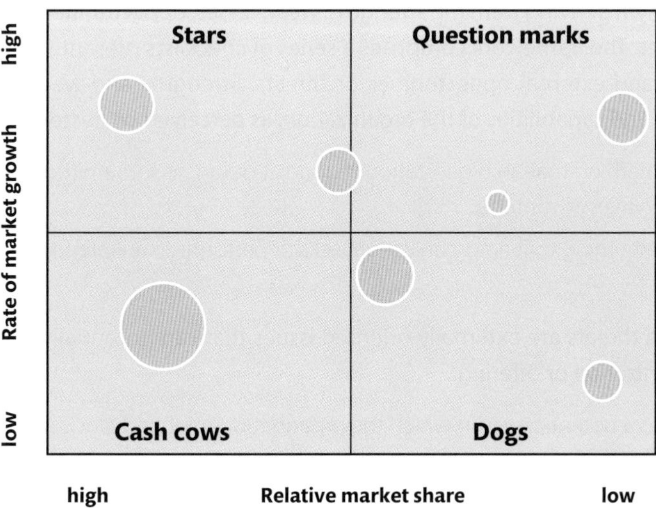

Figure 4.4 The Boston box

Source: Reprinted from B. Hedley, 'Strategy and the business portfolio', *Long Range Planning*, 10, 1, 12. © 1977, with permission from Elsevier.

- *Cash cows* exist in fairly stable, low-growth markets and require little ongoing investment. Their high market share draws both positive cash flows and high levels of profitability.
- *Dogs* experience low growth and low market share, and generate negative cash flows. These indicators suggest that many of them are operating in declining markets and that they have no real long-term future.

Essentially, excess cash generated by cash cows should be utilized to develop question marks and stars, which are unable to support themselves. This enables stars to become cash cows and self-supporting. Dogs should be retained only as long as they contribute to positive cash flow, and do not restrict the use of assets and resources elsewhere in the business. Once they do so, they should be divested or ejected from the portfolio.

Divestment need not occur only because of low share, however: when pharmaceutical firm Merck sold Sirna Therapeutics to Alnylam Pharmaceuticals, the sale of the drug delivery subsidiary was heralded as enabling Merck to remain consistent with its strategy of reducing its emphasis on platform technologies. Merck's policy is to assess whether particular assets are core to its strategy, whether they provide competitive advantage, and whether they might generate greater value as part of Merck or outside Merck (Zhu, 2014).

By plotting all of a company's offerings within the Boston matrix, it becomes easy to appreciate visually whether a portfolio is well balanced (or otherwise). If offerings are distributed equally—or at least are not clustered in any single area—and market shares and cash flows equate with the offerings' market position, the portfolio is financially healthy and well balanced. An unbalanced portfolio, meanwhile, would see too many offerings clustered in one or two quadrants—and hence portfolio analysis would inform possible strategies to remedy this and allow us to project possible outcomes.

SWOT Analysis

Once the entire operating environment has been examined, it is essential to draw the information together in a form that can be easily understood. Perhaps the most common analytical tool is **SWOT analysis**, the acronym deriving from the strengths, weaknesses, opportunities, and threats on which the analysis centres. The framework comprises a series of checklists presented as internal strengths and weaknesses, and external opportunities or threats. Strengths and weaknesses relate to the internal resources and capabilities of the organization, as perceived by customers (Piercy, 2002).

- A *strength* is something that an organization is good at doing, or something that gives it particular credibility and market advantage.
- A *weakness* is something that an organization lacks or performs in an inferior way in comparison to others.

Opportunities and threats are externally oriented issues that can potentially influence the performance of an organization or offering.

- An *opportunity* is a potential way in which the organization might advance by developing and satisfying an unfulfilled market need.
- A *threat* is something that, at some time in the future, may destabilize and/or reduce the potential performance of the organization.

SWOT analysis helps us to sort through the information generated in the environmental analysis and to identify the key issues, and prompts us to think about converting weaknesses into strengths and threats into opportunities—that is, about generating conversion strategies.

Once the three or four elements of each part of the SWOT matrix have been derived, then a number of pertinent questions need to be asked, including the following.

1. Does the organization do something far better than its rivals? If it does, this is known as a 'competitive advantage' (or 'distinctive competence', or 'differential advantage'), and this can lead to a competitive edge.
2. Which of the organization's weaknesses does a strategy need to correct and is it competitively vulnerable?
3. Which opportunities can be pursued, and are there the necessary resources and capabilities to exploit them?
4. Which strategies are necessary to defend against the key threats?

Figure 4.5 depicts a SWOT matrix for a small digital media agency. The outcome of a successful SWOT analysis is a series of decisions that help the organization to develop and formulate strategy and goals. (Note that there are no more than four items in any one category, rather than a list of ten or so items. It is important to prioritize and make a judgement about what is really key.)

Strengths	**Weaknesses**
Quick to respond to changes in the marketing environment	Too much work from a few clients and at non-premium rates
Flat management encourages fast decision-making	Few project management skills
Use of contractors enables flexibility—lowers employment costs/finance and improves customers' perception of expertise	High office and finance costs
	Low customer base
Opportunities	**Threats**
Emerging markets such as professional services (e.g. dentists, lawyers, surveyors)	Larger media houses buying business
New distribution channels	Speed of technological advances
Tax incentives to encourage e-commerce	Contractors have low levels of loyalty

Figure 4.5 A SWOT analysis for a small digital media agency

Research Insight 4.3

To take your learning further, you might wish to read this influential paper.

Prahalad, C. K., and Hamel, G. (1990) 'The core competence of the organisation', *Harvard Business Review*, 68(3), 79–91.

This paper was incredibly important because it provided a first insight into the critical role of core competencies as a means of developing superior business performance.

 **Visit the online resources to read the abstract and access the full paper.**

Weaknesses need to be addressed, not avoided. Some can be converted into strengths; others, into opportunities. In this example, entering the professional services market would probably increase the number of customers and enable premium rates to be earned.

Threats need to be nullified. For example, by building relationships with key contractors (suppliers) and selected larger media houses, these threats might be dissipated—or even developed into strengths.

 Visit the **online resources** and complete Internet Activity 4.3 to learn more about the use of SWOT analysis.

Strategic Marketing Goals

The analysis of the environment and the company's position allows us to determine exactly what the marketing strategy should actually achieve—that is, what the **strategic marketing** goals should be. Strategic marketing is a process that leads to specific decisions on how to compete in the marketplace and how the company should best serve its customers.

There are five strategic objectives, as illustrated in Figure 4.6.

- *Niche* objectives are often the most suitable when firms operate in a market dominated by a major competitor and in which financial resources are limited. A niche can be either a small segment or a small part of a segment. The Australian government identified several **niche markets** when exploring the development of its tourism business. It identified sports, cycling seniors, culture and the arts, backpackers, health, people with disabilities, caravanning and camping, food, wine, and agri-tourism as potential niche markets.
- **Hold** objectives are concerned with defence. They are designed to prevent and fend off attack from aggressive competitors. Market leaders are the most likely to adopt a holding strategy, because they are prone to attack from new entrants and their closest rivals as they strive for the most market share.

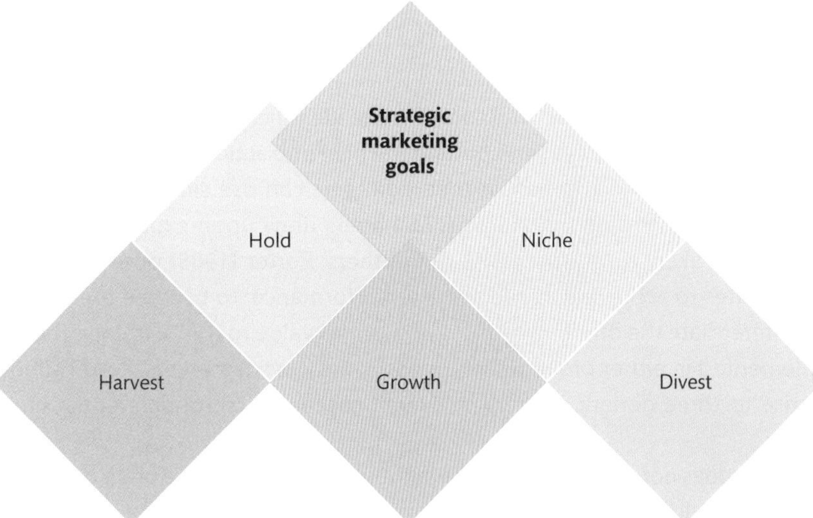

Figure 4.6 Five dimensions of strategic marketing goals

- **Harvesting** objectives are often employed in mature markets as firms/offerings enter a decline phase. The goal is to maximize short-term profits and stimulate a positive cash flow.
- *Divest* objectives are sometimes necessary when offerings continue to incur losses and generate negative cash flows, such as when General Motors sold off Saab to sports car manufacturer Spyker (Madslien, 2010).
- *Growth* is an objective that the vast majority of organizations consider to be primary. There are, however, different forms of growth. Ansoff (1957) proposed that organizations should first consider whether new or established products are to be delivered in new or established markets. His product–market matrix (see Figure 4.7) is an important first step in deciding what the marketing strategy should be.

Australia's tourism has been developed around the identification of niche markets.

Source: © James Fisher/Tourism Australia.

	Present products	**New products**
Present markets	Market penetration	Product development
New markets	Market development	Diversification

Figure 4.7 Ansoff's matrix

Source: Adapted from Ansoff (1957).

Strategic Market Action

An important marketing strategy activity concerns the identification of the most appropriate way of achieving the marketing goals set and putting the plan into action: the implementation phase.

There is no proven formula or toolkit that managers can use simply because of the many internal and external environmental factors. Managers draw upon experience to know which strategies are more likely to be successful than others. Porter (1985) proposed that there are two essential routes to achieving above average performance: to become the lowest cost producer or to differentiate the offering until it is of superior value to the customer. These strategies can be implemented in either broad (mass) or narrow (focused) markets. Porter suggested that these give rise to three generic strategies: overall **cost leadership**; differentiation; and focus strategies.

Cost leadership does not mean a lower price, although lower prices are often used to attract customers. By having the lowest cost structure, an organization can offer standard offerings at acceptable levels of quality, yet still generate above-average profit margins. If attacked by a competitor using lower prices, the low-cost leader has a far bigger cushion than its competitors. Charging a lower price than rivals is not the critical point. The competitive advantage is derived from *how* the organization exploits its cost–price ratio (see Market Insight 4.4). By reinvesting the profit, for example by improving product quality, investing more in product development, or building extra capacity, long-run superiority is more likely to be achieved.

Differentiation requires that all value chain activities are geared towards the creation of offerings that are valued by, and which satisfy, the needs of particular broad segments. By identifying particular customer groups, each of which has a discrete set of needs, a product can be differentiated from its competitors. Fashion brand Zara differentiated itself by reformulating its value chain so that it became the fastest high-street brand from design, through production and distribution, to delivery of fashion clothing to the customer in store.

Customers are sometimes prepared to pay a higher price—that is, a premium—for offerings that deliver superior or extra value. The Starbucks coffee brand, for example, is strongly differentiated and valued, with consumers willing to pay higher prices to enjoy the Starbucks experience. However, differentiation can equally be achieved by low prices, as evidenced through the success of low-cost airlines such as Ireland's Ryanair.

Focus strategies are used by organizations that seek gaps in broad market segments or find gaps in competitors' ranges. In other words, focus strategies seek out unfulfilled market needs. There are two options for a company wishing to follow a **focus strategy**: one is low cost and the other is differentiation—but both occur within a particular, narrow segment. The difference between a broad differentiator and a focused differentiator is that the former bases its strategy on attributes valued across a number of markets, whereas the latter seeks to meet the needs of particular segments within a market.

Porter argues that, to achieve competitive advantage, organizations must achieve one of these three generic strategies. He argues that to fail to be strategically explicit results in organizations being 'stuck in the middle'—that is, they achieve below-average returns and have no

Market Insight 4.4 **Primark: Low-Cost Leadership in the Face of Brexit?**

Primark (known as Penneys in the Republic of Ireland) is an Irish fashion retailer owned by Associated British Foods (ABF). The retailer has grown considerably since its establishment in 1969 and boasted 360 stores in eleven different countries across Europe and the USA in 2019. Primark has 187 stores in the UK alone and opened its biggest ever store in Birmingham in 2019, with this superstore occupying a whopping 160,000 square feet. Despite a long list of fashion retailers running into financial difficulties, Primark thrives, turning over a healthy profit of €8.1 billion in 2018.

Primark operates in a very competitive market and is a cost leader. While there is a threat of substitutes, few of its competitors, such as Zara, ASOS, H&M, New Look, and M&S, offer a similar vast range of products at low prices. Cheap and affordable clothing has been a hallmark of Primark's existence and providing fashionable clothing at affordable rates is extremely important to its success. The retailer has been able to achieve this with little or no advertising costs and most products are manufactured in countries such as Bangladesh, Pakistan, India, and China with low labour costs, creating barriers to entry. Buying in bulk helps improve Primark's bargaining power, while the bargaining power of customers is not very strong as not many other retailers can compete on Primark's low prices. Primark does not have an e-commerce website, instead choosing to focus on selling its produce in-store only. Some argue that Primark's success is due to the fact that it has not deviated from its core purpose: fast, accessible, fun fashion with quick turnarounds in stock.

However, Primark is faced with a turbulent marketing environment and needs to be attuned to the many political, economic, social, technological, legal, and environmental factors that have the potential to affect its business. One strong concern in 2019 was Britain's decision to leave the EU, a move that was predicted to cause political and economic upheaval. Uncertainty over Brexit and its impact on the pound has made it hard to predict the future profitability of retailers such as Primark. As Primark celebrates its fiftieth anniversary, its trading performance has improved with further expansion into Slovenia, Poland, and the Czech Republic. There doesn't seem to be an end in sight for Primark's growth.

1. **How is Brexit likely to affect Primark's operations? What are the negative and positive impacts that are likely to ensue?**
2. **Technological developments have resulted in a move away from in-store shopping. Do you think Primark's lack of an e-commerce website will make it more vulnerable going forward, particularly as consumers shift their spending online?**
3. **Analyse Primark's performance environment using Porter's five forces industry analysis model.**

Sources: Nazir (2019); O'Brien (2019); Percival (2019); RTE (2019).

This market insight was kindly contributed by Marie O' Dwyer, Waterford Institute of Technology, Republic of Ireland.

competitive advantage. It has been observed, however, that some organizations have been able to pursue both low-cost and differentiated strategies simultaneously. For example, an organization that develops a large market share through differentiation and by creating very strong brands or through technological innovation may well also become the cost leader.

Visit the **online resources** and access Internet Activity 4.4 to learn more about business planning in the airline market.

Marketing Planning

The three key activities associated with strategic marketing planning cover strategic market analysis, the setting of strategic marketing goals, and defining strategic marketing action, each area of which we consider in the preceding sections. For organizations to be able to develop, implement, and control these activities at the offering and brand levels, marketing plans are developed. This final section considers the characteristics of the marketing planning process.

Marketing planning is a sequential process involving a series of activities leading to the setting of marketing objectives and the formulation of plans for achieving them (McDonald, 2016: 39). A marketing plan is the key output from the overall strategic marketing planning process. It details a company's or brand's intended marketing activity. Marketing plans can be developed for periods of one, two, or five years—even up to twenty-five years. Too many organizations, however, regard marketing plans as a development of the annual round of setting sales targets, which are then extrapolated into quasi-marketing plans. In doing so, they fail to take into account the marketplace, customer needs, and resources available.

The first step in the planning process should be a phase of strategic appraisal and evaluation. This will cover a period of between three and five years, and provide a strategic insight into the markets, competitors, and organizational resources that will shape the direction and nature of the way in which the firm has decided to compete. Once agreed, these should be updated on an annual basis, and modified to meet changing internal and external conditions. Only once the strategic marketing plan has been developed should detailed operational or functional marketing plans, covering a one-year period, be developed (McDonald, 2016). This makes marketing planning a continuous process, not something undertaken once a year or, worse, only when a new product is launched.

A marketing plan designed to support a particular offering consists of a series of activities that should be undertaken sequentially. These are presented in Table 4.1.

Many of the corporate-level goals and strategies and internal and external environmental analyses that are established within the strategic marketing planning process can be replicated within each of the marketing plans written for individual products, product lines, markets, or even strategic business units (SBUs). As a general rule, only detail concerning offerings, competitors, and related support resources need change prior to the formulation of individual marketing mixes and their implementation, within functional level marketing plans.

The strategic marketing planning process starts with a consideration of the organization's goals and resources, and an analysis of the market and environmental context in which the organization seeks to achieve its goals. It culminates in a detailed plan, which, when implemented, is measured to determine how well the organization performs against the marketing plan.

Table 4.1 Key activities within a marketing plan

Activity	Explanation
Executive summary	Brief, one-page summary of key points and outcomes
Overall objectives	Makes references to the organization's overall mission and corporate goals—i.e. the elements that underpin the strategy
Product/market background	Summarizes the product and/or market to clarify understanding about target markets, sales history, market trends, main competitors, and the organization's own product portfolio
Marketing analysis	Provides insight into the market, the customers, and the competition; should consider segment needs, current strategies, and key financial data; is supported by the marketing audit and SWOT analysis
Marketing strategies	States the market(s) to be targeted, the basis on which the firm will compete, the competitive advantages to be used, and the way in which the product is to be positioned in the market
Marketing goals	Expresses the desired outcomes of the strategy in terms of the volume of expected sales, the value of sales and market share gains, levels of product awareness, availability, profitability, and customer satisfaction
Marketing programmes	Develops a marketing mix for each target market segment; specifies who is responsible for the various activities and actions, and the resources that are to be made available
Implementation	Sets out: • the way in which the marketing plan is to be controlled and evaluated; • the financial scope of the plan; and • the operational implications in terms of human resources, R&D, and system and process needs
Supporting documentation	Any relevant supporting documentation too bulky to be included in the plan itself, but necessary for reference and detail, e.g. the full PESTLE and SWOT analyses, marketing research data, and other market reports and information, plus key correspondence

Chapter Summary

To consolidate your learning, the key points from this chapter are summarized below.

- **Describe the key characteristics associated with the marketing environment.**

  The marketing environment incorporates the external environment, the performance environment, and the internal environment. The external environment incorporates macro-environmental factors, which are largely uncontrollable and which organizations generally cannot influence. The performance environment incorporates key factors within an industry, impacting on strategic decision-making. The internal environment is controllable and is the principal means, through its resource base, by which an organization influences its strategy.

  The external environment comprises political, social, and technological factors, and organizations often have very limited, if any, control of these. The performance environment consists of competitors, suppliers, and indirect service providers, who shape the way and extent to which organizations achieve their objectives. Here, organizations have a much stronger level of influence. The internal environment concerns the resources, processes, and policies with which an organization achieves its goals, factors it can influence directly.

- **Explain the environmental scanning process and show how PESTLE analysis can be used to understand the external environment.**

  The environmental scanning process consists of the data-gathering phase, the environmental interpretation and analysis phase, and the strategy formulation phase. The three processes are interlinked, but, over time, more attention is focused on each one more than the others so that at the end of the process, greater effort is expended on using knowledge gleaned from the external and competitive environments to formulate strategy based on changes occurring and identified in the company's environment.

  We considered the various components of the external marketing environment that may impact on any particular organization using the PESTLE framework, which comprises political, economic, sociocultural, technological, legal, and ecological factors. Some of these factors are more important than others in any particular industry.

- **Analyse the performance environment using the Porter's five forces industry analysis model.**

  The most common technique used to analyse the performance environment is Porter's 'five forces' model of competitive analysis. Porter concludes that the more intense the rivalry between the industry players, the lower will be their overall performance. On the other hand, the lower the rivalry, the greater will be the performance of the industry players. Porter's five forces comprise supplier bargaining power, buyer bargaining power, the threat of new entrants, rivalry among competitors, and the threat of substitutes.

- **Analyse an organization's product/service portfolio to aid resource planning.**

  An organization's principal resources relate to its portfolio of offerings and the financial resources at its disposal. We use portfolio analysis—specifically, the Boston box approach—to determine whether different SBUs or product/service formulations are 'stars', 'dogs', 'question marks', or 'cash cows', each category characterised by differing levels of cash flow and resource requirements. It is important to undertake a marketing audit as a preliminary measure to allow proper development of marketing strategy.

- **Analyse current conditions and formulate marketing strategies.**

  SWOT analysis is used to determine an overall view of the organization's strategic position, and highlights the need to produce a strong fit between the internal capability (strengths and weaknesses) and the external situation (opportunities and threats). SWOT analysis serves to identify the key issues, and then prompts thought about converting weaknesses into strengths and threats into opportunities.

- **Explain the different types of strategic marketing goal and associated growth strategies.**

  There are several types of strategic objective, but the main ones are niche, hold, harvest, growth, and divest goals. The vast majority of organizations consider growth to be a primary objective.

Review Questions

1. What are the three main marketing environments?
2. How might changes in the political environment affect marketing strategy?
3. How might changes in the economic environment affect marketing strategy?
4. How might changes in the sociocultural environment affect marketing strategy?
5. How might changes in the technological environment affect marketing strategy?
6. How might changes in the legal environment affect marketing strategy?
7. How might changes in the ecological environment affect marketing strategy?
8. What are Porter's 'five forces'?
9. Identify the key characteristics of SWOT analysis. What actions should be taken once the SWOT grid is completed?
10. List the core parts of a marketing plan.

Worksheet Summary

To apply the knowledge you have gained from this chapter, and to test your understanding of how the PESTLE framework, five forces model, and Boston box can be used to analyse the marketing environment, visit the **online resources,** and complete Worksheet 4.1.

Discussion Questions

1. Having read Case Insight 4.1, how would you advise 3scale with regard to Amazon's entry into the market?
2. Search the Internet for further information on the rise of vegetarian and vegan products and the increasing number of meat substitute options in the UK, and then answer the following questions.
   - A What changes have taken place in the external environment to bring an increase in the number of meat-free and dairy-free products in supermarkets?

B How should supermarkets like Tesco and Sainsbury's ensure that they keep up to date with trends in consumer lifestyles and foods as well as competitor new proposition development?

C What strategies in relation to proposition development and promotion could supermarkets in other European countries (e.g. France or Spain) adopt to accommodate vegetarian and vegan consumers?

3 **Undertake an environmental analysis using PESTLE, by searching the Internet for appropriate information and by using available market research reports, for each of the following markets.**

A The automotive market (e.g. VW, Renault, BMW, Ford, Toyota, or Tesla)

B The global multiple retail grocery market (e.g. Walmart, Carrefour, or Tesco)

C The beer industry (e.g. InBev, Carlsberg, Heineken, Miller Brands, or Budweiser Budvar)

4 **After a successful period of twenty years' trading, a bicycle manufacturer notices that its sales, rather than increasing at a steady rate, are starting to decline. The company, Rapid Cycles, produces a range of bicycles to suit various segments and distributes them mainly through independent cycle shops. In recent years, however, the number of low-cost cycles entering the country has increased, with many distributed through supermarkets and national retail chains. The managing director of Rapid Cycles feels that he cannot compete with these low-cost imports and asks you for your opinion about what should be done. Discuss the situation facing Rapid Cycles and make recommendations regarding its marketing strategy.**

Visit the **online resources** and complete the multiple-choice questions to assess your knowledge of the chapter.

Glossary

Boston box a popular portfolio matrix, developed by the Boston Consulting Group, commonly also referred to as the 'BCG matrix'.

competitive advantage achieved when an organization has an edge over its competitors on factors that are important to customers.

cost leadership a strategy involving the production of goods and services for a broad market segment, at a cost lower than those of all other competitors.

differentiation a strategy through which an organization offers products and services to broad particular customer groups, who perceive the offering to be significantly different from, and superior to, its competitors.

divestment a strategic objective that involves selling a business or killing a product when that business or product continues to incur losses and generate negative cash flows.

environmental scanning a management process designed to identify external issues, situations, and threats that may impinge on an organization's future and its strategic decision-making.

focus strategy a strategy based on developing gaps in broad market segments or gaps in competitors' product ranges.

government the system of organization of a nation state.

gross domestic product (GDP) a measure of the output of a nation—that is, of the size of its economy; calculated as the market value of all finished goods and services produced in a country during a specified period, typically available annually or quarterly.

harvesting a strategic objective based on maximizing short-term profits and stimulating positive cash flow; often used in mature markets as firms or products enter a decline phase.

hold a strategic objective based on defending against attacks from aggressive competitors.

inflation rising prices.

niche market a small part of a market segment that has specific and specialized characteristics that make it uneconomic for the leading competitors to enter.

performance environment refers to the organizations that directly or indirectly influence an organization's ability to achieve its strategic and operational goals.

PESTLE a framework that examines the external environment, named as an acronym of the political, economic, sociocultural, technological, legal, and ecological factors on which it focuses.

political environment that part of the macro environment concerned with impending and potential legislation and how it may affect a particular firm.

portfolio analysis an assessment of a company's mix of products, services, investments, and other assets aiming to optimize the use of resources and to assess its suitability, level of risk, and expected financial return.

price sensitivity the extent to which a company or consumer increases or lowers its purchase volumes in relation to changes in price. A company or customer is price *in*sensitive when unit volumes drop proportionately less than increases in prices.

public relations (PR) a non-personal form of communication used by companies to build trust, goodwill, interest, and ultimately relationships with a range of stakeholders.

purchasing power parity (PPP) a way of establishing the relative value of currencies between countries, so that there is an equivalence of purchasing power.

recession a fall in a country's GDP for two or more successive quarters in any one year.

relative price denotes the price of company A's product/service as a proportion of the price of a comparable product/service of company B (typically the market leader) or its nearest competitor (where A is the market leader).

reverse engineering the process of developing a product from the finished version (e.g. from a competitor's prototype) to its constituent parts rather than the usual approach from component parts to a finished product.

society the customs, habits, and nature of a nation's social system.

stakeholders people with an interest—that is, a 'stake'—in the levels of profit an organization achieves, its environmental impact, and its ethical conduct in society.

strategic marketing the organizational process that leads to decisions on how the company should compete in the marketplace (against its rivals) and how it should serve its customer base.

sustainable competitive advantage when an organization is able to offer a superior product to those of competitors that is not easily imitated and which enjoys significant market share as a result.

switching costs the psychological, economic, time, and effort-related costs associated with substituting one product or service for another, or changing a supplier from one to another.

SWOT analysis a methodology used by organizations to understand their strategic position; involves analysis of an organization's strengths, weaknesses, opportunities, and threats.

values the standards of behaviour expected of an organization's employees.

References

Aguilar, F. Y. (1967) *Scanning the Business Environment*, New York: Macmillan.

Albright, K. S. (2004) 'Environmental scanning: Radar for success', *Information Management Journal*, 38(3), 38–45.

Amberber, E. (2014) 'Vodafone launches Africa's digital money M-Pesa in India; Now your SIM is powered to pay for everything', *Your Story*, 1 April. Retrieve from: http://yourstory.com/2014/04/vodafone-m-pesa-india/ (accessed 30 November 2019).

Anand, G., and Kumar, H. (2016) 'Narendra Modi defends currency move as millions in India scramble for cash', *New York Times*, 13 November. Retrieve from: https://

www.nytimes.com/2016/11/14/world/asia/narendra-modi-defends-currency-move-as-millions-in-india-scramble-for-cash.html?searchResultPosition=1 (accessed 30 October 2020).

Anon. (2017) 'Η νέα εποχή της STEROPAL [trans. The new era of STEROPAL]'. *Epipleon Magazine*, 8 May. Retrieve from: https://epipleon.gr/steropal/ (accessed 13 September 2020).

Ansoff, I. H. (1957) 'Strategies for diversification', *Harvard Business Review*, 35(2), 113–24.

Buzzell, R. D., Gale, B. T., and Sultan, R. G. M. (1975) 'Market share: A key to profitability', *Harvard Business Review*, 53(1), 97–106.

Danciu, V. (2013) 'The future of marketing: An appropriate response to the environment changes', *Theoretical and Applied Economics*, 20(5), 33–52.

Deloitte (2019) 'Plant-based alternatives: Driving industry M&A'. Retrieve from: https://content.deloitte.com.au/20200113-cpr-inb-plant-based-alternatives-reg#:~:text=Plant-based%20alternatives%20Driving%20industry%20M%26A%20The%20global%20meat,growth%20of%20viable%20plant-based%20alternatives%20across%20many%20categories. (accessed 30 October 2020).

DiMasi, J. A., Grabowski, H. G., and Hansen, R. W. (2016) 'Innovation in the pharmaceutical industry: New estimates of R&D costs', *Journal of Health Economics*, *47*, 20–33.

Fleming, A. (2019) 'Table for one: How eating alone is radically changing our diets', *The Guardian*, 6 May. Retrieve from: https://www.theguardian.com/lifeandstyle/2019/may/06/table-for-one-how-eating-alone-changing-our-diets (accessed 30 October 2020).

Forsyth, J. (2013) 'Consumer tastes are changing—But wine has been slow to adapt', *Mintel Blog*, 23 May. Retrieve from: https://www.mintel.com/blog/drink-market-news/wine-consumer-tastes-are-changing (accessed 30 November 2019).

GTP (2019) 'Report: Greece's construction industry set to grow by 2022', 3 May. Retrieve from: https://news.gtp.gr/2019/05/03/report-greeces-construction-industry-set-grow-2022/ (accessed 30 October 2020).

Hedley, B. (1977) 'Strategy and the business portfolio', *Long Range Planning*, 10(1), 9–15.

Hillman, A., Keim, G. D., and Schuler, D. (2004) 'Corporate political activity: A review and research agenda', *Journal of Management*, 30(6), 837–57.

Hotten, R. (2019) 'Watch industry's times are changing', *BBC News*, 13 January. Retrieve from: https://www.bbc.co.uk/news/business-46822929 (accessed 30 October 2020).

Iyengar, R. (2017) 'India poised for smartphone revolution', *CNN Business*, 28 September. Retrieve from: http://money.cnn.com/2017/09/26/technology/indiamobile-congress-market-numbers/index.html (accessed 30 October 2020).

Kalavalapalli, Y., and Nair, V. (2016) 'Digital payments in India seen touching $500 billion by 2020', *LiveMint*, 28 July. Retrieve from: https://www.livemint.com/Industry/M6SPyd4vUcC7QIQRnjBqaO/Digital-payments-in-India-seen-touching-500-billion-by-2020.html (accessed 30 October 2020).

Lawton, T., and Rajwani, T. (2011) 'Designing lobbying capabilities: Managerial choices in unpredictable environments', *European Business Review*, 23(2), 167–89.

Levitt, T. (1960) 'Marketing myopia', *Harvard Business Review*, 38(4), 45–56.

McDonald, M. (2016) *Marketing Plans: How to Prepare Them, How to Profit from Them* (8th edn), Chichester: Wiley.

Madslien, J. (2010) 'Spyker boss outlines Saab plans', *BBC News*, 12 February. Retrieve from: http://news.bbc.co.uk/1/hi/business/8512224.stm (accessed 30 October 2020).

May, R. C., Stewart, W. H., Jr., and Sweo, R. (2000) 'Environmental scanning behaviour in a transitional economy: Evidence from Russia', *Academy of Management Journal*, 43(3), 403–27.

Nazir, S. (2019) 'Primark enters 12th market with launch of new Slovenia store', 14 June. Retrieve from: https://www.retailgazette.co.uk/blog/2019/06/primark-enters-12th-market-launch-new-slovenia-store/ (accessed 30 October 2020).

O'Brien, S. (2019) 'How this Irish woman helped shape a global retail empire', *Irish Central*, 30 May. Retrieve from: https://www.irishcentral.com/news/breege-o-donoghue-primark-penneys (accessed 30 November 2019).

Orsato, R. J. (2006) 'Competitive environmental strategies: When does it pay to be green?', *California Management Review*, 48(2), 127–43.

Percival, G. (2019) 'Primark upbeat on Ireland as sales rise 4%', *Irish Examiner*, 4 July. Retrieve from: https://www.irishexaminer.com/business/arid-30934842.html (accessed 30 October 2020).

Piercy, N. (2002) *Market-Led Strategic Change: Transforming the Process of Going to Market*, Oxford: Butterworth-Heinemann.

Porter, M. E. (1979) 'How competitive forces shape strategy', *Harvard Business Review*, 57(2), 137–45.

Porter, M. E. (1985) *The Competitive Advantage: Creating and Sustaining Superior Performance*, New York: Free Press.

Prno, J., and Slocombe, S. D. (2012) 'Exploring the origins of "social license to operate" in the mining sector: Perspectives from governance and sustainability theories', *Resources Policy*, 37(3), 346–57.

Rao, P. M. (2005) 'Sustaining competitive advantage in a high-technology environment: A strategic marketing perspective', *Advances in Competitiveness Research*, 13(1), 33–47.

RTE (2019) 'Primark-owner AB Foods warns of volatile pound as Brexit nears', *RTE*, 10 September. Retrieve from: https://www.rte.ie/news/business/2018/0910/992746-associated-british-foods/ (accessed 30 October 2020).

Sen, S. (2014) 'Inclusion by mobile', *Business Today*, 23 November. Retrieve from: https://www.businesstoday.in/magazine/case-study/case-study-vodafone-mpesa-mobile-cash-transfer-service-future/story/211926.html (accessed 30 October 2020).

Tiwari, M. and Deepti, K.C. (2013) 'Mobile payment systems: What can India adopt from Kenya's Success?, *CGAP*, 2 April. Retrieve from: https://www.cgap.org/blog/mobile-payment-systemswhat-can-india-adopt-kenyas-success (accessed 30 October 2020)

Wade, S. (2017) 'How India is surviving postdemonetization', *Forbes*, 29 July. Retrieve from: https://www.forbes.com/sites/wadeshepard/2017/07/29/how-india-is-surviving-post-demonetization/?sh=9c3443811643 (accessed 30 October 2020).

Wiebe, A. (2015) 'A problematic process: The memorandum of understanding between Barrick Gold and Diaguita communities of Chile'. Retrieve from: http://miningwatch.ca/sites/default/files/barrick_mou_pascua_lama_eng_15sep1015.pdf (accessed 30 October 2020).

Younglai, R. (2014) 'Barrick reaches agreement with indigenous groups over Pascua Lama mine', *The Global and the Mail*, 28 May. Retrieve from: https://www.theglobeandmail.com/report-on-business/industry-news/energy-and-resources/barrick-reaches-deal-with-indigenous-groups-over-pascua-lama-mine/article 18899708/#:~:text=Although%20Barrick%20is%20nowhere%20close%20to%20restarting%20the,in%20April%20with%2015%20Diaguita%20communities%20in%20Chile. (accessed 30 October 2020).

Zhu, K. (2014) 'Top 4 reasons to divest', *Axial*, 12 February. Retrieve from: http://www.axial.net/forum/top-4-reasons-divest/ (accessed 30 November 2019).

Chapter 5
Market Segmentation and Positioning

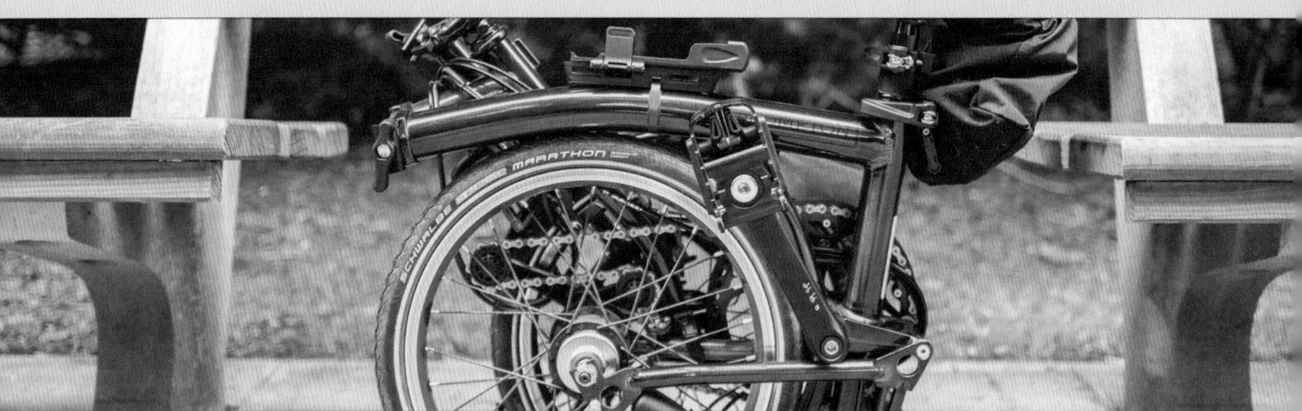

Learning Outcomes

After studying this chapter, you will be able to:

- describe the principles of market segmentation and the segmentation, targeting, and positioning (STP) process;
- list the characteristics and differences between market segmentation and product differentiation;
- explain consumer and business-to-business (B2B) market segmentation;
- describe different targeting strategies;
- discuss the concept of 'positioning'; and
- consider how the use of perceptual maps can assist in the positioning process.

Case Insight 5.1
Lanson International

Market Insight 5.1
Brompton: Just for You

Market Insight 5.2
Banking on the 'Life Escalator'

Market Insight 5.3
Recapturing Lost B2B Customers

Market Insight 5.4
Positioning Premium Beer

Case Insight 5.1 **Lanson International**

Founded in 1760, Champagne Lanson is one of the oldest existing champagne houses in France, making some of the world's finest champagnes. We speak to Paul Beavis (pictured), managing director of Lanson International, to find out more about how the company looks to further develop its presence in international markets, including the UK.

Lanson currently operates in more than thirty countries around the world and this has been developed over a number of years, driven by the increase in demand for champagne in the UK, which started more than fifteen years ago. Generally, we believe that a company should look at international markets when its appetite for growth supersedes the current in-market capacity. Obviously, however, general economic market conditions apply and these need to be considered before we enter into any new markets. For us, a key success factor for successfully entering a new market is having data, data, and more data! Having the absolute facts about your markets is essential: it's a case of examination (of the market), diagnosis (of the entry method, what channels to use, and how to promote our brand), and prescription (of the operational approach).

Before we enter a market, we look at the current shape and size of the markets, but also (and this is seldom easy) we try to forecast how the category will be shaped in the next three to five years. One key trend that we can see in the global economy today is a concentration of spending power across and within certain markets. To tap into those segments, internationalization has to be a core part of our strategy for the future. So we evaluate a potential market's economic conditions, searching for market data not only about current volumes, but also more about consumer trends, the knowledge gap (what we know versus what we don't know about consumers' attitudes and behaviour), and we look at other drinks categories, such as spirits, and growth in wine consumption generally.

All of this insight helps us to plan our route-to-market strategy primarily. This also involves ascertaining more generally what strategy we should deploy, in terms of market **positioning**, whether or not we should use a subsidiary brand model or a distributor/agency model, and then considering the financial implications of each of those.

In the UK, part of the problem is that, as categories get more mature, as the UK is now, there is a real need to be able to explain why your brand is essential in the marketplace. The hardest question any business should ask itself is: what is my true competitive advantage?

In the UK market, champagne (with sales of £141.3 million in 2014) has generally seen strong competition from sparkling wine brands, particularly prosecco (with sales of £181.8 million in 2014), and especially in the off-licence trade, but Lanson enjoys the position of being the leading rosé brand and the second non-vintage champagne brand. Meanwhile, Spanish cava has seen a recent decline in sales.

Lanson therefore faced a key question in relation to its international market development strategy: how should a French brand such as Lanson seek to differentiate itself in a category that is dominated, in the UK, by a competitor focus on 'advertising' and the colour of the label?

Introduction

Have you ever wondered how we decide to target certain market segments with our marketing activities? Think about fashion retailers for a moment: how do they determine which people to communicate with about their new ranges? In this chapter, we consider how organizations decide on which segments of a market to concentrate their efforts. This process is known as **market segmentation** and it is an integral part of marketing strategy. After defining 'market segmentation', we explore the differences between market segmentation and **product differentiation.** We consider consumer and **business-to-business (B2B)** market segmentation in detail. The method by which whole markets are subdivided into different segments to allocate marketing programme activity is referred to as the **STP process**, referring to segmentation, targeting, and positioning (see Figure 5.1).

The STP Process

Segmentation, targeting, and positioning is a core component of the strategic marketing process, and the STP process is used because of the prevalence of mature markets and greater diversity in customer needs, and its ability to help us to identify specialized, niche segments. Marketers segment markets and identify attractive segments (i.e. whom to focus on and why), identify new proposition opportunities, develop suitable positioning and **communication** strategies (i.e. what message to communicate), and allocate resources to prioritized marketing activities (i.e. how much to spend and where). Organizations commission segmentation research to revise their marketing strategies, to investigate a declining brand, to launch a new offering, or to restructure their pricing policies. When operating in highly dynamic environments, segmentation research should be conducted at regular intervals.

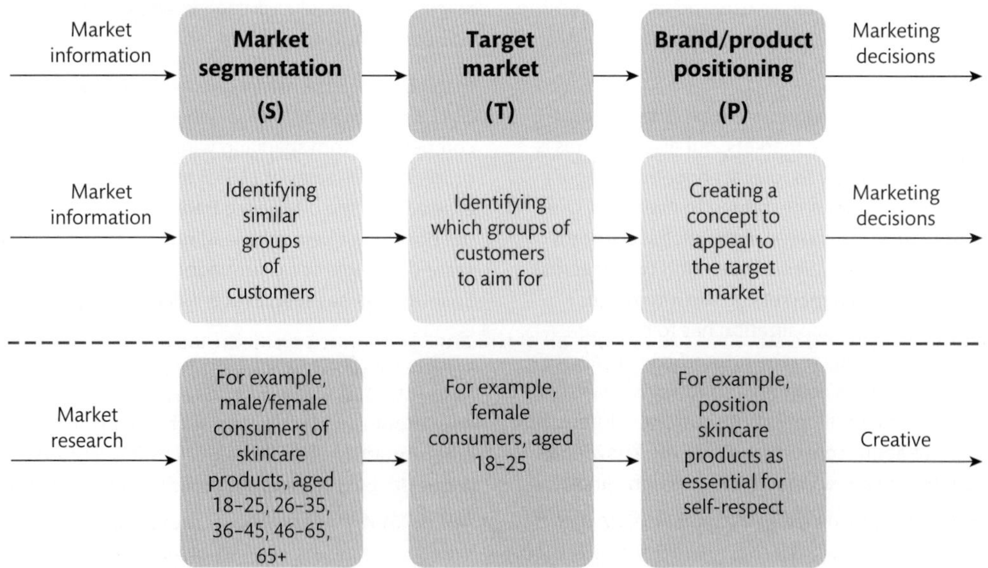

Figure 5.1 The STP process

The key benefits of the STP process include the following.

- It enhances a company's competitive position, providing direction and focus for marketing strategies, including targeted advertising, new proposition development, and brand differentiation. For example, Unilever's PG Tips, a traditional tea brand in the UK, released in 2018 a 'Perfect with Dairy-Free' blend, specifically targeted at soya, almond, and oat milk drinkers (Selwood, 2018). This new product enabled PG Tips to target a growing number of health and ethically conscious consumers.

PG Tips developed its 'Perfect with Dairy-Free' blend to target a specific segment: non-dairy milk tea drinkers.
Source: © Sophie Whitehouse.

- It allows an organization to identify market growth opportunities by means of the identification of new customers, growth segments, or proposition uses, for example when Lucozade repositioned itself away from an offering that sick people used to rebrand itself as an energy drink.
- It allows for the effective and efficient matching of company resources to targeted market segments, promising greater return on marketing investment (ROMI). For example, Asda and Carrefour use data-informed segmentation strategies to target direct marketing messages (online and offline) and to offer rewards to customers representing long-term value to the company.

The Concept of Market Segmentation

'Market segmentation' is the division of a mass market into distinct and identifiable groups or segments, within which individuals have common characteristics and needs, and display similar responses to marketing actions.

Market segmentation was first defined as 'a condition of growth when core markets have already been developed on a generalized basis to the point where additional promotional expenditures are yielding diminishing returns' (Smith, 1956: 7). It forms an important foundation for successful marketing strategies and activities (Wind, 1978). The purpose of market segmentation is to ensure that elements of the marketing mix—namely, price, place (or distribution), products, and promotion (plus people, process, and physical evidence for service offerings)—meet different customer groups' needs. Because companies have finite resources, it is not feasible to produce all of the required offerings, for all of the people, all of the time. We cannot be all things to all people; the best that we can do is provide selected offerings for selected groups of people, most of the time. This enables the most effective use of an organization's scarce resources.

Market segmentation is related to product differentiation (see Figure 5.2). Companies vary their product offering on the basis of the specific needs of the segments they have identified. In fashion retailing, for example, if you adapt your clothing range so that your skirts are more colourful, use lighter fabrics, and have very short hemlines, this styling might appeal to younger women. This is product differentiation—a focus on the product offering (see Market Insight 5.1).

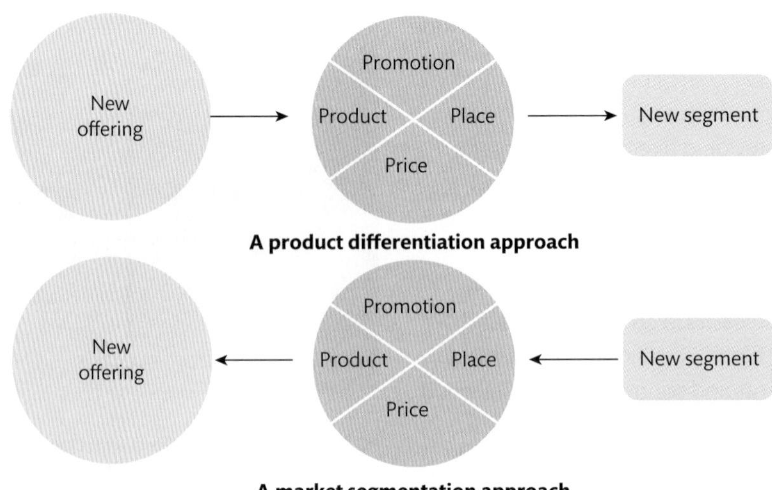

Figure 5.2 The difference between market segmentation and product differentiation

Market Insight 5.1 **Brompton: Just For You**

First launched in 2017, Brompton Bicycles is a niche British engineering company producing around 50,000 folding bikes and e-bikes per year, from its base in Brentford, West London. The Brompton bicycle was first produced by innovative owner, Andrew Ritchie in 1975, from his apartment overlooking the Brompton Oratory, from which the company and the bike originally took its name. The bike product retails at a starting price of around £745 per bike and the e-bike product price starts at £2,595. In both cases, each one is custom-made. One of Brompton Bicycles' key selling points is the portability of its bikes as they can fold into such a small package and can be taken on buses and trains, and even stored under office desks and in cloakrooms. The company also offers city apparel (jackets, gilet, gloves, socks), bags and parts and through a sister company, Brompton Bike Hire, bikes are also available throughout Britain on a hire basis.

Each bike is quality-checked before being packed for dispatch. Bikes are particularly popular with city commuters. More than 80 per cent of the company's production is exported, particularly to Japan, South Korea, and Germany where there is a strong cycling culture. Since a partnership agreement was signed in 2019 Brompton bikes are also available at British retailer Halfords, including by click and collect, and at Halfords.com. Other established bike manufacturers like Giant and Specialized built huge markets worldwide for bicycles for leisure use. Instead, Brompton saw a market opportunity for a revived market for bicycles as a mode of transport, particularly given the trend for both keeping fit and reducing usage of cars and, therefore, carbon emissions.

1. **Take a look at Brompton.com. Do you think the company is operating a market segmentation or a product differentiation approach?**
2. **How does the fact that the bike is customized link to product differentiation and/or market segmentation?**
3. **What segments do you think might be attracted to the e-bike offer?**

Sources: Butler (2019), Harker (2019); www.brompton.com.

Research Insight 5.1

To take your learning further, you might wish to read this influential paper.

Smith, W. R. (1956) 'Product differentiation and market segmentation as alternative marketing strategies', *Journal of Marketing*, 21(1), 3–8.

In this seminal paper, the author distinguishes between product differentiation and market segmentation. It is emphasized that product differentiation is concerned with distinguishing one's product characteristics from those of competitors. The distinguishing aspects of the product are then marketed to consumers, to persuade them to purchase from a particular seller. Market segmentation instead acknowledges the broad range of needs of the consumers and alters the design and marketing of the product to meet those needs.

 **Visit the online resources to read the abstract and access the full paper.**

The Process of Market Segmentation

There are two main approaches to segmentation. The first adopts the view that markets consist of customers who are similar; the task is to identify groups that share particular differences. This is known as the **breakdown method**. The second approach considers that markets consist of customers who are different; the task is to find similarities. This is known as the **build-up method** (Griffith and Pol, 1994).

The breakdown method is the most established method for segmenting consumer markets. The build-up method seeks to move from the individual level, at which all customers are different, to a more general level of analysis based on the identification of similarities (Freytag and Clarke, 2001). The build-up method is customer-oriented, seeking to determine common customer needs. The aim of both methods is to identify market segments in which identifiable differences exist between segments—segment heterogeneity—but similarities exist between members within each segment—member homogeneity (see Figure 5.3).

In **business markets**, segmentation should reflect the relationship needs of the organizations involved. However, problems remain concerning the practical application and implementation of B2B segmentation. Managers frequently report that the analytical processes are reasonably clear, but it is unclear how they should choose and evaluate the various market segments (Naudé and Cheng, 2003). Segmentation theory has developed in an era in which a transactional goods-centric approach to marketing was predominant, rather than the service-dominant logic existing today. Under the transactional approach, resources are allocated to achieve designated marketing mix goals. But customers within various segments have changing needs and therefore these customers may change their segment membership (Freytag and Clarke, 2001). Consequently, market segmentation programmes should use current customer data.

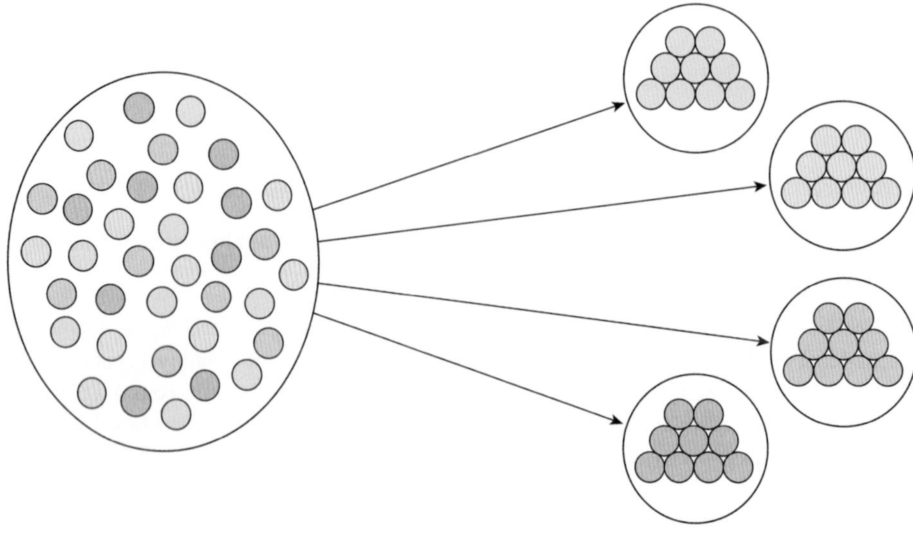

Figure 5.3 Segment heterogeneity and member homogeneity

Market Segmentation in Consumer Markets

To segment consumer markets, we use market information based around key customer-, product-, or situation-related criteria. These are classified as 'segmentation bases' and include profile (e.g. 'who are my market and where are they?'), behavioural (e.g. 'where, when, and how does my market behave?'), and psychological criteria (e.g. 'why does my market behave that way?') (see Figure 5.4). A fourth segmentation criterion is contact data—that is, customers' names and full contact details beyond their postcodes (e.g. postal and email addresses, and mobile and home telephone numbers). Contact data are useful for tactical-level marketing activities, such as direct and digital marketing.

Table 5.1 illustrates the key characteristics associated with each of the main approaches to consumer market segmentation.

When selecting different segmentation bases, the trade-off between data acquisition costs and the ability of the data to predict customer choice behaviour should be considered. Demographic and geo-demographic data are relatively easy to measure and obtain; however, these bases suffer from low levels of accuracy in predicting consumer behaviour (see Figure 5.5). In contrast, behavioural data (such as product usage, purchase history, and media usage), although more costly to acquire, provide a more accurate means to predict future behaviour: for example, the brand of toothpaste you purchased previously is more likely to be the brand of toothpaste that you purchase in future. However, customer choices are also influenced by susceptibility to marketing communications.

One way of segmenting consumer markets is to use profile criteria to determine who consumers are and where they are located. To do this, we use demographic methods (e.g. age, gender, race), socio-economics (e.g. determined by social class or income levels), and geographic location

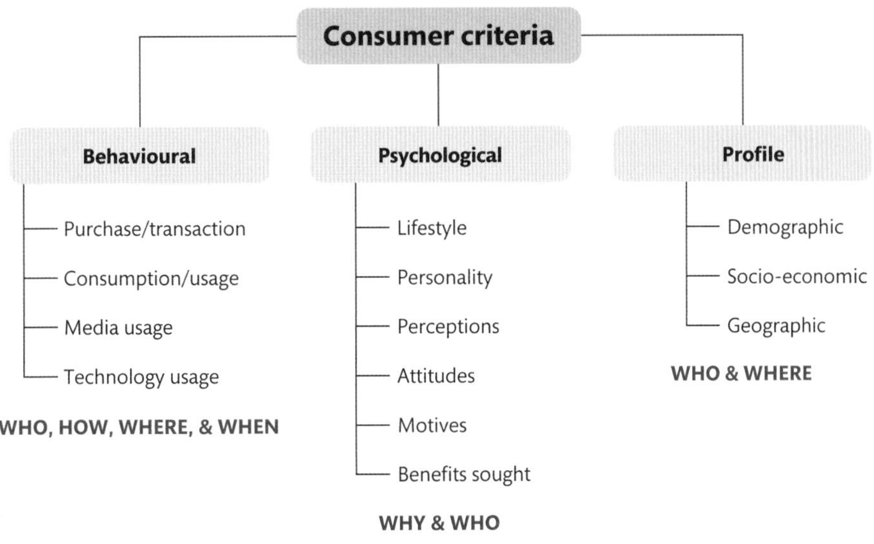

Figure 5.4 Segmentation criteria for consumer markets

(e.g. using postcodes). A utility company might segment households based on geographical area to assess regional brand penetration; an insurance company might segment the market based on age, employment, income, and asset net worth to identify attractive market segments for a new investment portfolio. These are all examples of segmentation based on profile criteria.

Demographic

Demographic variables relate to age, gender, family size, and life cycle, generation (such as 'baby boomers', 'Generation Y', 'Generation Z', 'Generation Alpha'), income, occupation, education, ethnicity, nationality, religion, and social class. They indicate the profile of a consumer and are useful in media planning. For example, gender differences have spawned a raft of offerings targeted at women, including beauty and fragrance offerings (such as Clinique, Chanel), magazines (such as *Cosmopolitan*, *Marie Claire*), hairdressing (such as Pantene, Clairol), and clothes (such as H&M, New Look). Offerings targeted at men include magazines (such as *GQ*) and beverages (such as Carlsberg, Coke Zero). Some brands develop offerings targeted at both men and women, for example fragrances (such as Calvin Klein) and watches (such as Rolex). Some companies and categories are taking advantage of the trend towards a more gender-fluid world by also developing unisex offerings in their ranges, such as in kids' clothing (e.g. Abercrombie & Fitch), perfume (e.g. Calvin Klein's CK2), and beauty products (e.g. Walmart's unisex shaving cream).

Designer clothing targeting men and women
Source: © Richard Levine/Getty.

Table 5.1 Segmentation criteria

Base type	Segmentation criteria	Explanation
Profile	Demographic	Key variables concern age, sex, occupation, level of education, religion, social class, and income characteristics.
	Life stage	This is based on the principle that people need different offerings at different stages in their lives (e.g. childhood, adulthood, young couple, and retirement).
	Geographic	The needs of potential customers in one geographic area are often different from those in another area owing to climate, custom, or tradition.
	Geo-demographic	There is a relationship between the type of housing and location in which people live and their purchasing behaviours.
Psychological	Psychographic (lifestyle)	By analysing consumers' activities, interests, and opinions, we can understand individual lifestyles and patterns of behaviour affecting their buying behaviour and decision-making processes. We can also identify similar offering and/or media usage patterns.
	Benefits sought	The motivations customers derive from their purchases provide an insight into the benefits they seek from the use of an offering.
Behavioural	Purchase/ transaction	Data about customer purchases and transactions provide scope for analysing who buys what, when, and how often, how much they spend, and through what transactional channel they purchase.
	Product usage	Segments can be derived on the basis of customer usage of the offering, brand, or product category. This may be in the form of usage frequency, time of usage, and usage situations.
	Media usage	What media channels are used, by whom, when, where, and for how long provides useful insights into the reach potential for certain market segments through differing media channels, as well as insight into the segment's media lifestyle.

Life Cycle

Lifestage analysis posits that people have varying amounts of disposable income and different needs at different times in their lives. Adolescents need different offerings from single 26-year-olds, who need different offerings compared with 26-year-old married people with young children. Major supermarkets (such as Asda, Tesco) have all invested in the development of offerings targeted at singles with high levels of disposable income and busy lifestyles by offering 'meal for one' ranges,

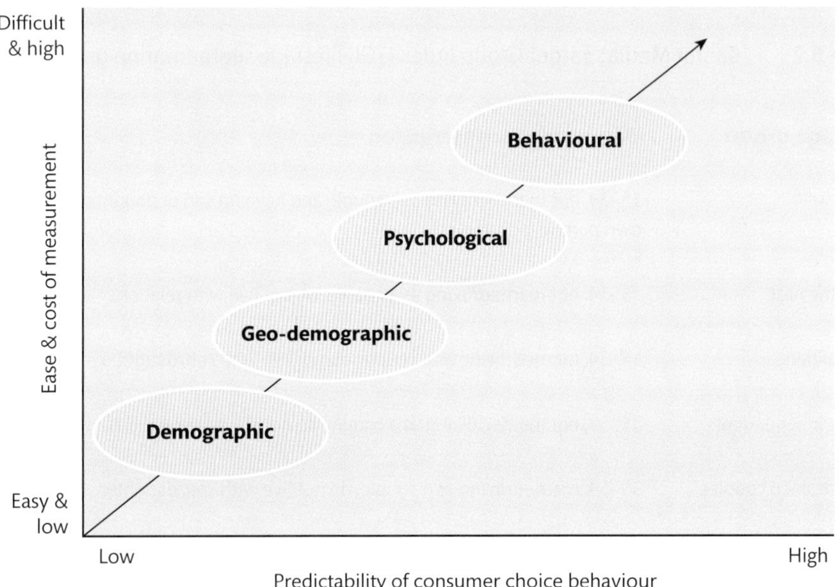

Figure 5.5 Considerations for segmentation criteria accessibility and use

Source: From SHIMP. *Integrated Marketing Communications in Advertising and Promotion*®, International Edition, 7E. © Profile Criteria.

which compare with 'family value' and 'multipacks' targeted at families. As families grow and children leave home, the needs of parents change and their disposable income increases (see Table 5.2).

Geographics

A geographical approach is useful when there are clear locational differences in tastes, consumption, and preferences. These consumption patterns provide an indication of preferences according to differing geographical regions. Markets can be considered by country or region, by size of city or town, by postcode, or by population density, such as urban, suburban, or rural. It is often said that American beer drinkers prefer lighter beers, compared with their UK counterparts, whereas German beer drinkers prefer a much stronger drink.

In addition to proposition selection and consumption, geographical segmentation is important for retail location, advertising and media selection, and recruitment. Direct sales operations (e.g. catalogue sales) can use census information to develop better customer segmentation and predictive models. Book publishers have long segmented based on geographical markets, frequently charging consumers in developing countries much less for a book than those in the developed world and trying to enforce a non-import policy so that these cheaper books do not enter Western markets.

Geo-demographics

Geo-demographics is a natural outcome when combining demographic and geographic variables. The marriage of geographics and **demographics** has become an indispensable market analysis tool, because it can lead to a rich mixture of who lives where.

Table 5.2	Kantar Media's Target Group Index (TGI) lifestage segmentation groups

Lifestage group	Demographic description
Fledglings	15–34, not married/living as a couple and have no son or daughter; living with own parents
Flown the nest	15–34, not married/living as a couple, do not live with relations
Nest builders	15–34, married/living as a couple, do not live with son/daughter
Mid-life independents	35–54, not married/living as a couple, do not live with relations
Unconstrained couples	35–54, married/living as a couple, do not live with son/daughter
Playschool parents	Live with son/daughter and youngest child 0–4
Primary school parents	Live with son/daughter and youngest child 5-9
Secondary school parents	Live with son/daughter and youngest child 10–15
Hotel parents	35+, live with son/daughter and have no child 0–15
Senior sole decision makers	55+, not married/living as a couple and live alone
Empty nesters	55+, married/living as a couple, and do not live with son/daughter
Non-standard families	Not married/living as a couple, live with relations, do not live with son/daughter, and do not live with parents if 15–34
Unclassified	Not in any group

Source: Reproduced with the kind permission of Kantar Media.

Visit the **online resources** and complete Internet Activity 5.1 to learn more about how we use databases compiled with geo-demographic data to profile market segments effectively.

The best-known UK geo-demographic system is A Classification of Residential Neighbourhoods (ACORN). Developed by British market research group CACI, ACORN demonstrates how postcode areas are broken down into six categories, eighteen groups, and sixty-two types. ACORN is a geo-demographic tool used to segment the UK population and their demand for a variety of offerings to assist marketers so that they can determine where to locate operations, field sales forces, retail outlets, and so on. ACORN can also be used to determine where to plan marketing communications and social media marketing campaigns.

Visit the **online resources** and follow the web link to CACI to learn more about the ACORN system.

Mosaic is a consumer classification system developed by Experian which enables companies to gain insight into their customers across all marketing channels (e.g. offline, TV). Mosaic is available in multiple declinations dedicated to different sectors and markets, including Mosaic Digital, Mosaic Public Sector and Mosaic Scotland. For example, Mosaic Scotland has identified 57 person types across 14 groups from 850 million samples (Experian, 2019). Market Insight 5.2 discusses one of Experian's methods of segmentation in the individual finance sector.

Visit the **online resources** and follow the web link to Experian to learn more about the Mosaic system.

Psychological Criteria

Psychological criteria used for segmenting consumer markets include the types of benefit sought by customers from brands in their consumption choices, attitudes, and perceptions (e.g. their feelings about fast cars), and **psychographics** or the lifestyles of customers (e.g. extrovert, fashion-conscious, high achiever).

Benefits Sought

The 'benefits sought' approach is based on the principle that we should provide customers with exactly what they want, based on the benefits they derive from use (Haley, 1968). This might sound obvious, but what are the real benefits, both rational and irrational, for the different offerings that people buy, such as mobile phones and sunglasses? Major airlines often segment on the basis of the benefits that passengers seek from transport by differentiating between first-class passengers (given extra luxury benefits in their travel experience), business-class passengers (who get some of the luxury of the first-class passenger), and economy-class passengers (who get none of the luxury of the experience, but enjoy the same flight).

Psychographics

Psychographic approaches rely on analysis of consumers' activities, interests, and opinions to understand their individual lifestyles and behaviour patterns. Psychographic segmentation includes understanding the values that are important to different customer types. A traditional form of lifestyle segmentation is AIO, based on customers' activities, interests, and opinions. Taylor Nelson Sofres (TNS), now Kantar, developed a UK lifestyle typology based on lifestyle, comprising 'belonger', 'survivor', 'experimentalist', 'conspicuous consumer', 'social resistor', 'self-explorer', and 'the aimless'.

Fix it quickly: John Deere outperformed rivals thanks to its service network and ability to minimize productivity losses for farmers.
Source: © smereka/Shutterstock.

International Harvester undertook value-based segmentation to discover why farmers consistently rated the equipment of John Deere, its main competitor, as 'more reliable'. International Harvester had invested heavily to minimize breakdowns, but John Deere continued to lead in the reliability rankings. Surveys about repair problems revealed that it was the downtime caused by breakdowns that most affected farmers, because of the days of lost productivity waiting for repairs. John Deere's customers perceived reliability to be much less of a problem because of the company's extensive, service-oriented dealer network, which stocked spare parts and offered temporary tractors that served to get a farmer working again quickly. John Deere was serving a different segment of farmers: those driven by the value of a total-service solution, which John Deere complemented well (Anon., 2013).

Behavioural Criteria

Product-related methods of segmenting consumer proposition markets include using behavioural methods (e.g. product usage, purchase, and ownership) as bases for segmentation. Observing consumers as they use offerings or consume services can be an important source of ideas for new uses or proposition design and development. Furthermore, new markets for existing offerings can be signalled, as well as appropriate communication themes for promotion. Purchase, ownership, and usage are three very different behavioural constructs that can be used to aid consumer market segmentation.

Usage

A company may segment a market based on how often a customer uses its offerings, categorizing these into high, medium, and low users. This allows the development of service specifications or marketing mixes for each user group. For example, heavy users of public transport might be targeted differently from heavy users of private vehicles by a coach-operating company. Consumer usage of offerings can be investigated from three perspectives, as follows.

1. *Social interaction perspective*—This considers the symbolic aspects of usage and the social meanings attached to the consumption of socially conspicuous offerings, such as a car or house (Belk et al., 1982; Solomon, 1983). For example, clothing company Patagonia published an advertisement in the *New York Times* called 'Don't Buy This Jacket'. The ad critiqued Black Friday, emphasized the waste created to produce one of its recycled best-selling jackets and highlighted the social stigma of overconsumption.
2. *Experiential consumption perspective*—This considers emotional and sensory experiences as a result of usage—especially emotions such as satisfaction, fantasies, and fun (Holbrook and Hirschman, 1982). For example, playing on the cultural stereotype of Italian families, Dolmio pasta sauce campaigns have emphasized how usage of Dolmio brings families together, and express values such as love, sharing, and spending time together.
3. *Functional utilization perspective*—This considers the functional usage of products and their attributes in different situations (Srivastava et al., 1978; McAlister and Pessemier, 1982), for example how and when action cameras such as the GoPro are used, how often, and in what contexts.

Transaction and Purchase

The development of electronic technologies, such as electronic point-of-sale (EPOS) systems, standardized product codes, radio frequency identification (RFID) systems, QR (quick response) codes, and integrated purchasing systems (e.g. web, in-store, telephone), has facilitated a rapid growth in the collection of consumer purchase and transactional data. Browsing and purchase data allow Amazon to make recommendations of offerings that are more likely to appeal to its consumers; EPOS systems allow retailers to track who buys what, when, for how much, in what quantities, and with what incentives (such as sales promotions). Companies have the ability to monitor purchase patterns in various geographical regions, at different times or seasons of the year, for various offerings, and increasingly for differing market segments. Social media can also be analysed to track what people are saying once they have purchased and used particular offerings.

Transactional and purchase information is very useful for marketers to assess who are their most profitable customers. By analysing the recency, frequency, and monetary (RFM) value of purchases, marketers can identify their most profitable market segments.

Market Insight 5.2 **Banking on the 'Life Escalator'**

To keep up with trends in saving and spending habits, marketers must tailor products to meet the needs of a wide range of consumers. For example, the number of young first-time buyers has recently decreased and 'springboard' parents often help the next generation to get on the property ladder.

Experian's Financial Strategy Segments (FSS) tool is used to understand customers' financial habits and market trends by enriching companies' existing data. This tool covers more than 500 variables over 49 million UK adults and includes attitudes and lifestyles attributes such as inclination for service switching and saving habits. Benefiting from these insights, marketers can propose tailored options for financial services while targeting specific categories of consumers. FSS notably categorizes individuals based on their age and wealth. For example, 'Earning Potential' individuals are identified by FSS as the 1.9 million early career UK households with potential to earn more in the near future, 'Career Experience' are categorized as middle-aged workers with relatively high income and 'Home-equity Elders' as retired individuals reaping the fruits of past investments.

Furthermore, further FSS analysis reveals that individuals are likely to follow common wealth trajectories (the 'life escalator') as they progress through life stages. For instance, 'Earning Potential' individuals in their early careers are likely to transition to the 'Career Experience' category after some years (perhaps purchasing their first property) and finally to 'Home-equity Elders' once retired. After segmenting consumers into these categories, it is easier for marketers to identify differences in characteristics among the categories. For example, 'Savvy Switchers', those actively looking for better deals, are likely to be in wealthier and employed categories or in brackets with lower income but keen to find the best alternatives for their situations.

1. **What types of segmentation criteria are implied in Experian's FSS?**
2. **Other than personal finance, what are other contexts in which consumers change segments at different stages in their lives?**
3. **What criteria could be used to enrich the description of the different segments? Why do you think these criteria would be useful in this context?**

Source: Experian (2017)

Segmentation in Business Markets

Business-to-business market segmentation is the identification of 'a group of present or potential customers with some common characteristic which is relevant in explaining (and predicting) their response to a supplier's marketing stimuli' (Wind and Cardozo, 1974: 155). There are two main groups of interrelated variables used to segment B2B markets (see Table 5.3). The first involves organizational characteristics, such as **organizational size** and location, sometimes referred to as **firmographics**. Those seeking to segment might start with these variables. The second group is based on the characteristics surrounding the decision-making process. Those organizations seeking to establish and develop customer relationships would normally expect to start with these variables.

Organizational Characteristics

The organizational characteristic factors concern the buying organizations that make up a business market. There are a number of criteria that can be used to cluster organizations, including size,

Table 5.3 Segmentation bases used in business markets

Base type	Segmentation base	Explanation
Organizational characteristics	Organizational size	Grouping organizations by relative size (multinational corporations, or MNCs; international corporations; large companies; small and medium-sized enterprises, or SMEs) enables the identification of design, delivery, usage rates or order size, and other purchasing characteristics.
	Geographic location	The needs of potential customers in one geographic area are often different from those in another geographic area.
	Industry type (SIC codes)	**Standard industrial classification (SIC) codes** are used to identify and categorize industries and businesses.
Buyer characteristics	**Decision-making unit** (DMU) structure	Attitudes, policies, and purchasing strategies allow organizations to be clustered.
	Choice criteria	The types of offering bought and the specifications companies use when selecting and ordering offerings form the basis for clustering customers and segmenting business markets.
	Purchase situation	Segments are based on how the company structures its purchasing procedures, the type of buying situation, and whether buyers are involved at an early or late stage in the purchase decision process.

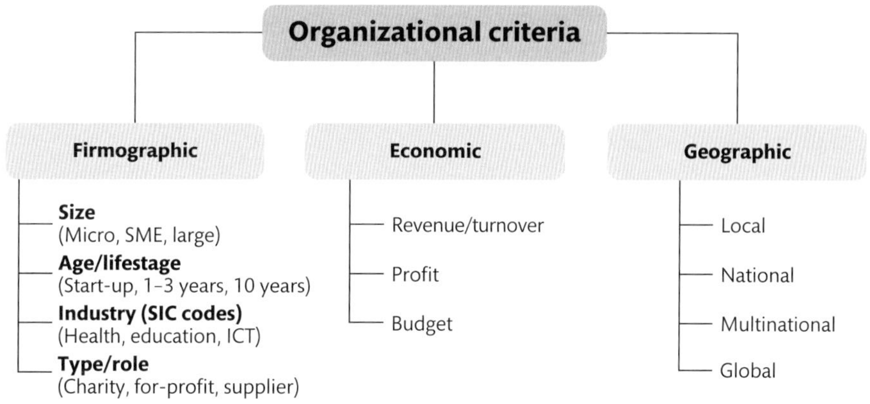

Figure 5.6 Segmentation by organizational characteristic

geography, market served, value, location, industry type, usage rate, and purchase situation. We discuss the main three categories used in Figure 5.6.

Organizational Size

By segmenting organizations by size, we can identify particular buying requirements. Large organizations may have particular delivery or design needs based on volume demand. Supermarkets such as France's Carrefour and the UK's Tesco, for example, pride themselves on purchasing goods in sufficiently large quantities to enable them to offer cheaply priced goods. The size of the organization often impacts on the usage rates of an offering, so organizational size is linked to whether an organization is a heavy, medium, or low buyer of a company's offerings.

Geographical Location

Geo-targeting is one of the more common methods used to segment B2B markets and is often used by new or small organizations attempting to establish themselves. This approach is useful because it allows the drawing of sales territories around particular locations that salespersons can service easily (e.g. Scotland, Scandinavia, Western Europe, the Mediterranean). Alternatively, sales territories may be based on specific regions within a country: in Eastern Europe, for example, they may be based on individual nations (e.g. Poland, Czech Republic, Romania, and Hungary). This approach however becomes less useful as the Internet cuts across geographic distribution channels (see Chapters 9 and 10).

SIC Codes

Standard industrial classification (SIC) codes are used to understand market size. They are easily accessible and standardized across most Western regions, for example the UK, Europe, and the United States. However, some marketers have argued that SIC codes comprise categories that are too broad to be useful. Consequently, SIC codes have received limited application, although they do provide an indication of the industrial segments in a market (Naudé and Cheng, 2003). More commonly, companies sometimes segment B2B markets using industry types (so-called verticals).

For example, a law firm might segment its customers into, among other sectors, financial services, utilities, transport, and retailing.

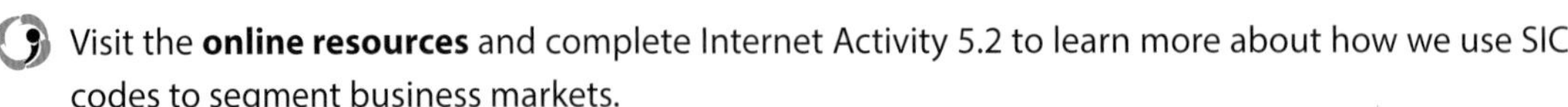

Visit the **online resources** and complete Internet Activity 5.2 to learn more about how we use SIC codes to segment business markets.

Customer Characteristics

Customer-specific factors concern the characteristics of buyers within the organizations that make up a business market. Numerous criteria could be used to cluster organizations including by decision-making unit (DMU), by purchasing strategy, by relationship type, by attitude to risk, by choice criteria, and by purchase situation.

Decision-Making Unit

An organization's DMU may have specific requirements that influence purchase decisions in a particular market, for example policy factors, purchasing strategies, a level of importance attached to these types of purchase, or attitudes towards vendors and risk. These characteristics can be used to segregate groups of organizations for particular marketing programmes. Segmentation might be based on the closeness and level of interdependence existing between organizations. Organizational attitudes towards risk and the degree to which an organization is willing to experiment through the acquisition of new industrial offerings varies. The starting point of any B2B segmentation is a good database or customer relationship management (CRM) system. It should contain customer addresses, contact details, and detailed purchase and transactional history. Ideally, it will also include the details of those buyers present within the customer company's DMU structure.

Market Insight 5.3 **Recapturing Lost B2B Customers**

Customer churn for firms such as FedEx, UPS, and XPO in the logistics industry can reach 20–25 per cent. Customers switch suppliers for a variety of reasons, but some of the more common ones concern core service failures, dissatisfactory service encounters, price, inconvenience in terms of time, location, or delays, poor response to service failure, competition, ethical problems, and involuntary switching. It is therefore important for all firms to understand these switch or defection behaviours to reduce their incidence, retrieve lost customers, and so lower their costs over the long run.

Segmenting B2B markets based on customers who have been lost is not necessarily the same as segmenting to find new customers. One of the reasons for this is that 'lost customers' leave a portfolio of transactions that the sales force can use to leverage a return. Research suggests that five distinct segments of lost customers can be identified and actioned, as follows.

- *Bought-away customers*—Often very price-orientated, these customers are attracted by competitive prices. A decision to regain this segment needs to take into account how easy and profitable it will be to retain them in light of their price vulnerability.
- *Pulled-away customers*—This segment is characterized by buyers seeking better overall value, who will collaborate with suppliers to achieve higher benefits and/or lower costs. The solution to win back these 'lost customers' is thus

Market Insight 5.3 (continued)

to co-develop with them value propositions that are unique and sustainable.

- *Unintentionally pushed-away customers*—These customers leave because they perceive that they have been mistreated or neglected. An apology is required, but where there have been service/product failures, service recovery and reacquisition may include compensation, reimbursement, and discounts. In severe cases, often when mistakes have been repeated, customers can be retrieved only after personnel changes in either or both the buying and sales centres.
- *Moved-away customers*—This segment is characterized by customers who no longer need or value the product/service offerings. They might have moved physically or to different markets that the selling company cannot serve. Although lost for good, a positive ending to the relationship is regarded as important to secure referrals and helpful word-of-mouth.
- *Intentionally pushed-away customers*—These problematic or unprofitable customers are deliberately let go because the selling company no longer wants their business. Allowing them to build relationships with competitors should be matched by a positive dissolution to help to maintain a strong reputation and brand image.

1 **Discuss the view that if retrieving lost customers is costly and keeping them problematic, then there is little point in segmenting and actively trying to get them back.**

2 **To what extent is a high churn rate a function of poor customer management?**

3 **Focusing on a different industry, determine how companies try to retain customers.**

Sources: Keaveney (1995); Lopes et al. (2001); Liu et al. (2015).

Choice Criteria

Business markets can be segmented on the basis of the specifications of offerings that they choose. An accountancy practice may segment its clients by those that seek compliance-type offerings, such as audits and tax submission work, companies that require management accounting services, and companies that require a complex mix of both. Companies do not necessarily need to target multiple segments, however; they might simply target a single segment, as RM Education, an information technology (IT) solutions provider, has done successfully in the UK education market.

Purchase Situation

Companies sometimes seek to segment the market on the basis of how organizations buy or do not buy (see Market Insight 5.3). There are three questions associated with segmentation by purchase situation that should be considered, as follows.

1. What is the structure of the buying organization's purchasing procedures: centralized, decentralized, flexible, or inflexible?
2. What type of buying situation is present: new task (i.e. buying for the first time), modified rebuy (i.e. not buying for the first time, but buying something with different specifications from previously), or straight rebuy (i.e. buying the same thing again)?
3. What stage in the purchase decision process have target organizations reached? Are they buyers in early or late stages and are they experienced or new?

Research Insight 5.2

To take your learning further, you might wish to read this influential paper.

Beane, T. P., and Ennis, D. M. (1987) 'Market segmentation: A review', *European Journal of Marketing*, 32(5), 20–42.

Beane and Ennis's article provides a useful insight into the main bases for market segmentation, and the strengths and weaknesses of the key statistical methods we use to analyse customer data to develop segmentation models. The article suggests that there are many ways in which to segment a market and that it is important to exercise creativity when doing so.

 **Visit the online resources to read the abstract and access the full paper.**

For example, a large global consulting and IT services company like Infosys from India might segment the market for IT project management services into public and private sectors. The focus might then be on fulfilling large government contracts, which are put out to tender, whereby a group of selected buyers are offered the opportunity to bid for an exclusive franchise to deliver agreed services for a defined period of time.

Target Markets

The second important part of the STP process is to determine which of the segments uncovered should be targeted and made the focus of a comprehensive marketing programme. Ultimately, managerial discretion and judgement determines which markets are selected and exploited. Kotler (1984) suggested that the acronym DAMP should be applied if market segmentation is to be effective—that is, all segments must be the following.

- *Distinct*—Is each segment clearly different from other segments? If so, different marketing mixes may be necessary.
- *Accessible*—Can buyers be reached through appropriate promotional programmes and distribution channels?
- *Measurable*—Is the segment easy to identify and measure?
- *Profitable*—Is the segment sufficiently large to provide a stream of constant future revenues and profits?

Another approach to evaluating market segments uses a rating approach for different segment attractiveness factors, such as market growth, segment profitability, segment size, competitive intensity within the segment, and the cyclical nature of the industry (e.g. whether or not the business is seasonal, as in retailing). Each of these segment attractiveness factors is rated on a 0–10 scale and loosely categorized in the high, medium, or low columns, based on either set criteria or subjective criteria, dependent on the availability of market and customer data and the approach adopted by the managers undertaking the segmentation programme (see Table 5.4).

Other examples of segment attractiveness factors might include segment stability (i.e. stability of the segment's needs over time) and mission fit (i.e. the extent to which dealing with a particular segment fits the mission of the company). Once the attractiveness factors have been determined, the importance of each factor can be weighed and each segment rated on each factor. This generates a segment attractiveness evaluation matrix (see Table 5.5).

Decisions need to be made about whether a single offering is made available to a range of segments, a range of offerings is made available to multiple segments or a single segment, or one offering should be presented to a single segment. Whatever the decision, a marketing mix strategy should be developed to meet segment needs that reflects the organization's capabilities and competitive strengths.

Targeting Approaches

Once segments are identified, an organization selects its preferred approach to targeting. Four differing approaches can be used, as follows (see Figure 5.7).

- **Undifferentiated approach**—In this approach to targeting, there is no delineation between market segments and the market is viewed as one mass market, with one marketing strategy for the entire market. Although expensive, this approach is used for markets in which there is limited or no segment differentiation, for example housing offered by local authorities.

Table 5.4 Examples of segment attractiveness factors

	Rating		
Segment attractiveness factors	***High (10–7)***	***Medium (6–4)***	***Low (3–0)***
Growth	2.5%	2.5–2.0%	2.0%
Profitability	15%	10–15%	10%
Size	£5m	£1m–£5m	£1m
Competitive intensity	Low	Medium	High
Cyclicality	Low	Medium	High

Source: McDonald and Dunbar (2004). Reproduced with permission. © Elsevier.

Table 5.5	Example of a segment attractiveness evaluation matrix

Segment attractiveness factors	**Weight**	**Segment 1**		**Segment 2**		**Segment 3**	
		Score	***Total***	***Score***	***Total***	***Score***	***Total***
Growth	25	6.0	1.50	5	1.25	10	2.50
Profitability	25	9.0	2.25	4	1.00	8	2.00
Size	15	6.0	0.90	5	0.90	7	1.05
Competitive intensity	15	5.0	0.75	6	0.90	6	0.90
Cyclicality	20	2.5	0.50	8	1.60	5	1.00
Total	100	5.9		5.65		7.45	

Source: McDonald and Dunbar (2004). Reproduced with permission. © Elsevier.

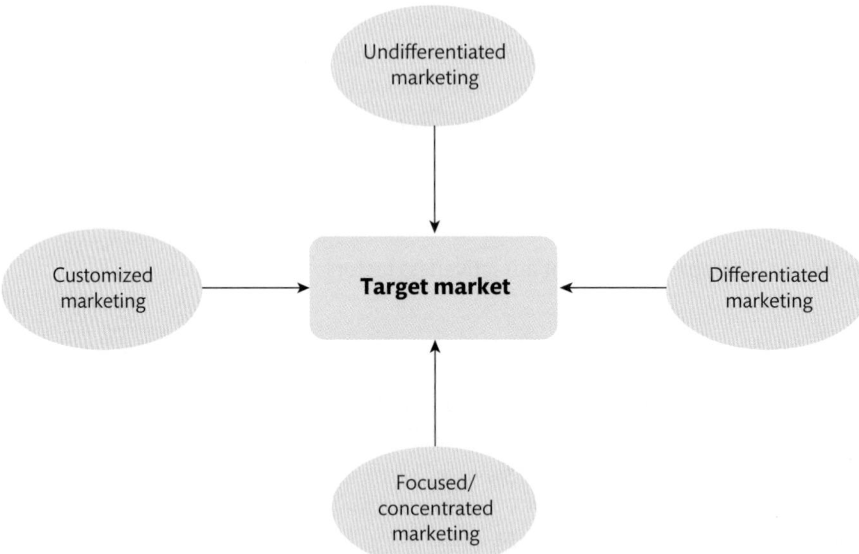

Figure 5.7 Target marketing approaches

- **Differentiated targeting approach**—This is used where there are several market segments to target, each being attractive to the marketing organization. To exploit them, a marketing strategy is developed for each segment. Hewlett Packard, for example, has developed its product range and marketing strategy to target the following user segments of computing equipment: home office users; small and medium-sized businesses; large businesses; and health, education, and government departments. A disadvantage of this approach is the loss of economies of scale owing to the resources required to meet multiple market segments' needs.

- **Concentrated, or niche, marketing strategy**—Where there are only a few market segments, this approach is adopted by firms with limited resources to fund their marketing strategies or which adopt a very exclusive strategy in the market. The UK's Co-operative Bank targets consumers interested in a bank with ethical lending and investment credentials. This approach is used frequently by small-to-medium- and micro-sized organizations with limited resources (e.g. an electrician, who may focus on local residences).
- **Customized targeting strategy**—This type of marketing strategy is developed for each customer rather than each segment. This approach predominates in B2B markets (e.g. marketing research or advertising services) or consumer markets with high-value, highly customized products (e.g. a custom-made car). A manufacturer of industrial electronics for assembly lines might target and customize its offering differently for Nissan, Unilever, and SCA, for example, given the differing requirements in assembly line processes for the manufacture of automobiles, foodstuffs, and hygiene products (such as hand dryers).

Segmentation Limitations

Whilst market segmentation is a useful process for organizations to divide customers into distinct groups, it has been criticized for the following reasons.

- The process approximates offerings to the needs of customer groups, rather than individuals, so there is a chance that customers' needs are not fully met. **Customer relationship marketing (CRM)** processes and software, however, allow companies to develop customized approaches for individual customers.
- There is insufficient consideration of how market segmentation is linked to competitive advantage (Hunt and Arnett, 2004). The product differentiation concept is linked to the need to develop competing offerings, but market segmentation does not stress the need to segment on the basis of differentiating the offering from those of competitors.
- It is unclear how valuable segmentation is to managers. Suitable processes or models to measure market segmentation effectiveness have yet to be developed.

Microtargeting

With recent progress in digital technologies to collect and process a large volume of consumers' personal data, it is now possible for companies to identify and focus on smaller groups of consumers or individuals with fast-changing characteristics (Erevelles et al., 2016). As opposed to traditional marketing segmentation that focuses on a relatively fixed and well-defined profile of consumers, **microtargeting** identifies clusters of consumers with similar personal details that are constantly evolving, such as purchase intentions and online behaviours (NGDATA, 2016). Once focused segments are identified, it is possible to send highly customized messages to these small groups of consumers based on the specific information collected and in a timely manner.

For example, Tabi et al. (2014) carried out in-depth statistical analysis of the results of a consumer survey in Germany to investigate the characteristics of subscribers of green electricity tariffs. Compared to non-subscribers who favour electricity generated in Germany, they identified that existing subscribers perceive green energy prices as lower and have changed energy tariffs more recently. These results encourage marketers to better communicate the origin and price of green electricity to potential adopters.

Research Insight 5.3

To take your learning further, you might wish to read this influential paper.

Erevelles, S., Fukawa, N. and Swayne, L. (2016) 'Big data consumer analytics and the transformation of marketing', *Journal of Business Research*, 69(2), 897–904.

In this paper, the authors explain recent advances in technology to collect and analyse customers' data in real time. In particular, they focus on the five 'Vs' of big data: volume, velocity, variety, veracity and value. They propose that companies that utilize big data analysis techniques to uncover hidden consumer insights will be more successful at marketing their products.

 **Visit the online resources to read the abstract and access the full paper.**

Positioning

Having segmented the market, determined the size and potential of market segments, and selected specific target markets, the third part of the STP process is to position a brand within the target market(s). Positioning is the means by which offerings are differentiated from one another to give customers a reason to buy. It encompasses two fundamental elements. The first concerns the attributes, functionality, and capability that a brand offers (e.g. a car's engine specification, its design, and carbon emissions). The second positioning element concerns the way in which a brand is communicated and how customers perceive the brand relative to competing brands. This element of communication is important because it is not what you do to an offering that is important, but 'what you do to the mind of a prospect' (Ries and Trout, 1972: 35) that determines how a brand obtains its market positioning (see Market Insight 5.4).

Positioning concerns the overall perception of an offering and not only its features. Positioning is therefore about how customers judge an offering's value relative to those of competitors. To develop a sustainable position, we must understand the market in which the offering is competing.

At a simple level, the positioning process begins during the target market selection process. Key to this process is identifying those attributes considered to be important by consumers. For a car manufacturer, these attributes may be tangible (e.g. the gearbox, transmission system, seating, and interior design) and intangible (e.g. the reputation, prestige, and allure that a brand generates). By understanding what customers consider to be the ideal standard that each attribute needs to attain, and how they rate the attributes of each brand in relation to the ideal level and each other, it becomes possible to see how a brand's attributes can be adapted and communicated to become more competitive.

Perceptual Mapping

Understanding the complexity associated with the different attributes and brands can be made easier by developing a visual representation of each market. These are known as 'perceptual maps'. The 'maps' are used to determine how various brands are perceived according to the key attributes that customers value. **Perceptual mapping** allows the geometric comparison of how competing products are perceived (Sinclair and Stalling, 1990). Typically, the closer offerings or brands are clustered on a perceptual map, the greater the competition. The further apart the positions, the greater the opportunity for new brands to enter the market. For example, in the non-vintage champagne market, there are numerous brands competing with each other across differing attributes. Figure 5.8 shows the positioning of key champagne brands in the non-vintage market. Here, the positions are based on attributes relating to the type of fruit used and the taste. It can be seen that leading brands Lanson, Bollinger, and Moët et Chandon occupy distinct positions in their 'own' quadrants. (See Case Insight 5.1 for more information about Lanson International, a leading champagne house.)

Perceptual mapping data reveal strengths and weaknesses that can inform strategic decisions about how to differentiate in terms of the attributes that matter to customers the most.

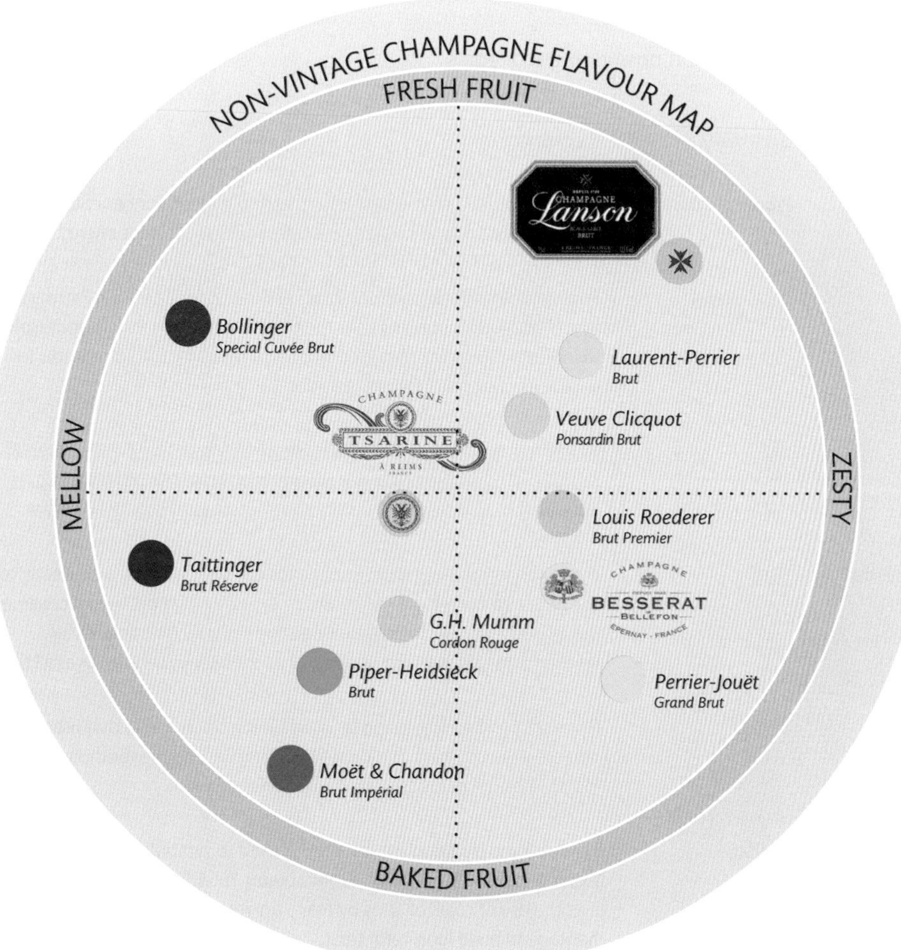

Figure 5.8 Perceptual map for non-vintage champagne

Source: Reproduced with kind permission of Lanson International UK Ltd

Positioning and Repositioning

Marketing communications try to adjust customers' brand perceptions and can be used to position brands either functionally or expressively (symbolically) (see Table 5.6). *Functionally* positioned brands emphasize features and benefits, whereas *expressive* brands emphasize the ego, social, and hedonic satisfactions a brand brings. Different positioning approaches are likely to be more successful than others, with particular offerings. For example, in the compact car market, Fuchs and Diamantopoulos (2010) found that direct benefit positioning (based on functional aspects) is likely to be more effective than indirect benefit positioning (based on experiential or symbolic dimensions) and that expressive positioning is more effective than functional approaches. User positioning can also provide a sound alternative to benefit positioning.

Technology, customer tastes, and competitors' new offerings are reasons why markets might change. Disney acquired Lucasfilm in 2012 and have released another five Star Wars films since; to be successful, however, Disney needed to reposition and target the new films at the generation who grew up with the *Clone Wars* cartoon and Lego *Star Wars* characters rather than those

Table 5.6 Proposition positioning strategies

Position	Strategy	Explanation
Functional	Product features	Brand positioned on the basis of attributes, features, or benefits relative to the competition, e.g. Volvos are safe; Red Bull provides energy.
	Price quality	Price can be a strong communicator of quality. John Lewis & Partners (the UK department store) uses the tagline 'never knowingly undersold' to indicate how it will match competitors' prices on the same items to ensure its customers always get good value.
	Use	By informing when or how an offering can be used, we create a mental position in buyers' minds, e.g. Kellogg's repositions its offerings (e.g. Special K) to be consumed throughout the day, not only at breakfast.
Expressive	User	By identifying the target user, messages can be communicated clearly to the right audience. Flora margarine was initially for men, then it became 'for all of the family'. Some hotels position themselves as places for weekend breaks, as leisure centres, or as conference centres, or as all three.
	Benefit	Positions can be established by proclaiming the benefits that usage confers on consumers. The benefit of using Sensodyne toothpaste is that it alleviates the pain associated with sensitive teeth.
	Heritage	Heritage and tradition are sometimes used to symbolize quality, experience, and knowledge. Kronenbourg 1664, 'Established since 1803', and the use of coats of arms by many universities are designed to convey heritage to build long-term trust.

Market Insight 5.4 **Positioning Premium Beer**

The history of Belgian beer brand Leffe can be traced back to 1240. Its current success, however, can be accredited to its positioning and association with contemporary food and lifestyles, rather than its taste and the historic values associated with traditional brewing and ingredients.

Despite its super-premium price, the brand has experienced strong growth in France, nearly doubling its market share between 2008 and 2013.

This growth has been achieved by associating the brand as an 'aperitif'—that is, at a time when social interaction occurs before a meal, normally associated with wine. The brand was positioned as the ideal first drink of the evening, particularly when accompanied by traditional foods such as dry-cured ham and cheese.

Leffe's repositioning strategy focused on presenting the product as the perfect aperitif.
Source: © Shutterstock/mandritoiu.

The bottle uses foil wrapping around the neck, similar to champagne, reinforcing the premium cue. Rather than using conventional media, Leffe uses an online newsletter called *Leffervescense*. In addition to featuring its own products, Leffe uses the newsletter to introduce readers to celebrity chefs and artisanal food producers. Heineken in the United States has now followed this path by aligning itself with hand-crafted products that 'embody Heineken's aspirational and metropolitan essence'.

In Italy, Peroni is priced below the average for mass-market brands. Nastro Azzuro is Peroni's upmarket brand offering, premium priced, and does not carry the Peroni name.

When owner SABMiller launched Peroni in the UK, it recoupled the names and positioned 'Peroni Nastro Azzuro' against its Italian origins. Research identified the target audience as confident, socially mobile, 25–34-year-old status seekers, who were optimistic about the future and their ability to control it. They were referred to as 'modern sophisticates'. Using conventional media, the brand was associated with 'the golden age of Italy'. Television advertising uses stereotypical images of Italy, 1960s nostalgia, and premium brand cues, such as flying boats, a carefree lifestyle, and powerboats.

1 **Identify two other ways in which Leffe and Peroni could be positioned.**

2 **What problems might arise when positioning museums and other cultural attractions?**

3 **Choose a market (such as fashion, haircare, air travel) and determine how any three brands in that market are positioned. Is that positioning successful?**

Sources: Hollis (2014); http://www.brandunion.com.

Research Insight 5.4

To take your learning further, you might wish to read this influential book.

Ries, A., and Trout, J. (2006) *Positioning: The Battle for your Mind*. London: McGraw-Hill.

Al Ries and Jack Trout's book, originally published in 1981, remains the bible of advertising strategy. They define 'positioning' not as what you do to an offering to make it acceptable to potential customers, but as what you do to the mind of the prospect. Positioning requires an outside-in rather than an inside-out thinking approach.

 **Visit the online resources to read more about the book.**

who watched the original trilogy in the late 1970s and 1980s (Garrahan, 2012). Thus if the brand positioning adopted is strong and the position is continually reinforced with clear messages, there may be little need to alter the position originally adopted. Sometimes, marketers need to reposition their offering relative to those of competitors. Repositioning is often difficult to accomplish because of the entrenched perceptions and attitudes held by customers towards brands and the cost of the vast (media) resources required to make these changes.

There are four approaches to repositioning, depending on the individual situation facing a brand.

1 Change the tangible attributes and then communicate the new proposition to the same market. UBS, the Swiss financial services firm whose reputation was shattered following an estimated US$2 billion loss owing to insider trading, spent four years transforming itself internally before relaunching and repositioning as a wealth management company (Rooney, 2015).

2 Change the way *in which* a proposition is communicated to the original market. Norwegian oil and gas company Statoil Hydro was repositioned globally as Statoil by communications agency Hill & Knowlton Strategies, raising its profile in key markets across Europe, including in the UK.

3 Change the target market and deliver the same proposition. On some occasions, repositioning can be achieved through marketing communications alone, but targeted at a new market. For example, soft drink Orangina was repositioned as a premium adult drink, targeting those who remember it from childhood French holidays.

4 Change both the proposition (attributes) and the target market. For example, Xerox has repositioned itself from a document company to a diversified business services company, running call centres, and processing insurance claims and even toll payments (Carone, 2013).

Chapter Summary

To consolidate your learning, the key points from this chapter are summarized below.

- **Describe the principles of market segmentation and the segmentation, targeting, and positioning (STP) process.**

  Whole markets are subdivided into different segments through the STP process. 'STP' refers to the three activities that should be undertaken, sequentially, if segmentation is to be successful: segmentation, targeting, and positioning. Market segmentation is the division of a market into different groups of customers with distinctly similar needs and offering requirements. The second part of the STP process determines which segments should be targeted with a comprehensive marketing mix programme. The third part of the STP process involves positioning a brand within the target market(s).

- **List the characteristics and differences between market segmentation and product differentiation.**

  Market segmentation is related to product differentiation. Given an increasing proliferation of tastes, marketers have sought to design offerings around consumer demand (market segmentation) more than around their own production needs (product differentiation).

- **Explain consumer and business-to-business (B2B) market segmentation.**

  Data, based on differing consumer, user, organizational, and market characteristics, are used to segment a market. These characteristics differ for business-to-consumer (B2C) and business-to-business (B2B) contexts. To segment consumer goods and service markets, market information based on certain key customer-, product-, or situation-related criteria (variables) is used. These are classified as segmentation bases, and include profile, behavioural and psychological criteria. To segment business markets, two main groups of interrelated variables are used: organizational characteristics and buyer characteristics.

- **Describe different targeting strategies.**

  Once identified, the organization selects its target marketing approach. Four differing approaches exist: undifferentiated; differentiated; concentrated, or niche marketing; and customized target marketing.

- **Discuss the concept of 'positioning'.**

  Positioning provides the means by which offerings can be differentiated from one another and gives customers reasons to buy. It encompasses physical attributes, the way in which a brand is communicated, and how customers perceive the brand relative to competing brands.

- **Consider how the use of perceptual maps can assist in the positioning process.**

  Perceptual maps are used in the positioning process to illustrate the differing attributes of a selection of brands. They also illustrate: existing levels of differentiation between brands; how a brand and competing brands are perceived in the marketplace; how a market operates; and strengths and weaknesses that can assist with making strategic decisions about how to differentiate the attributes that matter to customers to compete more effectively in the market.

Review Questions

1. **Define 'market segmentation' and explain the STP process.**
2. **What is the difference between market segmentation and product differentiation?**
3. **Identify four different ways in which markets can be segmented.**
4. **How do market segmentation bases differ in B2B and consumer markets?**
5. **How can market segmentation bases be evaluated when target marketing?**
6. **What are the different approaches to selecting target markets?**
7. **Describe the principle of positioning and why it should be undertaken.**
8. **What are perceptual maps and what can they reveal?**
9. **Explain three ways in which brands can be positioned.**
10. **Make a list of four reasons why organizations need to reposition brands.**

Worksheet Summary

To apply the knowledge you have gained from this chapter, and to test your learning about the STP process used to develop whom to market to, in what way, and while differentiating from the competition, visit the **online resources** and complete Worksheet 5.1.

Discussion Questions

1. Having read Case Insight 5.1, how would you recommend that Lanson position itself in the UK market?
2. In a group, with other colleagues from your seminar or tutor group, discuss answers to the following questions.
   - A Using the information in Table 5.7 on the champagne market and a suitable calculator, determine which segments have the greatest potential profit.
   - B What other data do we need to determine the size of the market (market potential)?
3. Discuss which market segmentation bases might be most applicable to the following.
   - A A fashion retailer segmenting the market for menswear.
   - B A media production company such as Netflix looking to commission a new TV series.
   - C A Belgian chocolate manufacturer supplying multiple retail grocers and confectionery shops across Europe, for example Godiva.
   - D The Absolut Company, headquartered in Sweden, supplying high-quality vodka around the world.
   - E A digital bank such as UK-based company Monzo, when segmenting the market for its credit card.

Table 5.7	Champagne and sparkling wine market by segment			
Social class	**Enthusiasts (%)** **AP = £20** **F = 5/yr**	**Sparkling sceptics (%)** **AP = £10** **F = 3/yr**	**Price driven (%)** **AP = £8.50** **F = 3/yr**	**Uneducated (%)** **AP = £15** **F = 2/yr**
AB (n = 8m)	25	31	30	14
C1 (n = 14m)	23	23	32	21
C2 (n = 8m)	27	26	33	14
DE (n = 10m)	20	26	40	14

Notes: AP = average price, F = no. of bottles purchased per year, ***n*** = population size (all data hypothetical).
Source: Percentage segment sizes per socio-economic group and segment descriptions only from Mintel (2016).

4 Write a one-sentence description of the attributes and benefits that are attractive to target consumers for an offering with which you are particularly familiar (e.g. Apple, in the computer category, or Samsung, in the mobile phones category), using the statement provided. Explain how these attributes and benefits are different from those of competitors. Your positioning statement might be as follows:
[Product A] provides [target consumers] with [one or two salient product attributes]. This distinguishes it from [one or two groups of competing product offerings] that offer [attributes/benefits of the competing products].
   A Briefly describe the target market segment. This should summarize the defining characteristics of the segment (e.g. demographic, psychographic, geographic, or behavioural).
   B Briefly explain your reasons for believing that the attributes or benefits of your positioning statement are important for your target segment. Draw a perceptual map which summarizes your understanding of the market and shows the relative positions of the most important competing products.

Visit the online resources and complete the multiple-choice questions to assess your knowledge of the chapter.

Glossary

benefits sought by understanding the benefits that customers derive from their purchases, it is possible to have an insight into the motivations behind product use.

breakdown method an approach to segmentation based on the view that the market consists of customers who are essentially the same, so the task is to identify groups that share particular differences.

build-up method an approach to segmentation based on the view that a market consists of customers that are all different, so the task is to find similarities.

business markets those characterized by organizations that consume products and services for use within the manufacture of other products or for use in their daily operations.

business-to-business (B2B) activities undertaken by one company that are directed at another.

choice criteria the principal dimensions on the basis of which we select a particular product or service, for example, for a hairdresser, price, location, range of services, level of expertise, friendliness, and so on.

communication the sharing of meaning created through the transmission of information.

concentrated, or niche, marketing strategy a marketing strategy that recognizes that there are segments in the market; implemented by focusing on only one or two, or a few, of those market segments.

customer relationship marketing (CRM) a strategy whereby all marketing activities aim to retain customers, achieved by providing customers with relationship-enhancing products and/or services that are perceived to be of value to the individual customer and superior to those offered by a competitor.

customized targeting strategy a marketing strategy that is developed for each customer as opposed to each market segment.

decision-making unit (DMU) a structure on which segmentation can focus whereby organizations' attitudes, policies, and purchasing strategies can be clustered.

demographics key variables concerning age, sex, occupation, level of education, religion, and social class, many of which determine a potential buyer's ability to purchase a product or service.

differentiated targeting approach an approach that recognizes several market segments to target, each being attractive to the marketing organization, whereby a distinct marketing strategy is developed for each.

firmographics criteria such as company size, geography, standard industrial classification (SIC) codes, and other company-oriented classification data used to inform an approach to segmentation of B2B markets.

geo-demographics criteria informing an approach to segmentation that presumes that there is a relationship between the type of housing and location in which people live and their purchasing behaviours.

lifestage analysis one based on the principle that people need different products and services at different stages in their lives (e.g. childhood, adulthood, young couples, retired, etc.).

market segmentation the division of customer markets into groups of customers with distinctly similar needs.

microtargeting a highly focused targeting approach made possible by recent advances in data collection and analysis techniques.

organizational size a criterion by means of which organizations can be grouped—for example multinational corporations (MNCs, international corporations, large companies, small and medium-sized enterprises (SMEs))—which enables the identification of common design, delivery, usage rates, or order size and other purchasing characteristics.

perceptual mapping a diagram, typically two-dimensional, of 'image space' derived from attitudinal market research data, which displays the differences in perceptions that customers, consumers, or the general public have of different products or services specifically, or brands in general.

positioning the way in which an audience of consumers or buyers perceives a product or service, particularly as a result of the marketing communications process aimed at a target audience.

product differentiation a strategy that involves companies seeking to produce offerings that are different from those of competing firms.

product usage a criterion whereby segments derive from analysing markets on the basis of their usage of the product offering, brand, or product category, in terms of frequency, timing, and circumstances of use.

psychographics criteria relating to consumers' activities, interests, and opinions that allow us to understand individual lifestyles and patterns of behaviour, which in turn affect their buying behaviour and decision-making processes, on which basis we can also identify similar product and/or media usage patterns.

purchase situation an approach to segmentation that clusters organizational buyers in terms of the way in which a buying company structures its purchasing procedures, the type of buying situation, and whether buyers are at an early or late stage in the purchase decision process.

standard industrial classification (SIC) codes used to identify and categorize all types of industry and business.

STP process the method by which whole markets are subdivided by means of Segmentation, for subsequent Targeting and Positioning of products, services, and brands.

undifferentiated approach an approach to segmentation in which there is no delineation between market segments, with the market viewed instead as a single mass market and only one marketing strategy applied to the whole.

References

Anon. (2013) 'Berger to reposition Sherwin Williams brand', *Chemical Business*, 27(10), 60.

Beane, T. P., and Ennis, D. M. (1987) 'Market segmentation: A review', *European Journal of Marketing*, 32(5), 20–42.

Belk, R. W., Bahn, K. D., and Mayer, R. N. (1982) 'Developmental recognition of consumption symbolism', *Journal of Consumer Research*, 9(1), 4–17.

Butler, S. (2019) 'Straight outta Brompton: Company predicts ebikes future', *The Guardian*, 24 June. Retrieve from: https://www.theguardian.com/business/2019/jun/24/brompton-company-predicts-ebikes-future-folding-bicycle (accessed 30 October 2020).

Carone, C. (2013) 'Xerox's brand repositioning challenge', *Ad Age*, 12 March. Retrieve from: https://adage.com/article/cmo-strategy/xerox-s-brand-repositioning-challenge/240285 (accessed 30 October 2020).

Erevelles, S., Fukawa, N., and Swayne, L. (2016) 'Big data consumer analytics and the transformation of marketing', *Journal of Business Research*, 69(2), 897–904.

Experian (2017) 'Consumer finances today: A fresh perspective on the UK's changing behaviours, attitudes and preferences'. Retrieve from: https://www.experian.co.uk/assets/marketing-services/whitepapers/consumer-finances-today-white-paper.pdf (accessed 30 October 2020).

Experian (2019) 'Mosaic Scotland: The consumer classification solution for consistent cross-channel marketing'. Retrieve from: https://www.experian.co.uk/assets/marketing-services/brochures/mosaic-brochure-scotland.pdf (accessed 30 October 2020).

Freytag, P. V., and Clarke, A. H. (2001) 'Business-to-business segmentation', *Industrial Marketing Management*, 30(6), 473–86.

Fuchs, C., and Diamantopoulos, A. (2010) 'Evaluating the effectiveness of brand-positioning strategies from a consumer perspective', *European Journal of Marketing*, 44(11–12), 1763–86.

Garrahan, M. (2012) 'Disney grabs a galaxy of opportunity', *Financial Times*, 19 November.

Griffith, R. L., and Pol, L. A. (1994) 'Segmenting industrial market', *Industrial Marketing Management*, 23, 39–46.

Haley, R. I. (1968) 'Benefit segmentation: A decision-oriented research tool', *Journal of Marketing*, 32(3), 30–5.

Harker, J. (2019) 'Brompton to retail in 49 Halfords stores and C&C in further 76', *Cycling Industry News*, 13 September. Retrieve from: https://cyclingindustry.news/brompton-to-retail-in-49-halfords-stores-and-cc-in-further-76/ (accessed 30 October 2020).

Holbrook, M. B., and Hirschman, E. C. (1982) 'The experiential aspects of consumer behaviour: Consumer fantasies, feelings and fun', *Journal of Consumer Research*, 9(2), 132–40.

Hollis, N. (2014) 'Justify your brand's price premium, and grow', *MMG*, 8 December. Retrieve from: http://www.mandmglobal.com/justify-your-brands-price-premium-and-grow/ (accessed 30 October 2020).

Hunt, S. D., and Arnett, D. B. (2004) 'Market segmentation strategy, competitive advantage and public policy: Grounding segmentation strategy in resource-advantage theory', *Australasian Marketing Journal*, 12(1), 7–25.

Keaveney, S. M. (1995) 'Customer switching behaviour in service industries: An exploratory study', *Journal of Marketing*, 59(2), 71–82.

Kotler, P. (1984) *Marketing Management* (international edn), Upper Saddle River, NJ: Prentice Hall.

Liu, A., Leach, M., and Chugh, R. (2015) 'A sales process framework to regain B2B customers', *Journal of Business & Industrial Marketing*, 30(8), 906–14.

Lopes, L., Alves, H., and Brito, C. (2001) 'Lost customers: Determinants and process of relationship dissolution'. Paper presented at the 40th EMAC Conference, May, Ljubljana, Slovenia.

McAlister, L., and Pessemier, E. (1982) 'Variety seeking behaviour: An interdisciplinary review', *Journal of Consumer Research*, 9(3), 311–22.

McDonald, M., and Dunbar, I. (2004) *Market Segmentation: How to Do It; How to Profit from It*, Oxford: Elsevier.

Mintel (2016) 'Wine and sparkling wine in the UK (2016)—Market sizes'. Retrieve from: https://store.mintel.com/report/wine-sparkling-wines-in-uk-2016-market-sizes (accessed 30 October 2020).

Naudé, P., and Cheng, L. (2003) 'Choosing between potential friends: Market segmentation in a small company'. Paper presented at the 19th IMP Conference, September, Lugano, Switzerland.

NGDATA (2016) 'How to implement more effective micro-targeting programs'. Retrieve from: https://www.ngdata.com/wp-content/uploads/2016/08/NGD-eBook-micro-targeting-2016.pdf (accessed 30 October 2020).

Ries, A., and Trout, J. (1972) 'The positioning era cometh', *Advertising Age*, April 24, 35–8.

Rooney, L. (2015) 'UBS unveils major brand overhaul', *Forbes*, 1 September. Retrieve from: https://www.forbes.com/sites/jenniferrooney/2015/09/01/ubs-unveils-major-brand-overhaul/ (accessed 30 November 2019).

Selwood, D. (2018) 'PG Tips adds black tea blend optimised for dairy-free cuppas', *The Grocer*, 23 February. Retrieve from: https://www.thegrocer.co.uk/new-product-development/pg-tips-adds-black-tea-blend-optimised-for-dairy-free-cuppas/563684.article (accessed 06 October 2019).

Sinclair, S. A., and Stalling, E. C. (1990) 'Perceptual mapping: A tool for industrial marketing—A case study', *Journal of Business and Industrial Marketing*, 5(1), 55–65.

Smith, W. R. (1956) 'Product differentiation and market segmentation as alternative marketing strategies', *Journal of Marketing*, 21(1), 3–8.

Solomon, M. R. (1983) 'The role of products as social stimuli: A symbolic interactionism perspective', *Journal of Consumer Research Conference*, 10(3), 319–29.

Srivastava, R. K., Shocker, A. D., and Day, G. S. (1978) 'An exploratory study of the influences of usage situations on perceptions of product markets', *Advances in Consumer Research*, 5, 32–8.

Tabi, A., Hille, S. L., & Wüstenhagen, R. (2014) 'What makes people seal the green power deal? Customer segmentation based on choice experiment in Germany', *Ecological Economics*, 107, pp. 206–15.

Wind, Y. (1978) 'Issues and advances in segmentation research', *Journal of Marketing Research*, 15(3), 317–37.

Wind, Y., and Cardozo, R. N. (1974) 'Industrial market segmentation', *Industrial Marketing Management*, 3(3), 155–66.

Part 3

Implementing the Marketing Mix

Chapter 6
Proposition and Branding Decisions

Learning Outcomes

After studying this chapter, you will be able to:

- explain the different levels of a proposition and the product life cycle;
- explore the processes associated with innovating new propositions and how propositions are adopted;
- explain the characteristics and principal types of brand and branding; and
- explain how brands can be built.

Case Insight 6.1
Micro-Fresh

Market Insight 6.1
Kopparberg: the Unconventional Brand

Market Insight 6.2
Personal(ity) Branding

Market Insight 6.3
Semi-globalization of Starbucks Coffee

Market Insight 6.4
Building a Responsible Brand: Nestlé's Case

Case Insight 6.1 **Micro-Fresh**

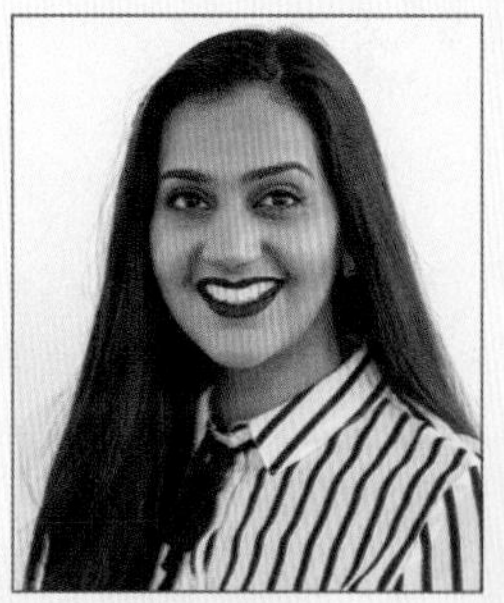

We speak to Jigna Varu, the chief commercial officer, to find out how Micro-Fresh® has helped to maintain distribution of its product with the Away from Home Channel throughout the Covid-19 crisis.

Micro-Fresh® is an antimicrobial product, originally developed and crafted in 2006 to prevent the growth of mould on products in transit from around the world. While sales of the original application continue to grow, Micro-Fresh® has now evolved into a smart technology, to be added during the manufacture of all kinds of homeware, footwear, and clothing to prevent the growth of odour-causing bacteria. The result is that Micro-Fresh® keeps sheets, duvets, towels, shoes, and clothes fresher for longer. Research has shown that fabrics made with Micro-Fresh® technology stay fresh for the lifetime of the product, regardless of how many times they are washed or at whatever temperature. It is gentle on skin and products enhanced with Micro-Fresh® are ideal even for babies and are hypoallergenic.

Micro-Fresh®, when used in hospitals/schools/office locations or in other buildings, is integral to the prevention of mould and the growth of pathogenic bacteria. As Micro-Fresh® prevents the growth of mould spores in the air it aids in the fight against respiratory issues associated with fungal growth in homes and the phenomenon known as 'sick building syndrome' (SBS). SBS is where construction factors in a building such as hermetically sealed environments (which coincide with energy-saving measures such as double glazing to restrict heat loss and air flow and increase thermal efficiency) can give rise to illnesses with associated headaches and respiratory problems simply by being in a particular building.

The Micro-Fresh® technology also provides antibacterial protection on hospital surfaces in the fight against hospital-acquired infections and also, by adding it during the laundry cycle rinse phase into uniforms, towels, masks, and gloves, restricts the risk of cross-contamination. Adding Micro-Fresh® as a final rinse imparts residual antibacterial properties to the laundry and leads to resultant lower wash temperatures as there is no requirement for the higher temperature to kill bacteria. There is also a corresponding reduction in energy, detergent, and water, resulting in a vastly reduced carbon footprint and a significant cost saving. The application can be integrated in three ways:

(1) during the manufacturing process: the active ingredient in Micro-Fresh® is natural and sustainable; free from nano technology and effective in reducing bacteria by up to 99.9 per cent;

(2) as a water-miscible formulation dosed into laundry; and

(3) as an antimicrobial spray or wipe.

Today Micro-Fresh® is used as an 'added-value' ingredient brand by over fifty household names, including John Lewis, Tesco, Asda, Dunelm, and Emirates. In April 2020 it was even featured in *Vogue* for high-fashion anti-bacterial gloves! The technology offers an opportunity to live a fresh, odour-free life on the go, 24/7.

We first formulated Micro-Fresh® in 2006 as a product, but the brand journey didn't start until around 2010. In the early stages, we needed to educate consumers on what Micro-Fresh® was.

Case Insight 6.1 (continued)

As the brand name became recognized, we changed our communications to inform the consumer of its value-in-use, e.g. runners' trainers no longer need to stink! Also, typically the lifespan of kids' new school shoes hinges on two main factors: they grow out of them or the shoes start to smell. Because Micro-Fresh® prevents odours, wastage is eliminated, so trainers last longer and fewer end up in landfill.

The fashion retailer, Next, was the first to sell the benefits of this revolutionary new technology in store, using our brand name to give their products a marketing edge. At the same time, we started a Facebook page in the halcyon days of emerging social media. Today, we have evolved to build the Micro-Fresh community via Instagram, Twitter, and Facebook where we educate consumers, run competitions, and aim to improve their well-being and lifestyle. We also undertake B2B marketing communications, through LinkedIn and our website www.microfresh.com. As trends change, we adapt our campaigns, newsletters, and podcasts. Innovation is at the heart of our business, from our product to the service we provide. Being innovative is what makes us a thriving business. Ultimately, we want all product designers to see Micro-Fresh® as a way to give their own products an edge, and to get consumers thinking 'has this product been Micro-Fresh'd?'.

We regularly request feedback to continually improve. In client meetings, we've presented treated and untreated Micro-Fresh® samples. Clients have tended to pick up the item and smell it, despite the fact that Micro-Fresh® is an invisible technology (you cannot see or smell it). This sparked an idea. We thought, 'when we talk about freshness, what is it that people imagine?'. After carrying out large-sample market research, we found that answers ranged from clinical smells, to freshly cut grass, to lavender fields, to freshly washed sheets. Taking all this into consideration, we are launching a scented version of Micro-Fresh® for Autumn/Winter 2020.

As the Covid-19 pandemic hit, resulting in mass closure of businesses worldwide and self-imposed quarantine for many people, we had to rethink our approach. For us in the biotechnology sector, Covid-19 brought up new marketing opportunities but we wanted to approach these with measured sensitivity. The first thing we did was test our technology against Coronavirus to get a new version that's both anti-viral and anti-Covid-19. During the pandemic, we felt it was crucial to leverage the trusted Micro-Fresh® brand name but we didn't want to frighten our customers or follow others with inappropriate promotions in the media.

The question for us was: how should we develop our branding and product development activities given the new growth opportunities in the Covid-19 environment?

Introduction

After studying how companies define their marketing strategies (see Chapters 4 and 5), we focus now on how they can implement these strategies. The first step is the study of **propositions** and **brands**.

A Samsung smartphone, an Interrail train journey from Kraków, Poland to Dubrovnik, Croatia, a latte at Costa in Stockholm, and the Italian *Corriere della Sera* newspaper are all commercial propositions or offerings. The term 'proposition' includes the tangible and intangible attributes related not only to physical goods, but also to services, ideas, people, places, experiences, and even a mix of these various elements. Anything that can be offered for use and consumption, in exchange for money or some other form of value, is referred to as a proposition, or offering. In this chapter, we consider the nature of propositions, before exploring issues associated with their innovation and development.

The second part of the chapter examines how brands can be developed to help customers to identify specific propositions and appreciate their value. Our world is full of brands—from soap powders and soft drinks, to airlines, and financial services. So what exactly is a 'brand'? How are they developed? Who really creates them? These are key questions explored in this chapter.

Product Levels, Types, and Lifecycles

The taste of coffee granules is an important benefit arising from the purchase of a jar of instant coffee. However, in addition to this core benefit, people are also attracted to the packaging, the price, the strength of the coffee, and also some of the psychosocial associations that we have learned about a brand. The Cafédirect brand, for instance, seeks to help people to understand its ties with the Fairtrade movement and so to provide some customers with a level of psychosocial satisfaction through their contribution to that movement.

To understand these different elements and benefits, we refer to three different proposition forms: the core, the embodied, and the augmented forms (see Figure 6.1).

- The *core* proposition consists of the real core benefit or service. This may be a functional benefit, in terms of what the offering will enable you to do, or it may be an emotional benefit, in terms of how the product or service will make you feel.
- The *embodied* proposition consists of the physical good or delivered service that provides the expected benefit. For example, cars are supplied in different styles, with different engines, seats, colours, and boot space.
- The *augmented* proposition consists of the embodied offering plus all of those other factors that are necessary to support the purchase and any post-purchase activities, such as credit and finance, training, delivery, installation, guarantees, and the overall perception of customer service.

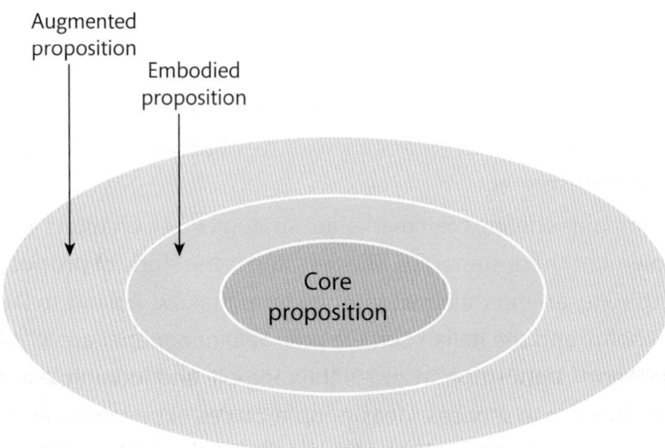

Figure 6.1 The three proposition forms

Each individual combination, or 'bundle', of benefits constitutes added value and serves to differentiate, for example, one sports car from another sports car and one tablet from another.

Consumer Products

The first way of classifying consumer products is to consider them in terms of their durability. **Durable goods**, such as bicycles, smartphones, and refrigerators, can be used repeatedly and provide benefits each time they are used. **Non-durable goods**, such as yoghurt and newspapers, have a limited duration and are often used only once.

Durable goods often require the purchaser to have high levels of involvement in the purchase decision. There is a high perceived risk in these decisions, and so consumers can spend time, care, and energy searching, formulating, and making the 'right' decision.

Non-durable goods—typically, food and grocery items—reflect low levels of involvement and buyers are seldom concerned with which particular product they buy. Risk is seen to be low and so there is little or no need to shop around for the best possible price. Buyers may base their choice on availability, price, habit, or brand experience.

A deeper and more meaningful way of classifying consumer products is to consider how and where consumers buy them. In Chapter 2, we considered how consumers make purchases. In particular, we looked at **extensive problem-solving**, **limited problem-solving**, and **routinized response behaviour**. Classifying products according to the behaviours that consumers demonstrate when buying them enables marketing managers to develop more suitable and appropriate marketing strategies. Four main behavioural categories have been established: **convenience products**; **shopping products**; **specialty products**; and unsought products.

Convenience products are non-durable and are bought because the consumer does not want to put very much, if any, effort into the buying decision. Routinized response behaviour corresponds most closely to convenience products, because they are bought frequently and are inexpensive. Most decisions in this category are made habitually, and if a usual brand is unavailable, an alternative brand is selected, or none at all if it is seen to be too inconvenient to visit another store.

Shopping products are not bought as frequently as convenience products and, as a result, consumers do not always have sufficient up-to-date information to make a buying decision. The purchase of shopping products such as furniture, electrical appliances, jewellery, and smartphones requires some search for information, if only to find out about the latest features. Consumers dedicate time and effort to planning these purchases, if only because the level of risk is more substantial than that associated with convenience products. They will visit several stores, and use the Internet and word-of-mouth, to make price comparisons, to find out product information, and to learn from the experiences of other customers.

Product Life Cycles

Underpinning the concept of the **product life cycle** is the belief that offerings move through a sequential, predetermined pattern of development similar to the biological path that lifeforms follow. This pathway, known as the 'product life cycle', consists of five distinct stages—namely, development, introduction, growth, maturity, and decline. Sales and profits rise and fall across the various life stages of the product, as shown in Figure 6.2.

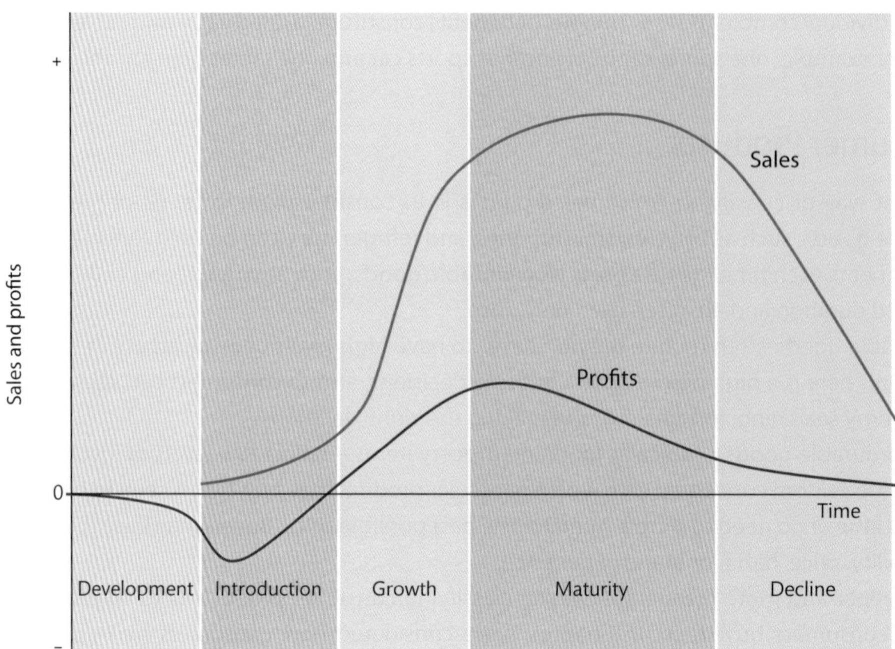

Figure 6.2 The product life cycle

Products move through an overall cycle that consists of different stages. Speed of movement through the stages will vary, but each product has a limited lifespan. Although the life of a product can be extended in many ways, such as introducing new ways of using the product, finding new users, and developing new attributes, the majority of products have a finite period during which management needs to maximize its returns on the investment made.

Different marketing strategies, relating to the offering and its distribution, pricing, and promotion, need to be deployed at particular times in the product life cycle so as to maximize financial returns. Moreover, the concept does not apply to all offerings in the same way. For example, some offerings reach the end of the introduction stage and then die as it becomes clear that there is no market to sustain them. Other products follow the path into decline, but then linger, sustained by heavy advertising and sales promotions, or are recycled back into the growth stage by repositioning activities. Yet other products grow really quickly and then fade away rapidly. Fashion products are pertinent examples of this latter instance, with leading retailers such as H&M and Zara having fifty-two 'micro-seasons' per year, one for every week of the year (Boström et al., 2019: 295).

The concept of the product life cycle can apply to a product class (such as computers), a product form (such as a laptop), or a brand (such as Lenovo). The shape of the lifecycle curve varies, with product classes having the longest cycle as the mature stage is often extended.

Despite its usefulness, the concept has several limitations. One problem is identifying which stage an offering has reached in the cycle. Some brands do not follow the classical S-shaped curve (see Figure 6.3), but rise steeply and then fall away immediately after sales reach a crest.

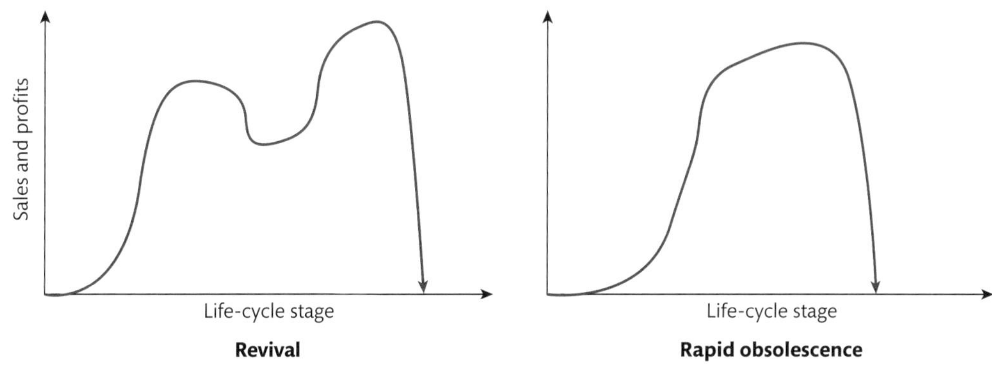

Figure 6.3 Types of product life cycle

Other possible shapes are generated when demand for a brand or product is rejuvenated, such as the revival of vinyl records (Friedlander, 2019), and when a product becomes rapidly out of date (e.g. the shift from wired headphones to Bluetooth headphones). The model works reasonably well when the environment is relatively stable and not subject to dynamic swings or short-lived customer preferences.

Developing New Product Propositions

An organization needs continually to offer superior value to its customers. A key management task is therefore to control the organization's range, or portfolio, of products and to anticipate when one product will become tired, and when new ones will be necessary to sustain the organization and to help it to grow.

The term 'new products' can be misleading. This is because there is a range of newness, relevant to both the organization and to customers: some new products might be totally new to both the organization and the market, whereas others might be only minor product adaptations that have no real impact on a market other than to introduce an interesting new feature, for example features such as new colours, flavours, and pack sizes.

To ensure a stream of new propositions, organizations have the following three main options:

- to buy in finished products from other suppliers, perhaps from other parts of the world, or to license the use of other products for specific periods of time, as does Samsung with its processor technology;
- to develop products through collaboration with suppliers or even competitors, as did the three largest record companies, Universal Music Group, Sony Music Entertainment and Warner Music Group when they developed online video platform Vevo; or
- to develop new products internally, often by means of research and development (R&D) departments or by adapting current products through minor design and engineering changes, as Dyson did with its vacuum cleaner.

The success rate of new products is consistently poor. No more than one in ten new consumer products succeed and, according to Drucker (1985), there are three main reasons for this:

1 that no market exists for the product—as was the case with the Nissan Murano Crosscabriolet which was released in 2011. A hybrid of an SUV and a convertible, it was discontinued in 2014 after being branded 'weird' for its unusual combination of features (Stock, 2018);
2 that there is a market need, but the product fails to meet customer requirements—for example the online social network Google+ launched in 2011 and subsequently closed in 2019 due to low user engagement and design flaws which compromised user privacy (Smith, 2018); or
3 the product's ability to meet the market need, although satisfactory, is not adequately communicated to the target market—as was the case for Buckler, a very low-alcohol beer in the Dutch market in the 1980s (Institute of Brilliant Failures, n.d.).

The development of new propositions is a complex and high-risk task, so organizations usually adopt a procedural approach. The procedure consists of several phases (stages and gates) that enable progress to be monitored, test trials to be conducted, and the results analysed before there is any commitment to the market. The most common new product development process (NPDP) is set out in Figure 6.4.

The NPDP is generally (but not necessarily) perceived to be linear in that new proposition development occurs only after managers are satisfied with progress of the development project at each stage. There is a therefore a 'go–no go' decision at each stage (i.e. a gate) and hence this process is often referred to as a 'stage–gate model'.

Idea Generation

Ideas can be generated through customers, competitors (through websites and sales literature analysis), market research data (such as reports), social media analyses, R&D, customer service employees, the sales force, project development teams, and secondary data sources such as sales records. What this means is that organizations should foster a corporate culture that

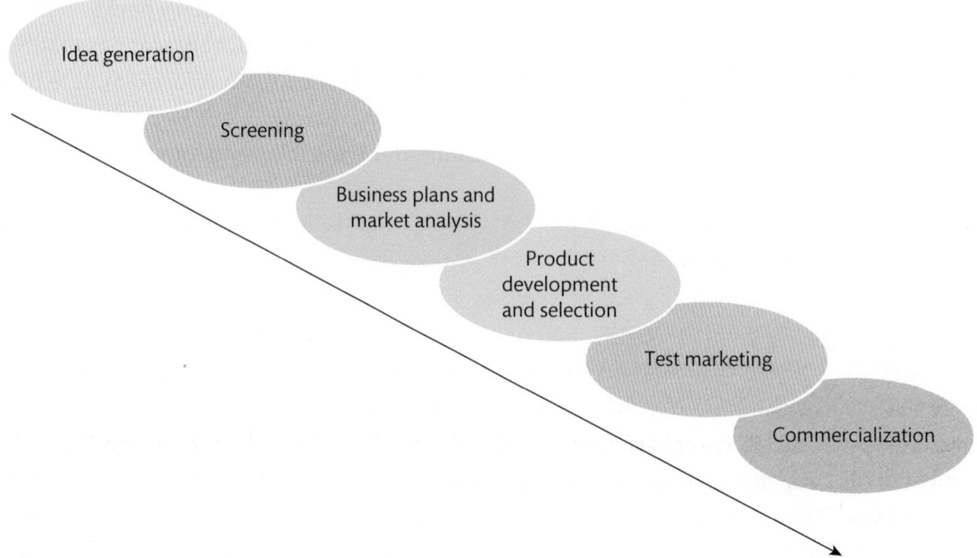

Figure 6.4 Stages in the new product development process

encourages creativity, supporting people when they propose new ideas for product enhancements and other improvements. 3M famously allows its engineers and scientists to spend 15 per cent of their time pursuing projects of their own choice and 30 per cent of a division's revenue must come from products developed in the last four years. Over the years, the company has introduced such pioneering products as the Post-It note, Scotch tape, and the first electronic stethoscope with Bluetooth technology (Govindarajan and Srinivas, 2013).

Screening

All ideas need to be assessed so that only those that meet predetermined criteria are advanced. Key criteria include the fit between the proposed new idea and the overall corporate strategy and objectives. Another consideration involves the views of customers, determined using concept testing. Other approaches consider how the market will react to the idea and what effort the organization will need to make if the offering is to be brought to market successfully. Whatever approaches are used, screening must be a separate activity to the idea generation stage; if it is not, creativity might be impaired.

Business Planning and Market Analysis

The development of a business plan is crucial, simply because it will indicate the potential and relative profitability of the product. To prepare the plan, important information about the size, shape, and dynamics of the market should be determined. The resultant profitability forecasts will be significant in determining how and when the product will be developed, if at all.

Product Development and Selection

In many organizations, several product ideas are considered simultaneously. It is management's task to select those that have commercial potential and are in the best interests of the organization, in terms of its longer-term strategy, goals, and use of resources. There is a trade-off between the need to test and reduce risk and the need to go to market and drive income to get a return on the investment committed to the new proposition. This phase is expensive, so only a limited number of projects are allowed to proceed into development. Prototypes and test versions are developed for those projects that are selected for further development. These are then subjected to functional performance tests, design revisions, manufacturing requirements analysis, distribution analysis, and a multitude of other testing procedures.

Test Marketing

Before committing a new product to a market, most organizations decide to test market the finished product. By piloting and testing the product under controlled real-market conditions, many of the genuine issues that only customers may perceive can be raised and resolved, while minimizing any damage or risk to the organization and the brand. **Test marketing** can be undertaken using a particular geographical region or specific number of customer locations. The intention is to evaluate the product and the whole marketing programme under real-world working conditions. Test marketing, or field trials, enables the product and marketing plan to be refined or adapted in the light of market reaction, before the product's release to the whole market. British supermarket group Sainsbury's, for example, has built a central London lab and hired 500 specialists to test new ways of shopping, especially on mobile apps, given that customers' lives have changed and they have become more 'promiscuous shoppers' (Ghosh, 2015).

It is vital for organizations to set up systems with which to measure the success or failure of new product development. Criteria for measuring success and failure include (but are not limited to) measures based on customer acceptance, financial performance, and product- and firm-level considerations (Griffin and Page, 1993), such as the following.

- Customer acceptance measures:
  - Customer acceptance
  - Customer satisfaction
  - Net revenue goals
  - Net market share goals
  - Net unit sales goals
- Financial performance measures:
  - Break-even period
  - Margin goals
  - Profitability goals
  - Internal rate of return (IRR)/return on investment (ROI)
- Product level measures:
  - Development cost
  - Launched on time
  - Product performance level
  - Net quality guidelines
  - Speed to market
- Firm level measurements:
  - Percentage of sales attained as a proportion of new products/services

Commercialization

To commercialize a new product, a launch plan is required. This considers the needs of **distributors**, end-user customers, marketing communication agencies, and other relevant stakeholders. The objective is to schedule all of those activities that are required to make the launch successful. These include communications (to inform audiences of the product's capabilities, and to position and persuade potential customers), training, and product support for all customer-facing employees.

Any perceived rigidity in this formal process should be disregarded. Many new offerings come to market via different routes, at different speeds and different levels of preparation.

Product Launch: Adoption and Diffusion

Adoption

The process by which individuals accept and use new propositions is referred to as 'adoption' (Rogers, 1983). The different stages in the **process of adoption** are sequential and are characterized by the different factors that are involved at each stage (e.g. the media used by each individual).

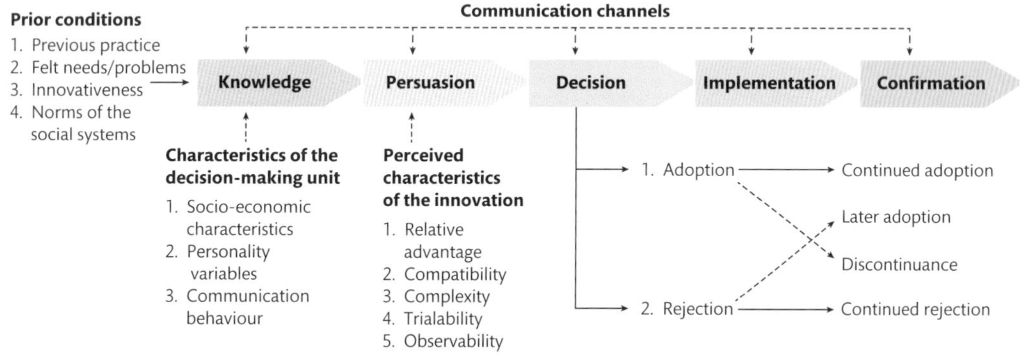

Figure 6.5 Stages in the innovation decision process of adoption

Source: Reprinted with the permission of Free Press, a Division of Simon & Schuster, Inc., from *Diffusion of Innovations* (5th edn) by Everett M. Rogers. Copyright © 1995, 2003 by Everett M. Rogers. Copyright © 1962, 1971, 1983, by Free Press, a Division of Simon & Schuster, Inc. All rights reserved.

The process starts with people gaining awareness of a proposition, then moves through various stages of adoption, before a purchase is eventually made. Figure 6.5 sets out the various stages in the process of adoption.

1. In the *knowledge* stage, consumers become aware of the new proposition. They have little information and have yet to develop any particular attitudes towards the product. Indeed, at this stage, consumers are not interested in finding out any more information.
2. The *persuasion* stage is characterized by consumers becoming aware that the innovation may be of use in solving a potential problem. Consumers become sufficiently motivated to find out more about the proposition's characteristics, including its features, price, and availability.
3. In the *decision* stage, individuals develop an attitude toward the proposition and they reach a decision about whether the innovation will meet their needs. If this is positive, they will experiment with the innovation.
4. During the *implementation* stage, the innovation is tried for the first time. Sales promotions are often used as samples to allow individuals to test the product without any undue risk. Individuals accept or reject an innovation on the basis of their experience of the trial. Consider, for example, the way in which supermarkets or duty-free airport retailers use sampling to encourage people to try new food and drink products.
5. The final *confirmation* stage is signalled when an individual successfully purchases the proposition on a regular basis without the help of the sales promotion or other incentives.

Product sampling in supermarkets is used as a tactic to facilitate the adoption of new products.

Source: © Tyler Olson/Shutterstock.

The adoption stages do not always occur in sequence. Rejection of the innovation can occur at any point—even during implementation and the very early phases of the confirmation stage. Generally, mass communications are more effective in the earlier phases of the adoption process for propositions in which buyers are actively interested and more interpersonal forms are more appropriate in later stages—especially implementation and confirmation.

Diffusion Theory

Consumers may have both functional and emotional motives when purchasing, but customers adopt new propositions differently. Their different attitudes to risk, and their levels of education, experience, and needs, mean that different groups of customers adopt new propositions at varying speeds. The rate at which a market adopts an innovation is referred to as the **process of diffusion** (Rogers, 1962). According to Rogers, there are five categories of adopter, as shown in Figure 6.6.

- **Innovators**—This group, which constitutes 2.5 per cent of the buying population, is important because it has to kick-start the adoption process. These people like new ideas, and are often well educated, young, confident, and financially strong. They are more likely to take risks associated with new propositions. Innovative attitudes and behaviour can be specific to only one or two areas of interest.
- **Early adopters**—This group, which comprises 13.5 per cent of the market, is characterized by a high percentage of opinion leaders. These people are very important for speeding up the adoption process. Consequently, marketing communications need to be targeted at these people, who in turn will stimulate word-of-mouth communications to spread information. Although early adopters prefer to let innovators take all of the risks, they enjoy being at the leading edge of innovation, tend to be younger than any other group, and have above-average levels of education. Other than innovators, this group reads more publications and consults more salespeople than all others.
- **Early majority**—This group, which forms 34 per cent of the market, is more risk-averse than the previous two groups. Individuals require reassurance that the offering works and has been proven in the market. They are above average in terms of age, education, social status, and income. Unlike the early adopters, they tend to wait for prices to fall and prefer more informal sources of information, and they are often prompted into purchase by other people who have already purchased.

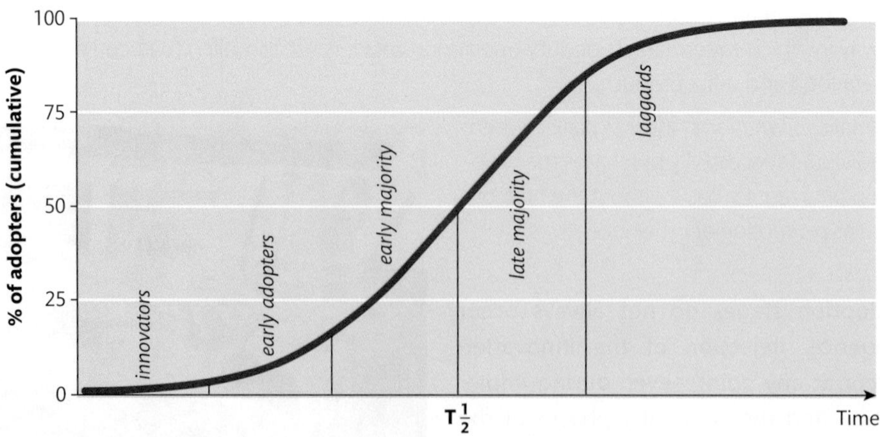

Figure 6.6 The process of diffusion

Source: Reprinted with the permission of Free Press, a Division of Simon & Schuster, Inc., from *Diffusion of Innovations* (5th edn) by Everett M. Rogers. Copyright © 1995, 2003 by Everett M. Rogers. Copyright © 1962, 1971, 1983, by Free Press, a Division of Simon & Schuster, Inc. All rights reserved.

Research Insight 6.1

To take your learning further, you might wish to read this influential paper.

Chang, Y. T., Yu, H. and Lu, H. P. (2015) 'Persuasive messages, popularity cohesion, and message diffusion in social media marketing', ***Journal of Business Research*****, 68(4), 777–82.**

Consumers are increasingly exposed to a range of influences beyond traditional advertising, including electronic word-of-mouth communications. With the proliferation of social media platforms such as Instagram, YouTube, and Facebook, consumers tend to seek information about products or services from friends and influential users online whom they perceive as trustworthy. In this paper, the authors examine the characteristics of marketing messages on Facebook which persuade users to like and share posts. Forwarding messages via liking and sharing ultimately contributes to the process of diffusion, as the information can spread and be viewed by a wide audience. Findings suggest that post popularity is a key factor which encourages users to like or share, alongside the quality of the argument and the attractiveness of the post.

Visit the online resources to read the abstract and access the full paper.

- **Late majority**—Of a similar size to the previous group (34 per cent), the late majority are sceptical of new ideas and adopt new offerings only because of social or economic factors. They read few publications and are below average in terms of education, social status, and income.
- **Laggards**—This group of people, comprising 16 per cent of the buying population, are suspicious of all new ideas and their opinions are very hard to change. Laggards have the lowest income, social status, and education of all of the groups, and take a long time to adopt an innovation, if they adopt it at all.

The What, Why, and How of Branding

What is a Brand?

A 'brand' can be distinguished from its proposition or unbranded commodity counterparts by means of the perceptions and feelings consumers have about its attributes and its performance. Bottled water, for example, is essentially a commodity, but brands such as Highland Spring in Scotland, Evian in France, and Font Vella in Spain have all developed their offerings with imagery that serves to enhance customer feelings and emotions about the actual water in the packaging. Ultimately, a brand resides in the minds of the consumer (Achenbaum, 1993).

Brand positioning is a strategic activity used to differentiate and distinguish a brand so that a consumer understands the brand, not only remembers it. As Tudor and Negricea (2012) rightly assert, branding and positioning are interrelated: a credible position cannot be sustained without a strong brand, and a brand cannot be developed or preserved without the audience perceiving a justifiable position.

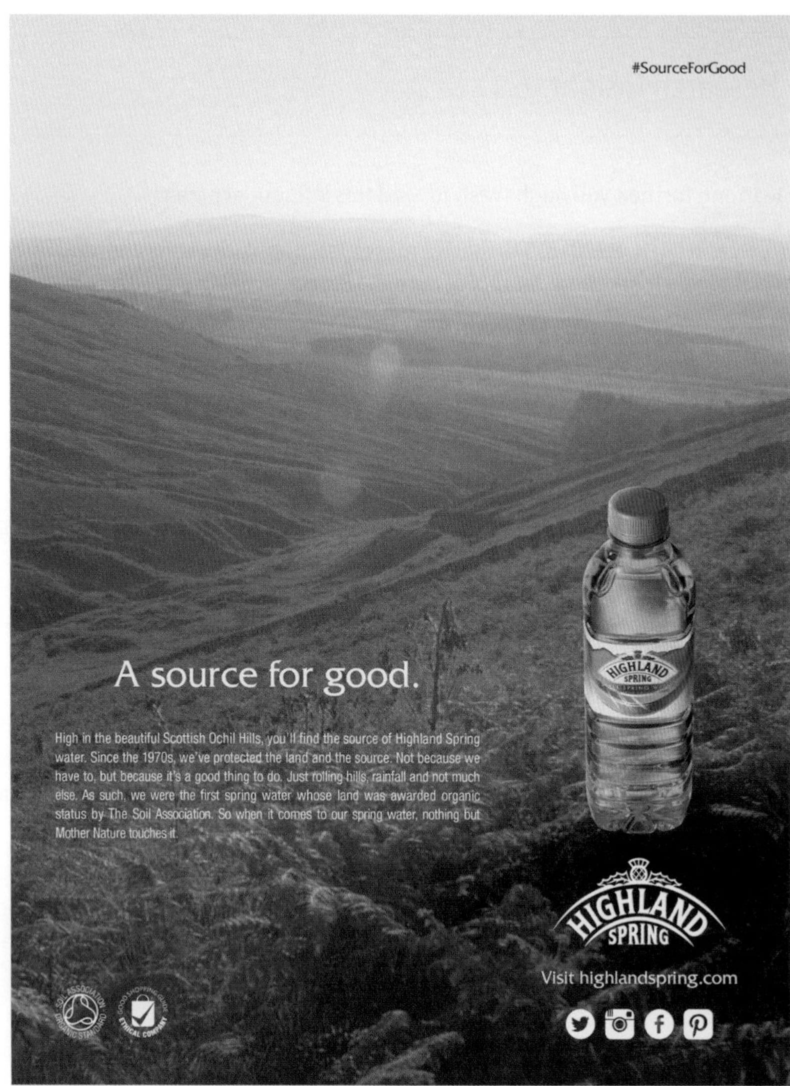

Even basic commodities like water can be successfully branded.

Source: Courtesy of Highland Spring.

Successful brands capture three core brand elements: promises, positioning, and performance—that is, the 'three brand Ps' (3BPs) (see Figure 6.7). At the core of this concept is communication, which enables a promise to be known (known as 'brand awareness'), positions the brand correctly (known as 'brand attitude'), and delivers brand performance (known as 'brand response').

Commonly, a brand is represented by a name, symbol, words, or mark that identifies and distinguishes a proposition or company from its competitors. However, brands consist of much more than these various elements. As Aaker (2014: 1) remarks, 'far more than a name or a logo it is an organization's promise to a customer to deliver what a brand stands for . . . in terms of functional benefits but also emotional, self-expressive and social benefits'.

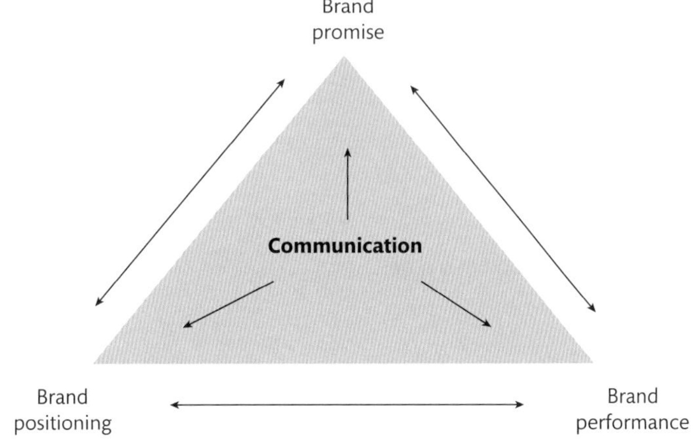

Figure 6.7 The triangulation of the 3BPs

Source: Fill and Turnbull (2016).

Why Brand?

Brands represent opportunities for both consumers and organizations (manufacturers and retailers) to buy and to sell products and services easily, more efficiently, and relatively quickly. The benefits can be considered from each perspective.

Consumers like brands because they:

- help people to identify their preferred offerings;
- reduce levels of perceived risk and, in doing so, improve the quality of the shopping experience;
- help people to gauge the level of quality of a product/service or experience;
- reduce the amount of time that a customer must spend making proposition-based decisions and, in turn, decrease the time spent shopping;
- provide psychological reassurance or reward, especially for offerings bought on an occasional basis; and
- inform consumers about the source of an offering (in terms of country or company).

Many brands are deliberately imbued with human characteristics, to the point at which they are identified as having particular personalities. These **brand personalities** might be based around being seen as 'friendly', 'approachable', 'distant', 'aloof', 'calculating', 'honest', 'fun', or even 'robust' or 'caring'. For example, Timberland is 'rugged', Victoria's Secret, 'glamorous', Virgin is associated with youthfulness and rebelliousness, and management consultancies such as PricewaterhouseCoopers (PwC) seek to be seen as successful, accomplished, and influential. Marketing communications play an important role in communicating the essence of a brand's personality. By developing positive emotional links with a brand, a company can reassure consumers about their brand purchases.

Manufacturers and retailers use brands because they:

- can increase the company's financial valuation;
- enable premium pricing;

- help to differentiate the proposition from competitive offerings;
- can deter competitors from entering the market;
- encourage cross-selling of other brands owned by the manufacturer;
- help the company to develop customer trust, customer loyalty and retention, and repeat-purchase buyer behaviour;
- help in the development and use of integrated marketing communications;
- contribute to corporate identity programmes; and
- provide some legal protection.

Visit the **online resources** and complete Internet Activity 6.1 to learn more about how major organizations perceive the importance of branding and their brands.

How Brands Work: Associations and Personalities

The development of successful brands requires customers to be able to make appropriate brand-related associations. Normally, these should be based on utilitarian, functional issues, as well as emotions and feelings towards a brand.

Clayton and Heo (2011) refer to brand image, perceived quality, and brand attitude as the main dimensions of **brand associations**, citing work by Aaker (1991), Keller (1993), and Low and Lamb (2000) in this area.

Keller (1993) believes that brand associations themselves are made up of the physical and non-physical attributes and benefits aligned with attitudes to create a brand image in the mind of the consumer. Belk (1988), meanwhile, suggested that brands offer a means of self-expression, whether this is in terms of who they want to be (the 'desired self'), who they strive to be (the 'ideal self'), or who they think they should be (the 'ought self'). Brands therefore provide a means for individuals to indicate to others their preferred personality.

This emotional and symbolic approach is intended to provide consumers with additional reasons to engage with a brand, beyond the normal functional characteristics that a brand offers (Keller, 1998), which are so easily copied by competitors. Aaker (1997) developed the **brand personality scale**, which consists of five main dimensions of psychosocial meaning, subdivided into forty-two personality traits (see Figure 6.8):

- sincerity ('wholesome', 'honest', 'down-to-earth');
- excitement ('exciting', 'imaginative', 'daring');
- competence ('intelligent', 'confident');
- sophistication ('charming', 'glamorous', 'smooth'); and
- ruggedness ('strong', 'masculine').

Aaker's initial research was conducted in the mid-1990s and revealed that, in the United States, MTV was perceived to be best at excitement, CNN best on competence, Levi's best on ruggedness, Revlon best on sophistication, and Campbell's best on sincerity. More recent research has applied Aaker's brand personality scale to investigate how consumers perceive the personality

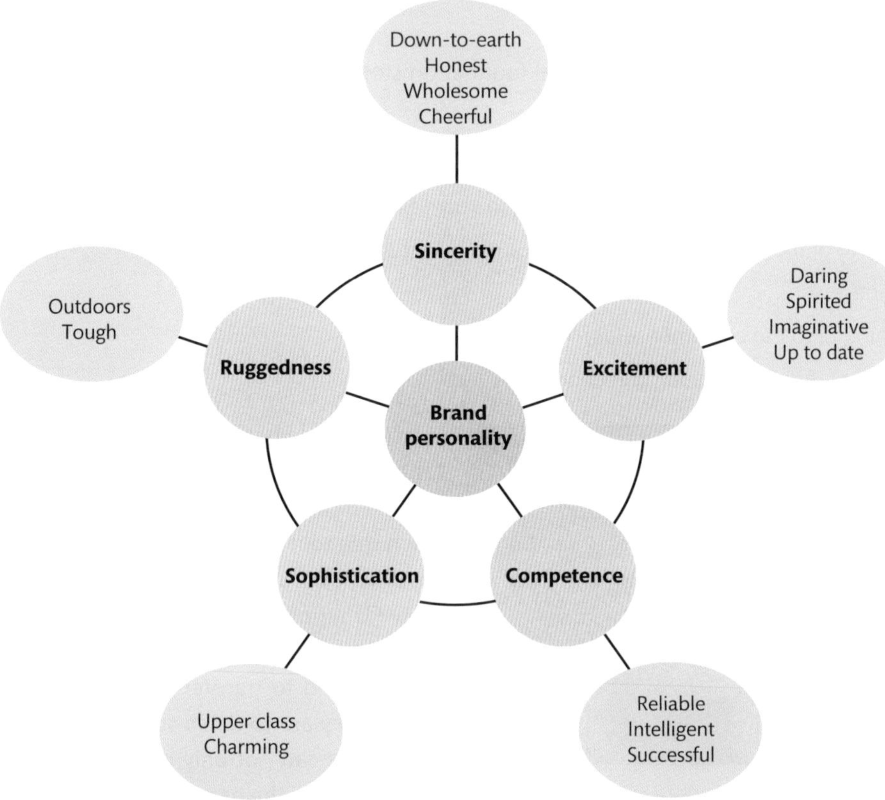

Figure 6.8 Five dimensions of psychosocial meaning

Source: Reprinted with permission from Aaker, J. (1997) 'Dimensions of brand personality', *Journal of Marketing Research*, 34(August), 347–56, published by the American Marketing Association.

traits of a variety of brands in different contexts. For example, Gómez Aguilar et al. (2016) studied the destination branding of two popular tourist destinations in southern Spain: Granada and Torremolinos. They found that British tourists perceived the beach destination Torremolinos to be best on competence and the more cultural destination Granada to be best at both competence and sophistication.

These psychosocial dimensions have subsequently become enshrined as dimensions of brand personality. Aaker developed a five-point framework around these dimensions to provide a consistent means of measurement. Various studies have found that consumers choose brands that reflect their own personality (Linville and Carlston, 1994; Phau and Lau, 2001)—that is, they prefer brands that project a personality that is consistent with their self-concepts. As Arora and Stoner (2009: 273) indicate, 'brand personality provides a form of identity for consumers that expresses symbolic meaning for themselves and for others'. Brand personality can therefore be construed as a means of creating and maintaining consumer loyalty, if only because this aspect is difficult for competitors to copy.

Brand Names

Choosing a name for a brand is a critical foundation stone because, ideally, it should enable the brand to be:

- easily recalled, spelled, and spoken;
- strategically consistent with the organization's branding policies;
- indicative of the offering's major benefits and characteristics;
- distinctive;
- meaningful to the customer; and
- capable of registration and protection.

Cadbury—the company prefix to a range of different brand names.
Source: © Ekaterina_Minaeva/Shutterstock.

Sometimes, changes in a brand's macro-environment can stimulate a change of name. For example, Danone's 'Bio' yoghurt, labelled as such due to its use of probiotics, was renamed Activia in 2006 in France and Spain because of new EU regulations which stipulated that only organic produce could be labelled as 'bio'. Brand names need to transfer easily across markets, and if they are to do so successfully, it helps if customers can not only pronounce the name, but also recall the name unaided.

Brand names should have some internal strategic consistency and be compatible with the organization's overall positioning. Ford Transit, Virgin Atlantic, and Cadbury Dairy Milk are names that reflect the parent company's policies because the company name prefixes the product brand names.

Increasingly, brands are being developed through the use of social media. This is essentially about people talking—either spontaneously to one another, or through broadcasts such as blogs, vlogs, and posts, within formal or informal communities—about brands that they have experienced in some way. The role of brand managers has transitioned from one of guardian to that of a brand host (Christodoulides, 2009), who now listens to these conversations and then adapts the brands accordingly. What this suggests is that the control and identity of a brand has moved from the company to the consumer.

Visit the **online resources** and complete Internet Activity 6.2 to learn more about generating brand names.

Branding Strategies

An overall branding strategy can provide direction, consistency, and brand integrity within an organization's portfolio of brands. This provides the basis of the brand architecture. There are three core brand strategies: individual, family, and corporate.

Individual Branding

Once referred to as a 'multibrand policy', individual branding requires that each product offered by an organization is branded independently of all of the others. Grocery brands offered by Unilever (such as Knorr, Cif, and Dove) and Procter & Gamble (such as Fairy, Crest, and Head & Shoulders) typify this approach.

One of the advantages of this approach is that it is easy to target specific segments and to enter new markets with separate names. If a brand fails or becomes subject to negative media attention, the other brands are not likely to be damaged. However, there is a heavy financial cost, because each brand needs to have its own promotional programme and associated support.

Family Branding

Once referred to as a 'multiproduct brand policy', family branding requires that all of the products use the organization's name, either entirely or in part. Microsoft, Heinz, and Kellogg's all incorporate the company name, because it is hoped that customer trust will develop across all brands and that therefore promotional investment need not be as high. The idea is that there will always be a halo effect across all of the brands when one is communicated and that brand experience will stimulate word-of-mouth following usage. A prime example of this is Google, which has pursued a family brand strategy across Google Ads, Google Maps, and Google Scholar, to name only a few.

A family of cereals: Kellogg's image reinforces the image of the individual brands in its product lines.

Source: © DenisMArt/Shutterstock.

Corporate Brands

Many retail brands adopt a single **umbrella brand**, based on the name of the organization. This name is then used at all locations, and is a way of identifying the brand and providing a form of consistent differentiation, and of recognition, whether on the high street or online. Major supermarkets such as Tesco in the UK, Carrefour in France, and Asda use this branding strategy to attract, and to help to retain, customers.

Corporate branding strategies are also used extensively in business markets, such as IBM, Cisco, and Caterpillar, and in consumer markets in which there is technical complexity, such as financial services. Companies such as HSBC and Prudential adopt a single name strategy. One of the advantages of this approach is that promotional investments are limited to one brand. However, the risk is similar to that of family branding, whereby damage to one offering or operational area can cause problems across the organization. The British Broadcasting Corporation (BBC), for example, experienced editorial problems with its *Newsnight* programme that resulted in extensive and persistent negative media coverage. In this instance, not only did the director-general decide to resign, but also questions surfaced about declining trust and reputation concerning the whole of the BBC.

How to Build Brands

The development of successful brands is critical to an organization's success. Keller (2009) believes that this is best accomplished by considering the brand-building process in terms of steps. The first step is to enable customers to identify with the brand and help them to make associations with a specific product class or customer need (see Market Insight 6.1). The second is to establish what the brand means, by linking various tangible and intangible brand associations. The third step is concerned with encouraging customer responses based around brand-related judgements and feelings. The final step is about fostering an active relationship between customers and the brand.

Figure 6.9 depicts these rational steps on the left-hand side, with the emotional counterpart shown on the right-hand side. In the centre are six blocks that make up a pyramid, echoing these rational and emotional steps. To achieve a successful brand, or 'brand resonance', Keller argues that a foundation is necessary and that these building blocks need to be developed systematically.

Let us apply the brand pyramid to a shampoo brand to understand the terminology further.

- *Brand salience*—How easily and often do customers think of the shampoo brand when thinking about haircare brands or when shopping?
- *Brand performance*—How well do customers believe the shampoo brand cleans and conditions their hair?

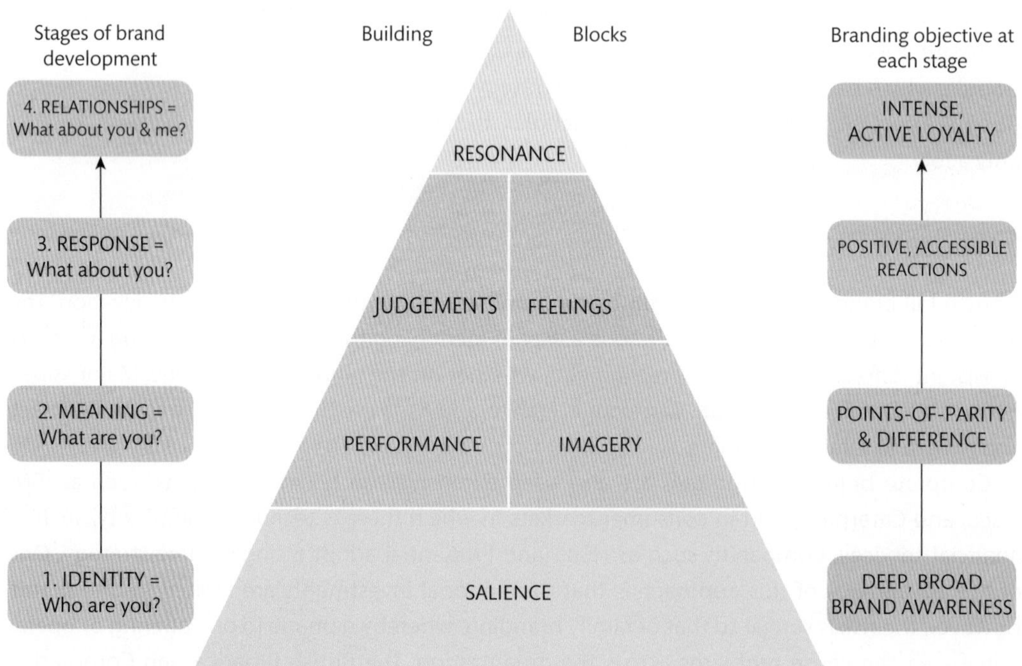

Figure 6.9 Brand pyramid: building blocks

Source: K. L. Keller, 'Building strong brands in a modern marketing communications environment', *Journal of Marketing Communications*, July 2009, Taylor & Francis. Reprinted by permission of the publisher (Taylor & Francis Ltd, http://www.tandf.co.uk/journals).

- *Brand imagery*—What are the extrinsic properties of the shampoo (the colour, the packaging, the product consistency, associations) and to what level do these satisfy customers' psychological or social needs?
- *Brand judgements*—What are customers' own personal opinions and evaluations about the shampoo?
- *Brand feelings*—What are customers' emotional responses and reactions to the shampoo brand when prompted by communications, friends, or when washing their own hair?
- *Brand resonance*—What is the nature of the relationship that customers have with the shampoo brand and to what extent do they feel loyal to the brand?

Brand resonance is most likely to result when marketers create proper salience and breadth and depth of awareness. From this position, 'points of parity' and 'points of difference' need to be established, so that positive judgements and feelings can be made that appeal to both the head and the heart, respectively.

Market Insight 6.1 **Kopparberg: the Unconventional Brand**

In 1882, local brewers in the Swedish town of Kopparberg joined up to form Kopparberg's Bryggeri AB. Today, the company is led by brothers Peter and Dan-Anders Bronsman. Peter bought a disused mineral water bottling plant, and began making lager and cider. Kopparberg capitalizes on natural soft water in the area, which has low mineral content and enables natural tastes to come through unchanged. Even though cider is claimed to be a way of life in Sweden, traditional apple cider was seen as too dull and unexciting for the younger generation. A gap in the market existed for a fruitier and sweeter cider aimed at young people. Kopparberg therefore decided to innovate with non-traditional flavours for ciders, such as 'naked apple', 'toffee apple', 'kiwi fruit', 'blackcurrant and raspberry', 'strawberry and lime', 'elderflower and lime', and 'cranberry and cinnamon'.

Kopparberg often uses innovative events to build its image. TV presenters Lilah Parsons and A. J. Odudu were two of the opinion formers who participated in the latest Kopparberg Urban Forest in London.
Source: © Getty/David M. Benett/Contributor.

However, a difficulty arose when launching and marketing the new ranges of cider in Sweden owing to a government ban on alcohol advertising. Kopparberg found a way around the problem by focusing its advertising in Ibiza, Greece, and Majorca, where young people from Sweden and other European countries go to party every summer. The idea was that, while partying, they would be drinking Kopparberg's fruitier and sweeter ciders. When they returned home from their summer holidays, they would bring back with them awareness and knowledge about the taste and the brand. This was how Kopparberg launched its products and brand to a young Swedish market without advertising in Sweden.

When Kopparberg expanded its market to the UK in 2007, it found itself a small fish swimming in a big cider pond! It faced strong competition from players such as Magners, Bulmers, and Strongbow. Since then, Kopparberg's fruity ciders have grown to become the most popular amongst UK cider drinkers. In 2018, it was the UK's second best-selling cider, and

Market Insight 6.1 (continued)

with 9.3 per cent value growth, it is beating its major competitors in spite of smaller marketing budgets.

Differentiation and innovation have been the key to Kopparberg's success. Instead of investing in traditional advertising, it identified opinion formers—that is, people who were more adventurous and willing to try new fruity ciders. These people could also influence and spread popularity of these cool, innovative products through word-of-mouth. Cool pubs and bars where young hipsters hang out were targeted in the main UK cities, such as London, Manchester, and Glasgow; free ciders were also supplied to events organized in art galleries and bars in east London: these activities acted as an advert for the brand. Based on product differentiation and its unconventional marketing approach, Kopparberg is now sold in more than 40 countries. In 2015, 75 million litres were sold worldwide, with £225 million in revenue.

1 **What do you think was the most important factor in Kopparberg's success in Sweden: the unconventional advertising, or the new product development?**
2 **Why do you think Kopparberg has been successful in the UK market, given the strong competition?**
3 **How might Kopparberg innovate further to keep ahead of the competition?**

Sources: Forbes (2018); Torrance (2014); Eads (2015); Trott (2016).

This market insight was kindly contributed by Dr Ning Baines, De Montfort University, UK.

Brand Relationships and Co-creation

Although branding has its roots in identification and differentiation, a 'brand-mark is a relational asset whose value to the firm is contingent on past, present and future interactions with various firm stakeholders' (Ballantyne and Aitken, 2007: 366).

Fournier (1998) was one of the first researchers to introduce and utilize relationship theory to understand the roles that brands play in the lives of consumers. She explored ideas about consumers who think about brands as if they were human characters—that is, the personification of brands. She also found that consumers accept attempts by marketers to personalize brands, for example through advertising, which suggests interaction and relationship potential. She identified six facets that characterize brand relationship quality: love and passion; a connection between the brand and self; a high degree of interdependence; a high level of commitment; intimacy; and a positive evaluation of brand quality.

Fournier (1998) believes that it is important to understand consumer–brand relationships and that, by understanding how consumers interact with brands and the meaning that brands represent to people through consumption, marketing theory and practice can be advanced. She argues that it is necessary to consider the broad context of consumers' lives to understand the role and relationship that brands play in them. In addition, meaningful consumer–brand relationships can be observed when the brand represents the key dimension, 'perceived ego significance' (Fournier, 1998: 366). Fournier stresses the importance of understanding what consumers do with brands that adds meaning to their lives (see Market Insight 6.2).

Market Insight 6.2 **Personal(ity) Branding**

The recent development of social media platforms has enabled two-way interactions between brands and their consumers. It is now possible for brands to ask questions to their audience and reply to their comments almost instantly and in an unmediated manner.

As it is now easier for consumers to develop close and personal relationships with their favourite brands, they can attribute humanlike characteristics to often impersonal brands, in a process referred to as 'brand anthropomorphism'. This has led marketers to focus on identifying and conveying real human traits such as honesty and integrity via their brand's social media pages. Other techniques include communicating in the first person, giving a nickname to the brand, or using personified profile pictures.

A prime example of building a humanlike brand on social media is Toronto-based mobile phone accessories creator dbrand. In 2019, the brand boasted more than 1.4 million followers on its Twitter account and about half that number on Instagram. The brand is also known for personalizing its products and packaging accompanied by handwritten notes to add a personal touch. dbrand also carries out special and sometimes unusual requests from customers to convey humour.

On social media, dbrand regularly addresses its followers in a provocative and often offensive way, either by promoting one of their products or reacting promptly to the posts and photos of their proud customers after receiving their orders. Ironically, dbrand pretends that the company and social media account are run by robots.

1 **How do dbrand's personalized deliveries contribute to the humanlike qualities that its customers attribute to the brand?**

2 **Why does the company communicate in a provocative and offensive manner?**

3 **Which aspects of Fournier's brand relationship quality are executed by dbrand?**

Sources: Hudson et al. (2016); https://twitter.com/dbrand; https://dbrand.com/

Research Insight 6.2

To take your learning further, you might wish to read this influential paper.

Fournier, S. (1998) 'Consumers and their brands: Developing relationship theory in consumer research', *Journal of Consumer Research*, 24(4), 343–73.

The article has already been characterized as a modem classic by Bengtsson (2003), such is its significance and contribution to our understanding about marketing and consumer research. The paper discusses the need to incorporate relationship marketing theory with branding and explores the types of relationship that people form with brands.

 Visit the **online resources** to read the abstract and access the full paper.

The managerial perspective assumes that manufacturers or service providers develop and manage brands, while individual consumers are passive and can influence only brand meaning or perception of a brand. This requires marketers to perform three essential branding activities, which Pennington and Ball (2009) suggest are to enable identification and differentiation, to maintain consistency, and to communicate the existence and attributes to customer and marketing channel audiences.

In recent years, this perspective and process has been challenged by increasing evidence that customers can create brands. In **customer branding**, customers attach a name, term, or other feature that enables them to identify one undifferentiated seller's goods or service as distinct from those of other sellers (Pennington and Ball, 2009: 455). This is commonly referred to as 'co-creation' and although many indicate that this is not a recent phenomenon, France et al. (2015: 6) point out that there is no exact understanding of the co-creation construct and that there is 'some confusion in the literature, especially in the area of brand co-creation and brand engagement'.

In conventional branding processes, a business is able to influence external stakeholders and customers, through promises of value creation, and internal stakeholders as a means of employee branding and organizational identity. Where there is customer branding, however, the organization surrenders control of the brand's ability to convey these and other clear messages to customers and employees (Pennington and Ball, 2009).

Pennington and Ball (2009) identify three key conditions that need to be met if customer branding is to occur: first, there must be a variety of offerings in the market; second, the delivery and quality of offerings must be unacceptable; and, third, customers must be able to obtain a reliable and satisfactory alternative from within the marketing channel. As they phrase it, 'for the customer to expend the effort to take over branding activities that the marketer is not performing, the customer must show certain needs, perceptions and abilities' (Pennington and Ball, 2009: 459).

In addition to customer branding, customers can co-create in different ways, most of which are rooted in brand value. France et al. (2015) refer to co-creation in the context of exchanges with and experiences of a brand, influencing customer perception of a brand, customer-generated advertising, new product development, social media, and word-of-mouth.

The development of the Web 2.0 has resulted in an increase in the number of 'working consumers' who help producers create new brands and shape existing ones (Gabriel and Lang, 2015: 210). For example, the online travel and accommodation platform CouchSurfing was principally developed by its members (both hosts and guests) to create authentic travelling experiences (Cova and White, 2010).

Ideas about brand co-creation are not confined to product or service offerings. For example, Juntunen (2012) found that a range of stakeholders, not only customers, are involved in corporate brand co-creation. These include employees, relatives, friends, university researchers, students, employees and managers of other companies, advertising agencies, financiers, lawyers, graphic designers, and customers. She revealed that stakeholders engage in various sub-processes of corporate brand co-creation, even before a company is formed (Kollmann and Suckow, 2007). These sub-processes include inventing the corporate name before a company is established, developing a new corporate name, updating the logo and communications material, and developing the proposition and the business after establishment of the company.

Global Branding

Brands can be considered in terms of the markets in which they operate, sometimes referred to as 'scope'. **Brand scope** can vary, spanning operating in local and domestic markets, operating in selected foreign markets, and operating across a range of international markets. Townsend et al. (2010) provide a useful typology of brands (see Table 6.1).

The scope, or reach, of a brand is a result of decisions to enter different geographic regions to achieve particular goals. As organizations extend their scope, so their branding and marketing strategies must adapt to influence local cultures and customer needs (see Market Insight 6.3).

Table 6.1 A hierarchy of brand scope

Brand scope	Criteria and characteristics	Examples
Domestic brand	A brand with a presence only in the home market and managed locally.	Thorntons (UK) Selver (Estonia) Panaché (France) Chufi (Spain)
International brand	Sold across a few country markets and managed largely by the home market, often using local agents in international markets. Positioning, identity, image, distinguishing characteristics including attributes, associations, and identifiers of the brand virtually identical to the home market.	Eddie Stobart Ideal Standard
Multi-domestic brand	Sold across multiple country markets and managed through decentralized management, with local control. Positioning, identity, image, distinguishing characteristics including attributes, associations, and identifiers of the brand varying across markets.	Caterpillar Diageo Ferrero GM Philips Samsung
Global brand	Sold across multiple country markets, with distribution located in three major developed continents. Centralized brand management coordinates local execution, but core essence of the brand remains unchanged. Positioning, identity, image, distinguishing characteristics including attributes, associations, and identifiers maintain a high degree of consistency across worldwide markets.	Apple Coca-Cola Google IBM McDonald's

Source: Adapted from Townsend, Cavusgil and Baba (2010).

Research Insight 6.3

To take your learning further, you might wish to read this influential paper.

Holt, D. B., Quelch, J. A., and Taylor, E. L. (2004) 'How global brands complete', *Harvard Business Review*, 82(9), 68–81.

This is an important paper that all those interested in global marketing and global brands should read. The authors review the ways in which global brands compete and reflect on the need for companies to manage their national identities, as well as their 'globalness'.

Visit the online resources to read the abstract and access the full paper.

However, global branding is characterized by a consistency of marketing strategies—a transfer of the same strategy across all markets, as practised by IBM, AT&T, and China Mobile.

Whatever the merits, the purity of the global brand concept has not been entirely realized, because issues of adaptation to local market needs, including social and cultural issues, have led to a need to achieve a balance between these two extremes. Coca-Cola, for example, adapts the taste of its products to meet the needs of local markets, even across Europe. So, because the consumption of different offerings naturally varies across countries (such as chocolate, milk, coffee, cars), it is unsurprising that we find manufacturers and producers varying their marketing strategies. What this means is that marketers need to determine which elements can be standardized (e.g. products, name, packaging, service) and which need to be adapted (typically, language, communications, and voiceovers) to meet local needs.

Measuring Brand Value: Brand Equity

Brand equity is a measure of the value and strength of a brand. It is an assessment of a brand's wealth, sometimes referred to as 'goodwill'. Financially, brands consist of their physical assets plus a sum that represents their reputation, or goodwill, with the latter far exceeding the former. So when Capri Holdings Limited, which owns Michael Kors and Jimmy Choo, paid £1.6 billion to buy the Italian luxury fashion brand Versace, it bought the physical assets and the reputation of Versace (Neate, 2018).

Brand equity is considered important because of the increasing interest in measuring the return on promotional investments and pressure by various stakeholders to value brands for balance-sheet purposes. A brand with a strong equity is more likely to be able to preserve its customer loyalty and to fend off competitor attacks (see Market Insight 6.4).

There are two main views about how brand equity should be valued, one from a financial and the other from a marketing perspective (Lasser et al., 1995). The financial view is founded on a consideration of a brand's asset value that is based on the net value of all of the cash the brand

Market Insight 6.3 Semi-globalization of Starbucks Coffee

The Chinese society and economy has been going through a period of great transformation since the early 1980s. Embarking upon former leader of the People's Republic of China Deng Xiaoping's open market reforms, the previously communist regime has turned China into a socialist market economy. Paced with unprecedented growth, it is considered today the largest economy by purchasing power.

Many Western global brands are increasingly interested and reliant upon China's growing middle-class consumption growth. Since the turn of the century, luxury, automobile, and technology brands have been fiercely competing to attract the attention of several Chinese market segments based on age, income, gender, and of course geographical location. Coffee brands constitute an excellent example of emerging brand propositions and market penetration. In particular, Starbucks has been one of the key protagonists in this story.

The Chinese market for coffee is expanding and the traditionally tea-drinking country is turning into the world's most promising market for international coffee chains. Driven by busier lifestyles and a youth culture, coffee is about to overtake tea as China's favourite drink of choice. Coffee Business Intelligence reports that coffee consumption in urban China has developed a growth rate of about 20 per cent over the last few years. Moreover, apart from the urban middle classes and young professionals, female Chinese consumers show a preference for drinking coffee in a relaxed environment. This desire is fulfilled by the thousands of new coffee shops across the country.

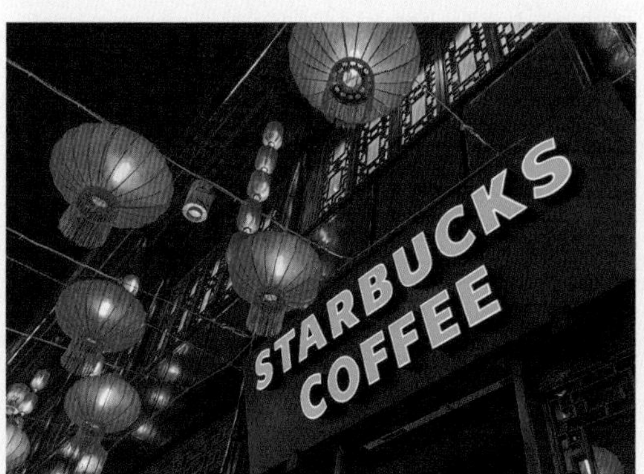

In China, Starbucks approaches consumers who enjoy a mix of global and local brands.

Source: © testing/Shutterstock.

Global coffee brands such as Starbucks approach Chinese consumers based on:

- a highly localized segment (rural areas in Central and Western China);
- a **semi-globalized segment** with a mix of global preferences (Dalian, Fuzhou, and Qingdao); and
- a highly globalized segment (Beijing and Shanghai).

The semi-globalized segment is characterized by consumers who embrace global branding practices but, at the same time, remain loyal to local products and services. It can be found in smaller Chinese cities and some rural areas. The growth of Starbucks in the country (3,500 stores as of 2019) shows that Western coffee brands have successfully penetrated both urban centres and parts of the traditionally tea-drinking central China.

1 **What do coffee companies need to take into consideration when positioning their brand in urban versus rural China?**

2 **Identify Chinese consumers' perceptions towards Fair Trade coffee. To what extent do Chinese consumers in the semi-globalized segment require more information about the nature of Fair Trade coffee?**

3 **How likely is it that Fair Trade coffee brands will manage to capture the attention of Chinese millennials in the next twenty years?**

Sources: Zakkour (2017); CoffeeBI (2019).

This market insight was kindly contributed by Dr Georgios Patsiaouras, Lecturer in Marketing and Consumption, School of Business, University of Leicester.

is expected to generate over its lifetime. The marketing perspective is grounded in the images, beliefs, and core associations that consumers have of and with particular brands, and the degree of loyalty or retention that a brand is able to sustain. Measures of market awareness, penetration, involvement, attitudes, and purchase intervals (frequency) are typical. Feldwick (1996), however, suggests that there are three parts associated with brand equity:

- brand value, based on a financial and accounting base;
- brand strength, measuring the strength of a consumer's attachment to a brand; and
- brand description, represented by the specific attitudes customers have towards a brand.

Market Insight 6.4 **Building a Responsible Brand: Nestlé's Case**

Nestlé is the largest multinational corporation (MNC) in the world in the food and beverage sector. Nestlé also has equally ambitious targets on sustainability and human rights. In particular, the multinational giant has an impressive policy on responsible sourcing, with commitments to working conditions of suppliers of an array of resources, including:

- fish and seafood, in relation to which Nestlé promises 'continuous improvement' on its traceability;
- coffee, in relation to which its Nescafé Plan has the concrete goal to 'source 100% of the coffee for Nespresso's permanent range through its AAA Sustainable Quality Program on coffee sourcing, and improve farmer social welfare'; and
- cocoa, in relation to which Nestlé aims to eliminate all forms of child labour from its supply chain.

To implement these polices and to meet its goals, Nestlé works with different non-governmental organizations (NGOs) and supplier auditor firms. However, during 2015 and 2016, Nestlé was accused by different human rights activist NGOs of sourcing cocoa from suppliers using child labour in the Ivory Coast, shrimp from suppliers using slaves in Thailand, and coffee from Brazilian plantations with forced labour.

In an innovative and bold manner, Nestlé responded to these claims by admitting that it did indeed have these issues in its supply chains, because these are systemic problems associated with political governance in many developing countries. Nestlé has claimed that it is impossible for any large company to eliminate these human rights abuses from its supply chain when sourcing cocoa from Ivory Coast, fish or seafood from Thailand, and coffee from Brazil.

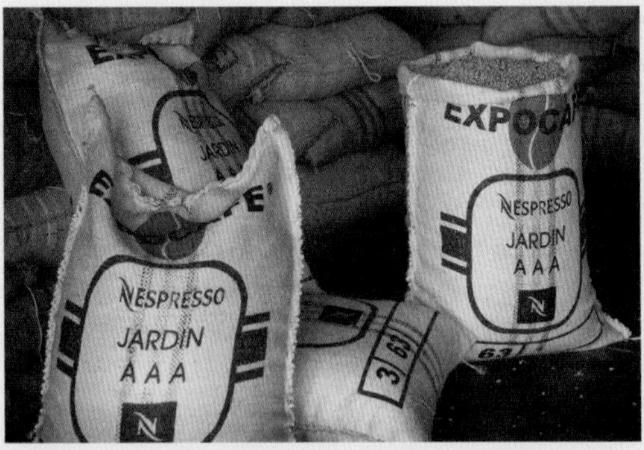

Retaining ethical standards across the supply chain can be very difficult as demonstrated by the challenges faced by Nestlé.
Source: Courtesy of Nespresso.

With regard to Brazil, but equally applicable to the difficulties involved in upholding human rights globally in a supply chain, Nestlé has said: 'Unfortunately, forced labour is an endemic problem in Brazil and no company sourcing coffee and other ingredients from the country can fully guarantee that it has completely removed forced labour practices or human rights abuses from its supply chain.'

1 **What do you think are the implications of Nestlé's statement for its branding strategy? What are the strengths and weaknesses of Nestlé's reaction?**

Market Insight 6.4 (continued)

2 Discuss how Nestlé can work with its local partners to try to live up fully to its ethical sourcing commitments.

3 What more can global corporations do to ensure that their marketing commitments on responsible sourcing are consistent with their practices?

Sources: Perego and Kolk (2012); Rodríguez-Garavito (2015); Hodal (2016); Nespresso (n.d.).

The market insight has been kindly contributed by Dr Rajiv Maher, postdoctoral researcher at the Pontifical Catholic University of Chile.

Chapter Summary

To consolidate your learning, the key points from this chapter are summarized below.

- **Explain the different levels of a proposition and the product life cycle.**

Propositions encompass three levels, including: the *core* proposition, consisting of the real core benefit or service (e.g. bottled water is thirst-quenching); the *embodied* proposition, consisting of the physical good or delivered service that provides the expected benefit (e.g. the packaging); and the *augmented* proposition, consisting of the embodied offering plus all those other factors that are necessary to support the purchase and any post-purchase activities. Propositions are thought to move through a sequential pattern of development, referred to as the 'product life cycle'. It consists of five distinct stages—namely, development, birth, growth, maturity, and decline. Each stage of the cycle represents a different set of market circumstances and customer expectations that need to be met with different strategies.

- **Explore the processes associated with innovating new propositions and how propositions are adopted.**

The development of new propositions is complex and high risk, so organizations usually adopt a procedural approach. The procedure consists of several phases. The process by which individuals accept and use new propositions is referred to as 'adoption' (Rogers, 1983). The different stages in the adoption process are sequential and are characterized by the different factors that are involved at each stage. The rate at which a market adopts an innovation differs according to an individual's propensity for risk and is referred to as the 'process of diffusion' (Rogers, 1962).

- **Explain the characteristics and principal types of brand and branding.**

Brands are products and services that have added value. Brands help customers to differentiate between the various offerings and to associate certain attributes or feelings with a particular brand. Brands are capable of triggering associations in the minds of consumers. These associations may sometimes enable consumers to construe a psychosocial meaning associated with a particular brand. This psychosocial element can be measured in terms of the associations consumers make along five key dimensions: sincerity, excitement, competence, sophistication, and ruggedness. Brand personality provides a form of identity for consumers that expresses symbolic meaning for themselves and for others.

- **Explain how brands can be built.**

Keller's (2009) brand pyramid consists of several building blocks and posits that brands are built through a series of steps. The first aims to enable customers to identify with the brand and help them to make associations with a specific product class or customer need. The second aims to establish what the brand means by linking various tangible and intangible brand associations. The third step encourages customer responses based around brand-related judgements and feelings. The final step is about fostering an active relationship between customers and the brand.

Review Questions

1. **Identify the three levels that make up a proposition.**
2. **Describe the four types of good by behavioural category and find examples to illustrate each one.**
3. **What is the product life cycle and what key characteristics make up each of its stages?**
4. **What are the main stages associated with the development of new product propositions?**
5. **Why is knowledge about the process of adoption useful to marketers?**
6. **Why is branding important to consumers and to organizations?**
7. **Why is it necessary to consider the broad context of consumers' lives to understand the role and relationship that brands play in them?**
8. **What are Aaker's (1997) five dimensions of psychosocial meaning?**
9. **Draw Keller's (2009) brand pyramid and label the individual building blocks.**
10. **Write brief notes explaining the two main views about brand equity.**

Worksheet Summary

To apply the knowledge you have gained from this chapter, and to test your understanding of branding insight, visit the **online resources** and complete Worksheet 6.1.

Discussion Questions

1. Having read Case Insight 6.1, how would you advise Micro-Fresh on developing its branding and product development activities in the midst of the Covid-19 pandemic?

2. Prepare a brief report in which you explain the nature of the product life cycle for a grocery brand of your choice. Consider how it might be used to improve your chosen brand's marketing activities and, from this, highlight any difficulties that might arise when using the product life cycle to develop strategies.

3 In 2018, IKEA launched its co-creation programme to work closely with customers to generate new product ideas. What are the benefits of this initiative for IKEA and how could it build on these new products to reinforce its mission of 'putting people first'?

4 When Ingrid Stevenson was appointed brand manager for a range of well-established fruit juices, one of her first tasks was to understand the market and how consumers related to the brand. How might an understanding of Aaker's (1997) brand personality scale help her in this task?

 Visit the **online resources** and complete the multiple-choice questions to assess your knowledge of the chapter.

Glossary

brand multidimensional and emotional construct that people use to embrace an abstract object or a set of associations.

brand associations the physical and non-physical product attributes and benefits aligned with attitudes that consumers use to create an image of a brand.

brand equity a measure of the value and strength of a brand. It is an assessment of a brand's wealth, sometimes referred to as 'goodwill'.

brand personalities the associations and images that enable consumers to construe a psychosocial meaning associated with a particular brand.

brand personality scale a framework of dimensions used to measure brand personality, developed by Aaker (1997).

brand positioning a strategic activity used to differentiate and distinguish a brand.

brand scope the range of international markets in which a brand operates.

C2C marketing consumer-to-consumer marketing, for example, through product reviews, social media comments, online direct messaging.

convenience products non-durable goods or services, often bought with little pre-purchase thought or consideration.

customer branding the name, term, or other feature devised by customers that enables them to identify otherwise undifferentiated or unbranded products.

distributors organizations that buy goods and services, often from a limited range of manufacturers, and normally sell them to retailers or resellers.

durable goods those bought infrequently, which are used repeatedly and which involve a reasonably high level of consumer risk.

early adopters a group of people in the process of diffusion who enjoy being at the leading edge of innovation and buy into new products at an early stage.

early majority a group of people in the process of diffusion who require reassurance that a product works and has been proven in the market before they are prepared to buy it.

extensive problem-solving occurs when consumers give a great deal of attention and care to a purchase decision, in circumstances in which there is no previous or similar product purchase experience.

influentials people who have the ability to persuade others to think, believe, or behave in a certain way.

innovators a group of people in the process of diffusion who like new ideas and who are most likely to take risks associated with new products.

laggards a group of people in the process of diffusion who are suspicious of all new ideas and whose opinions are very hard to change.

late majority a group of people in the process of diffusion who are sceptical of new ideas and adopt new products only because of social or economic factors.

limited problem-solving occurs when consumers have some product and purchase familiarity.

non-durable goods low-priced products that are bought frequently, used only once, and incur low levels of purchase risk.

process of adoption the process through which individuals accept and use new products. The different stages in the adoption process are sequential and each is characterized by different factors.

process of diffusion the rate at which a market adopts an innovation.

product anything that is capable of satisfying customer needs.

product life cycle the pathway that a product assumes over its lifetime, in which there are said to be five main stages: development, introduction, growth, maturity, and decline.

proposition a product or service that represents a promise made to customers and stakeholders.

routinized response behaviour a form of purchase behaviour that occurs when consumers have suitable product and purchasing experience and they perceive low risk.

semi-globalized segment a consumer segment that embraces global branding practices, yet remains loyal to local products and services.

shopping product a type of consumer product that is bought relatively infrequently and requires consumers to update their knowledge prior to purchase.

specialty product a type of consumer product that is bought very infrequently, is very expensive, and represents very high risk.

test marketing a stage in the new product development process, undertaken when a new product is tested with a sample of customers or is launched in a specified geographical area, to judge customers' reactions prior to a national launch.

umbrella brand a type of branding in which a unique brand name is used for several products to portray a sense of uniformity to consumers.

value-in-use what benefits the customer gets from actually using the product or service.

References

Aaker, D. A. (1991) *Managing Brand Equity*, New York: The Free Press.

Aaker, D. A. (2014) *Aaker on Branding*, New York: Morgan James.

Aaker, J. (1997) 'Dimensions of brand personality', *Journal of Marketing Research*, 34(3), 347–56.

Achenbaum, A. A. (1993) 'The mismanagement of brand equity'. Presented at: ARF Fifth Annual Advertising and Promotion Workshop, 1 February, New York.

Arora, R., and Stoner, C. (2009) 'A mixed method approach to understanding brand personality'. *Journal of Product & Brand Management*, 18(4), 272–83.

Ballantyne, D., and Aitken, R. (2007) 'Branding in B2B markets: The service-dominant logic'. *Journal of Business & Industrial Marketing*, 22(6), 363–71.

Belk, R. (1988) 'Possessions and the extended self', *Journal of Consumer Research*, 15(2), 139–68.

Bengtsson, A. (2003) 'Towards a critique of brand relationships', *Advances in Consumer Research*, 30(1), 154–8.

Boström, M., Micheletti, M., and Oosterveer, P. (2019) *The Oxford Handbook of Political Consumerism*, Oxford: Oxford University Press.

Chang, Y. T., Yu, H., and Lu, H. P. (2015) 'Persuasive messages, popularity cohesion, and message diffusion in social media marketing', *Journal of Business Research*, 68(4), 777–82.

Christodoulides, G. (2009) 'Branding in the post-Internet era', *Marketing Theory*, 9(1), 141–4.

Clayton, M., and Heo, J. (2011) 'Effects of promotional-based advertising on brand associations', *Journal of Product & Brand Management*, 20(4), 309–15.

CoffeeBI (2019) 'China, 7 reasons why coffee consumption is growing', *Coffee Business Intelligence*, 11 February. Retrieve from: https://coffeebi.com/2019/02/11/china-7-reasons-of-coffee-consumption-grow/#:~:text=%20Here%20below%20some%20reasons%3A%20%201%20Coffee,%E2%80%9Cenvironment%E2%80%9D%20and%20%E2%80%9Cservice%E2%80%9D%20targeted%20on%20Chinese...%20More (accessed 30 October 2020).

Cova, B., and White, T. (2010) 'Counter-brand and alter-brand communities: The impact of Web 2.0 on tribal marketing approaches', *Journal of Marketing Management*, 26(3–4), 256–70.

Drucker, P. F. (1985) 'The discipline of innovation', *Harvard Business Review*, 63(3), 67–72.

Eads, L. (2015) 'UK cider market suffers £35m loss', *Drink Business*, 2 October. Retrieve from: https://www.thedrinksbusiness.com/2015/10/uk-off-trade-cider-market-suffers-35m-loss/ (accessed 30 October 2020).

Feldwick, P. (1996) 'What is brand equity anyway, and how do you measure it?', *Journal of Marketing Research*, 38(2), 85–104.

Fill, C., and Turnbull, S. (2016) *Marketing Communications: Discovery, Creation, and Conversations* (7th edn), London: Pearson Education.

Forbes, S. (2018) 'Weston's cider report 2018: Time to refresh your approach to cider'. *Imbibe*, 1 May, Retrieve from: https://imbibe.com/news/westons-cider-report-2018 (accessed 30 October 2020).

Fournier, S. (1998) 'Consumers and their brands: Developing relationship theory in consumer research', *Journal of Consumer Research*, 24(4), 343–73.

France, C., Merrilees, B., and Miller, D. (2015) 'Customer brand co-creation: A conceptual model', *Marketing Intelligence & Planning*, 33(6), 848–64.

Friedlander, J. P. (2019) 'Mid-year 2019 RIAA music revenues report'. Retrieve from: https://www.riaa.com/wp-content/uploads/2019/09/Mid-Year-2019-RIAA-Music-Revenues-Report.pdf (accessed 30 October 2020).

Gabriel, Y., and Lang, T. (2015) *The Unmanageable Consumer*, London: SAGE Publications.

Ghosh, S. (2015) 'Sainsbury's trials connected kitchens to understand "promiscuous" shoppers', *Campaign*, 11 May. Retrieve from: http://www.campaignlive.co.uk/article/1346564/sainsburys-trials-connected-kitchens-understand-promiscuous-shoppers (accessed 19 December 2019).

Gómez Aguilar, A., Yagüe Guillén, M. J., and Villaseñor Roman, N. (2016) 'Destination brand personality: An application to Spanish tourism', *International Journal of Tourism Research*, 18(3), 210–19.

Govindarajan, V., and Srinivas, S. (2013) 'The innovation mindset in action: 3M Corporation', *Harvard Business Review*, 6 August. Retrieve from: https://hbr.org/2013/08/the-innovation-mindset-in-acti-3 (accessed 19 December 2019).

Griffin, A., and Page, A. L. (1993) 'An interim report on measuring product development success and failure', *Journal of Product Innovation Management*, 10(4), 291–308.

Hodal, K. (2016) 'Nestlé admits slave labour risk on Brazil coffee plantations', *The Guardian*, 2 March. Retrieve from: https://www.theguardian.com/global-development/2016/mar/02/nestle-admits-slave-labour-risk-on-brazil-coffee-plantations (accessed 30 October 2020).

Holt, D. B., Quelch, J. A., and Taylor, E. L. (2004) 'How global brands compete', *Harvard Business Review*, 82(9), 68–81.

Hudson, S., Huang, L., Roth, M. S., and Madden, T. J. (2016) 'The influence of social media interactions on consumer–brand relationships: A three-country study of brand perceptions and marketing behaviors', *International Journal of Research in Marketing*, 33(1), 27–41.

Institute of Brilliant Failures (n.d.) 'Buckler beer on the Dutch market'. Retrieve from: http://www.briljantemislukkingen.nl/EN/failures/submit-reaction/buckler-beer-on-the-dutch-market/ (accessed 19 December 2019).

Juntunen, M. (2012) 'Co-creating corporate brands in start-ups', *Marketing Intelligence & Planning*, 30(2), 230–49.

Keller, K. L. (1993) 'Conceptualizing, measuring, and managing customer-based brand equity', *Journal of Marketing*, 57(1), 1–22.

Keller, K. L. (1998) *Strategic Brand Management: Building, Measuring, and Managing Brand Equity*, Upper Saddle River, NJ: Prentice-Hall.

Keller, K. L. (2009) 'Building strong brands in a modern marketing communications environment', *Journal of Marketing Communications*, 15(2–3), 139–55.

Kollmann, T., and Suckow, C. (2007) 'The corporate brand naming process in the net economy', *Qualitative Market Research: An International Journal*, 10(4), 349–61.

Lasser, W., Mittal, B., and Sharma, A. (1995) 'Measuring customer based brand equity', *Journal of Consumer Marketing*, 12(4), 11–19.

Linville, P., and Carlston, D. E. (1994) 'Social cognition of the self', in P. G. Devine, D. L. Hamilton, and T. M. Ostrom (eds), *Social Cognition: Impact on Social Psychology*, San Diego, CA: Academic Press, 143–93.

Low, G. S., and Lamb, C. W. (2000) 'The measurement and dimensionality of brand associations', *Journal of Product and Brand Management*, 9(6), 350–368.

Neate, R. (2018) 'Michael Kors buys Versace in $2.1bn deal', *The Guardian*, 25 September. Retrieve from: https://www.theguardian.com/fashion/2018/sep/25/michael-kors-buys-versace-capri-donatella (accessed 19 December 2019).

Nespresso (n.d.) 'The Positive Cup'. Retrieve from: https://sustainability.nespresso.com/the-positive-cup (accessed 30 October 2020).

Pennington, J. R., and Ball, D. A. (2009) 'Customer branding of commodity products: The customer-developed brand', *Brand Management*, 16(7), 455–67.

Perego, P., and Kolk, A. (2012) 'Multinationals' accountability on sustainability: The evolution of third-party assurance of sustainability reports', *Journal of Business Ethics*, 110(2), 173–90.

Phau, I., and Lau, K. C. (2001) 'Brand personality and consumer self-expression: Single or dual carriageway?', *Journal of Brand Management*, 8(6), 428–44.

Rodríguez-Garavito, C. A. (2005) 'Global governance and labor rights: Codes of conduct and anti-sweatshop struggles in global apparel factories in Mexico and Guatemala', *Politics & Society*, 33(2), 203–333.

Rogers, E. M. (1962) *Diffusion of Innovations*, New York: Free Press.

Rogers, E. M. (1983) *Diffusion of Innovations* (3rd edn), New York: Free Press.

Smith, B. (2018) 'Project Strobe: Protecting your data, improving our third-party APIs, and sunsetting consumer Google+'. 8 October. Retrieve from: https://www.blog.google/technology/safety-security/project-strobe/ (accessed 30 October 2020).

Stock, K. (2018) 'The strange, ugly car that everyone wants', *Bloomberg*, 26 January. Retrieve from: https://www.bloomberg.com/news/articles/2018-01-26/theweird-nissan-murano-crosscabriolet-is-still-in-highdemand (accessed 30 October 2020).

Torrance, J. (2014) 'How Kopparberg use hipsters to take the UK market by stealth', *Real Business*, 10 February. Retrieve from: https://realbusiness.co.uk/how-kopparberg-used-hipsters-to-take-the-uk-market-by-stealth/ (accessed 30 October 2020).

Townsend, J. D., Cavusgil, S. T., and Baba, M. L. (2010) 'Global integration of brands and new product development at General Motors', *Journal of Product Innovation Management*, 27(1), 49–65.

Trott, D. (2016) 'A view from Dave Trott: Fear-free marketing', *Campaign*, 2 June. Retrieve from: https://www.campaignlive.co.uk/article/view-dave-trott-fear-free-marketing/1396946 (accessed 30 October 2020).

Tudor, E., and Negricea, I. C. (2012) 'Brand positioning: A marketing resource and an effective tool for small and medium enterprises', *Journal of Knowledge Management, Economics and Information Technology*, 11(1), 182–90.

Zakkour, M. (2017) 'Why Starbucks succeeded inChina: A lesson for all retailers', *Forbes*, 24 August. Retrieve from: https://www.forbes.com/sites/michaelzakkour/2017/08/24/why-starbucks-succeeded-in-china-a-lesson-for-all-retailers/ (accessed 30 October 2020).

Chapter 7
Pricing and Value Creation

Learning Outcomes

After studying this chapter, you will be able to:

- explain the concept of price elasticity of demand;
- describe how customers perceive price;
- understand pricing strategies and how to price new offerings;
- explain cost-, competitor-, demand-, and value-oriented approaches to pricing; and
- explain how pricing operates in the business-to-business (B2B) setting.

Case Insight 7.1
Ammon Zeus

Market Insight 7.1
Forking Out for Organic Foods

Market Insight 7.2
Is the Price Right?

Market Insight 7.3
Unbeatable Prices at Carrefour

Market Insight 7.4
Everlane: Pricing for Ethics

Case Insight 7.1 **Ammon Zeus**

Ammon Zeus is a leading luxury hotel in Halkidiki, the popular tourist destination, in northern Greece. We speak to Efrosini Psychopoulou, its vice president, to find out more about how the company sought to develop its value proposition.

Built during the 1960s, the Ammon Zeus Hotel was among the very first hotels to begin operating in the now famous Halkidiki. The land on which the hotel sits was originally owned by Mount Athos, an autonomous polity within the Greek Republic. At the time, it was serving as the Russian Monastery of St Panteleimon. You can still see the remains of the homonymous chapel as well as a medieval-style wall that have stood since 1860. During the excavation for the hotel, the owners stumbled upon what came to be one of the most important antique monuments in northern Greece—the remains of the Temple of Ammon Zeus, built during the 4th century BC. This was the inspiration for the hotel's illustrious name. Our management style is to flatter the customer, compared with other luxury seasonal hotels. We encourage our people to take the initiative towards meeting a common goal. We also encourage collaboration and the openness of ideas. We want every visitor to feel at home, in luxury.

Our client base has an 'affordable luxury vacation' profile. We serve people seeking a unique luxurious destination and one that values their privacy. The most common type of visitors are entrepreneurs, politicians, families, and young and older couples. Our customers seek a unique location (we are just a few metres from the sea), comfortable facilities, plenty of amenities, high-quality and fresh food, as well as personalized service. Consequently, the value proposition of the hotel is personalized luxury. We believe that luxury goes beyond the top-notch facilities, flamboyant food, and the amazing location we offer. Our staff are dedicated to ensuring that customers staying at Ammon Zeus can focus on enjoying their holiday, without having to make their own plans.

Our customers had tended to come through to us via two main channels: 70 per cent came through tour operators and 30 per cent came as individuals booking directly via the Internet. Tour operators, however, tend to bring in mostly price-sensitive customers via limited promotions, mainly via through brochures and websites. We felt it was time to 'fish' for our own customers. We wanted to bring in customers who were prepared to pay a higher price, recognizing that they would be more demanding in what customer service and facilities they wanted to receive. Since Halkidiki is not well known for high-budget tourists, unlike Mykonos or Santorini, and not promoted as much by the tour operators, or Greek tourism promotion organizations, as Crete and Rhodes, it was a real bet as to whether we could manage to attract high-value clients.

The dilemma of our business plan was: should we undertake a high-quality renovation to attract those guests wishing to spend more and implement a large increase in our prices, or should we initiate a more limited renovation with a smaller increase in prices?

Introduction

How do companies set **prices**? What procedures do they use? How do customers perceive prices for different products and services? How do companies determine their prices? These are some of the questions we set out to consider in this chapter.

Our understanding of pricing and costing has developed from accounting practice. Economics has also contributed to our understanding of pricing through models of supply and demand, operating at an aggregate level (i.e. across all customers in an industry). Psychology contributes greatly to our understanding of customers' perceptions of prices. Marketing, as a field, integrates all of these components to provide a better understanding of how the firm sets price to achieve higher profits and maintain satisfied customers. Pricing is the most difficult aspect of the marketing mix to comprehend, because an offering's price is linked to the cost of the many different components that make up a particular proposition. The marketing manager rarely controls costs and prices of a particular offering, and usually refers to the accounting and finance department, or the marketing/financial controller, to set prices.

In this chapter, we provide insight into how customers respond to price changes. We define price, quality, costs, and value, and outline the relationship between them. We provide insights into how customers perceive and learn about prices—a necessary step prior to evaluating them and their fairness, which impacts on customers' willingness to pay. We describe the four main approaches to pricing, based on evaluating costs and adding a margin, copying competitors' prices, basing prices on demand, and pricing according to perceived customer value. We also consider the two principal means by which to price a new proposition—that is, skim and market penetration pricing. Finally, we consider what pricing tactics are used in the business-to-business (B2B) setting.

Price Elasticity of Demand

The concept of '**price elasticity** of demand' was first developed in the field of economics. It grants us an insight into how demand shifts with changes in price. Such information is useful, but the data needed to determine price elasticities require detailed research of price and quantity changes over time. Price elasticity is affected by both brand and category characteristics, as well as general economic conditions, including such factors as time, product category, brand (manufacturer versus own-label), stage of product life cycle, country, household disposable income, and inflation rates (Bijmolt et al., 2005).

In some categories, for example cigarettes but not washing powder, changes in price (whether positive or negative) lead to smaller changes in demand. For instance, a 10 per cent increase in cigarette prices might lead to only a 2 per cent decrease in quantity sold, while a 10 per cent increase in washing powder prices might lead to a 20 per cent decrease in sales. In this case, we say that washing powder is the more 'price elastic' offering. We define 'price elasticity' as the percentage change in quantity demanded as a proportion of the percentage change in price. Mathematically, this is displayed as:

$$\textit{Price elasticity of demand} = \eta \text{ (Pronounced } \textit{eta}) = \frac{\text{Precentage change in quantity demanded}}{\text{Percentage change in price}} \quad (1)$$

When the price of an offering rises or falls, the quantity demanded falls or rises. When the percentage change in price is positive (negative), the percentage change in quantity demanded is negative (positive). Consequently, the price elasticity of demand is always negative. The price elasticity of demand for most marketed goods is somewhere between –9 and –1. In a meta-analysis of a set of 1,851 price elasticities, based on 81 studies, the average price elasticity was found to be –2.62 (Bijmolt et al., 2005). In other words, for these goods (including **consumer durables** and other types of product), a 10 per cent increase in price would produce an average 26.2 per cent decrease in quantity demanded. This, however, is an average across offerings. Individual products and services can vary greatly from this average.

Generally, we can refer to three main extremes of price elasticity, as follows.

1. ***Unit price elasticity of demand*** ($\eta = 1$)—For example, a 10 per cent increase (decrease) in price produces a 10 per cent decrease (increase) in quantity demanded.
2. ***Zero price elasticity of demand*** ($\eta = 0$)—In this situation, any change in price, either positive or negative, has absolutely no, or only an infinitesimal, impact on quantity sold. Such a situation is highly unlikely ever to occur.
3. ***Infinite (or perfect) price elasticity of demand*** ($\eta = \infty$)—In this case, a decrease in price causes an infinite increase in demand, whereas a price increase causes demand to fall to zero. This situation is also highly unlikely to occur.

Governments use price elasticity data to determine which offerings to tax. For example, petrol and tobacco have tended to be taxed because increases in prices resulting from tax increases have a lesser impact on quantity supplied compared to other offerings. Marketing managers should seek to understand whether or not their offerings are price elastic or inelastic, because this allows them to predict how price changes will affect the total quantity supplied in the market (see Market Insight 7.1 for discussion of the price elasticity of demand for organic products).

Market Insight 7.1 **Forking Out for Organic Foods**

Recent trends in sustainable and environment-friendly consumption have boosted the sales of organic foods in high-income countries. In 2019, the UK Soil Association reported that the organic food market had developed for the eighth year in a row and will be worth £2.5 billion by 2020. In Denmark, 13.3 per cent of all food sales are now organic. This is also emphasized by the multiplication of new box subscription schemes and home delivery platforms such as Ocado that propose a large range of organic products.

Although the prices of organic products have decreased in recent years, a price gap still exists between non-organic and organic products. This can be explained by the more expensive process involved with managing organic crops, the small scale of the associated supply chain, and the limited availability of organic bulk offers in supermarkets.

The price of organic products has been reported as the main barrier to wider consumption. Whereas regular consumers perceive the health

Market Insight 7.1 (continued)

and sustainability benefits, other consumers refer to the high price tag of organics to justify their existing groceries habits. However, the adoption of organic products also depends on non-economic factors such as education level and the number of young children in the household. Even though non-organic consumers tend to overestimate the price difference of organic products such as fish, meat, and milk, regular consumers are keen to pay a 30 per cent premium for organic products and even more for non-essential items such as wine.

Consumers are not sensitive to price variations of organic produce.

Sources: © indukas/Shutterstock.

Overall, the price elasticity of demand for organics is low (between −0.46 and −1.43 for most products and close to zero for rice, milk, and cereal). This can be explained by the fact that most consumers regularly purchase the same groceries out of habit and are not made aware of price reductions by supermarkets and independent farm shops. Consumers are also less likely to start purchasing organic products in food categories already driven by price promotions.

1 **Do you think that the decreasing price of organic products will eventually lead to their wider adoption by consumers?**

2 **Visit the website of your preferred supermarkets. How are organic products differentiated from non-organic products?**

3 **How could the UK Soil Association further promote organic foods to increase their adoption by non-organic consumers?**

Sources: Bunte et al. (2010); Doward (2017); Aschemann-Witzel and Zielke (2017); Soil Association (2019).

The Concept of Pricing and Cost

Pricing

The term 'price' has come to encompass:

> *noun.* the amount of money expected, required, or given in payment for something; an unwelcome experience or action undergone or done as a condition of achieving an objective.
>
> *verb.* to decide the amount required as payment for (something offered for sale); discover or establish the price of (something for sale).
>
> (Lexico, 2019)

In marketing terms, we consider price to be the amount the customer has to pay or exchange to receive an offering. For example, when purchasing a classic super club sandwich from Pret A Manger, the price exchanged for it might be, say, €5.50 in France or £3.99 in the UK. The £3.99

element is the price—that is, the assigned numerical monetary worth of the sandwich in the UK. However, the notion of pricing an offering is often confused with a number of other key marketing concepts—particularly cost and value.

Proposition Costs

To price properly, we need to know what the offering costs us to make, produce, or buy. Cost represents the total money, time, and resources sacrificed to produce or acquire an offering. For example, the costs incurred to produce the Pret A Manger classic super club sandwich includes the cost of heat and light in the shop, advertising and sales promotion costs, costs of rent or of the mortgage interest accrued from owning the shop, management and staffing costs, taxes, and the franchise fees paid to Pret's central headquarters to cover training, management, and marketing. There are additionally costs associated with the distribution of the product **components** to and from farms and other catering suppliers to the restaurants. There are also the costs to acquire and maintain computer and purchasing systems, and the costs of the packaging, napkins, cutlery, and so on.

Typically, a firm determines what its fixed costs are and what its variable costs are for each proposition. These items vary for individual industries. Fixed costs do not vary according to the number of units of goods made or services sold and are independent of sales volume. In a Pret A Manger shop, fixed costs are the costs of heating and lighting, rent, and staffing. In contrast, variable costs vary according to the number of units of goods made or services sold. For example, with the production of Pret A Manger food and drink, when sales and demand decrease, fewer raw goods, such as salad ingredients, product packaging, and accompanying items such as cutlery and napkins are required, so less spending on raw materials is necessary. Conversely, when sales increase, more raw materials are used and spending rises.

The Relationship between Pricing and Proposition Costs

The relationship between price and costs is important, because costs should be substantially less than the price assigned to a proposition; otherwise, the firm will not sell sufficient units to obtain sufficient revenues to cover costs and make long-term profits (see Equations (2) and (3)):

$$\textit{Total revenue} = \text{Volume sold} \times \text{Unit price} \tag{2}$$

$$\textit{Profit} = \text{Total revenue} - \text{Total costs} \tag{3}$$

The price at which a proposition is set is important, because increases in price have a disproportionately positive effect on profits and decreases in price have a disproportionately negative effect on profits. For example, in one study (Baker et al., 2010: 5), it was identified that:

- a 1 per cent improvement in price achieves an 8.7 per cent improvement in operating profit;
- a 1 per cent improvement in variable costs achieves only a 5.9 per cent improvement in operating profit;
- a 1 per cent improvement in volume sales achieves a 2.8 per cent improvement in operating profit; and
- a 1 per cent improvement in fixed costs achieves only a 1.8 per cent improvement in operating profits.

Until recently, organizations have had fairly rudimentary methods of assessing the effectiveness of their pricing decisions, but changes in computing power and the availability of data now allow companies to simulate thousands of 'what if?' pricing scenarios to predict likely demand and profit levels (Michard, 2016). Whenever possible, we should therefore aim to increase prices.

Customer Perceptions of Price, Quality, and Value

Marketers are concerned with how individuals react to the way in which offerings are priced, questioning how consumers perceive prices and why they perceive them as they do. Here, we consider individual perceptions of proposition quality and value, and their relationship to customer response to prices.

Proposition Quality

Quality is important in setting proposition pricing levels. 'Quality' is defined as 'the standard of something as measured against other things of a similar kind; the degree of excellence of something; a distinctive attribute or characteristic possessed by someone or something' (Lexico, 2019). In this context, the quality of goods and services relates to standards to which that offering performs as a need satisfier. For example, a very high-quality car (such as the Porsche Panamera or even the Lamborghini Huracán) will satisfy both our aesthetic needs for aerodynamic beauty and our ego, and functional needs for high-performance road-handling, speed, and power.

Expensive cars are not necessarily of better quality. Quality, much like beauty, is in the eye of the beholder.
Source: © Stefan Ataman/Shutterstock.

Quality is multifaceted (i.e. comprising different functional and non-functional needs) and multilayered (i.e. comprising degrees of satisfaction). Because people all have their own definitions of quality, we prefer to talk of **perceived quality**: one person might be very dissatisfied and another highly satisfied with the same offering.

The Relationship between Quality and Pricing Levels

There is an assumption that as price increases, so does quality and that, in general, price reflects quality. However, research has demonstrated that there is only a weak relationship between price and perceived quality, although this is category-dependent (Gerstner, 1985). The idea that price indicates quality (perceived quality) assumes that prices are objectively determined by market forces. In truth, people within firms set prices, often dispassionately, to try to obtain the maximum profit possible. Völckner and Hofmann (2007) gathered data from multiple studies on the degree to which price is seen to reflect quality, suggesting there are several potential determinants. They propose that familiarity with products, as well as the type of good (e.g. durable, fast-moving consumer goods or services) and country, each impact the price-perceived quality effect size.

The Relationship between Perceived Value, Product Quality, and Pricing Levels

'**Value**' is defined as:

> the regard that something is held to deserve; importance, worth, or usefulness of something; principles or standards of behaviour; one's judgement of what is important in life; the numerical amount denoted by an algebraic term; a magnitude, quantity, or number.
>
> (Lexico, 2019)

In marketing terms, value refers to the quality of what we get for what we pay. Leszinski and Marn (1997), consultants at McKinsey, suggest Equation (4) to calculate the value to the customer:

$$\textit{Value} = \text{Perceived benefits} - \text{Perceived price} \tag{4}$$

In this equation, the customer perceives positive value if the perceived benefits (a proxy for quality) outweigh the price paid for those benefits. Usefully, if the price paid is zero (i.e. if an item is given away), the value to the customer is the value of the perceived benefits (which makes sense), and if there are no benefits, the value is the negative value of the price paid. When the benefits of an offering are reduced, the value is also seen to be reduced if customers notice the difference in offerings. An example of this occurred when British confectionery company Cadbury reduced the number of chocolate fingers in its traditional pack from 24, weighing 125 g, to 22, weighing 114 g, with an increase in price from around £1.19 in 2014 to around £1.43 in 2015 (Hayward, 2015), changing the cost of each chocolate finger from 4.96 pence to 6.5 pence (for a marginally lighter chocolate finger at 5.18 g compared to 5.21 g).

Influences on Customer Price Perceptions

A Framework for Price Perception Formation

How we perceive prices as customers can be summarized in a theoretical framework (see Figure 7.1). Here, price perceptions are based on a variety of antecedents. Once we see a price, we make a judgement. This judgement is a newly formed price perception, which affects our willingness to pay, in turn affecting our purchase behaviour. Price perceptions are affected by prior beliefs, prior knowledge of **reference prices**, prior experiences with the offering or brand under consideration, price consciousness (i.e. how aware we are of prices), our own price sensitivities (how much extra we are prepared to pay for something), customer characteristics, and cultural factors. We compare the price we see with internal reference prices (price knowledge gained from experience) and external reference prices (what others tell us prices should be, perhaps in the form of price comparison websites). Reference prices are price bands against which customers judge the purchase price of offerings (see Market Insight 7.2). Reference prices can be viewed as predictive price expectations based on prior experience with those offerings or gained through word-of-mouth.

Price perception formation is influenced by exposure to reference prices (internal and external), quality perceptions, brand awareness, brand loyalty, product familiarity, memory of prices (paid previously and seen previously), and asymmetries of information (the extent to which

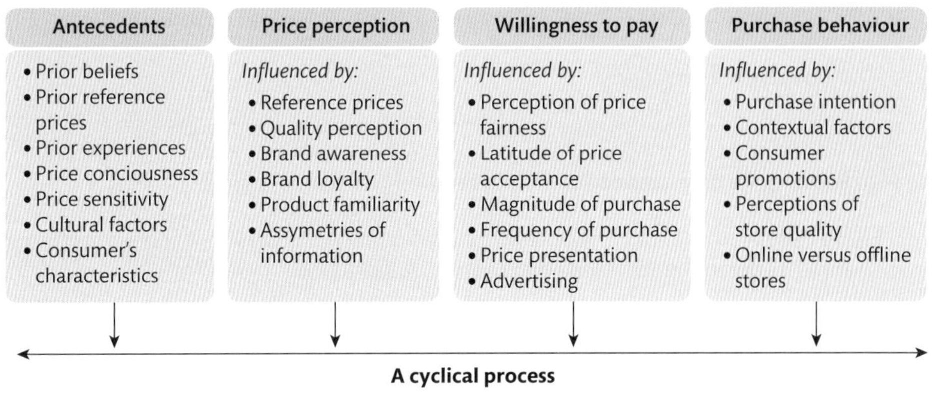

Figure 7.1 A framework for price perception formation

Source: Mendoza and Baines (2012).

customers do not know various factors about those offerings). Price perceptions affect customers' willingness to pay. Willingness to pay is influenced by perceptions of the fairness of prices set, latitude of price acceptance (customers appear willing to accept a price within a range of prices, suggesting a 'price zone of tolerance'), magnitude (absolute price) and frequency of purchase, price presentation (how prices are presented might produce different levels of willingness to pay), and advertising.

Actual purchase behaviour is influenced by purchase intention, contextual factors (such as store format, location, timing, and out-of-stock situations), promotions (such as in-store and external promotions), perceptions of store quality, and whether or not the customer is online or in-store, partly because it is much easier to comparison shop online than it is in-store. However, price perception formation is a dynamic process. In other words, the framework indicates that once the purchase behaviour occurs, there is a recalibration of the customer's price perception, because new purchase experiences and new information provide the stimulus for that recalibration. Therefore the process is cyclical.

Next, we consider key elements within the price perception process: willingness to pay, price consciousness, and **pricing cues**.

Willingness to Pay

We memorize certain prices for some items; when companies deviate from those prices, we perceive them as unfair. A key question is: why do some consumers see one proposition's price as fair and others do not? If we are to price an offering according to customer needs, we should understand which customers think a particular price is a fair price to pay, or what they expect to pay, or what they think others would pay. For example, in the UK, Superdrug was forced to review its 'sexist' pricing after an investigation by *The Times* revealed that women were being charged more than men on certain offerings, such as razors. In some retailers, the gender price surplus that women were expected to pay for similar products was 37 per cent (Hipwell and Ellson, 2016).

Research Insight 7.1

To take your learning further, you might wish to read this influential paper.

Völckner, F., and Hofmann, J. (2007) 'The price–perceived quality relationship: A meta-analytic review and assessment of its determinants', *Marketing Letters*, 18(3), 181–96.

This article uses a meta-analytic approach to evaluate various studies performed between 1989 and 2006, aiming to provide evidence that there is an increasingly weakening relationship between price and perceived quality.

 Visit the **online resources** to read the abstract and access the full paper.

Price Consciousness

What determines price fairness? Superdrug was accused of 'sexist' price discrimination.

Source: Konmac/Shutterstock.

In addition to deciding whether or not a price is fair, or what customers expect to pay, we also need to know whether or not customers are conscious of prices in a particular category. Most people do not have a good knowledge of prices. Think of your parents or of friends significantly older than you: do they know the monthly subscription price for streaming music tracks? Do you know the price of a quality dining table or £200,000 worth of life insurance cover? These examples indicate that our price experience contributes to what we know about reference prices. Our experience is limited to previous actual or considered purchases. So if people do not know the reference prices of particular offerings, how can they determine their fairness? In 2019, Irish beef farmers protested over a sharp decrease in the price of beef. Losses of €5 million per week compared with other European beef farmers were reported, which left many Irish farmers incurring financial losses which put their businesses at risk (O'Brien, 2019).

Pricing Cues

When customers assess prices, they estimate value using pricing cues, because they do not always know the true cost and price of the item that they are purchasing. These pricing cues include sale signs, odd-number pricing, the purchase context, and **price bundling** and rebates.

- *Sale signs*—Sale signs act as cues, indicating the availability of a bargain. This seduces the customer to buy, suggesting to the buyer that an item is desirable and may not be available if it is not bought quickly enough. The sale sign uses scarcity as a persuasive device, because the scarcer we perceive an offering to be, the more we want it (Cialdini, 1993)—sometimes regardless of whether or not we need it.

- *Odd-number pricing*—Another pricing cue is the use of odd-number endings, such as prices that end in the figure 9. Have you ever wondered why the Nintendo Switch was priced at US$299, or €299, or SEK3,649? According to Anderson and Simester (2003), raising the price of a woman's dress in a national mail order catalogue from US$34 to US$39 increased demand by 33 per cent, but demand remained unchanged when the price was raised to US$44! The question is: why did the increase in demand take place when there was a higher price? It is unlikely that demand would have increased if the item had been priced at US$38. The reason is that we perceive the first price as relative to a reference price of £30 (which is £34 rounded down to the nearest unit of ten) and more expensive, whereas the second price of US$39 we perceive as cheaper than a reference price of US$40 (which we rounded up to the nearest ten).
- *Purchase context*—Our perception of risk is greater if we are continually reminded of it than if we consider it only at the point of purchase. For example, gyms use the technique of charging a monthly fee, even though they often demand a yearly membership agreement, for precisely this reason. In fact, a monthly price (instead of an annual, semi-annual, or quarterly charge) drives a higher level of gym attendance, because customers are more regularly reminded of their purchase. So the way you set your price not only influences demand, but also drives consumption (Gourville and Soman, 2002).

Visit the **online resources** and complete Internet Activity 7.1 to learn more about the impact that the purchase context (e.g. time of day, week, online versus telephone booking, etc.) has on the pricing of budget airline services.

Pricing Strategies

Companies establish their pricing strategy based on what their pricing objectives are. The four main pricing strategies include the following.

- *Premium pricing*—This focuses on pricing an offering to indicate its distinctiveness in the marketplace. For example, Lamborghini prices its Huracán in this way, at around €180,000 for an entry-level model.
- *Penetration pricing*—This occurs when the price is set low relative to the competition to gain market share. Amazon has adopted this approach to build its now substantial customer base.
- *Economy pricing*—This strategy sees prices set at the bare minimum to attract price-sensitive customers. Supermarkets often use this approach with their everyday low-pricing approach (e.g. Leader Price in France, Aldi all over Europe, and Jumbo in the Netherlands).

Market Insight 7.2 **Is the Price Right?**

ICA is Sweden's largest grocery retailer, with a market share in 2015 of 36 per cent, more than 1,300 stores in four different formats, and total store sales of €11.7 billion. The company was founded in 1917 as a purchasing federation of independent retailers, which remains its basic operating structure to this day.

Two critical components of any offer in retailing are price and quality. Price can determine store

Market Insight 7.2 (continued)

choice, patronage behaviour, basket size, and overall customer satisfaction. Retail managers have to consider two dimensions of their chain's positioning: the actual prices to use ('on shelf'); and how customers perceive them ('in mind'). These two sometimes diverge.

When comparing prices between the chains, baskets of everyday groceries are typically used to create an index of actual prices, in which 100 denotes a market average price for the basket. In a perfect world, the 'in mind' position closely tracks the 'on shelf' prices indicated by this index.

In the Swedish market, the in-mind discount price position is occupied by the largest European discount chain Lidl, with the price-fighting local supermarket chain Willy's as runner-up. ICA and some other local Swedish actors, such as Hemköp and City Gross, are perceived as quality players, with a good value-for-money offer.

In ICA's case, however, many consumers perceive the prices to be somewhat higher than they actually are. This is reflected in a misalignment between consumer rankings of grocery chains as 'low price' or giving 'good value for money' and ICA's performance on price index comparisons. In the United States, Whole Foods Market suffers from a similar misalignment. Paradoxically, this phenomenon can then affect discount actors positively, meaning that they are sometimes perceived as somewhat less expensive than they actually are.

In conclusion, price perception is an important concept for any manager to understand. A poor price perception can lead to lost sales and a pressure on prices and profits. The manager has to learn how to work with both sides of the value equation: actual price levels and added value. This can help the manager to balance the perceptions of the firm's customer offer.

Lidl is the largest discounter in Europe—lower prices is a key differentiator for this supermarket chain
Source: © Getty/Francis Dean.

1. **Under what circumstances is misalignment between actual prices ('on shelf') and customers' price perceptions ('in mind') beneficial for a retailer?**
2. **Under what circumstances is misalignment between actual prices ('on shelf') and customers' price perceptions ('in mind') troublesome for a retailer?**
3. **Why do you think price perceptions are sometimes misaligned for premium retailers (e.g. ICA, Whole Food Markets)?**
4. **Why do you think price perceptions are sometimes misaligned for discount retailers (e.g. Lidl)?**

Sources: Hamilton and Chernev (2013); Mägi et al. (2016); http://www.ica.se.

This market insight was kindly contributed by Dr Jonas Gunnarsson, market and consumer research manager at ICA AB, Sweden.

Research Insight 7.2

To take your learning further, you might wish to read this influential paper.

Gourville, J., and Soman, D. (2002) 'Pricing and the psychology of consumption', *Harvard Business Review*, 80(9), 90–6.

This is a useful article summarizing how marketing managers should consider not only the price at which customers are likely to purchase an offering, but also how the way in which price is set also affects consumption. This article suggests that marketers might counter-intuitively want to draw customers' attention to the price paid, so that they can achieve greater value in using the offering and generate a longer-term impact on customer retention. The article has strong implications for organizations selling subscriptions and memberships.

Visit the online resources to read the abstract and access the full paper.

- *Price skimming*—In this model, the price is initially set high, then lowered in sequential steps. Apple iPhone adopted this strategy, for example. This strategy is frequently used for the launch of new offerings (which we look at next).

Launch Pricing

When launching new offerings, organizations tend to adopt one of two classic pricing strategies. With the first approach, price skimming, they charge an initially high price and then reduce the price over time, recouping the cost of the research and development (R&D) investment from sales to the group of customers that is prepared to pay the higher price (hence 'skimming' the market). In the second approach, they charge a lower price in the hope of generating a large volume of sales and recouping R&D investment that way (hence 'penetration pricing'). Figure 7.2 shows both market-skimming and market penetration price strategies, along with their hypothetical impact on quantity demanded (Q1 and Q2, respectively).

The price-skimming approach is a fairly standard approach for high-technology offerings or those offerings that require substantial R&D investment initially (such as games consoles and prescription pharmaceuticals). For example, Microsoft dropped the price for its Xbox One machine, bringing the official base price to US$299 in 2016, having opened with a launch price of US$500 (Thier, 2016). The price-skimming approach is also particularly appropriate when demand is likely to be inelastic and there are few economies of scale in the product or category (Dean, 1950; Doyle, 2000).

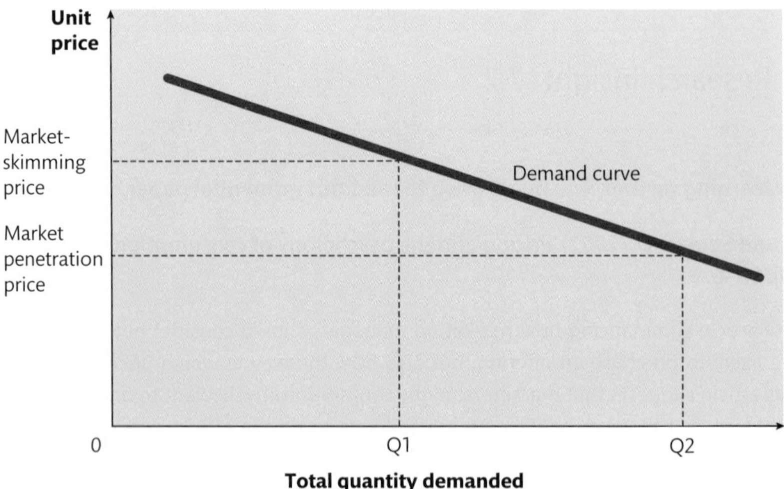

Figure 7.2 Launch-pricing strategies

Source: Adapted from Burnett (2002). Reproduced with the kind permission of the author, John Burnett.

The market penetration pricing approach is used for fast-moving consumer goods and consumer durables, when the new offering introduced is not demonstrably different from existing formulations. Items aimed at capturing price-sensitive customers might use this approach. The penetration approach is more effective when there is a strong threat from competition and demand is very elastic (Dean, 1950; Doyle, 2000).

Pricing Approaches

Price setting depends on various factors, including how price affects demand, how sales revenue is linked to price, how cost is linked to price, and how investment costs are linked to price (Doyle, 2000). Broadly, there are four types of underlying pricing approach:

- the *cost-oriented* approach (i.e. prices set based on costs);
- the *demand-oriented* approach (i.e. prices set based on price sensitivity and demand);
- the *competitor-oriented* approach (i.e. prices set based on competitors' prices); and
- the *value-oriented* approach (i.e. prices based on what customers believe to offer value).

The Cost-Oriented Approach

The cost-oriented approach advances the idea that the most important element of pricing is the cost of the component resources that constitute the offering. Therefore the marketer sells output at the highest price possible, regardless of the buyer's preferences or costs. If that price is sufficiently high compared with the seller's costs, the firm earns a profit and survives; if not, the seller must find a way of either increasing the price or lowering costs, or both, or it will not survive (Lockley, 1949). The cost-oriented approach considers the total costs of a proposition in the pricing equation, but does not take into account non-cost factors, such as brand image, degree of prestige in ownership, or effort expended.

One approach to determining price is using mark-up pricing, often found in the retail sector. This method operates on the basis of a set percentage mark-up. When used, the cost-oriented method leads to the use of list prices, with single prices set for all customers. We simply add a mark-up to the cost of X per cent and this constitutes the price. In British supermarket retailing, the mark-up is around 6–8 per cent, but in American supermarket retailing, it is often around 4 per cent or less. Mark-ups on wine served in restaurants are typically between 200 per cent and 300 per cent. The cost-oriented approach requires us first to determine the price we set that just covers our costs. This is known as 'breakeven pricing'. It represents the point at which our total costs and our total revenues are exactly equal.

To exemplify the concept of mark-up pricing further, we might use the example of a computer company selling high-quality laptops costing £1,000 per unit to manufacture. Suppose that the computer company uses the mark-up pricing method, adding 66.7 per cent. The final price set can be calculated as:

$$\text{Sales price (£)} = (\text{mark-up}^* \times \text{cost}) + \text{cost} = (0.67 \times 1{,}000) + 1{,}000 = £1{,}670$$

(*Note that mark-up is expressed as a decimal between 0 and 1—that is, we divide the mark-up percentage by 100 to get a mark-up figure.)

It is important to note that the gross profit margin (i.e. that proportion of the revenue which is profit) is not the same as the mark-up percentage (which is a proportion of cost). The gross profit margin in the preceding example can be calculated as:

$$\text{Gross margin (\%)} = (\text{mark-up/sales price}) \times 100 = (670/1{,}670) \times 100 = 40.11\%$$

The cost-oriented approach does not mean that we have to use a mark-up pricing approach. In some industries, prices are instead based on fixed formulae, set with a supplier's costs in mind. For example, in the ethical prescription pharmaceutical industry in Spain, Italy and France, government-fixed formulae have tended to dictate prices, with limited scope for pharmaceutical manufacturers to negotiate, whereas in the UK and Germany, the tradition has been for the country's national health authorities not to fix individual product prices, but to set an overall level of profitability with which the pharmaceutical manufacturer must agree, based on a submission of its costs (Attridge, 2003).

The Demand-Oriented Approach

With the demand-oriented approach to pricing, the firm sets prices according to how much customers will pay. This approach is prevalent in marketing services, but again could be used in B2B or consumer marketing contexts. Airline companies frequently operate this approach, with customers paying different amounts for seats with varying levels of service attached, as illustrated in Figure 7.3. Most airline companies operate three types of cabin service. Emirates, for instance, offers first class, business class, and economy, with varying benefits according to the price paid based on the seat pitch (and availability as a bed), the entertainment package, the quality of the meal options, the availability and quality of airport lounges, transportation to and from the airport, the in-flight service offered, and the experience through immigration and security.

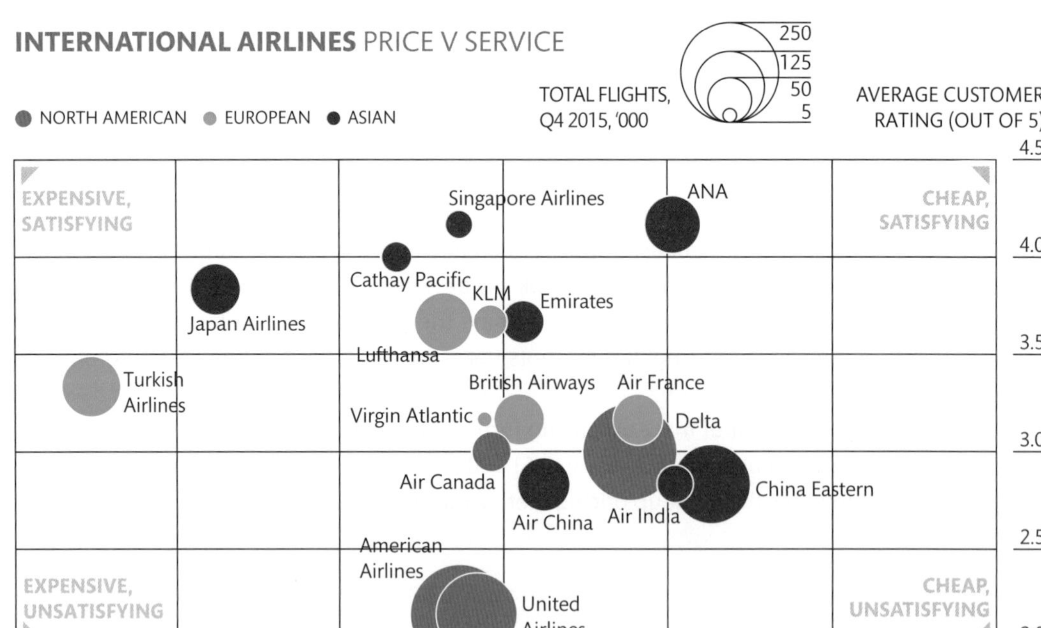

Figure 7.3 International airlines: price vs service

Source: From *1843* magazine © 2016 The Economist Newspaper Limited. All rights reserved.

The Competitor-Oriented Approach

Companies can also set prices based on competitors' prices—that is, the so-called going rate—sometimes known as 'me too' pricing. This approach is used in B2B, services, and consumer marketing contexts. The advantage here is that when your prices are lower than those of the competition, customers are more likely to purchase from you—provided that they know your prices are lower.

Price guarantee schemes like that outlined in Market Insight 7.3 seek to provide customers with the peace of mind of knowing that the price paid is a competitive one. In reality, such schemes are expensive to operate, requiring continuous monitoring of the full range of competitors' prices and a strong focus on cost control. It is also worth considering that adopting a competitor-oriented pricing strategy can lead to price wars.

Visit the **online resources** and complete Internet Activity 7.2 to learn more about how French supermarket chain Carrefour has used price promises in its advertising.

Price wars occur when competitors' pricing policies are almost exclusively focused on competitors rather than customers, when price is pushed downwards, and when pricing results in interactions between competitors that lead to unsustainable prices. For example, in 2003, when Dutch supermarket retailer Albert Hejn slashed its prices in response to competition from Aldi and Lidl, the resulting battle saw an 8.2 per cent reduction in food prices, costing Dutch supermarkets €900 million (£700 million) and 30,000 jobs in only one year (van Heerde et al., 2008; Blackhurst, 2014)—although by 2005, after the price war had ended, Albert Hejn had managed to regain lost market share to regain market leadership (Reinemoeller, 2014).

Calculating and anticipating competitor response is important when setting prices and responding to competitors' price cuts. We should analyse consumer responses when a competitor starts to cut prices, but if purchase behaviour changes only modestly or temporarily, other marketing mix elements (such as promotion, place or distribution, or product differentiation) may be more likely to win back customers (van Heerde et al., 2008). We do not always have to respond to a price war with a price cut; instead, we might promote increased service quality (Rust et al., 2000) or customer value improvements more generally.

The Value-Oriented Approach

Even in the consumer durables category (e.g. furniture, **white goods**, carpets), in which we might expect customers to be less price sensitive, firms practise pricing approaches with customers' considerations in mind (Foxall, 1972). We term this the value-oriented approach to pricing, because prices are set based on buyers' perceptions of specific product or service attribute values rather than on costs or competitors' prices. This approach can be used in B2B, services, and consumer contexts. With value-based pricing, the pricing process begins with customers, determining what value they derive from the offering and then determining price, rather than the opposite approach used in cost-oriented pricing, whereby costs are determined first and then the price is set.

In value-based pricing, deciding what is of value to the customer is based on customer research. The result may be that the company does not necessarily offer a cheaper price. In fact, it could mean a higher-priced offering. If that offering were to represent true value to customers, they must feel that it has more benefits than equivalent offerings. A recent study of 1,812 pricing professionals demonstrated that a value-based pricing strategy is positively linked to firm performance, whereas a cost-based approach is not (Liozu and Hinterhuber, 2013). A good example of a brand using this approach is L'Oréal, which has advertised its products using spokesmodels, such as South Korean model Soo-Joo Park, Chinese model Xiao Wen Ju, Dutch model Lara Stone, Cuban singer-songwriter Camila Cabello and Hollywood actress Naomi Watts, on the basis that we should use its products 'because we're worth it'.

Market Insight 7.3 **Unbeatable Prices at Carrefour**

In 2019, the French multinational corporation Carrefour Group reportedly owned more than 12,000 stores, consisting of hypermarkets, supermarkets, convenience stores, and cash-and-carry stores across worldwide locations. Carrefour stores provide customers with a wide range of products, including fresh produce globally and locally sourced. The chain is known for its attractive prices in all categories of products as well as daily promotions. Such an offering has resulted in Carrefour becoming one of the leading French supermarkets, second only to the hypermarket chain Group E. Leclerc.

Carrefour recently launched its 'prix imbattables' (which translates to unbeatable prices) offer. This initiative guarantees that a large variety of products are sold for a lower price by Carrefour than any of its competitors. This not only includes short-term promotions but also 500 food and non-food products available all year round. Carrefour also promises to pay double the price difference if customers find a cheaper product elsewhere.

Market Insight 7.3 (continued)

Carrefour's unbeatable prices are available all year round.
Source: © aureliefrance/Shutterstock.

In September 2019, Carrefour launched its first 'Supeco' stores (blending the two words 'supermarket' and 'eco') in the north of France after having trialled this new concept in Spain and Romania. Supeco stores have been designed for French consumers and mix the traditional supermarket layout with the cash-and-carry shopping experience specific to discount chains like Aldi and Lidl. Supeco stores stock fewer products than Carrefour's other supermarkets and convenience stores (e.g. Carrefour Market and Carrefour City) and feature a dedicated zone for discounted products over short offer periods. By opening these new stores, Carrefour can compete with American rival Costco which successfully opened its first warehouse stores in France in 2017.

1. **Why does Carrefour guarantee the lowest prices on products all year round and not only for short promotions?**
2. **What do you think are the benefits of using the Supeco name instead of using the Carrefour brand?**
3. **What data does Carrefour need to collect to determine the efficacy of its aggressive pricing strategy?**

Sources: Sicard (2019); https://www.carrefour.fr.

Research Insight 7.3

To take your learning further, you might wish to read this influential paper.

Reinemoeller, P. (2014) 'How to win a price war', *Sloan Management Review*, 55(3), 15–17.

This article, based on a study of Albert Hejn in the Netherlands, explains that companies can win price wars by leveraging five strategic capabilities, including:

- the ability to affirm the need for a price war;
- the ability to carefully select an appropriate battlefield using advanced analytics capabilities;
- the ability to pick a single target competitor;
- staying under the radar (by targeting former customers rather than explicitly poaching new customers); and
- the ability to align revenues with reformed cost structures.

 **Visit the online resources to read the abstract and access the full paper.**

When setting value-based prices, it is important to consider the following questions (Anderson et al., 2010).

1 What is the market strategy for the segment? What does the supplier want to accomplish?
2 What is the differential value that customers are likely to perceive (i.e. the value between this offering and the next-best alternative, assuming that the differential value can be verified with the customer's own data)?
3 What is the price of the next-best alternative?
4 What is the cost of the supplier's offering?
5 What pricing tactics will be used initially (e.g. price discounting)?
6 What is the customer's expectation of a 'fair' price?

Pricing Tactics

In reality, when setting prices, an organization trades off the different approaches against each other by considering all of the following factors.

- *Competition*—How much are competitors charging for similar offerings?
- *Cost*—How much do the individual components that make up our offering cost?
- *Demand*—How much of this product or service will we sell at what price?
- *Value*—What components of the offering do customers value and how much are they prepared to pay for them?

Pricing Management

In the information era, marketing information systems, database technologies, and Internet-enabled technologies have changed how companies make pricing decisions. Pricing strategies such as 'real-time' or 'dynamic' pricing have increasingly developed in both consumer and B2B markets, sometimes through online price comparison sites, online auctions, and companies' own websites, because prices can be changed easily. For example, Amazon updates its price list every ten minutes based on constant data analysis (Anon., 2016). Dynamic pricing even allows changes at the customer level (Grewal et al., 2011).

Airline companies have been practising a similar technique for years, relying on software guided by a programmer who remains in charge of making pricing decisions. More recently, artificial intelligence (AI) has made it possible to automate pricing without the need for human intervention. In such scenarios, the software learns about and responds to its environment autonomously, resulting in optimized prices (Calvano et al., 2018). For example, ride-sharing company Uber uses AI to determine in real time the price its app users are willing to pay for a ride based on time of day, location, flow of traffic, and history of rides (Martin, 2019).

Comparison sites have developed large customer databases covering all types of offering, including complex services such as gas and electricity supply, insurance, mobile phone packages, and travel, as well as standard offerings such as cars and breakdown cover. Marketers are working in an increasingly price-transparent environment and they should recognize that pricing is a capability at which some companies are better than others. Those companies that are excellent at pricing manage their costs and price complexity well, and offer sustainability and innovation in pricing approaches (Hinterhuber and Liozu, 2012). See, for example, Market Insight 7.4. Online retailers are increasingly recognizing that it is not only the price that matters, but also how easy it is to pay online, because a more efficient payment process can lead to more time shopping.

Market Insight 7.4 **Everlane: Pricing for Ethics**

Pricing in the fashion industry is probably one of the biggest mysteries in marketing. One can find products that are incredibly cheap, while other consumers are willing to pay an exorbitant price for brands, the value of which is determined by intangible traits such as prestige and design.

Everlane, a US-based apparel start-up, challenges this status quo by offering consumers a new solution under its 'Radical Transparency' policy.

The company identified factories that produce for high-end fashion brands around the world. By establishing direct and close relationships with these factories, and selling exclusively online, Everlane can deliver high-quality products at a reasonable price. More importantly, it outlines the cost breakdown of all of the products it sells at each stage of the value chain on its website, from material, labour, duties, and transport, to the mark-up it takes.

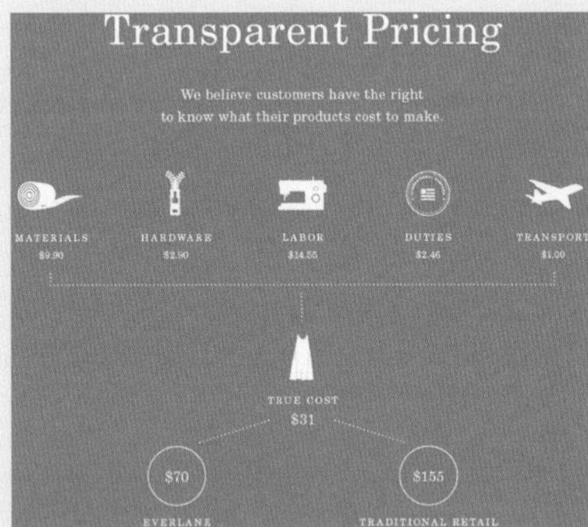

This infographic offers an example of the type of information Everlane provides to its customers.
Source: Courtesy of Everlane

Against a backdrop of recent scandals about some fashion brands whose products are manufactured by suppliers in factories in which workers' rights are not respected and conditions are often very poor, Everlane's transparent pricing strategy has a meaningful implication for business ethics. All of the factories that work with Everlane are well documented on its website, with clear information on and photos of the working environment, products manufactured, and the reasons why Everlane chose the factory. This not only shows customers where and how the products they purchase are made, but also serves as a 'reason to believe' to justify the pricing structure presented by the company. Additionally, this approach also educates customers on the hidden costs behind cheap clothing, because it shows a clear breakdown of costs across the supply chain.

In 2016, five years after it was founded, Everlane recorded US$51 million in sales and was reported to have a valuation of US$250 million.

1 **What are the implications of this type of pricing transparency for price perception in the clothing industry?**

2 **What are the barriers to consumers' understanding and learning of this pricing approach? (Think about what you learned in Chapter 2 on customer behaviour.)**

3 **In what way might Everlane's pricing strategy help in the promotion of business ethics?**

Source: O'Toole (2016).

This Market Insight was kindly contributed by Jenny Li, Adjunct Lecturer in Marketing, NEOMA Business School, France.

Business-to-Business (B2B) Pricing

In B2B markets, buyers are professionally trained procurement executives, often with qualifications from professional institutes (e.g. the Association for Supply Chain Management, Procurement and Logistics (BME) in Germany and Central Europe, the Swedish National Association of Purchasing and Logistics, or the Chartered Institute of Purchasing and Supply in the UK). Their function is often highly technical, even for apparently simple offerings. For example, to produce a pen, a manufacturer might buy the pens in Italy, packaging and printing in China, refills in Germany, and the final product assembly in Bulgaria.

In the B2B context, the discussion of price takes place between the buyer and the seller in an atmosphere in which both are trying to make the best commercial decision for their organizations. The seller wants to maximize profit (by getting a high price), and the buyer wants to procure at a low price to lower costs and maximize their profits. Their task is to resolve their mutual needs in a win–win situation. From the seller's perspective, there are numerous pricing tactics that can be adopted, including the following.

- *Geographical pricing*—Prices may be based on customer location. For example, pharmaceutical companies (sometimes controversially) sell their prescription drugs at different prices in different countries.
- *Negotiated pricing*—Prices may be set according to specific agreements between a company and its clients or customers (e.g. professional services, such as architectural or structural engineering). This approach occurs where a sale is complex and consultative, although sales representatives should not concede on price too quickly before properly understanding a client's needs (Rackham, 2001).
- *Discount pricing*—Companies may reduce the price on the basis that a customer commits to buying a large volume of that offering now or in the future, or is prepared to pay for it quickly. Large retailers work on the discount principle when buying for their stores.
- *Value-in-use pricing*—This approach focuses attention on customer perceptions of the attributes of offerings and away from cost-oriented approaches. It prices offerings based on what the customer is prepared to pay for individual benefits received from that proposition, so the company must first ascertain what benefit components the customer perceives to be important, quantify those benefit values, determine the price equivalence of value, rate competitive and alternative products to provide a benchmark for price determination, and quantify the value-in-use (i.e. the value in using the product vis-à-vis those of competitors), and only then is the price actually fixed. (See Christopher, 1982, for a detailed discussion.) This approach is particularly used for industrial propositions.
- *Relationship pricing*—This approach seeks to understand customers' needs before pricing the offering around those needs to generate a long-term relationship. This means offering excellent financial terms, credit or more lenient time periods for payment, or discounts based on future sales revenue or the risk involved in the purchase.
- *'Pay what you want' pricing*—This approach allows customers to pay whatever they want for an offering. For example, legal services firm CMS Cameron McKenna has offered this pricing approach to its corporate clients (Taylor, 2010).

- **Transfer pricing**—This occurs in large organizations in which considerable internal dealing between different company divisions occurs, often across national boundaries. Prices may be set at commercial rates, on the basis of negotiated prices between divisions, or using a cost-based approach, depending on whether the division is a cost or profit centre. Internal dealings can sometimes mean that the final offering is overpriced for a given customer. The European aircraft manufacturer Airbus adopts this approach when constructing its planes built from components made in different countries.
- *Economic value to the customer pricing*—With this approach, a company prices an offering according to its perceived value by the purchasing organization (i.e. total profit generated less the costs paid), typically by means of a comparison with a reference or market-leading offering, taking into consideration not only the actual purchase price of the offering, but also the start-up and post-purchase costs, to give an overall indication of how much better its pricing structure is compared with that of a competitor. The final price is then set based on a negotiation between the buyer and seller over the difference in value and how likely this value is to be achieved. This kind of pricing approach might be used by a large consultancy solutions company such as IBM, when it sells its system solutions.
- *Tendering and bid pricing*—With this approach, organizations invite other organizations to bid for the right to deliver a particular job or task (a tender) and to name their own price. This approach is used heavily by public-sector organizations. The difficulty arises in that organizations do not always provide a budgetary range to allow bidders an idea of what price would be accepted. The manager should know the profitability of a bid when determining the price, and aim to discover the winning bidder's name and price on lost jobs, where possible (Walker, 1967). Ross (1984) argues that it is often better not to ask 'What price will it take to win this order?', but 'Do we want this order, given the price our competitors are likely to quote?' Where the winning bidder obtains an unprofitable contract that it is duty-bound to deliver, because its bid price was set so low, this is known as the 'winner's curse'.

Chapter Summary

To consolidate your learning, the key points from this chapter are summarized below.

- **Explain the concept of price elasticity of demand.**

Price elasticity of demand allows us to determine how the quantity of an offering relates to the price at which it is offered. Inelastic propositions are defined as such because increases or decreases in price produce relatively smaller decreases or increases in sales volumes, whereas elastic offerings have larger similar effects. Understanding price elasticity helps us to devise demand-oriented pricing mechanisms.

- **Describe how customers perceive price.**

Understanding how customers and consumers perceive pricing helps in the setting of prices. Customers have an idea of reference prices based on what they ought to pay for an offering, what others would pay, or what they would like to pay. Their knowledge of actual prices is limited to well-known and frequently bought and advertised offerings. Consequently, customers tend to rely on price cues, such as odd-number pricing, sale signs, the purchase context, and price bundles, when deciding whether or not value exists in a particular proposition.

- **Understand pricing strategies and how to price new offerings.**

There are four main pricing strategies, including premium pricing (pricing an offering to indicate its distinctiveness in the marketplace), penetration pricing (pricing low relative to the competition to gain market share), economy pricing (pricing at the bare minimum to attract price-sensitive customers), and price skimming (setting the price high initially, then lowering in sequential steps).

- **Explain cost-, competitor-, demand-, and value-oriented approaches to pricing.**

There are a variety of different pricing policies that can be used depending on whether we are pricing a consumer, service, or industrial offering. These are cost-oriented (based on what we paid for it and what mark-up we intend to add), competitor-oriented (based on the so-called going rate or on at what price competitors sell an offering), demand-oriented (based on how much of an offering can be sold at what price), or value-oriented (what attributes of the offering are of benefit to our customer and what they will pay for them) approaches.

- **Explain how pricing operates in the business-to-business (B2B) setting.**

A variety of pricing tactics are used in the B2B setting, including geographical, negotiated, discount, value-in-use, relationship, 'pay what you want', transfer, economic value to the customer, and bid pricing. Business-to-business pricing differs in that buyers are frequently expert in purchasing for their organizations. They are likely to pay particular attention to the value that they derive from the offering.

Review Questions

1. Define 'price', 'cost', 'quality', and 'value', and how they relate to each other.
2. Explain the concept of 'price elasticity of demand', giving examples of offerings that are both price elastic and price inelastic.
3. What are pricing cues?
4. How does odd-number pricing work?
5. What are the four main pricing strategies?
6. When might you use price skimming as a pricing approach?
7. When might you use penetration pricing?
8. Name four B2B pricing tactics.
9. Under what circumstances does the 'pay what you want' pricing approach work best?
10. How does pricing operate in tender and bidding exercises?

Worksheet Summary

 To apply the knowledge you have gained from this chapter and to test your understanding of price decisions, visit the **online resources** and complete Worksheet 7.1.

Discussion Questions

1 Having read Case Insight 7.1, how would you advise Ammon Zeus with regards to the renovation of its hotel and the increase in price to attract new guests with higher expectations?

2 A range of scenarios are presented in which you are given some information on the price context. What pricing policy would you use when setting the price in each of the following situations? (State the assumptions under which you are working when you decide on each one.)

A The owner of a newly refurbished themed Irish pub in a central city location (e.g. Amsterdam or Oslo) wants to set the prices for his range of beers, with the objective of attracting a new customer base.

B The product manager at American car manufacturer Ford wants to set the price range for the Ford Mustang in the UK launched in Summer 2016 (http://www.ford.co.uk/Cars/newmustang).

C You are the manager at a large, well-known legal services firm (such as Bird & Bird) in Denmark, and your client, from a €20 million turnover medium-sized import/export company, commissions work in relation to a recent company acquisition. What further information would you require to price such work and what pricing approaches could you offer?

3 How would you go about determining the price sensitivity of your customers if you were a cinema marketing manager and you wanted your cinemas to operate at full capacity throughout the week, including for matinée and late (after 10 pm) seats, and not only at weekends and in the evenings?

4 Research and examine the prices of five different items in two different supermarkets (where possible, selling similar or identical products and pack sizes in each to allow comparison). What are the average prices for each of the items and how does each supermarket compare with the other?

Visit the **online resources** and complete the multiple-choice questions to assess your knowledge of the chapter.

Glossary

components a part of something larger, for example an engine as part of a car, or the casing, ink, and packaging as parts of a pen.

consumer durables manufactured consumer products that are relatively long-lasting (e.g. cars or computers) as opposed to non-durables (e.g. foodstuffs).

perceived quality a relative subjective measure of quality. We talk of 'perceived' quality because there is no truly objective absolute measure of product or service quality.

price the amount that the customer has to pay to receive a good or service.

price bundling when a product or service is offered together with another typically complementary product or service, which is not available separately, to make the original product or service seem more attractive (e.g. a CD with a music magazine).

price elasticity the percentage change in volume demanded as a proportion of the percentage change in price, usually expressed as a negative number. A score close to zero indicates that a product or service price change has little impact on quantity demanded, whereas a score of –1 indicates that a product or service price change effects an equal percentage quantity change. A value above –1 indicates a disproportionately higher change in quantity demanded as a result of a percentage price change.

pricing cues proxy measures used by customers to estimate a product or service's reference price, such as quality, styling, packaging, sale signs, and odd-number endings.

reference price the price band against which customers judge the purchase price of goods and services.

transfer pricing typically occurs in large organizations and represents the pricing approach used when one unit of a company sells to another unit within the same company.

value the regard that something is held to be worth, typically, although not always, expressed in financial terms.

white goods large electrical goods used in residences, typically, but not necessarily, white in colour, such as refrigerators and washing machines.

References

Anderson, E., and Simester, D. (2003) 'Mind your pricing cues', *Harvard Business Review*, 81(9), 96–103.

Anderson, J. C., Wouters, M., and Van Rossum, W. (2010) 'Why the highest price isn't the best price', *Sloan Management Review*, 51(2), 69–76.

Anon. (2016) 'Schumpeter: Flexible figures', *The Economist*, 30 January. Retrieve from: https://www.economist.com/business/2016/01/28/flexible-figures (accessed 30 October 2020).

Aschemann-Witzel, J., and Zielke, S. (2017) 'Can't buy me green? A review of consumer perceptions of and behavior toward the price of organic food', *Journal of Consumer Affairs*, 51(1), 211–51.

Attridge, J. (2003) 'A single European market for pharmaceuticals: Could less regulation and more negotiation be the answer?', *European Business Journal*, 15(3), 122–43.

Baker, W. L., Marn, M. V., and Zawada, C. C. (2010) *The Price Advantage* (2nd edn), Hoboken, NJ: Wiley.

Bijmolt, T. H. A., van Heerde, H. J., and Pieters, R. G. M. (2005) 'New empirical generalisations on the determinants of price elasticity', *Journal of Marketing Research*, 42(2), 141–56.

Blackhurst, C. (2014) 'Check out the Dutch for supermarket price wars', *Evening Standard*, 2 October, 47.

Bunte, F. H. J, Van Galen, M. A., Erno Kuiper, W., and Tacken, G. (2010) 'Limits to growth in organic sales', *De Economist*, 158(4), 387–410.

Burnett, J. (2002) *Core Concepts in Marketing*, Chichester: Wiley.

Calvano, E., Calzolari, G., Denicolò, V., and Pastorello, S. (2018) 'Artificial intelligence, algorithmic pricing and collusion'. Discussion Paper DP13405, Centre for Economic Policy Research.

Christopher, M. (1982) 'Value-in-use pricing', *European Journal of Marketing*, 16(5), 35–46.

Cialdini, R. B. (1993) *Influence: The Psychology of Persuasion*, New York: Quill William Morrow.

Dean, J. (1950) Pricing policies for new products. *Harvard Business Review*, 54(6), 45–53.

Doward, J. (2017) 'Organic food sales soar as shoppers put quality before price', *The Guardian*, 19 February. Retrieve from: https://www.theguardian.com/environment/2017/feb/19/sales-of-organic-food-soar-fruit-vegetables-supermarkets (accessed 30 October 2020).

Doyle, P. (2000) *Value-Based Marketing: Marketing Strategies for Corporate Growth and Shareholder Value*, Chichester: Wiley.

Foxall, G. (1972) 'A descriptive theory of pricing for marketing', *European Journal of Marketing*, 6(3), 190–4.

Gerstner, E. (1985) 'Do higher prices signal higher quality?', *Journal of Marketing Research*, 22(2), 209–15.

Gourville, J., and Soman, D. (2002) 'Pricing and the psychology of consumption', *Harvard Business Review*, 80(9), 90–6.

Grewal, D., Ailawadi, K. L., Gauri, D., Hall, K., Kopalle, P., and Robertson, J. R. (2011) 'Innovations in retail pricing and promotions', *Journal of Retailing*, 87(S1), S43–52.

Hamilton, R., and Chernev, A. (2013) 'Low prices are just the beginning: Price image in retail management', *Journal of Marketing*, 77(6), 1–20.

Hayward, S. (2015) 'So this is what Cadbury thinks of biscuit lovers', *Sunday Mirror*, 12 April, 24.

Hinterhuber, A., and Liozu, S. (2012) 'Is it time to rethink your pricing strategy?', *Sloan Management Review*, 53(4), 69–77.

Hipwell, D., and Ellson, A. (2016) 'Superdrug takes razor to sexist pricing', *The Times*, 5 February. Retrieve from: https://www.thetimes.co.uk/article/superdrug-takes-razor-to-sexist-pricing-5fm9gtv7r6p (accessed 30 October 2020).

Leszinski, R., and Marn, M. V. (1997) 'Setting value, not price', *McKinsey Quarterly*, February. Retrieve from: https://www.mckinsey.com/business-functions/

marketing-and-sales/our-insights/setting-value-not-price (accessed 30 October 2020).

Lexico (2019) '"Price", "quality", "value"'. Retrieve from: https://www.lexico.com/en/definition/price; https://www.lexico.com/en/definition/quality; https://www.lexico.com/en/definition/value (accessed 30 November 2019).

Liozu, S. M., and Hinterhuber, A. (2013) 'Pricing orientation, pricing capabilities, and firm performance', *Management Decision*, 51(3), 594–614.

Lockley, L. C. (1949) 'Theories of pricing in marketing', *Journal of Marketing*, 13(3), 364–7.

Mägi, A., Gunnarsson, J., and Rosengren, S. (2016) 'Consumer updating of store price perceptions'. Paper presented at the 2016 Academy of Marketing Science Annual Meeting, 18–21 May. Lake Buena Vista, FL.

Martin, N. (2019) 'Uber charges more if they think you're willing to pay more', *Forbes*, 30 March. Retrieve from: https://www.forbes.com/sites/nicolemartin1/2019/03/30/uber-charges-more-if-they-think-youre-willing-to-pay-more/ (accessed 30 October 2020).

Mendoza, J., and Baines, P. (2012) 'Towards a consumer price perception formation framework: A systematic review'. Retrieve from: https://webarchive.nla.gov.au/awa/20121203115234/http://pandora.nla.gov.au/pan/25410/20140311-1105/anzmac.org/conference/2012/papers/173ANZMACFINAL.pdf (accessed 30 October 2020).

Michard, Q. (2016) 'Why brands should be using data analytics to inform pricing strategy', *Impact*, 8, 68–9.

O'Brien, B. (2019) 'Irish beef price "over €5 million a week" behind UK and EU prices', *AgriLand*, 22 November. Retrieve from: https://www.agriland.ie/farming-news/irish-beef-price-over-e5-million-a-week-behind-uk-and-eu-prices/ (accessed 30 October 2020).

O'Toole, M. (2016) 'At Everlane, transparent is the new black', *Forbes*, 5 January. Retrieve from: https://www.forbes.com/sites/mikeotoole/2016/01/05/at-everlane-transparent-is-the-new-black/ (accessed 30 October 2020).

Rackham, N. (2001) 'Winning the price war', *Sales and Marketing Management*, 253(11), 26.

Reinemoeller, P. (2014) 'How to win a price war', *Sloan Management Review*, 55(3), 15–17.

Ross, E. B. (1984) 'Making money with proactive pricing', *Harvard Business Review*, 62(6), 145–55.

Rust, R. T., Danaher, P. J., and Varki, S. (2000) 'Using service quality data for competitive marketing decisions', *International Journal of Service Industry Management*, 11(5), 438–69.

Sicard, C. (2019) 'Carrefour lance en France Supeco, son enseigne a prix reduits', *Business Insider France*, 4 September. Retrieve from: https://www.businessinsider.fr/carrefour-se-preparerait-a-lancer-supeco-en-france-une-nouvelle-enseigne-a-prix-reduits/ (accessed 30 October 2020).

Soil Association (2019) *The Organic Market Report 2019*. Retrieve from: https://www.soilassociation.org/certification/trade-news/2019/february/06/uk-organic-market-hits-233b (accessed 30 November 2019).

Taylor, M. (2010) 'Camerons invites legal clients to pay what they want for legal work', *The Lawyer*, 5 August. Retrieve from: https://www.thelawyer.com/issues/online/camerons-invites-clients-to-pay-what-they-want-for-legal-work/ (accessed 30 October 2020).

Thier, D. (2016) 'Microsoft just dropped the Xbox One price again', *Forbes/Tech*, 18 March. Retrieve from: https://www.forbes.com/sites/davidthier/2016/03/18/microsoft-just-dropped-the-xbox-one-price-again/ (accessed 30 October 2020).

van Heerde, H. J., Gijsbrechts, E., and Pauwels, K. (2008) 'Winners and losers in a major price war', *Journal of Marketing Research*, 45(5), 499–518.

Völckner, F., and Hofmann, J. (2007) 'The price–perceived quality relationship: A meta-analytic review and assessment of its determinants', *Marketing Letters*, 18(3), 181–96.

Walker, A. W. (1967) 'How to price industrial products', *Harvard Business Review*, Sept–Oct, 125–32.

Chapter 8
Marketing Communications

Learning Outcomes

After studying this chapter, you will be able to:

- describe the nature, purpose, and scope of marketing communications;
- understand the models used to explain how marketing communications and advertising work;
- describe the different steps in the strategic marketing communications planning process;
- describe the role and configuration of the marketing communications mix;
- explain the characteristics of each of the primary tools, media, and messages; and
- consider the principles and issues associated with integrated marketing communications.

Case Insight 8.1
The Guardian

Market Insight 8.1
Influencing the Beauty Community on YouTube

Market Insight 8.2
Reinventing Advertising for the Digital Age

Market Insight 8.3
Variable Mixes

Market Insight 8.4
Do it for Denmark!

Case Insight 8.1 *The Guardian*

How could an organization realize its objective not only to shift audience perceptions, but also to change behaviours? We speak to Agathe Guerrier (pictured), strategy director at advertising agency Bartle Bogle Hegarty, to find out more about the work it undertook for its client *The Guardian*.

The Guardian is a truly impartial media organization that is rooted in the principles of independent journalism. The Scott Trust was set up to protect this independence and, to this day, *The Guardian*'s sole purpose remains the pursuit of the truth. This philosophy shapes the way it communicates: 'Facts are sacred, but comment is free.'

The Guardian is made by progressives, for progressives. A progressive is a curious and connected individual who welcomes change as a positive force. Progressives are not defined by income, age, or any other demographic data.

Today's *Guardian* is defined by its open operating system (OOS). By encouraging participation and debate, by welcoming contributions and challenges, it seeks to provide the broadest, most comprehensive view of the world. Openness means that it does not put its content behind a pay wall—a radical stance in today's media landscape. It also means that it does not believe journalists to be the only voices of authority or to be able to complete the entire editorial process on their own; instead, what they do is initiate the creation of content, and then invite bloggers, contributors, readers, and commentators to enrich and evolve it.

The Guardian uses marketing communications to support the key drivers of its commercial strategy. The first of these is to drive newspaper sales, which, although in structural decline, still represent nearly half of *The Guardian*'s revenues. Therefore it is strategically crucial that it defends them in a competitive marketplace.

A second driver concerns the digital reach of the brand via desktop and mobile products. As a media brand, its reach is a key driver of digital advertising revenue. Marketing and communications aim to grow its UK and international reach.

The third driver is digital engagement. Known, active, engaged users of digital products are more valuable to *The Guardian* than anonymous and disengaged visitors. To this end, a strand of the marketing and communications strategy is dedicated to increasing digital engagement—registrations, participation, time spent, and frequency.

However, *The Guardian* has had to face certain problems. The first concerns its potential audience of progressives. It was known from brand health tracking that they were not aware of how much *The Guardian* had changed (mainly the OOS philosophy), and it scored low on image items such as 'modern', 'innovative', and 'dynamic'.

Second, from its trade audience (advertisers and media agencies), it knew that it was struggling with being perceived as a worthy, left-wing, pedantic, and niche newspaper brand.

In terms of direct competition, most of the traditional newspaper sector was actually suffering from a similar fate. The real threat was from the new entrants in the knowledge sector, those of the digital age—Twitter, TED, YouTube—that are really redefining people's attitudes and behaviours when it comes to seeking, consuming, and understanding news content.

Case Insight 8.1 (continued)

For a long time, there had been little investment in the brand, with marketing spend focused on tactical campaigns, such as promoting a certain supplement or feature. The challenge now was to find a way of changing perceptions of *The Guardian* (as a dusty left-wing newspaper brand) among a large potential audience of digitally connected, inquisitive news readers. *The Guardian* wanted this audience to realize that it had evolved and was now a radically innovative leader of the digital age.

The problem was therefore not only how *The Guardian* could go about shifting perceptions, but also how it could change behaviours by driving a larger online audience to the desktop product.

Introduction

Have you ever wondered how organizations such as *The Guardian* manage to communicate effectively with so many different people and organizations? Just how do companies go about planning communication campaigns? This chapter explains how this can be accomplished through the use of 'marketing communications'. This chapter also describes the different aspects of the **marketing communications mix**: a set of tools, a variety of media, and messages that can be used in various combinations, and with different degrees of intensity, to communicate successfully with target audiences.

In the first half of the chapter, we discuss the scope and functions of marketing communications, from its definition and via communication theory to how it is planned for and implemented. Then, we explore the elements of the marketing communication mix, including tools, messages, and media. On completing this chapter, you should also appreciate that, by reconfiguring the mix, it is possible to achieve different goals. Finally, the chapter explains how an integrated approach to marketing communications delivers a more efficient and effective outcome.

Defining 'Marketing Communications'

'Marketing communications' is the management process through which an organization engages with its various audiences. By conveying messages that are of significant value, audiences are encouraged to offer attitudinal and behavioural responses (Fill and Turnbull, 2019).

There are three main aspects associated with this definition, as follows.

- *Engagement*—What are the audiences' communications needs and is it possible to engage with them on their terms using one-way, two-way, or dialogic communications?
- *Audiences*—Which specific audience(s) do we need to communicate with, and what are their various behaviour and information-processing needs?

- *Responses*—What are the desired outcomes of the communication process? Are they based on changes in perception, values, and beliefs, or are changes in behaviour required?

Engagement deals with the way in which communication influences its audiences (see the section after next, 'How marketing communication works'). What to expect in terms of engagement is largely dependent on the decisions made with regards to the target audience and target responses for different marketing communication activities (see 'Marketing communication planning').

The Scope of Marketing Communications

As discussed in Chapter 1, promotion is one of the 'P's of the marketing mix and encompasses the communication of the proposition to the target market. 'Marketing communications' is a more contemporary term for promotion. They are used to communicate the various elements of an organization's offerings to target audiences.

Marketing communications should be regarded as an audience-centred activity comprising three elements: (i) a set of tools; (ii) the media; and (iii) the messages. The five common *tools* are advertising, sales promotion, personal selling, direct marketing, and public relations (PR). In addition, a range of *media*, such as television, radio, press, and the Internet, are used to convey *messages* to target audiences.

These tools, media, and messages are not, however, the only sources of information for consumers. There is also implicit and important communication through the other elements of the marketing mix (such as a high price being symbolic of high quality), as well as unplanned or unintended experiences (such as empty stock shelves or accidents) in relation to the offer.

Figure 8.1 highlights the breadth and the complexity of managing marketing communications. Our focus in this chapter will be on *planned* marketing communications (Duncan and Moriarty, 1998). This component is really important because it has the potential not only to present offers in the best possible way, but also to influence people's expectations about both product and service experiences.

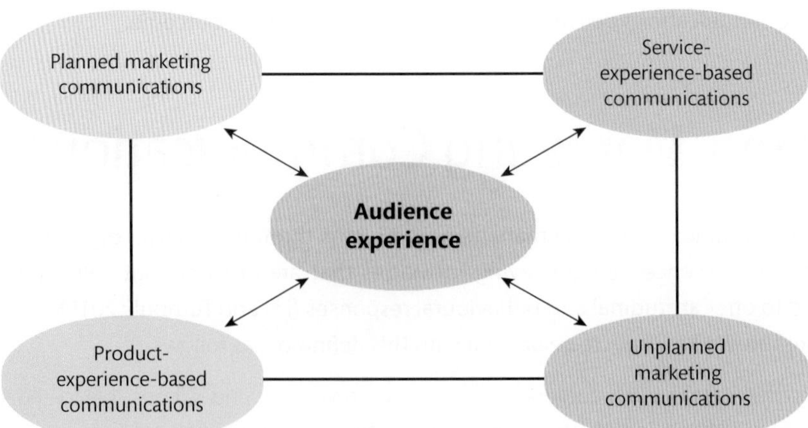

Figure 8.1 The scope of marketing communications

Source: Hughes and Fill (2007). Adapted with the kind permission of Emerald Group Publishing Ltd and Westburn Publishers.

How Marketing Communications Works

Ideas about how marketing communications works have been a constant source of investigation. Although no firm conclusion has been reached, some ideas have played a very influential role in shaping our thinking about this fascinating topic.

Communication Theory

Communication theory explains how and why certain marketing communication activities take place. Communication is the process by which individuals share meaning. Therefore, it is necessary for participants to be able to interpret the meanings embedded in the messages they receive and then, as far as the sender is concerned, be able to respond coherently. The act of responding is important because it completes an episode in the communication process. Communication that travels only from the sender to the **receiver** is essentially a one-way process and the full communication process remains incomplete. This type of communication is depicted in Figure 8.2.

When Swedish chocolate brand Marabou displays its chocolate bars on a poster in the Stockholm metro, the person standing on the platform can read the poster, understand it, and may even be entertained by it. However, the person does not have any immediate opportunity to respond to the poster in such a way that Marabou can hear, understand, and act on the person's comments and feelings. When that same advert is presented on a website or a sales promotion representative offers that same person a chunk of Marabou milk chocolate when they are shopping in a supermarket, there are opportunities to hear, record, and even respond to the comments that the person

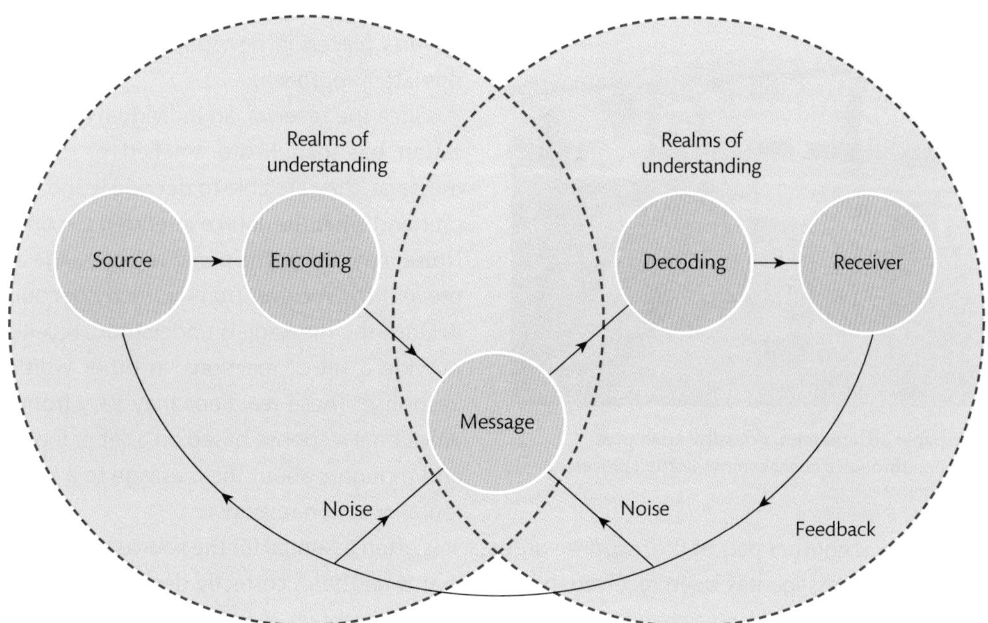

Figure 8.2 A linear model of communications

Sources: Based on Schramm (1955) and Shannon and Weaver (1962).

makes. This form of communication travels from a sender (Marabou) to a receiver (the person in the supermarket) and back again to Marabou. It is referred to as a two-way communication and represents a complete communication episode.

There are three main models or interpretations of how communication works: the linear model, the two-way model, and the interactive model of communication. Each of these is considered further below.

The Linear Model of Communication

The linear model of communication, first developed by Wilbur Schramm (1955), is regarded as the basic model of mass communications. The key components of this model of are set out in Figure 8.2.

The model describes a number of phases that occur in a particular sequence—a linear progression—which, according to Theodorson and Theodorson (1969: 13–14), enables the 'transmission of information, ideas, attitudes, or emotion from one person or group to another (or others), primarily through symbols'. The quality of the linkages between the various elements in the process determine whether the communication will be successful.

The source is an individual or organization, which identifies a problem requiring transmission of a message as well as a receiver. **Encoding** is the process by which the source selects a combination of appropriate words, pictures, symbols, and music to represent the message to be transmitted. Once encoded, the message must be put into a form that is capable of transmission. It may be oral or written, verbal or non-verbal, in a symbolic form or in a sign.

The channel is the means by which the message is transmitted from the source to the receiver. These channels may be targeted at one individual (personal) or not (non-personal). Personal channels involve face-to-face contact and word-of-mouth, which can be extremely influential. Non-personal channels are characterized by mass media advertising, which can reach large audiences. Adverts placed in newspapers are typical of this latter approach.

A newspaper ad represents a classical attempt at persuasion through a linear communication process.
Source: © Getty/AFP/Stringer.

Once the receiver, an individual or organization, has seen, heard, smelled, or read the message, they are able to **decode** it and comprehend what the source intended to convey. **Noise** may distort the perceived message and prevent the receiver from correctly decoding it. Once the message is understood, receivers provide a set of reactions, in other words a 'response'. These reactions may vary from an emotional response based on a set of feelings and thoughts about the message to a behavioural or action response.

Feedback is another part of the response process. It is often essential for the source to know not only that the message has been received, but also that it has been correctly decoded. However, feedback through mass media channels is generally difficult to obtain, mainly because of the inherent time delay involved in the feedback process. Feedback through personal selling, meanwhile, can be instantaneous, through explicit means such as questioning, raising objections, or signing an order form.

The final component in the linear model concerns the source and the receiver's 'realms of understanding' and, where they merge, a shared 'realm of understanding'—this is the common ground between the source and receiver. This understanding concerns the attitudes, perceptions, values, behaviour, and experience of both parties in the communication process.

Today, people engage with interactive-based communications and, in some circumstances such as online gaming, organizations and individuals can be involved in real **dialogue**. The linear model is consequently no longer sufficient to explain how consumers react to communications in modern contexts.

The Two-Step Model of Communication

One interpretation of the linear model is that it is a one-step explanation: information is directed at prospective audiences. However, people can have a significant impact on the communication process and the **two-step model**, sometimes referred to as the 'influencer model', goes some way towards reflecting their influence. This type of communication is depicted in Figure 8.3.

The two-step model recognizes the importance of personal influences when informing and persuading audiences to think or behave in particular ways. This model depicts information flowing via various media channels to particular types of person, to whom other members of the audience refer for information and guidance.

There are two main types of **influencers**: one is referred to as an 'opinion leader'; the other, as an 'opinion former'. **Opinion leaders** are simply ordinary people who have a heightened interest in a particular topic. They belong to the same peer group as the people whom they influence. For example, *Vogue* magazine has an 'Influencer Network', a panel of 1,000 women who, as opinion leaders, provide feedback on a range of issues, including new offerings, upcoming fashion collections, and advert creatives. They are encouraged to talk about particular offerings on their social networks, raising awareness of them and of *Vogue* itself (Moses, 2011).

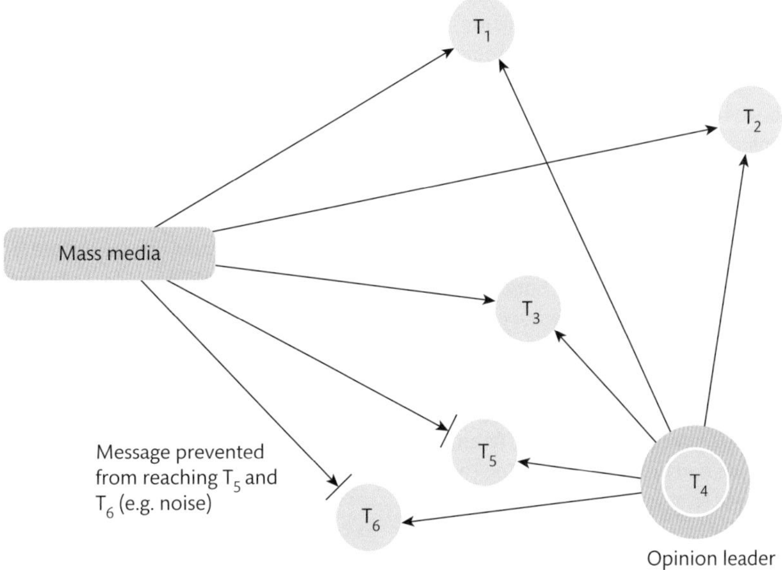

Figure 8.3 The two-step model of communications

Source: Marketing Communications (8th edn) Fill, C. and Turnbull, S. (2019). Reproduced with the kind permission of Pearson Education Limited. © Pearson Education Limited 2019.

Opinion formers are involved professionally in the topic of interest. Their defining characteristic is that they exert personal influence because their profession, authority, education, or status is associated with the object of the communication process. For example, shop assistants in music equipment shops are often experienced musicians in their own right. Aspiring musicians seeking to buy their first proper guitar will often consult these perceived 'experts' about guitar brands, styles, models, and associated equipment, such as amplifiers.

Both leaders and formers have enormous potential to influence audiences. This may be because messages from personal influencers provide reinforcement and message credibility, or it may be because this is the only way of reaching the end-user audience (see Market Insight 8.1).

Market Insight 8.1 **Influencing the Beauty Community on YouTube**

Make-up and beauty videos attract 700 million views a month and total over 14.6 billion views on YouTube. A key voice within this community is 25-year-old Dutch make-up artist Nikkie de Jager, who began posting video content to the website in June 2008 under the pseudonym 'NikkieTutorials'. While her nickname suggests she only creates and uploads beauty tutorials, her content actually stretches further to include beauty challenges, reviews, and product testing videos.

Her channel rose to notoriety from the success of her 2015 viral video 'The Power of MAKEUP!', which currently has forty million views. In October 2020, her videos had accumulated a total of 1.4 billion views while her YouTube channel had nearly fourteen million subscribers. Her creativity, fun personality, and positive attitude to body image all contribute to her monumental online success.

While de Jager continues to practise make-up artistry, most of her career now focuses on her online presence and influence upon her followers within the community. SocialBlade, a website that tracks statistics across the YouTube platform, states that her channel earns an estimated £484k yearly. Despite tremendous earning potential, brand sponsorship plays a major role throughout the entire YouTube community—most specifically the marketing of make-up. As an individual, Nikkie has had brand deals with Too Faced, Maybelline, Ofra, and NYX.

Furthermore, de Jager recently became global beauty adviser for premium brand Marc Jacobs. While this is not seen as an official sponsorship, her opinion will be integral within the product development process across the entire cosmetic line. On her YouTube channel, a disclaimer explains that despite being affiliated to certain brands all opinions are her own, although she will be inhibited from speaking negatively about Marc Jacob's product offerings and will undoubtedly earn significant financial reimbursement for her role.

At a time when consumers are losing trust and interest in certain social influencers, NikkieTutorials is managing to stay relevant through continually posting engaging, inventive, and consistent content. Additionally, following the trends of the community, posting videos on certain topics or brands, and having notable celebrity guest appearances on her channel attracts her viewership from notoriously fickle audiences. This creative professionalism has enlisted and maintained her channel as one of the top ten most influential within the YouTube beauty sphere.

1. **At what stage would you say that de Jager moved from being an opinion leader to becoming an opinion former? Is it possible to say?**
2. **Visit the NikkieTutorials YouTube channel. To what extent is de Jager's communication with her followers based on interaction and dialogue?**
3. **Visit the NikkieTutorials YouTube channel. What opportunities does it offer to marketers?**

Sources: Golbeck (2012); Sykes (2014); Social Blade (2019).

This market insight was kindly contributed by Caitlin Sear, master's student, University of Bath

The Interaction Model of Communications

In the **interaction model** of communications, the parties interact among themselves and communication flows among all of the members in what is regarded as a communication network (see Figure 8.4). The interaction model recognizes that messages can flow through various channels, and that people can influence the direction and impact of a message. It is not necessarily one-way, but interactive communication that typifies much of contemporary communications.

What is important here is interaction that leads to mutual understanding. This type of interaction concerns 'relationship-specific knowledge' (Ballantyne, 2004)—that is, the interaction is about information that is relevant to both parties. Once this is established, increased levels of trust develop between the participants so that, eventually, a dialogue emerges between communication partners. Therefore interactivity is a prelude to dialogue—the highest or purest form of communication.

Dialogue occurs through reasoning, which requires both listening and adaptation skills. Dialogue is concerned with the development of knowledge that is specific to the parties involved and is referred to as 'learning together' (Ballantyne, 2004: 119). The development of digital technologies has been instrumental in enabling organizations to provide increased interaction opportunities with their customers and other audiences (see Market Insight 8.2): consider for example the dialogue box that often pop's up on a retailer's website asking you if you want to talk to an agent (or sometimes **chatbot**).

Marketing Communication Theory

An early important idea about how advertising works centred on how the personal selling process works. Developed by Strong (1925), the **AIDA** model remains very well known and used by many practitioners. The acronym 'AIDA' refers to the need to, first, create *awareness*, then generate *interest*

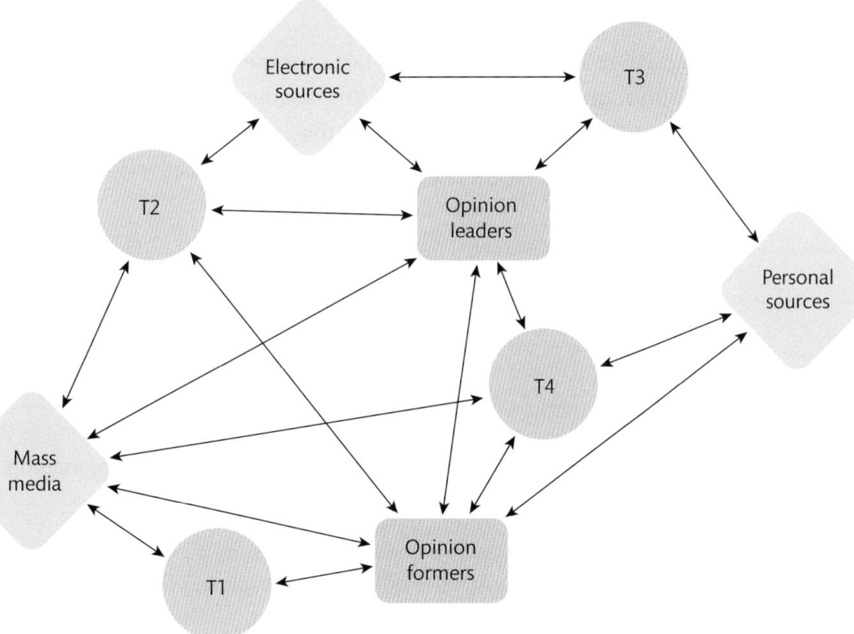

Figure 8.4 An interaction model

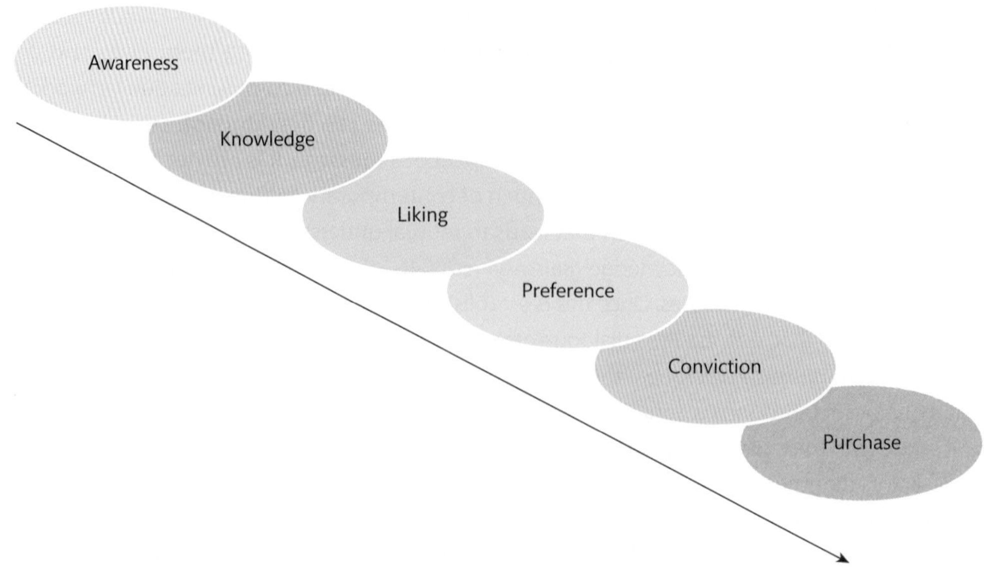

Figure 8.5 Stages in the HoE model

and drive *desire*, from which *action* (a sale) emerges. As a broad interpretation of the sales process, this is generally correct, but it fails to provide insight into the depths of how advertising works. Thirty-six years later, Lavidge and Steiner (1961) presented a model known as the **hierarchy of effects (HoE)** approach. Similar in nature to AIDA, it assumes that a prospect must pass through a series of steps for a purchase to be made. It is assumed that advertising cannot generate an immediate sale because there are a series of thought processes that need to be fulfilled prior to action. These steps are represented in Figure 8.5.

These models are known as 'hierarchy of effects' because the effects (on audiences) occur in a top-down sequence. Although attractive, however, this sequential approach has several drawbacks. People do not always process information nor do they always purchase offerings following a series of sequential steps. This logical progression is not reflected in reality when, for example, an

Research Insight 8.1

To take your learning further, you might wish to read this influential paper.

Duncan, T., and Moriarty, S. (1998) 'A communication-based marketing model for managing relationships', *Journal of Marketing*, 62(2), 1–13.

This is one of the most important academic papers in the field of marketing communications. It is important because it led the move from a functional perspective of integrated marketing communications to one that emphasized its role within relationship marketing.

 **Visit the online resources to read the abstract and access the full paper.**

impulse purchase is followed by an emotional feeling towards a brand. There are also questions about what actually constitutes adequate levels of awareness, comprehension, and conviction. How can one know which stage the majority of the target audience has reached at any one point in time and whether this purchase sequence is applicable to all consumers for all purchases?

The Strong and Weak Theories of Advertising

According to Jones (1991), advertising has a *strong* effect, because it can persuade people to buy an offering not previously purchased. Advertising can also generate long-run purchase behaviour. Under the **strong theory**, advertising is capable of increasing sales for a brand and for the **product class**. These upward shifts are achieved via manipulative and psychological techniques, deployed against largely passive consumers who, possibly because of apathy, are either generally incapable of processing information intelligently, or have little or no motivation to become involved.

Contrary to the strong perspective is the view that a consumer's brand choices are driven by purchasing habit rather than by exposure to promotional messages. One of the more prominent researchers in this area, Ehrenberg (1974), believed that advertising represents a *weak* force. According to the **weak theory**, advertising is employed as a defence, to retain customers and to increase brand usage. Advertising is used to reinforce existing attitudes, not necessarily to drastically change them. This means that when people say that they 'are not influenced by advertising', they are, in the main, correct. Ehrenberg proposed that an awareness–trial–reinforcement (**ATR**) framework would be a more appropriate interpretation of how advertising works.

Both Jones and Ehrenberg agree, however, that *awareness* is required before any purchase can be made, although the elapsed time between awareness and action may be very short or very long. Of the mass of people exposed to a message, a few will be sufficiently intrigued to want to try an offering (*trial*)—the next phase. *Reinforcement* follows, to maintain awareness and provide reassurance, encouraging customers to repeat the pattern of thinking and behaviour. Advertising's role is to breed brand familiarity and identification (Ehrenberg, 1997).

Both the strong and the weak theories of advertising are important because they are equally right and equally wrong. The answer to the question 'how does advertising work?' lies somewhere between the two and is dependent on the context. For advertising to work, involvement is likely to be high, and so here the strong theory is the most applicable. However, the vast majority of product purchase decisions generate low involvement and so decision-making is likely to be driven by habit. Here, advertising's role is to maintain a brand's awareness with the purchase cycle, so the weak theory is most applicable.

 Visit the **online resources** and complete Internet Activity 8.1 to learn more about the strong and the weak theories of advertising.

A Composite Approach

The frameworks presented so far have their roots in advertising. If we are to establish a model that explains how marketing communications works, a different perspective is required—one that draws on all of the models. This is possible because the three key components of the attitude construct lie within these different models. Attitudes are regarded as an important focus for marketing communications activities and advertising is thought to be capable of influencing the development of positive attitudes towards brands (see also Chapter 2).

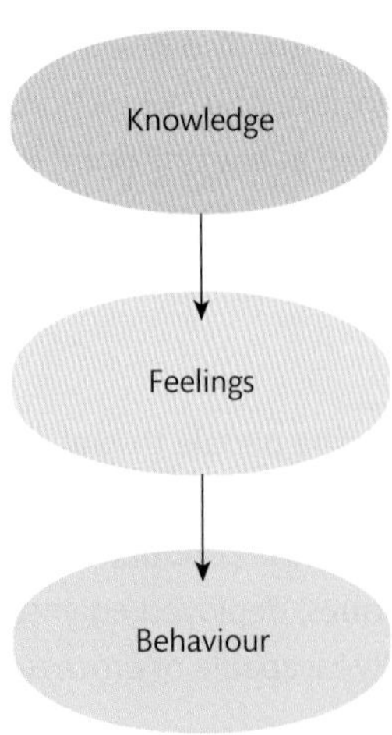

Figure 8.6 Attitude construct: linear

The three stages of attitude formation are that we learn something (i.e. a cognitive or learning component), feel something (i.e. an affective or emotional component), and then act on our attitudes (i.e. a behavioural or conative component). So, in many situations, we learn something, feel something towards a brand, and then proceed to buy or not to buy. These stages are set out in Figure 8.6.

The HoE models and the strong theory contain this sequential approach of learn–feel–do. However, we do not always pass through this particular sequence, and the weak theory puts greater emphasis on familiarity and reminding (awareness) than the other components.

If we look at Figure 8.7, we can see that these components are organized into a circular format. This means that, when using marketing communications, it is not necessary to follow each component sequentially. The focus can be on what the audience requires and this might be on the learning, feeling, or doing components, as the audience determines. In other words, for marketing communications to be audience-centred, we should develop campaigns based on the overriding need of the audience at any one time—that is, based on their need to learn, feel, or behave in particular ways.

Word-of-Mouth

The development of technologies such as social media, which facilitate interaction between customers, has intensified the importance of word-of-mouth for marketers. This type of communication does not involve any payment for media because communication is freely given through conversation. Word-of-mouth communication is 'interpersonal communication regarding products

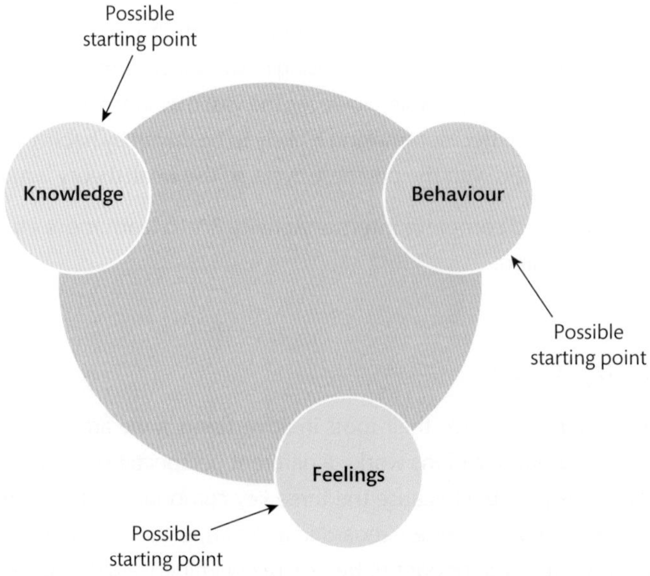

Figure 8.7 Attitude construct: circular

Research Insight 8.2

To take your learning further, you might wish to read this influential paper.

Gilliland, D. I., and Johnston, W. J. (1997) 'Toward a model of business-to-business marketing communications effects', *Industrial Marketing Management*, 26(1), 15–29.

In this paper, the authors develop a marketing communications model that can be used to understand and analyse advertising effects in business-to-business (B2B) contexts. The authors introduce the concept of 'buy task involvement' (BTI) as the personal relevance felt by individuals forming the buying centre of a company during the purchasing process. They also emphasize the importance of the psychological and emotional state of members of the buying centre in shaping their company's purchases.

Visit the online resources to read the abstract and access the full paper.

or services where the receiver regards the communicator as impartial' (Stokes and Lomax, 2002: 350), although this is not always the case, as we saw with the initial furore over sponsored tweets when they were introduced around 2009.

Customers perceive word-of-mouth recommendations as objective and unbiased. In comparison with advertising messages, word-of-mouth communications are more robust (Berkman and Gilson, 1986). They are used either as information inputs prior to purchase, or as a support and reinforcement of their own purchasing decisions.

For every positive comment, however, there are ten negative comments. For this reason, word-of-mouth communication was once seen as negative, unplanned, and having a corrosive effect on a brand's overall communications. Today, organizations actively manage word-of-mouth communications to generate positive comments and as a way of differentiating themselves in the market. Viral marketing, or electronic word-of-mouth, communication is an electronic version of the spoken endorsement of an offering. Both online and offline word-of-mouth has become increasingly important in influencing consumers' attitudes toward products and brand credibility (Chu and Kim, 2018).

Visit the **online resources** and complete Internet Activity 8.2 to learn more about the importance of word-of-mouth in contemporary advertising.

Marketing Communications Tasks

Marketing communications can be used to engage audiences by undertaking one of four main tasks, referred to by Fill and Turnbull (2019) as the '**DRIP** model'. The acronym refers to the ways in which communications can be used to *differentiate* brands and organizations, to *reinforce* brand memories and expectations, to *inform* audiences (i.e. to make them aware or to educate them), and to *persuade* them to do things or to behave in particular ways (see Table 8.1).

Table 8.1 DRIP tasks for marketing communications

Marketing communication tasks	Explanation
To differentiate	Marketing communications can help to *differentiate* one brand from another and position them, so that consumers develop positive attitudes and make purchasing decisions.
To reinforce	Communications may *remind* people of a need they might have or of the benefits of past transactions, with a view to convincing them that they should enter into a similar exchange. In addition, they can provide *reassurance* or comfort either immediately prior to an exchange or, more commonly, post-purchase.
To inform	One of the most common uses of marketing communications is to *inform* and make potential customers aware of the features and benefits of an organization's offering.
To persuade	Communication may attempt to *persuade* current and potential customers of the desirability of entering into an exchange relationship.

Market Insight 8.2 **Reinventing Advertising for the Digital Age**

Digital hit advertising like a wrecking ball! It smashed existing power structures into smithereens and empowered ordinary people to create their own mass communications. It broke the consumer decision journey into pieces, leaving advertisers to figure out how the new reality fits together. Consequently, the following three important changes are shaping the future of advertising.

1 *The zero moment of truth* (ZMOT)—The first effect the digital age had was to end the illusion of control. Brands no longer control what is being said about their brand, if they ever did, and in what order or form their communications reach the masses. People have the power to universally share and access actual experiences of a brand, influencing the choices of people only starting their own decision journey. The experience of initial users moves 'upstream' to affect future users. Google dubbed this the 'zero moment of truth' (ZMOT). This phenomenon is most clearly illustrated by Yelp and TripAdvisor reviews, where real customer experiences trump restaurant reviews and promotions. A brisk smartphone search is now the starting point for many brand experiences, and the bridge between initial need and final decision.

2 *The attention economy*—The second effect of the digital age made it increasingly difficult to buy attention. The media landscape has grown more user-centric, putting pressure on brands

Market Insight 8.2 (continued)

to earn attention—that is, to engage rather than interrupt. A successful campaign now goes beyond bought media, straight into the news and our personal newsfeeds. Increasingly, this means that the new aim of advertising is to create either fame or friendship: to make the brand a celebrity that creates a big splash; or to make the brand a 'friend', providing relevant updates in social media (H&M on Instagram being a good example). The brand needs to have a social role that makes it earn attention—again and again—and builds salience and preference over time.

3 *The brand purpose*—The third effect is a shift from communication to action—from message to mission, and from talk to walk. It is no longer enough for a brand to claim a benefit; it also needs to prove and believably act on it. This creates a need to find a clear purpose—that is, a brand mission, ideal, or theme that it can put into practice in all contact points, and which serves as a platform for innovation and relationship building. This is a property shared by many great brands, but well exemplified by Red Bull's mission to uplift mind and body—'to give you wings'—put into practice through numerous sponsorships, bold stunts, and, of course, the product itself.

Real customer experiences are important to consider in marketing communications.
Source: © Gil C/Shutterstock.

Red Bull sponsorships reinforce its brand proposition using the 'Red Bull gives you wings' tagline.
Source: © David Acosta Alley/Shutter stock.

These key changes mark the end of the age of interruption and the beginning of an age of disruption—for the people, by the people—in which smartphones act as decision guides, entertainment centres, and voting booths, all rolled into one. The new advertising model is being built right now, with advertisers looking for new ways in which to create experiences that are emotional, relevant, and shareable, and which will launch brands to fame, familiarity, and (hopefully) fortune.

1 **Do you agree with the changes described in the insight?**

2 **How might each of the three changes impact on marketing communications?**

3 **What examples have you seen of marketing communications that seem to have been developed with each of the three changes in mind?**

Source: Based on the author's own experience.
This market insight was kindly contributed by Karl Wikström, planner, TBWA Stockholm, Sweden.

 Visit the **online resources** and complete Internet Activity 8.3 to learn more about the way in which fashion house Burberry uses marketing communications.

These tasks are not mutually exclusive; indeed, campaigns might target two or three of them. For example, the launch of a new brand will require that audiences be informed—that is, made aware of its existence—and enabled to understand how it is different from competitor brands. A brand that is well established might try to reach lapsed customers by reminding them of the key features and benefits, and offering them an incentive (persuasion) to buy again.

Marketing Communications Planning

Management's task is to formulate and implement a communication strategy that blends the right mix of tools and media to deliver the right messages in the right place, at the right time, for the right audience. Strategically, the main decisions are concerned with defining the appropriate target audience and setting the right objectives.

To understand what a marketing communications plan should achieve, it is helpful to appreciate the principal tasks facing marketing communications managers. These are to decide the following.

- Who should receive the messages?
- What should the messages say?
- What image of the organization or brand are the receivers expected to retain?
- How much is to be spent establishing this new image?
- How are the messages to be delivered?
- What actions should the receivers take?
- How do we control the whole process once implemented?
- What was achieved?

For many reasons, planning is an essential management activity, and if planned marketing communications are to be developed in an orderly and efficient way, it is helpful to use a suitable framework. A framework for integrated marketing communications plans is presented in Figure 8.8.

The marketing communications planning framework (MCPF) provides a visual guide to what needs to be achieved and brings together the various elements in a logical sequence of activities. It also provides a suitable checklist of activities that need to be considered. The MCPF represents a sequence of decisions that marketing managers undertake when preparing, implementing, and evaluating communication strategies and plans. This framework reflects a deliberate or planned approach to strategic marketing communications.

However, in practice, marketing communications planning is not always developed as a linear process, as depicted in this framework. Indeed, many marketing communications decisions are made outside of any recognizable framework, because some organizations approach the process as an integrative and sometimes spontaneous activity.

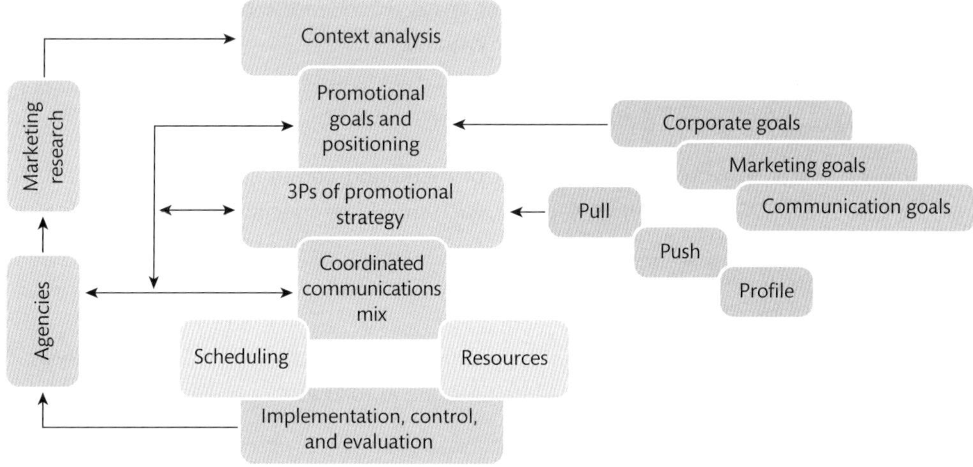

Figure 8.8 The marketing communications planning framework

Source: Marketing Communications (8th edn) Fill, C. and Turnbull, S. (2019). Reproduced with the kind permission of Pearson Education Limited. © Pearson Education Limited 2019.

Elements of the MCPF

A marketing communications plan should be developed for each level of communications activity, from strategy to individual tactical aspects of a campaign.

Context Analysis

The first and vital step is to analyse the context in which marketing communications activities are to occur. The context analysis provides the rationale for the rest of the plan. It is from the context analysis that the marketing objectives (from the marketing plan) and the marketing communications objectives are derived. The marketing plan will already have been prepared and contains important information about the target segments, the business and marketing goals, the competitors, and the timeframes within which the goals are to be achieved. The following four aspects need to be analysed and understood as part of the context analysis:

- the needs, motivations, and attitudes of *customers*;
- the *business*, or *marketing*, context in general, and the marketing communications environment in particular;
- the *internal* context, including people, financial and technological resources; and
- the wider *external* context, including the political, economic, societal, ecological, and technological conditions.

Marketing Communications Objectives

Having performed a context analysis, the next step is to define marketing communication objectives. Ideally, marketing communications objectives should consist of the following three main elements:

- *Corporate* objectives refer to the mission and the business area that the organization believes it should be in.

- *Marketing* objectives might be market share, sales revenues, volumes, return on investment (ROI), and other profitability indicators.
- *Communications* objectives refer to levels of awareness, perception, comprehension/knowledge, attitudes, and overall degree of preference for a brand.

These three elements constitute the overall set of marketing communications objectives. They should be set out in SMART terminology—that is, each should be specific, measurable, achievable, realistic, and timed.

Marketing Communications Strategy

The marketing communications strategy is derived from the objectives and context analysis. The three types of strategies, often used at the same time, are as follows:

- A traditional *pull* strategy uses marketing communications at the consumer or end-user level (e.g. a supermarket advertising to shoppers). It should be supported by a core message to differentiate (position), remind or reassure, inform, or persuade the audience to think, feel, or behave in a particular way.
- A *push* strategy, targeting trade buyers, should be treated in a similar way (e.g. manufacturers advertising to retailers).
- An organization wishing to signal a change of strategy and/or a change of name following a merger or acquisition may choose to use a profile *strategy*.

Communications Method

The communications method part of the plan is relatively complex and a number of activities need to be accomplished. A creative message needs to be developed for each specified target audience in the strategy and should be based on the positioning requirements. Simultaneously, it is necessary to formulate the right mix of communication tools to reach each particular audience. In addition, the right media mix needs to be determined, for both online and other delivery routes.

The Schedule

The next step is to schedule the way in which the campaign is to be delivered. Events and activities should be scheduled according to the goals and the strategic thrust. So, if it is necessary to communicate with the trade prior to a public launch, those activities tied into the push strategy are scheduled prior to those calculated to support the pull strategy.

Resources

The resources necessary to support the plan need to be determined. These refer not only to the financial issues, but also to the quality of available marketing expertise. This means that, internally, the right sort of marketing knowledge may not be present and may have to be recruited. For example, if a customer relationship management (CRM) system initiative is launched, it will be important to have people with knowledge and skills related to running CRM programmes.

Control and Evaluation

Once launched, campaigns are then monitored. This is to ensure that, should there be any major deviance from the plan, opportunities exist to get back on track as soon as possible.

The market for toothpaste is crowded and competitive: a push strategy is necessary to grab customers' attention.
Source: © defotoberg/Shutterstock.

Feedback

The marketing communications planning process is completed when feedback is provided. Not only should information regarding the overall outcome of a campaign be considered, but so too should individual aspects of the activity. For example, the performance of the individual tools used within the campaign, whether or not sufficient resources were invested, the appropriateness of the strategy, and the relative ease with which the objectives were accomplished, are all aspects that need to be fed back to the various internal and external parties associated with the planning process.

The Role of the Marketing Communications Mix

The marketing communications mix consists of five main tools, four forms of message or content, and three types of medium. These are depicted in Figure 8.9 and each is explored later in this chapter.

Traditionally, organizations have been able to use a fairly predictable and stable range of tools and media. There have, however, been some major changes in the environment and in the way in which organizations communicate with their target audiences. Digital technology has given rise to a raft of different media and opportunities for advertisers to reach their audiences. As the Internet has transformed the way in which we communicate, educate, inform, and entertain ourselves, we now have access to a wide range of media, including hundreds of commercial television channels as well as programmes and podcasts on streaming platforms.

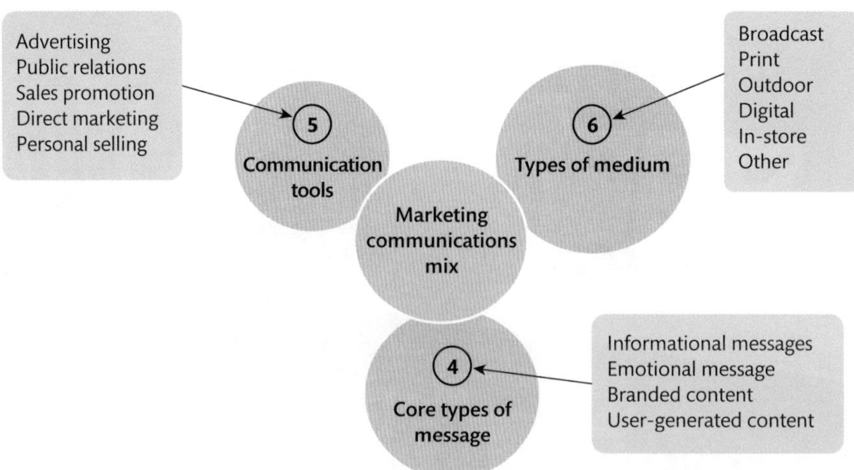

Figure 8.9 The elements of the marketing communications mix

This expansion of the media is referred to as **media fragmentation**. At the same time, people have developed a whole host of new ways in which to spend their leisure time; they are no longer restricted to a few media. This expansion of an audience's choice of media is referred to as **audience fragmentation**. So, although the range and type of media have expanded, the size of audiences that each medium commands has generally shrunk.

The development of the Internet has created new opportunities to engage consumers at different points in their day and at different stages in their purchase decision-making journeys. Many organizations have found that the principles through which particular tools work offline do not necessarily apply in an interactive environment.

For organizations, one of the key challenges is to find the right mix of tools, messages, and media that will enable them to reach and engage with their target audiences effectively and economically. Now, the Internet and digital technologies have enabled new interactive forms of communication in which receivers have far greater responsibility for their part in the communication process and are encouraged to interact with the sender.

Market Insight 8.3 **Variable Mixes**

Airbnb

Online lodging marketplace Airbnb partnered with the Natural History Museum in London to organize sleepovers for children and their parents in a unique location. 'Dino Snores for Kids' allows families to spend a night in one of the UK's most prestigious museums and to explore the exhibitions at night while staying at an exclusive Airbnb Base Camp. The deal also includes activities such as night-time trails among real-sized dinosaurs. The **sponsorship** aimed to develop a memorable visitor experience, while also promoting the family values of the Airbnb brand and increasing awareness within this customer demographic.

Market Insight 8.3 (continued)

Gillette

In 2019, shaving company Gillette launched an advertising campaign in the form of a short film entitled 'We Believe: The Best Men Can Be', a play on their tagline of thirty years, 'The best a man can get'. The film depicted media footage from the #MeToo movement against sexual harassment and assault, as well as scenes of everyday sexism, violence, and bullying among men and boys. The intention was to raise awareness of what Gillette referred to as 'toxic masculinity', challenging traditional masculine stereotypes and advocating a more positive understanding of what it means to be masculine. With more than four million views on YouTube in the space of forty-eight hours, this **viral marketing** campaign divided its viewers, receiving both praise and criticism. Regardless of how the message was interpreted, the campaign resulted in increased publicity for Gillette.

KFC

Following an extreme shortage of chicken leading to the closure of most of KFC outlets in the UK, the company's marketers made the best of a difficult situation. As #KFCCrisis trended on Twitter, they responded with light-heartedness to the flood of tweets directed their way, including competitive banter with Burger King over their supply issues and shortage of not only their chicken but their fries, too. In addition, KFC issued a clever newspaper advertisement featuring their instantly recognizable KFC bucket with the letters rearranged to spell 'FCK', which unsurprisingly caught people's attention. Notably, the disclaimer beneath the ad acknowledged the absurdity of the problem, and thanked customers for their support during the crisis. This demonstrated transparency and openness in dealing with the situation, contributing positively to their brand image.

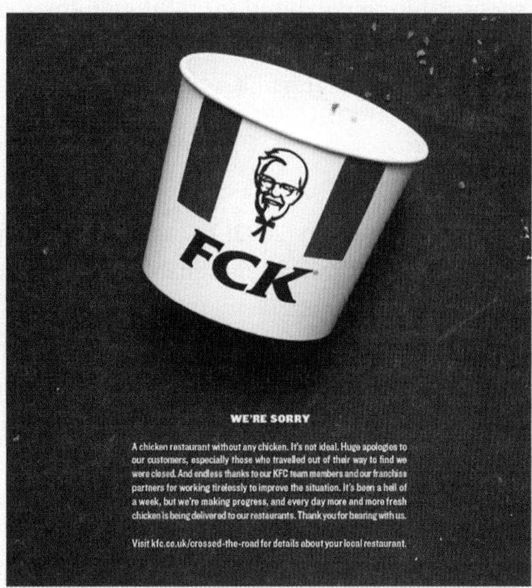

KFC issued an apology to its customers following the chicken shortage and the closure of its UK outlets.
Source: Ged Carroll via Flickr.

1. **Describe the key elements of the message in each of these campaigns.**
2. **How do the media used for these campaigns enable messages to reach target audiences?**
3. **Which of these three campaigns impresses you most? Why?**

Sources: Airbnb (2017); Topping (2018); Topping et al. (2019).

This has shifted the role of the media. Today, although a short-term focus still prevails for many firms, goals such as developing understanding and preference, reminding and reassuring customers, and building brand value are now accepted as important aspects of marketing communications. According to Binet and Field (2013), this longer-term brand-building perspective is a more profitable approach than a short-term direct-response focus on sales.

 Visit the **online resources** and complete Internet Activity 8.4 to learn more about how Toyota uses an interactive website to inform its target audience about a complex proposition, the Hybrid Synergy Drive.

Selecting the Right Tools

The principal or primary tools referred to above subsume other tools such as **brand placement**, sponsorship, and **exhibitions**. Although the tools can be seen as independent entities, each with its own skills and attributes, a truly effective mix works when the tools complement each other and work as an interacting unit.

Advertising

Richards and Curran (2002: 74) advanced a definition of 'advertising' as 'a paid, mediated form of communication from an identifiable source, designed to persuade the receiver to take some action, now or in the future'.

Dahlen and Rosengren (2016) have identified three particular dynamics that they believe need to be incorporated within any contemporary definition of advertising: (new) media and formats; (new) 'consumer' behaviours related to advertising; and the extended effects of advertising.

Sales Promotion

Sales promotions offer a direct inducement or an incentive to encourage customers to buy an offering. These inducements can be targeted at consumers, distributors, agents, and members of the sales force. The key forms of sales promotion are sampling, coupons, deals, premiums, contests, and sweepstakes, and (in the trade) various forms of allowance.

Public Relations

Public relations is used to influence how an organization is perceived by various groups of stakeholders, including employees, the public, supplier organizations, and the media. Public relations does not require the purchase of airtime or space in media vehicles, such as television

Research Insight 8.3

To take your learning further, you might wish to read this influential paper.

Dahlen, M., and Rosengren, S. (2016) 'If advertising won't die, what will it be? Towards a new definition of advertising', *Journal of Advertising*, 45(3), 334–45.

This paper provides a timely and interesting consideration of the way in which advertising has been, and should be, defined within an academic context. Talking to advertising academics and professionals and considering the changing nature of media, consumer behaviours and extended social influences, the authors propose a new definition of advertising as 'brand-initiated communication intent on impacting people'.

 Visit the **online resources** to read the abstract and access the full paper.

magazines or online. These types of message are low cost and are perceived to be extremely credible.

Different types of PR can be identified, but the main approach is referred to as 'media relations', and consists of press releases, conferences, and events. Other forms of PR include lobbying, investor relations, and corporate advertising.

Direct Marketing

The primary role of direct marketing is to drive a response and shape the behaviour of the target audience with regard to a brand. This is achieved by sending personalized and customized messages, often requesting a 'call to action', designed to provoke a change in the audience's behaviour.

Direct marketing is used to create and sustain a personal and intermediary-free communication with customers, potential customers, and other significant stakeholders. Some of the principal techniques are direct mail, telemarketing, email, and, increasingly, Internet-based communications, such as searches. One of its key benefits is its precision; messages are sent to, received by, processed by, and responded to by members of the target audience and no others. This is unlike advertising, whereby messages often reach some people who are not targets and are unlikely to be involved with the brand.

Personal Selling

Personal selling involves interpersonal communication through which information is provided, positive feelings developed, and behaviour stimulated. Personal selling is an activity undertaken by an individual representing an organization, or collectively in the form of a sales force. It is a highly potent form of communication simply because messages can be adapted to meet the requirements of both parties. Objections can be overcome, information can be provided in the context of the buyer's environment, and the conviction and power of demonstration can be brought to the buyer when requested.

Other

There are numerous other instruments used by organizations to reach their audiences. These can be regarded as secondary tools that are used to support the primary mix.

Sponsorship is regarded as 'a commercial activity in which one party permits another an opportunity to exploit an association with a target audience in return for funds, services, or resources' (Fill and Turnbull, 2019: 481).

Brand placement is also a form of sponsorship, and represents a relationship between film/television producers and managers of brands. Through this arrangement, brand managers are able, for a fee, to present their brands 'naturally' within a film or entertainment event.

Field marketing concerns the provision of support for the sales force and merchandising personnel. One key task concerns getting free samples of a product into the hands of potential customers; another is to create an interaction between the brand and a new customer.

Exhibitions are held for both consumers and business markets. Organizations benefit from meeting their current and potential customers, developing relationships, demonstrating products, building industry-wide credibility, placing and taking orders, generating leads, and gathering market information. For customers, exhibitions enable them to meet new or potential suppliers, find out about new offerings and leading-edge brands, and bring themselves up to date with market developments (examples include the Frankfurt Book Fair in Germany and the Ideal Home Show in the UK).

Viral marketing is based on the credibility and reach associated with word-of-mouth communications. Porter and Golan (2006: 33) define viral marketing as 'unpaid peer-to-peer communication of provocative content originating from an identified sponsor using the Internet to persuade or influence an audience to pass along the content to others' (see Market Insight 8.4).

Market Insight 8.4 **Do it for Denmark!**

Companies can sometimes rely on humorous campaigns to attract consumers' interest. This is the case of Spies Rejser, a Danish travel agency, which, in 2014, launched a bold advertising campaign to promote European city breaks as a way in which to address Denmark's declining birth rate. The country has an average of 1.7 children per couple, which is below replacement levels. The advert uses scientific data to claim that people are more likely to conceive when on holiday and offers tips to improve young couples' ability to become pregnant in the name of patriotism!

The advertisement is also linked with a direct-marketing response component. Customers are invited to register online for a tongue-in-cheek campaign in which couples are sent a pregnancy kit to use after their holiday. If the result is positive, Spies Rejser offers three years' free baby supplies.

The advert received a lot of publicity in national and international media (the advert has gained more than eleven million views on YouTube), leading the company to use the same theme in a more recent campaign. This time, Spies is inviting Danish couples to 'Do it for Mom!' Concerned parents are invited to participate through a direct-response element. In exchange for a discount on the holiday, parents can contribute to their children's vacation to show how much they want to become grandparents. Once again,

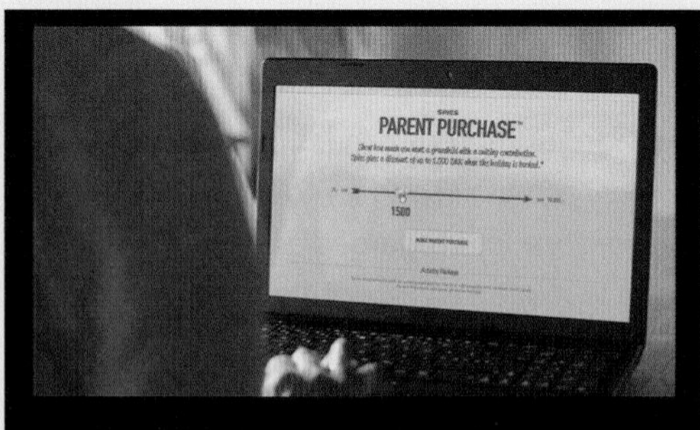

A humorous communications campaign that went viral: Do it for Denmark!
Source: Courtesy of Robert/Boisen & Like-minded.

Market Insight 8.4 (continued)

the campaign has received significant media attention (the advert has gained more than ten million views on YouTube) and has creatively linked a humorous appeal with an interactive dimension.

1 **What tasks is the campaign performing according to the DRIP taxonomy?**

2 **What are the potential strengths and weaknesses of this campaign?**

3 **Which tools and media were used for this campaign? Can you think of ways in which Spies might extend the campaigns to include additional tools and media?**

Sources: Saul (2014); Basu (2015).

Crisis communications have become increasingly necessary as the incidence of crises has increased. This appears to be the result of an increasing number of simple managerial mistakes, incorrect decision-making, technology failures, and uncontrollable events in the external environment (see the KFC example in Market Insight 8.3). Organizations are encouraged to plan for crisis events so that they can respond quickly using planned communications. Using websites, social media, and mobile technologies, managers of an afflicted organization can post up-to-date information quickly; through video and news media, they can attempt to reassure communities by explaining events honestly, by demonstrating concern and sympathizing with any affected groups, before explaining how the situation is being rectified.

Marketing Communications Messages

Our consideration of communication theory confirms the importance of sending the right message—that is, one that can be understood and responded to in context. We can identify four main forms of message content, considered further below, that are not independent entities: informational, emotional, user-generated, and branded content.

Informational Messages

When audiences experience high involvement (see Chapter 2), the emphasis of a message should generally be on the information content, emphasizing the key attributes and the associated benefits. For example, advertising campaigns for charities (such as Greenpeace and Oxfam), financial services (such as Allianz, Santander, and Aviva) and government campaigns for health, tax, and other state services normally make a

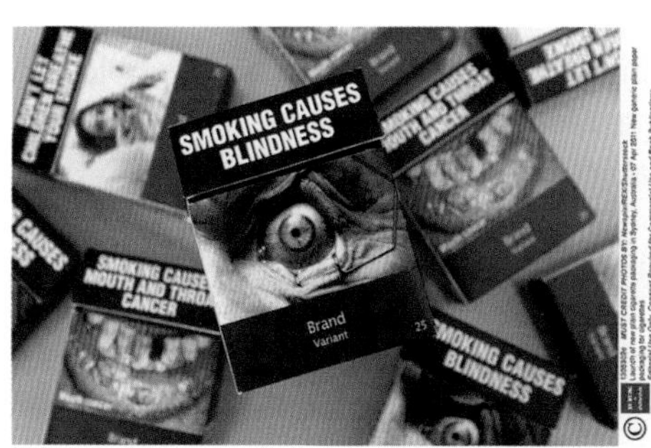

Tobacco packaging using informational, shock-based images to deter users.

Source: © Newspix/REX/Shutterstock.

A common strategy for advertisers is to generate an emotional response that can have a positive influence on brand perception.

Source: © Getty/Richard Levine/Contributor.

statement about the product ingredients, then deliver a rational reason why the receiver should behave in a particular way.

Emotional Messages

When audiences experience low involvement, messages should attempt to gain an emotional response. For example, adverts for fashion, cosmetics, fast food, and soft drinks often engage audiences by using fear, humour, animation, and storytelling. The use of celebrity endorsers and peer-to-peer word-of-mouth can also amplify these messages.

However, buyers often require both rational and emotional messages to make purchasing decisions of specific products and service. These include cars, smartphones, dentistry, energy suppliers, and apps, to name only a few.

Visit the **online resources** and complete Internet Activity 8.5 to learn more about how Bacardi uses product demonstration and a digital media format to inform target audiences how to make a Bacardi mojito.

User-Generated Content

The development of social media has enabled individuals to communicate with organizations, communities, friends, and family. The content of the message, creative and amateur in nature, can be about brands, experiences, or events, and is developed and publicly shared by individuals. This is referred to as **user-generated content (UGC)** and can be seen in action, for example, at YouTube, Instagram, and Twitter. Kaplan and Haenlein (2010) consider UGC to comprise all of the ways in which people make use of social media, and to refer to the various forms of media content that are publicly available and created by end-users.

Research Insight 8.4

To take your learning further, you might wish to read this influential paper.

Dahl, D. W., Frankenberger, K. D., and Manchanda, R. V. (2003) 'Does it pay to shock? Reactions to shocking and non-shocking advertising content among university students', *Journal of Advertising Research*, 43(3), 268–81.

This classic paper examines the effectiveness of shock advertising in comparison to fear and information appeals. The authors find that shocking content in an advertisement significantly increases attention, benefits memory, and positively influences behaviour. The literature review and consideration of different types of appeal is helpful.

Visit the online resources to read the abstract and access the full paper.

Although there have been instances of commercial involvement in UGC, the very nature of this type of content takes the communication initiative away from organizations. As a result, marketers are listening to and observing consumers through UGC. Through this approach, many are finding out the different meanings that consumers attribute to brands, helping in brand development and helping organizations to reposition brands. For example, home decor retailers often encourage customers to post and tag photos of their new furniture or ornaments on social media to generate unique content.

Branded Content

Branded content is the use of entertainment material delivered through paid or owned media, featuring a single company or brand. The recent growth in branded content rests with a drive to realize the potential that 'owned' media offers. Branded content enables conversations, particularly in social media, serving to raise a brand's profile and its credibility. Today consumers use a variety of platforms and so organizations, often through content agencies, need to develop content for use across a wide variety of digital media including social media. This provides an opportunity to integrate material and allow customers to form a coherent or interconnected experience of the brand. The entertainment material is still distributed to customers, but non-customers are also included. Distribution is entirely through media owned by the brand.

The Media

Once a client has decided to use a particular message, decisions need to be made about how and when the message is to be conveyed to engage target audiences. Some media are owned by a client organization, for example its website or the signage outside a building. In most circumstances, client organizations need to use the media owned by others, paying a fee for renting the space and time to convey their messages in order to reach a very large or targeted audience.

The development of digital media has had a profound impact on the way in which client organizations communicate with their audiences. Generally, the trend has been to reduce the amount of traditional media used, and to increase the amount of digital online and mobile media. **Direct-response media** are characterized by the provision of a contact mechanism, such as a telephone number or web address, and increasingly through Internet search activities. These mechanisms enable receivers to respond to messages. Direct-response media also allow clients the opportunity to measure the volume, frequency, and value of audience responses. This enables them to determine which direct-response media work best and so helps them become more efficient, as well as effective.

Visit the **online resources** and complete Internet Activity 8.6 to learn more about the differing media that were used for Ray-Ban's 'Never Hide' campaign.

Broadcast

Advertisers use broadcast media (television and radio) because they can reach mass audiences with their messages at a relatively low cost per target reached. Broadcast media allow advertisers to add visual and/or sound dimensions to their messages. This helps them to demonstrate the benefits of using a particular offering, and can bring life and energy to an advertiser's message.

Print

Newspapers and magazines are the two main media in the print media class; others include custom magazines and directories. Print is very effective at delivering messages to target audiences because it allows for explanation in a way that most other media cannot. This may be in the form of either a picture or a photograph demonstrating how an offering should be used.

Out-of-Home (OOH)

Out-of-home (OOH), or outdoor, media consist of three main formats: street furniture (such as bus shelters); billboards (which consist primarily of 96-, 48-, and 6-sheet poster sites); and transit (which includes buses, taxis, and trains, e.g. the London Underground). The key characteristic associated with OOH media is that they are observed by their target audiences at locations away from home and they are normally used to support messages that are transmitted through primary media—namely, broadcast and print.

Digital

Digital media enable two-way, interactive communication, with information flowing back to the source and again to the receiver, as each participant adapts its message to meet the requirements of its audience. For example, banner ads can provoke a click method by which the receiver is taken to a new website, where the source presents new information and the receiver makes choices, responds to questions (e.g. registers at the site), and the source again provides fresh information. Indeed, the identity of the source and receiver in this type of communication becomes blurred.

In-Store

There are two main forms of in-store media: point-of-purchase (POP) displays and packaging. Retailers control the former and manufacturers the latter. The primary objective of using in-store media is to get the attention of shoppers and to stimulate them to make purchases. There are a number of POP techniques, but the most used are window displays, floor and wall racks in which merchandise can be displayed, and posters and information cards, plus counter and checkout displays. Packaging has to protect and preserve products, but it also has a significant communication role and is a means of influencing brand choice decisions.

Other

Two main other media can be identified: cinema and ambient. *Cinema* advertising has all of the advantages of television-based messages, such as high-quality audio and visual dimensions, which combine to provide high impact on a generally younger audience. *Ambient* media are regarded as OOH media that fail to fit any of the established outdoor categories. Ambient media can be classified according to a variety of factors. These include posters (typically found in washrooms), distribution (e.g. adverts on tickets and carrier bags), digital media (in the form of video and LCD screens), sponsorships (as in golf holes and petrol pump nozzles), and aerials (in the form of balloons, blimps, or towed banners).

Integrated Marketing Communications

For the five tools, messages, and media discussed in this chapter to work most effectively and most efficiently, it makes sense to integrate them, so that they work together as a unit. In this way, they will have greater resonance. This bringing together of different communication media is referred to as **integrated marketing communications (IMC)**.

Integrated marketing communications is popular with both clients and communications agencies. IMC can represent both a strategic and tactical approach to the planned management of an organization's communications. IMC requires that organizations coordinate their various strategies, resources, and messages in order that they enable meaningful engagement with audiences. The main purposes are to develop a clear positioning and encourage stakeholder relationships that are of mutual value (Fill and Turnbull, 2019). IMC can also be used to support the development and maintenance of effective relationships.

One quite common use of an integrated approach can be seen in the use of the tools. For example, rather than using advertising, PR, sales promotions, personal selling, and direct marketing separately, it is preferable to use them in a coordinated manner. Organizations often use advertising or sales promotion to create awareness, then involve PR to provoke media comment, and then reinforce these messages through direct marketing or personal selling. The Internet can also be incorporated to encourage comment, interest, and involvement in a brand, yet still convey the same message in a consistent way.

Research Insight 8.5

To take your learning further, you might wish to read this influential paper.

Ots, M., and Nyilasy, G. (2015) 'Integrated marketing communications (IMC): Why does it fail?', *Journal of Advertising Research*, 55(2), 132–45.

This paper provides an interesting view of IMC implementation, explaining that implementation can be a reason for its failure. The researchers identify four aspects of IMC implementation dysfunction including: miscommunication, compartmentalization, loss of trust, and decontextualization.

 Visit the **online resources** to read the abstract and access the full paper.

Another important aspect of integration concerns the question: what else should be integrated? One element might be the planning and campaign development process. Using an integrated approach during the planning phase can serve to integrate clients, agencies, suppliers, and employees, as well as other resources.

Integrated marketing communications has emerged for two main reasons. First, organizations began to realize that their customers were more likely to understand a single message, delivered through various sources, rather than to try to appreciate a series of different messages transmitted through different tools and a variety of media. The second reason concerned costs. As organizations seek to lower their costs, it has become clear that it is far more cost-effective to send a single message, using a limited number of agencies and other resources, than it is to develop several messages via different agencies.

At first glance, IMC might appear to be a practical and logical development benefiting all concerned with an organization's marketing communications. There are issues, however, concerning the concept, including what should be integrated over and above the tools, media, and messages. For example, what about the impact of employees on a brand, and other elements of the marketing mix, as well as the structure, systems, processes, and procedures necessary to deliver IMC consistently through time?

Chapter Summary

To consolidate your learning, the key points from this chapter are summarized below.

- **Describe the nature, purpose, and scope of marketing communications.**

Marketing communications is a management process through which an organization attempts to engage with its various audiences. Marketing communications, or 'promotion' as it was originally called, is one of the 'P's of the marketing mix. It is used to communicate an organization's offer relating to products, services, or the overall organization. In broad terms, this management activity consists of several components. There are the communications experienced by audiences relating to both their use of products and their consumption of services. There are also communications arising from unplanned or unintended experiences, and there are planned marketing communications.

- **Understand the models used to explain how marketing communications and advertising work.**

Building on general models of communication, these models have evolved from sequential approaches such as AIDA (awareness, interest, desire, and action) and the hierarchy of effects (HoE) models. A circular model of the attitude construct helps us to understand the tasks of marketing communication—namely, to inform audiences, to create feelings and a value associated with offerings, and to drive behaviour.

- **Describe the different steps in the strategic marketing communications planning process.**

In order to differentiate, reinforce, inform, or persuade ('DRIP'), management's task is to formulate and implement a communication strategy that blends the right mix of tools and media to deliver the right messages in the right place, at the right time, for the right audience. The marketing communications planning framework (MCPF) identifies the following key steps in this process: context analysis; marketing communications objectives; marketing communications strategy; communications method; scheduling; resources; control and evaluation; and feedback.

- **Describe the role and configuration of the marketing communications mix.**

Organizations use the marketing communications mix to convey messages and to engage their various audiences. The mix consists of five tools, four main forms of messages or content, and three forms of media. These elements are mixed and adapted to meet the needs of the target audience and the context in which marketing communications operate. Tools and media are not the same, the former being methods or techniques and the latter, the means by which messages are conveyed to the target audience.

- **Explain the characteristics of each of the primary tools, media, and messages.**

Each of the tools—advertising, sales promotion, public relations (PR), direct marketing, and personal selling—communicates messages in different ways and achieves different outcomes. Messages are a balance of informational and emotional content. Some content can be branded and some can be generated by users. Each medium has a set of characteristics that enable it to convey messages in particular ways to and with target audiences.

- **Consider the principles and issues associated with integrated marketing communications.**

Rather than use advertising, PR, sales promotions, personal selling, and direct marketing separately, integrated marketing communications (IMC) is concerned with working with these tools (and media) as a coordinated whole. Hence organizations often use advertising to create awareness, then involve PR to provoke media comment, and sales promotion to create, trial, and then reinforce these messages through direct marketing or personal selling to persuade audiences. The Internet can also be incorporated to encourage comment, interest, and involvement in a brand, yet still convey the same message.

Review Questions

1. **What role does marketing communication ('promotion') play in the marketing mix?**
2. **Make brief notes outlining the meaning of interaction and how dialogue can develop.**
3. **What are the strong and weak theories of advertising?**

4. **Explain the key role of marketing communications and find examples to illustrate the meaning of each element in the DRIP framework.**
5. **Define a marketing communications plan and describe its main components.**
6. **Why do organizations like to use direct-response media?**
7. **What five criteria can be used to select the right mix of communication tools?**
8. **Make a list of the four main message formats and find an example to illustrate each.**
9. **Write brief notes explaining the differences between informational and emotional messages.**
10. **What are the principles of integrated marketing communications?**

Worksheet Summary

To apply the knowledge you have gained from this chapter and test your understanding of marketing communications, visit the **online resources** and complete Worksheet 8.1.

Discussion Questions

1. Having read Case Insight 8.1, how would you advise the marketing team at *The Guardian* to use marketing communications to change the perceptions and behaviour of progressive newspaper readers?
2. Consider the key market exchange characteristics that will favour the use of linear or one-way communication and then repeat the exercise with respect to interactional communication. Discuss the differences and find examples to illustrate these conditions.
3. Select an organization with which you are familiar or for which you would like to work. Visit its website and try to determine its use of the marketing communications tools, messages, and media. How might its mix be improved?
4. Zylog is based in Denmark, and manufactures and distributes a range of consumer electronic equipment. Ennike Christensen, Zylog's new marketing manager, has indicated that she wants to introduce an integrated approach to the firm's marketing communications. However, Zylog does not have any experience of IMC and Red Spider, its current communications agency, has started to become concerned that it may lose the Zylog account. Discuss the situation facing Zylog and suggest ways in which it might acquire the expertise it needs. Discuss ways in which Red Spider might acquire an IMC capability.

Visit the **online resources** and complete the multiple-choice questions to assess your knowledge of the chapter.

Glossary

AIDA a hierarchy of effects, or sequential, model used to explain how advertising works, as an acronym of awareness, interest, desire, and action (to create a sale).

ATR a framework developed by Ehrenberg (1974) to explain how advertising works, as an acronym of awareness–trial–reinforcement.

audience fragmentation the disintegration of large media audiences into many smaller audiences caused by the development of alternative forms of entertainment that people can experience. This means that, to reach large numbers of people in a target market, companies need to use a variety of media, not only rely on a few mass media channels.

brand placement the planned and deliberate use of brands within films, television, and other entertainment vehicles, with a view to developing awareness and brand values.

branded content use of entertainment material delivered through paid-for or owned media and which features a single company or product/service brand.

chatbot an automated online communication software system for users to interact with, often used to help them find what they look for.

crisis communications a part of public relations that is used to protect and defend a brand (individual or organization) when its reputation is damaged or threatened.

decoding that part of the communication process during which receivers unpack the various components of the message and begin to make sense of and give the message meaning.

dialogue the development of knowledge that occurs when all parties to a communication event listen, adapt, and reason with one another about a specific topic.

direct-response media those that carry advertising messages enabling audiences to respond immediately. Most commonly used in print, banner adverts, and on television (known as DRTV).

DRIP an acronym of the four primary tasks marketing communications can be expected to accomplish—that is, Differentiate, Reinforce, Inform, and Persuade.

encoding a part of the communication process during which the sender selects a combination of appropriate words, pictures, symbols, and music to represent a message to be transmitted.

exhibitions events at which groups of sellers meet collectively with the key purpose of attracting buyers.

field marketing a marketing communications activity concerned with providing support for the sales force and merchandising personnel.

hierarchy of effects (HoE) a type of general sequential model used to explain how advertising works. Popular in the 1960s–1980s, these models provided a template that encouraged the development and use of communication objectives.

integrated marketing communications (IMC) an approach associated with the coordinated development and delivery of a consistent marketing communication message(s) with a target audience.

interaction model the flow of communication messages that leads to mutual understanding about a specific topic.

marketing communications mix a set of five tools, a variety of media, and messages that can be used in various combinations, and with different degrees of intensity, to communicate with specific audiences.

media fragmentation the splintering of a few mainstream media channels into a multitude of media and channel formats.

noise influences that distort information in the communication process, which, in turn, make it difficult for the receiver to decode and interpret a message correctly.

opinion formers people who exert personal influence because of their profession, authority, education, or status associated with the object of the communication process. They are not part of the same peer group as the people whom they influence.

opinion leaders people who are predisposed to receiving information and then reprocessing it to influence others. They belong to the same peer group as the people whom they influence; they are not distant or removed.

packaging protects contents, and communicates key rational and emotional information about a brand.

product class a broad category referring to various types of related product, for example cat food, shampoo, or cars.

receiver an individual or organization who has seen, heard, smelled, or read a message.

sponsorship a marketing communications activity whereby one party permits another an opportunity to exploit an association with a target audience in return for funds, services, or resources.

strong theory a persuasion-based theory designed to explain how advertising works.

two-step model a communication model that reflects a receiver's response to a message.

user-generated content (UGC) content made publicly available over the Internet that reflects a certain amount of creative effort and is created by users, not professionals.

viral marketing the unpaid peer-to-peer communication of often provocative content originating from an identified sponsor, aiming to use the Internet to persuade or influence an audience to pass along the content to others.

weak theory a view that suggests advertising works only by reminding people of preferred brands.

word-of-mouth a form of communication founded on interpersonal messages regarding products or services sought or consumed. Receivers regard word-of-mouth communicators as impartial and credible, because they are not apparently attempting to sell products or services.

zero moment of truth (ZMOT) the initial point in the buying cycle at which consumers start researching a product or service, without direct control from the brand.

References

Airbnb (2017) 'Airbnb launches Base Camp at the Natural History Museum's "Dino Snores for Kids" sleepovers', *Airbnb Newsroom*, 11 August. Retrieve from: https://press.airbnb.com/en-uk/airbnb-launches-base-camp-natural-history-museums-dino-snores-kids-sleepovers/ (accessed 1 October 2019).

Ballantyne, D. (2004) 'Dialogue and its role in the development of relationship-specific knowledge', *Journal of Business and Industrial Marketing*, 19(2), 114–23.

Basu, T. (2015) 'Denmark encourages couples to "do it for Mom"', *Time*, 1 October. Retrieve from: https://time.com/4057865/do-it-for-mom-denmark/ (accessed 30 October 2020).

Berkman, H., and Gilson, C. (1986) *Consumer Behavior: Concepts and Strategies*, Boston, MA: Kent.

Binet, L., and Field, P. (2013) *The Long and Short of It*, London: IPA.

Chu, S. C., and Kim, J. (2018) 'The current state of knowledge on electronic word-of-mouth in advertising research', *International Journal of Advertising*, 37(1), 1–13.

Dahl, D. W., Frankenberger, K. D., and Manchanda, R. V. (2003) 'Does it pay to shock? Reactions to shocking and non-shocking advertising content among university students', *Journal of Advertising Research*, 43(3), 268–81.

Dahlen, M., and Rosengren, S. (2016) 'If advertising won't die, what will it be? Towards a new definition of advertising', *Journal of Advertising*, 45(3), 334–45.

Duncan, T., and Moriarty, S. (1998) 'A communication-based marketing model for managing relationships', *Journal of Marketing*, 62(2), 1–13.

Ehrenberg, A. S. C. (1974) 'Repetitive advertising and the consumer', *Journal of Advertising Research*, 14(3), 25–34.

Ehrenberg, A. S. C. (1997) 'How do consumers come to buy a new brand?', *Admap*, March, 20–4.

Fill, C., and Turnbull, S. (2019) *Marketing Communications: Touchpoints, Sharing and Disruption* (8th edn), Harlow: Pearson Education.

Gilliland, D. I., and Johnston, W. J. (1997) 'Toward a model of business-to-business marketing communications effects', *Industrial Marketing Management*, 26(1), 15–29.

Golbeck, J. (2012) *Analyzing the Social Web*, Waltham: Elsevier.

Hughes, G., and Fill, C. (2007) 'Redefining the nature and format of the marketing communications mix', *Marketing Review*, 7(1), 45–57.

Jones, J. P. (1991) 'Over-promise and under-delivery', *Marketing and Research Today*, 19(40), 195–203.

Kaplan, A. M., and Haenlein, M. (2010) 'Users of the world, unite! The challenges and opportunities of social media', *Business Horizons*, 53(1), 59–68.

Lavidge, R. J., and Steiner, G. A. (1961) 'A model for predictive measurements of advertising effectiveness', *Journal of Marketing*, 25(6), 59–62.

Moses, L. (2011) 'Vogue casts 1,000 "influencers" for network', *Adweek*, 11 July. Retrieve from: https://www.adweek.com/digital/vogue-casts-1000-influencers-network-133299/ (accessed 30 October 2020).

Porter, L., and Golan, G. J. (2006) 'From subservient chickens to brawny men: A comparison of viral advertising to television advertising', *Journal of Interactive Advertising*, 6(2), 30–8.

Richards, J. I., and Curran, C. M. (2002) 'Oracles on "advertising": Searching for a definition', *Journal of Advertising*, 31(2), 63–77.

Saul, H. (2014) 'Do it for Denmark: Competition calls for Danes to have more sex to tackle declining birth rates', *The Independent*, 28 March. Retrieve from: http://www.independent.co.uk/news/world/europe/do-it-fordenmark-competition-calls-for-danes-to-have-moresex-to-tackle-declining-birth-rates-9218490.html (accessed 30 October 2020).

Schramm, W. (1955) 'How communication works', in W. Schramm (ed.), *The Process and Effects of Mass Communications*. Urbana, IL: University of Illinois Press, 3–26.

Shannon, C., and Weaver, W. (1962) *The Mathematical Theory of Communication*, Urbana, IL: University of Illinois Press.

Social Blade (2019) 'Online website, statistic tracking for social influencers', NikkieTutorials. Retrieve from: https://socialblade.com/youtube/user/nikkietutorials (accessed 25 November 2019).

Stokes, D., and Lomax, W. (2002) 'Taking control of word-of-mouth marketing: The case of an entrepreneurial hotelier', *Journal of Small Business and Enterprise Development*, 9(4), 349–57.

Strong, E. K. (1925) *The Psychology of Selling*, New York: McGraw-Hill.

Sykes, S. (2014) 'Making sense of beauty vlogging', master's thesis, Carnegie Mellon University. Retrieve from: https://kilthub.cmu.edu/articles/thesis/Making_Sense_of_Beauty_Vlogging/6723560/1 (accessed 30 October 2020).

Theodorson, S. A., and Theodorson, G. R. (1969) *A Modern Dictionary of Sociology*, New York: Cromwell.

Topping, A. (2018) '"People have gone chicken crazy": What the KFC crisis means for the brand', *The Guardian*, 24 February. Retrieve from: https://www.theguardian.com/business/2018/feb/24/people-have-gone-chicken-crazy-what-the-kfc-crisis-means-for-the-brand (accessed 30 October 2020).

Topping, A., Lyons, K. and Weaver, M. (2019) 'Gillette #MeToo razors ad on "toxic masculinity" gets praise—and abuse', *The Guardian*, 15 January. Retrieve from: https://www.theguardian.com/world/2019/jan/15/gillette-metoo-ad-on-toxic-masculinity-cuts-deep-with-mens-rights-activists (accessed 30 October 2020).

Chapter 9
Managing Channels and Distribution

Learning Outcomes

After studying this chapter, you will be able to:

- describe the nature and characteristics of a marketing channel;
- explain the different types of intermediary and their roles in the marketing channel;
- understand the different marketing channel structures and their core characteristics;
- explain the factors that influence the design and structure of marketing channels;
- describe the main elements that constitute supply chain management; and
- consider the role and function of retailers in the marketing channel.

Case Insight 9.1
Pepsi Cola Colombia

Market Insight 9.1
Tesla's Drive towards Self-Sufficiency

Market Insight 9.2
Avocado: Distributing the Green Stuff

Market Insight 9.3
Luxury Goods Tracking via Blockchain

Market Insight 9.4
Programmatic Commerce

Case Insight 9.1 **Pepsi Cola Colombia**

Pepsi Cola Colombia Ltd has sold PepsiCo beverages in Colombia through Postobon SA since 1947, when PepsiCo Colombia signed an exclusive bottler agreement (EBA) for a lifetime, the only such agreement at PepsiCo in the world. We speak to Catalina Dixon, a customer management senior analyst, to find out how PepsiCo Colombia has helped maintain distribution of its product with the Away from Home Channel throughout the Covid-19 crisis.

In most countries outside the USA, PepsiCo franchises its business model by producing and selling its products through agreements with bottlers. The franchise model has a particular way of operating since all of the production, distribution, and selling of the products is the bottler's responsibility. The PepsiCo's management team in Colombia has three areas of responsibility and governance within the EBA in the following areas:

1 Operations: in charge of importing the product syrup (mainly from Uruguay), supervising Postobon's inventories and guaranteeing the quality of the products during the manufacturing process, and delivery of the final product in the marketplace.

2 Marketing: in charge of improving brand health, implementing marketing platforms, and global campaigns to ensure local relevance and activities that improve performance across all distribution channels (e.g. the marketing budget is cooperative, paid in equal parts between PepsiCo and the bottler).

3 Sales: in charge of supervising the bottler's selling performance, implementing sales incentives, sharing best practices, and managing key customer relationships.

The PepsiCo team is relatively small; our sole responsibility is to support the bottler to ensure they maintain our brand strength within the Colombian market. It's critical that we lead and influence the bottler. We proudly say that we work with a great bottler, because last year Postobon SA won the PepsiCo award for 'Bottler of the Year', recognizing them as the best bottler in the world.

I'm responsible for looking after the Away from Home channel (which accounts for a 67 per cent share of the whole market), managing the business-to-business (B2B) relationships with customers including KFC, Burger King, Subway, Pizza Hut, Sodexo, Compass, Marriott, as well as our local customers. Most international customers conduct business with PepsiCo in other countries, so they usually come with international negotiation guidelines, and the B2B relationship with them is crucial because any local problem can reverberate onto business in other countries. These local contracts, signed by the bottler, are usually for five to ten years. They include marketing funds (usually expressed as a percentage of sales) which are reinvested in the customer's marketing campaigns to build both the customer's brand and one of our brands.

My customers from the food service industry mainly buy soda in bag-in-box (BIB) packaging, designed especially for soda fountains. The fountain machines are owned by the bottler and provided to the customers as part of the commercial relationship. This is an advantage

Case Insight 9.1 (continued)

of the franchise model since all the equipment investments are undertaken by the bottler. This means the bottler too must be responsible for the operation, service, and maintenance of the equipment; indeed, this is a fundamental part of the customer relationship. Fortunately, in Colombia, Postobon has its own technical department which directly undertakes the maintenance work. Our customers value the service they provide highly and this gives us a competitive advantage. In Colombia, the selling process is undertaken by the bottler, which has around 2,000 salespeople who visit each point of sales around two to three times per week to take orders. The next day, trucks will deliver that order. An account manager coordinates with the customer discussing the product portfolio ordered, discounts, deliveries, payment method, and timings.

The Covid-19 pandemic has caused problems worldwide, with businesses shut down by governments and citizens ordered to stay at home. In Colombia, the government ordered a quarantine and shuttered businesses on 24 March, initially for nineteen days but they then subsequently extended the deadline. Consequently, the pandemic has particularly affected the Away from Home channel. Customers from the entertainment industry (e.g. cinemas, casinos, and theme parks) are 100 per cent closed and have little idea of when they might reopen. The hotel industry is operating at around 7 per cent of capacity, some of them offering the government the opportunity to use their facilities as hospitals. The food service industry is working at around 20 per cent of capacity, although only through delivery. The shutdown has significantly affected our business.

We have also had to deal with several customer problems given this tough and unprecedented situation. The problems largely revolve around three main areas: packaging, request for financial support from our customers, and costs of distribution.

1 Our main packaging sold is soda in BIB packaging, but carton cups are not ideal as packaging for drinks sold to customers outside the restaurant channel. Consequently, customers have shifted their demand to polyethylene terephthalate bottles and cans, more family combinations, multi-serve, and larger quantities. Our B2B customers also requested that we collect all the BIBs that they had not used so they weren't wasted (and didn't expire) and to offer them additional rebates.
2 Some customers have also asked for financial support in order to keep up with their payroll costs. For example, they wanted to use the marketing funds as cashflow for their payrolls and/or to settle their existing debts with us.
3 Finally, since distribution in Colombia mainly happens through third-party aggregators, they also wanted us to help them brainstorm and implement initiatives for our customers to achieve greater sales and sustain their businesses.

The question for us was: how should we respond to our B2B customers' requests—including the reorganization of our supply chain given the likely negative impact on our revenues and costs—because their own customers could no longer visit their premises?

Introduction

Have you ever considered the journey that a bottle of water, a laptop, or a bag of potatoes might take from its source (its manufacturer or producer) to be available for you to purchase at the point you prefer? In many cases, this journey can be complex, involving transactions between many organizations, countries, and people.

The organizations involved with any one journey are collectively termed a **distribution channel**, or a **marketing channel**. These are chains of organizations that are concerned with the management of the processes and activities involved in creating and moving products from producers and manufacturers to end-user customers. Each organization adds something of value before passing it to the next, and it is this interaction that provides mutual advantage (Kotler and Keller, 2009) and which underpins the concept of 'channel marketing'.

In this chapter, we consider three main elements. The first concerns the management of the intangible aspects or issues of ownership—that is, the control and flows of communication between the parties responsible for making an offering accessible for target customers, commonly referred to as 'marketing channel management'.

The second element concerns the management of the tangible or physical aspects of moving a product from the producer to the end user. This must be undertaken so that a customer can freely access an offering, and so that the final act of the buying process is as convenient and easy as possible. This is part of **supply chain management (SCM)**, which includes the logistics associated with moving products closer to end users.

The third and final element is about **retailing**, a critical element of the way in which consumers access the products they desire.

Channel Management

Europe's largest clothing maker and retailer Inditex has seen its clothing sales rise consistently in recent years, because it adds new stock to its fashion stores (e.g. Zara, Pull&Bear, and Massimo) twice a week, keeping the stock fresh and up to date with the latest fashion trends. It achieves this by manufacturing over 50 per cent of its stock in Spain or Portugal; although more costly in production, Inditex can get new designs into European and American stores twice as quickly than if it were to have to wait for delivery for stock manufactured in Asia. This shows that, by managing its marketing channels, Inditex has improved its overall business performance.

If we consider the skills that Inditex needs to design and assemble a range of garments, to source the materials, and to manufacture, package, and then distribute the final fashion garments to its stores and other customers, globally, we can see that a major set of complex operations are required. For many organizations, trying to undertake all of these operations is beyond their skillset or core activities. For all organizations, there is a substantial risk associated with producing too many or too few, too soon or too late, for the target market. There are risks associated with changing buyer behaviours, and with storage, finance, and competitors' actions, to name but a few of the critical variables.

By collaborating with other organizations that have the necessary skills and expertise, organizations can reduce these uncertainties. Working with organizations that can create customer demand or access and manage specialist financial issues, storage, or **transportation**, adds value and develops competitive advantage. For example, to reach the 600,000 rural villages in India, Samsung partnered with the Indian Farmers Fertiliser Cooperative Ltd to sell its handsets. With this new marketing channel, Samsung can now reach over 90 per cent of the villages in India.

Collectively, organizations that combine to enable offerings to reach end users quickly and efficiently constitute a 'marketing channel', sometimes referred to as a 'distribution channel'. Organizations that combine to reduce risk and uncertainty do so by exchanging offerings that are of value to each other. Marketing channels therefore enable organizations to share or reduce uncertainty. When the uncertainty experienced by all members in a channel is reduced, each is in a better position to concentrate on other tasks.

How Channels Help to Reduce Uncertainty

Marketing channels enable different types of uncertainty to be lowered in several ways (Fill and McKee, 2012). These include reducing complexity, increasing value and competitive advantage, routinization, and providing specialization.

Reducing Complexity

The number of transactions and the frequency of contact a producer might have with each individual end-user customer would be so high that the process would be unprofitable. This volume of activity can be seen in Figure 9.1.

Now, if an intermediary is introduced into the process, the number of transactions falls drastically, as demonstrated in Figure 9.2.

The fall in the number of transactions indicates not only that costs are reduced, but also that producers are better placed to redirect their attention to the needs of intermediaries. This allows them to focus on their core activities: production or manufacturing. In much the same way, end-user customers can get much improved individual support from channel intermediaries than they would be likely to get from a producer.

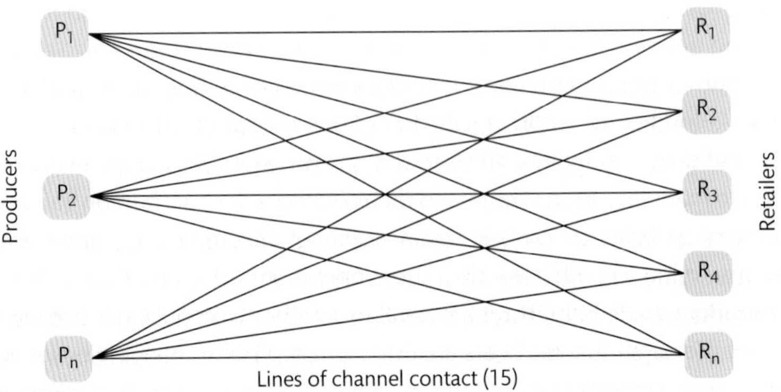

Figure 9.1 The complexity of channel exchanges without intermediaries

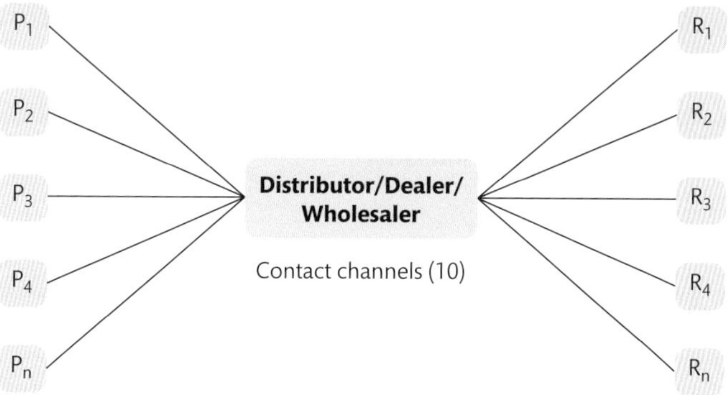

Figure 9.2 The impact of intermediaries on channel exchanges

Increasing Value and Competitive Advantage

By using intermediaries, producers can reduce purchase risk—that is, the uncertainty that customers might reject the offering. Intermediaries, rather than producers, have the skills and core competencies necessary to meet end-user requirements, for example retailing. By improving the overall value that customers perceive in an offering, relative to competing products and customer experience, it is possible to develop competitive advantage.

Routinization

Performance risk can be reduced by improving transaction efficiency. By standardizing or 'routinizing' the transaction process, perhaps by regulating order sizes, automating operations, or managing delivery cycles and payment frequencies, distribution costs can be reduced.

Specialization

By providing specialist training services, maintenance, installation, bespoke deliveries, or credit facilities, intermediaries can develop a service that has real value to other channel members or end-user customers. Value can also be improved for customers by helping them to locate offerings they want. Intermediaries can provide these specialist resources, whereas producers are not normally interested in doing or able to do so. This is because they prefer to produce large quantities of a small range of goods. Unfortunately, end-user customers want only a limited quantity of a wide variety of goods.

Intermediaries provide a solution by bringing together and sorting out all of the goods produced by different manufacturers in the category. They then represent these goods in quantities and formats that enable end-user customers to buy the quantities they wish, as frequently as they prefer.

Intermediaries provide other utility-based benefits. For example, they assist end users by bringing a product produced a long way away to a more convenient location for purchase and consumption—that is, they offer **place utility**. The product might be manufactured during the day, but purchased and consumed at the weekend. Here, manufacturing, purchase, and consumption occur at differing points in time, and intermediaries provide **time utility**.

Immediate product availability through retailers enables ownership to pass to the consumer within a short amount of time—that is, **ownership utility**. Finally, intermediaries can also provide information about the product to aid sales and usage. The Internet has led to the development of a new type of intermediary, an information intermediary (e.g. Expedia, Google). Here, the key role is to manage information to improve the efficiency and effectiveness of the distribution channel—that is, **information utility**.

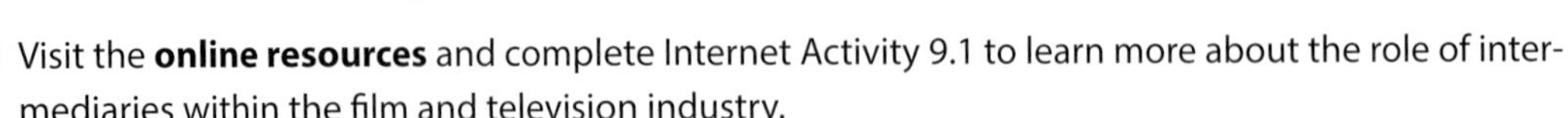

Visit the **online resources** and complete Internet Activity 9.1 to learn more about the role of intermediaries within the film and television industry.

Types of Intermediary

Having seen that intermediaries play a significant role in marketing channels, we now need to consider the different types that are available. Some of the more common ones are as follows.

- *Agents or brokers*—These act as a principal intermediary between the seller of an offering and buyers, bringing them together without taking ownership of the offering. These intermediaries have the legal authority to act on behalf of the manufacturer. For example, universities often use agents to recruit students in overseas markets (such as China, India).
- *Merchants*—A merchant undertakes the same actions as an agent, but takes ownership of a product.
- *Distributors or dealers*—These distribute the product. They offer value through services associated with selling inventory, credit, and aftersales service. Often used in B2B markets, they can also be found dealing directly with consumers, for example automobile distributors. (See Market Insight 9.1 for a view of Tesla's disruptive strategy in the automobile industry.)
- *Franchises*—A franchisee holds a contract to supply and market an offering to the requirements or blueprint of the franchisor, the owner of the original offering. The contract might cover many aspects of the design of the offering, such as marketing, product assortment, or service delivery. The uniformity of differing branches of McDonald's and KFC is an indication of franchisee contracts; however, franchise agreements are not used only in the fast-food or product sectors.
- *Wholesalers*—A wholesaler stocks goods before the next level of distribution, and takes both legal title and physical possession of the goods. In consumer markets, wholesalers do not usually deal with the end consumer, but with other intermediaries (e.g. retailers). In B2B markets, sales are made direct to end-user customers. Examples include Merkandi and BigBuy in Europe.
- *Retailers*—These intermediaries sell directly to end consumers and may purchase direct from manufacturers or deal with wholesalers. This is dependent on their purchasing power and the volume purchased. Leading retailers include Marks & Spencer (UK), Carrefour (France), Caprabo (Spain), and electronics retailers such as Media-Saturn (Germany).
- *Infomediaries*—These Internet-based organizations are intermediaries aiming to provide information to channel members, including end users.

Managing Marketing Channels

There are two main issues associated with the management of marketing channels. These are the design of the channel—that is, its structure and activities—and the relationships between channel members. These are considered in turn.

Channel Design

The design of an appropriate channel—that is, its structure, length, membership, and the roles of those members—varies according to context. For example, the channels necessary to support a new start-up product or organization are different from those needed when an existing structure must adapt to changing market conditions. The channel design decision process requires consideration of three main factors.

1. the level of purchase convenience required by the different end-user customer segments to be served, known as the 'distribution intensity decision';
2. the number and types of intermediary necessary to deliver products to the optimum number of sales outlets, known as the 'channel configuration decision'; and
3. the number of different types of channel to be used, known as the 'multichannel decision'.

This helps us to determine what is the most effective and efficient way of getting the offering to the customer.

Distribution Channel Strategy

When devising a distribution channel strategy, several key decisions need to be made to serve customers and to establish and maintain appropriate buyer–seller relationships. These are summarized in Figure 9.3. These choices are important because they can affect the benefits provided to customers.

Channel Structure

Distribution channels can be structured in a number of ways. There are three main configurations involving producers, intermediaries, and customers: a **direct channel structure** involves selling directly to end-user customers with little involvement from other organizations; an **indirect channel structure** uses intermediaries; and a **multichannel structure** combines both (see Figure 9.4). We now consider the advantages and disadvantages of each of type of channel structure.

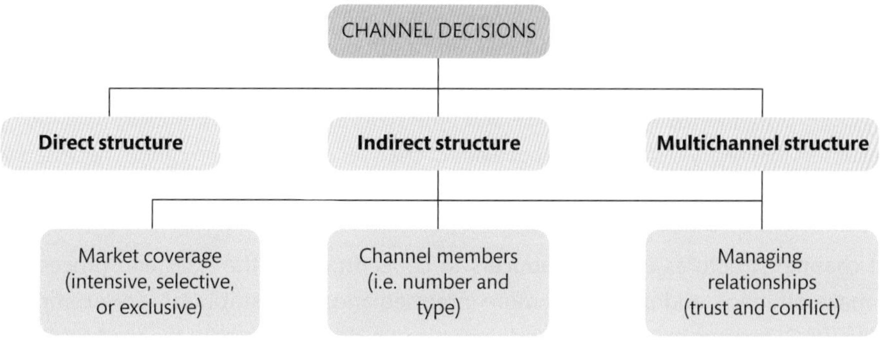

Figure 9.3 Distribution channel strategy decisions

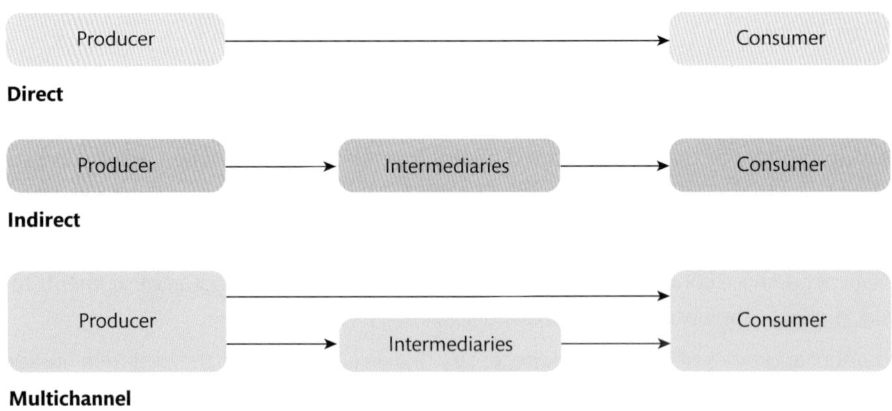

Figure 9.4 Distribution channel structure

Direct Channel Structure

In direct channels, the producer uses strategies to reach end users directly rather than dealing through an intermediary, such as an agent, broker, retailer, or wholesaler (see Figure 9.4). Have you ever been to a farmers' market and purchased produce directly from a farmer, or downloaded music directly from the website of a local band? These are examples of direct distribution. The advantages of this structure include the producer or manufacturer maintaining control over its product and profitability, and building strong customer relationships. This structure, however, is not suitable for all products. It is ideally suited to those products that require significant customization, technical expertise, or commitment on behalf of the producer to complete a sale (Parker et al., 2006).

Electronic technologies such as the Internet have enabled a greater number of product manufacturers to reach customers directly and can allow efficiency within the direct channel structure to be improved. Orders can be processed directly with customers and the communication of supporting information is also more efficient. For example, Dell sells computer equipment through its website, using telesales for product ordering, database technology for order processing, tracking, and inventory, and delivery management.

The disadvantages of a direct channel structure typically include the large amount of capital and resources required to reach customers. This means that there are virtually no economies of scale. Manufacturers might also suffer from offering a low variety of offerings, which may not meet the needs of buyers. This is especially apparent in consumer markets, such as fast-moving consumer goods (FMCGs). Imagine having to shop for bread, milk, and a soft drink at three differing retail outlets owned by each product manufacturer. Few consumers today would purchase their offerings from individual manufacturers owing to the inconvenience and time costs involved. Thus retailers fulfil the needs of end consumers for variety—something that a direct channel of distribution cannot necessarily do.

Indirect Channel Structure

Indirect channel structures enable producers to concentrate on the skills and processes necessary to make offerings, and use one or more intermediaries for distribution. For example, Procter & Gamble (P&G) focuses its resources and expertise on developing new types of FMCG, whereas Sainsbury's core retailing activity is to make P&G's products (and others) available to consumers.

Multichannel Structure

An increasing number of organizations adopt a hybrid, or multichannel, structure to distribute goods and services (Park and Keh, 2003). Here, the producer controls some marketing channels and intermediaries control others. For example, many airlines sell their tickets directly to consumers through the Internet, but also rely on travel agents. Consider the options for the purchase of a mobile device. This could occur directly from the Samsung website, from a service provider such as EE, or perhaps at Tesco, while picking up some bread and milk. Samsung, Lenovo, and LG Electronics use service providers, electronic retailers, and wholesale discount clubs alongside their own direct Internet and telesales channels to market and deliver their mobile phones.

The benefits of a multichannel structure include the following.

- *Increased reach*—By utilizing existing direct networks and the relationships of intermediaries, organizations can reach a wider target audience.
- *Producer control*—Producers have greater control over prices and communication, and can reach customers directly.
- *Greater compliance*—Intermediaries can perceive producers as competitors and so comply with channel rules.
- *Optimized margins*—Producers can improve margins from the direct channel element and increase their bargaining power as they become less dependent on intermediaries.
- *Improved market insight*—By developing relationships with their direct customers, producers can derive a better understanding of their needs and markets issues.

The use of multichannel strategies has been encouraged by the growth of the Internet, which has increased the efficiency with which consumers and manufacturers can interact (Park and Keh, 2003). At the same time, technologies are increasing the efficiency of information exchange between producers and intermediaries, for example through electronic data interchange (EDI) and extranets. However, the sharing of profits among channel members can be a source of conflict, especially when intermediaries perceive the producer as a competitor as well as a supplier. This structure may also confuse and alienate customers who are unsure about which channel they should use.

When implementing a multichannel strategy, the customer experience may differ depending on the touch point selected. **Omnichannel marketing** offers the customer a seamless experience

Research Insight 9.1

To take your learning further, you might wish to read this influential paper.

Rosenbloom, B. (2007) 'Multichannel strategy in business-to-business markets: Prospects and problems', *Industrial Marketing Management*, 36(1), 4–9.

Rosenbloom has written extensively about marketing channels and published several books on the topic. This paper provides an interesting insight into the issues of channel strategy within a B2B context.

 **Visit the online resources to read the abstract and access the full paper.**

across all touch points associated with a product or service, whether shopping online or in a physical store. For example, when purchasing the latest iPhone, you will find consistent branding and product information whether you are in a major retailer or an official Apple Store. Moreover, omnichannel experiences may also involve the blending of various touch points. For instance, when visiting Disneyland Paris, you can plan all aspects of your trip using the My Disney Experience app, which also functions as a digital companion while at the park (Larsen, 2017).

Market Insight 9.1 **Tesla's Drive towards Self-Sufficiency**

American automotive company Tesla, Inc. has disrupted the car industry since it was founded in 2003. Since then, the company has launched six electric vehicles with a much longer range—the distance travelled on one charge—than those of its competitors. Tesla has adopted an aggressive strategy to become a well-known brand among those established since the start of the last century such as Ford and BMW. To do so, the firm has mastered multiple technologies, including batteries and artificial intelligence. For example, its ground-breaking auto-pilot capabilities are present in all its new vehicles and can be improved through automatic updates as Tesla's expertise develops.

To reach new customers, Tesla stores are located in high traffic locations such as shopping centres.
Source: © Jer123/Shutterstock.

Tesla differs from other automotive companies as the brand does not have dealerships and cars are sold directly to customers. It is only possible to buy a Tesla car online or by visiting the company's official stores, located in highly frequented locations such as shopping centres. In this way, Tesla positions itself as a unique brand, educating new customers about electric vehicles as well as avoiding the costs associated with traditional dealers.

Tesla vehicles have short development cycles (the Model S was released in 2012, the Model X in 2015, the Model 3 in 2017) which can be difficult for its suppliers to match. As such, Tesla is also moving towards self-sufficiency with regards to most of its suppliers so that its tight delivery schedule can be met. For example, Tesla aims to manufacture battery cells in its 'Gigafactory' plant instead of solely relying on its main supplier, Panasonic. This process of **vertical integration** not only mitigates uncertainty but also reduces the cost associated with the transportation of materials from suppliers to Tesla's main plant in Fremont, California.

In doing so, Tesla can also build more expertise into key domains such as energy storage. The company already owns more than 15,000 car battery chargers around the world and sells integrated solar panels for domestic use. Tesla's vertical integration has become a key enabler to the company's ambition to pioneer a global and clean solar energy network.

1. **As a customer, what are the benefits associated with buying a car directly from the brand rather than one of its distributors?**
2. **What are the disadvantages for Tesla of not selling its cars via traditional dealerships?**
3. **What are the disadvantages of Tesla's vertical integration strategy?**

Sources: Fehrenbacher (2016); Kolodny (2019); https://tesla.com.

Channel Intensity

Sometimes referred to as 'channel coverage', 'channel intensity' refers to the number and dispersion of outlets that an end-user customer can use to buy a particular offering. This decision concerns the level of convenience that customers expect and suppliers need to provide to be competitive. The wider the coverage, the greater the number of intermediaries, which leads to higher costs associated with the management control of the intermediaries.

There are three levels of channel intensity: intensive, selective, and exclusive (see Figure 9.5).

- **Intensive distribution** involves placing an offering in as many outlets or locations as possible. It is used most commonly for offerings that consumers are unlikely to search for and which they purchase on the basis of convenience or impulse, such as magazines and soft drinks or confectionery.

- **Selective distribution** occurs when a limited number of outlets are used. This is because, when customers are actively involved with a purchase and experience moderate-to-high levels of perceived risk, they are prepared to seek out appropriate suppliers. Those that best match their overall requirements are successful. Producers determine and control which intermediaries are to deliver the required products and level of services. Electrical equipment, furniture, clothing, and jewellery are categories in which selective distribution is appropriate.

- **Exclusive distribution** occurs when intermediaries are given exclusive rights to market an offering within a defined 'territory'. This is useful where significant support is required from the intermediary, and the exclusivity is thus 'payback' for their investment and support. High-prestige goods, such as Ferrari sports cars, and designer fashion brands, such as Chanel and Gucci, adopt this type of distribution intensity.

Chocolates and other snacks are typical examples of impulse purchases characterized by intensive distribution.
Source: © Mawardi Bahar/Shutterstock.

Intensive	Selective	Exclusive
Distribution through every reasonable outlet in the market	Distribution through multiple, but not all, reasonable outlets in the market	Distribution through a single wholesaling intermediary and/or retailer

Figure 9.5 Intensity of distribution continuum

Table 9.1	Intensity of channel coverage		
Characteristics	**Intensive**	**Selective**	**Exclusive**
Objectives	Widespread market coverage; channel acceptance; volume sales	Moderate market coverage; solid image; some channel control and loyalty	Strong image channel control and loyalty; price stability
Channel members	Many in number; all types of outlet	Moderate in number; well established; better stores	Few in number; well established; reputable stores
Customers	Many in number; convenience-oriented	Moderate in number; brand-conscious; somewhat willing to travel to store	Few in number; trendsetters; willing to travel to store; brand-loyal
Marketing emphasis	Mass advertising; nearby location; items in stock	Promotional mix; pleasant shopping conditions; good service	Personal selling; pleasant shopping conditions; good service
Examples	Groceries; household products; magazines	Furniture; clothing; watches	Automobiles; designer clothes; caviar

Through the Internet, nearly all distribution is intensive because of the massive reach of the web. Even the smallest manufacturer can advertise and sell worldwide, using the same courier services to deliver its offerings as do major firms.

The decision about the number of intermediaries is often driven by cost considerations. The costs of intensive distribution are higher because of the number of outlets that must be served. The implications of these three strategies for distribution are summarized in Table 9.1.

Managing Relationships in the Channel

An important managerial issue concerns channel relationships. Because channels are open social systems (Katz and Kahn, 1978), some level of conflict between channel members is inevitable. Conflict follows a breakdown in the levels of cooperation between channel partners (Shipley and Egan, 1992) and may well affect channel performance. Gaski (1984: 11) defined 'channel conflict' as 'the perception on the part of a channel member that its goal attainment is being impeded by another, with stress or tension the result'.

Channel conflict may involve intermediaries on the same level (tier), for example between retailers or between agents (i.e. **horizontal conflict**). It may also occur between members on different levels (tiers), involving a producer, wholesaler, and a retailer (i.e. **vertical conflict**). (See Market Insight 9.2 for an example of vertical conflict in the avocado supply chain.)

Table 9.2 Conflict resolution strategies

Strategy	Explanation
Accommodation	Modifying expectations to incorporate requirements of others
Argument	Attempting to convince others of the correctness of one's position
Avoidance	Removing self from the point of conflict
Compromise	Meeting the requirements of others halfway
Cooperation	Mutual reconciliation through cooperation
Instrumentality	Agreeing minimal requirements to secure short-term agreement
Self-seeking	Seeking agreement on own terms or refusing further cooperation

Source: Fill and McKee (2012). Used with kind permission.

If strategies to prevent or avoid conflict have failed, it is necessary to resolve the conflict that erupts. The strategies depicted in Table 9.2 vary from selfishness or stubbornness and a refusal to work with other members, through cooperation and compromise, to seeking to accommodate all of the views of other parties, even to the extent of jeopardizing one's own position. The prevailing corporate culture, attitude towards risk, and sense of power that exists within coalitions shapes the chosen strategy.

 Visit the **online resources** and read about the conflict that has arisen in the supermarket industry in the UK.

Market Insight 9.2 **Avocado: Distributing the Green Stuff**

In Europe, consumer demand for avocados has increased steadily in the past few years. In 2017, Europeans consumed 3.4 billion avocados, a 27.5 per cent growth compared to 2016. This upward trend is most visible in France, the UK, and Germany, where individuals eat on average twelve, ten, and five avocados per year, respectively. This can be explained by the increased demand for healthy foods as many consumers are willing to spend more on unprocessed ingredients, including whole foods such as vegetables and fruits.

To stock European supermarkets throughout the year, avocados are sourced from several countries with hotter climates, predominantly located in South America. The journey of an avocado from a farm in Mexico or Colombia to the plate of French and German consumers is lengthy and requires cross-regional and cultural collaboration between

Market Insight 9.2 (continued)

Avocados can easily get bruised in transit between South American farms and European supermarkets.

Source: © Un fotografo mas/Shutterstock.

producers and distributors. However, a large proportion of avocado fruits are wasted during that process, due to rough transportation conditions or ineffective stock management and handling.

Post-harvest losses can be explained by the friction between members in the avocado distribution process. Parties tend not to share information with one another, both horizontally and vertically, for fear of losing their competitive advantage. Moreover, the goals of each party are not necessarily aligned and are often based on short-term individual gain rather than long-term global profit. For instance, the quality criteria may differ between producers, who focus on the size of the avocado, and distributors, who are mostly interested in the ease of handling and physical appearance of the fruit. There is also a general lack of trust between parties, due to the many intermediaries involved in the distribution of avocados. This is particularly true as the quality of avocados is difficult to assess until they are used by the end consumers, since the flesh of a ripe avocado can be bruised if handled incorrectly.

In global marketing channels, importers and distributors tend to have a significant amount of power that can sometimes lead to vertical conflict with their suppliers. For example, importers can modify their orders late, causing more avocado waste for the producers. Additionally, distributors have adapted quickly to the growing demand in European markets while producers located in developing countries still struggle to keep up with increasing local and global demand. A 2018 study concluded that developing effective partnerships between members of the distribution of avocados was at the root of solving the issue of avocado waste.

1 **How might producers and distributors improve their cooperation to reduce avocado waste?**

2 **How could members build long-term trust along the distribution channel?**

3 **What sources of conflict can you think of between an avocado producer in South America and an importer in Europe?**

Sources: Bustos and Moors (2018); https://avocadofruitoflife.com/.

Supply Chain Management

The second major issue associated with marketing channels concerns the movement of parts, supplies, and finished products. Melnyk et al. (2009) believe that SCM is concerned with the value creation chain of all of the activities associated with physical distribution. This embraces the chain of suppliers involved in providing raw materials (upstream), through the assembly and manufacturing stages, to distribution to end-user customers (downstream). This linkage is now referred to as a 'supply chain', formerly commonly called 'logistics' and, before that, 'physical distribution'.

Integrated SCM refers to the business processes associated with the movement of parts, raw materials, work-in-progress, and finished goods. Unlike marketing channels, which are concerned with the management of customer behaviour, finished goods, and interorganizational relationships, the goal of SCM is to improve efficiency and effectiveness with regard to the physical movement of products. Supply chain management is essentially about the management of all of the business activities necessary to get the right product, in the right place, for the right customer to access in a timely and convenient way (Fill and McKee, 2012).

SCM comprises four main activities: **fulfilment**, transportation, **stock management**, and **warehousing**. Brewer and Speh (2000) argue that it also seeks to accomplish four main goals: waste reduction, time compression, flexible response, and unit cost reduction (see Table 9.3).

By achieving these four goals, the efficiency of a supply chain is improved and, as a result, end-user customers can experience improved levels of channel performance. Figure 9.6 shows these activities and goals brought together to promote superior supply chain performance.

Management of Asda's supply chain is based on computerized scanning to inform suppliers very quickly of which products need delivery and in what quantities. More recent developments in electronic technologies, such as radio-frequency identification tags, are improving the efficiency and effectiveness with which supply chain activities are managed.

Cost control is a core SCM activity, given that about 15 per cent of an average product's price comprises shipping and transport costs alone. Ikea can sell its furniture 20 per cent cheaper than competitors because it buys furniture ready for assembly, thereby saving on transport and inventory costs. The Benetton **distribution centre** in Italy is run largely by robots, delivering numerous goods to 120 countries within twelve days. Benetton also uses just-in-time manufacturing, with some garments manufactured in neutral colours and then dyed to order, with very fast turnaround to suit customer

Table 9.3 Supply chain management goals

Goal	Explanation
Waste reduction	By reducing the level of duplicated and excess stock in the chain, it becomes possible to harmonize operations between organizations to achieve new levels of uniformity and standardization.
Time compression	Reducing the order-to-delivery cycle time improves efficiency and customer service outputs. A faster cycle indicates a smoother and more efficient operation and associated processes. Faster times mean less stock, faster cash flow, and higher levels of service output.
Flexible response	By managing the order-processing elements (size, time, configuration, handling), specific customer requirements can be met without causing them inconvenience, and this contributes to efficiency and service delivery.
Unit cost reduction	By understanding the level of service output that is required by the end-user customers, it then becomes possible to minimize the costs involved in delivering to that required standard.

Source: Fill and McKee (2012), adapted from Brewer and Speh (2000).

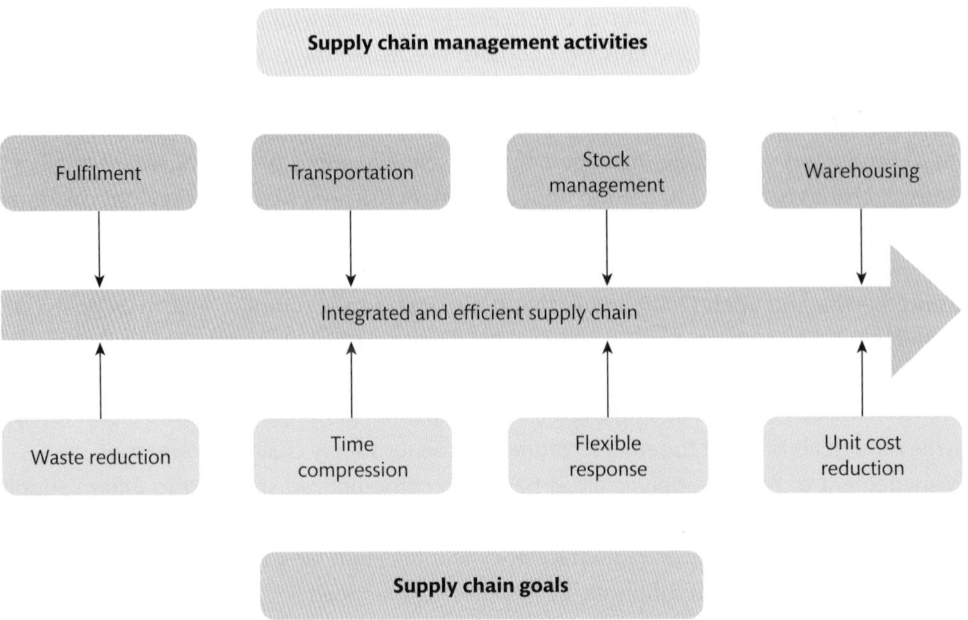

Figure 9.6 Developing high-performance supply chains

requirements. However, beyond lowering costs, many organizations are increasing their focus on managing activities to improve customer service, meet the explosion in product variety, and harness the improvements in information and communication technology.

Thanks to its superior SCM, Ikea can be significantly cheaper than its competitors.
Source: © Prachana Thong-on/Shutterstock.

Fulfilment

Fulfilment or materials handling is about locating and picking stock, packing and securing it, and then shipping the selected items or bundle to the next channel member. The increasing use of specialist software, IT, and equipment helps organizations to manage a range of fulfilment activities. Intra-warehouse stock movement needs to be minimized, while inter-warehouse movement is optimized (Fill and McKee, 2012). Automated emails are sent out to customers following online purchase of, for example, music from Apple Music, a book from Amazon, or a train ticket. Accuracy and speed of billing and invoicing customers is also vitally important, especially for customer relationships.

Transportation and Delivery

Transportation is considered to be the most important activity within SCM. Transportation involves the physical movement of products using, for example, road, rail, air, pipeline, and shipping. Sometimes, transportation is seen only as a way of supplying tangible goods, but it can also be as relevant to many service organizations and the delivery of electronic (or digital) products. Consultants, IT companies, and health organizations have to move staff around, incurring transport and accommodation costs. Management of transport usually involves making decisions between one or more transportation methods and ensuring vehicle capacity. Transportation methods also include electronic delivery modes, such as the telephone, Internet, and EDI.

Stock Management

Stock, or inventory, management involves trying to balance responsiveness to customer needs with the resources required to store stock. The management of both finished and unfinished goods can be critical to many organizations. A balance needs to be achieved between the number of finished goods to be available when customers need it (known as 'speculation') and a store of unfinished goods that can be assembled at a later date or when the stock of finished goods runs low (known as 'postponement').

Warehousing and Materials Handling

Supply chains involved with the exchange of goods usually require storage facilities for the periods between production, transportation, and purchase or consumption. Books, dry goods such as sugar and canned goods, and even clothing all require some level of storage between the time when they leave the producer or manufacturer and that at which they are required to be delivered to end-user customers.

Warehousing Tangible Goods and 'Digital' Products

For the storage of tangible goods, such as FMCGs, an organization can use either **storage warehouses** or distribution centres. Storage warehouses store goods for moderate-to-long periods (i.e. products that have long shelf lives), whereas distribution centres are designed to move goods, rather than only to store them. For products that are highly perishable with short shelf lives, such as fruit and vegetables, distribution centres are more appropriate.

Electronic warehousing systems, or database systems, are increasingly being used for the storage of products (or product components) that can be digitized (see Market Insight 9.3). For example, Emerald Publishing, ABI/INFORM, and ScienceDirect are electronic databases accessible through the Internet that store a vast array of documents electronically to facilitate customers' searches for information. In addition, many organizations use data warehousing facilities whereby product information, or even actual products, are stored in digital form awaiting distribution. Spotify, Apple Music, and Deezer are some of the largest online music streaming services in the world. As of December 2019, they each proposed more than fifty million songs available for users through a monthly subscription scheme. Customers can find, stream and sync in a fraction of the time it would take them to drive to a physical music store and flick through album covers.

We will now look more closely at one particular type of intermediary used in consumer markets: the retailer.

Market Insight 9.3 Luxury Goods Tracking via Blockchain

As of 2019, the number of counterfeit and fake products imported worldwide has increased, amounting to half a trillion American dollars or 3.3 per cent of total global trade. The most impacted countries include the USA, France, Italy, and Switzerland and the most common counterfeit products include clothing, leather goods, watches, and cosmetics. These current circumstances have pushed luxury companies to deploy new mechanisms to counteract this trend.

LVMH's flagship brand, Louis Vuitton, combatting counterfeit luxury goods by recording handbags on the blockchain.

Source: © Sergio Monti Photography/Shutterstock.

In 2019, French luxury conglomerate Louis Vuitton Moët Hennessey (LVMH), which owns Louis Vuitton, Bulgari, and Dior, announced the launch of the AURA platform as a cutting-edge solution to combat the increasing number of faked luxury goods. Leveraging the recent development of **blockchain** technology, AURA empowers LVMH to track products along an increasingly complex supply chain, from the raw materials (e.g. leather, diamonds, and silk) to the customer, as well as second-hand markets.

The AURA blockchain enables all LVMH suppliers to record every step of the production process in a transparent and secure manner. Upon purchase, customers can find out about the life cycle of their products, including ethical and environmental information, and verify their authenticity through a smartphone application. Customers can also record selling their products second-hand, transferring ownership of their goods, so that luxury products cannot be counterfeited even beyond LVMH's supply chain.

In doing so, LVMH not only increases control and transparency over the supply chain of its products but also reinforces the reputation of its brands. By providing fine-grained details of the life cycle of its handbags, watches, and jewellery, LVMH also adds value to its luxury products as their own unique story can be unveiled to its customers. For example, when purchasing a leather handbag from Louis Vuitton's exclusive store on the Champs-Élysées in Paris, customers could discover where the item was originally designed, which farm the leather comes from, and where it was manufactured.

1. **What other advantages are there of LVMH sharing information with its suppliers transparently?**
2. **Which other industries would benefit from providing customers with a transparent view of their supply chain?**
3. **What are the benefits of using blockchain technology for SCM?**

Sources: ConsenSys (2019); OECD (2019).

Retailing

Retailing encompasses all of the activities directly related to the sale of products and services to consumers for personal use. Retailers differ from wholesalers, which distribute the product to businesses, not consumers. Whether they are large retailers, such as Tesco (UK), Lidl (Germany), or

Carrefour (France), or one of the thousands of small owner-run retailers in India, all retailers provide a downstream link between producers and end consumers.

Retailers provide consumers with access to products. As such, it is very important for retailers to find out what consumers actually want if the retailer is to deliver value. Convenience and time utility is the primary concern for most consumers, with people increasingly being 'leisure time poor' and keen to trade off shopping time for leisure time (Seiders et al., 2000). Consequently, convenience drives most innovations in retailing, such as supermarkets, department stores, shopping malls, the Internet, and self-scanning kiosks, in pursuit of providing customer convenience (see also Market Insight 9.4). As noted by Seiders et al. (2000), from a customer's perspective, 'convenience' means speed and ease in acquiring a product, and consists of:

- *access* convenience—that is, being easy to reach;
- *search* convenience—that is, enabling customers to easily identify what they want;
- *possession* convenience—that is, ease of obtaining products; and
- *transaction* convenience—that is, ease of purchase and return of products.

These are outlined in more detail in Table 9.4.

Table 9.4 Retailing convenience: a customer's perspective

Element	Description
Access convenience	• The speed and ease with which customers can reach or engage with a retailer • Accessibility factors include location, availability, hours of operation, parking, and proximity to other outlets, as well as telephone, mail, and Internet • Convenience does not exist without access
Search convenience	• The speed and ease with which customers identify and select products they wish to buy • Identifying and selecting the products wanted is connected to product focus, intelligent outlet design and layout (servicescape), knowledgeable staff, interactive systems, product displays, package, signage, etc. • Solutions can be provided in the form of in-store kiosks, clearly posted prices, and mobile phones for sales staff linked to knowledge centres
Possession convenience	• The speed and ease with which customers can obtain desired products • Influenced by having merchandise in stock and available on a timely basis, with limitations for certain channels, e.g. highly customized products • Internet scores highly for search convenience, yet is generally low in terms of possession convenience
Transaction convenience	• The speed and ease with which consumers can effect and amend transactions before and after the purchase • Driven by a number of innovations, e.g. self-scanning in supermarkets • A significant issue on the Internet, with pure Internet retailers having problems with returns, and customers not prepared to pay for shipping and handling costs

Source: Based on Seiders et al. (2000). © 2007 by Massachusetts Institute of Technology. All rights reserved. Distributed by Tribune Media Services. Reproduced with the kind permission of MIT *Sloan Management Review*.

Research Insight 9.2

To take your learning further, you might wish to read this influential paper.

Glynn, M. S., Brodie, R. J., and Motion, J. (2012) 'The benefits of manufacturer brands to retailers', *European Journal of Marketing*, 46(9), 1127–49.

In this paper, the authors discuss the key value and benefits that consumers derive from retailing. They consider the key benefit of convenience in retailing strategy from a customer's perspective. They define 'convenience' as meaning speed and ease, and consisting of four key elements: access, search, possession, and transaction.

 **Visit the online resources to read the abstract and access the full paper.**

Types of Retailer

There are numerous types of retailer. These can be classified according to the marketing strategy employed (i.e. product, price, and service level) and the store presence (i.e. store or non-store retailing).

Table 9.5, although not exhaustive, provides a useful summary of these elements across the differing types of retailing channel.

The types of retailing establishment can be further distinguished as follows.

- *Department stores* are large-scale retailing organizations that offer a very broad and deep assortment of products (both hard and soft goods), and provide a wide array of customer service facilities for store customers. Debenhams, for example, has a wide array of products including home furnishings, foods, cosmetics, clothing, books, and furniture, and further provides variety within each category (such as brand, feature variety).
- *Discount retailers* are positioned based on low prices combined with the reduced costs of doing business. The key characteristics here involve a broad, but shallow, assortment of products, low prices, and very few customer services. Matalan in the UK, Lidl in Germany, and Tati in France are all examples of European discount retailers. To keep prices down, the retailers negotiate extensively with suppliers to ensure low merchandise costs.
- *Limited-line retailers* have a narrow, but deep, product assortment and customer services vary from store to store. Clothing retailers, butchers, baked goods, and furniture stores that specialize in a small number of related product categories are all examples. The breadth of product variety differs across limited line stores and a store may choose to concentrate on several related product lines (e.g. shoes and clothing accessories), a single product line (e.g. shoes), or a specific part of one product line (e.g. sports shoes).
- *Category killer stores*, as the name suggests, are designed to kill off the competition and are characterized by a narrow, but very deep, assortment of products, low prices, and few-to-moderate customer services. Successful examples include Ikea in home furnishings, Staples in office supplies, and B&Q in do-it-yourself goods.
- *Supermarkets*, founded in the 1930s, are large, self-service retailing environments that offer a wide variety of differing merchandise to a large consumer base. Tesco Extra in the UK stocks products from

Table 9.5	Marketing strategy and retail store classification			
Type of retail store	**Product assortment**	**Pricing**	**Customer service**	**Example**
Department	Very broad and deep, with layout and presentation of products critical	Minimize price competition	Wide array and good quality	Debenhams; Harrods; El Corte Inglés; Åhléns
Discount	Broad and shallow	Low-price positioning	Few customer service options	Dollar Dazzlers; Poundstretcher; Poundland
Convenience	Narrow and shallow	High prices	When high quality, can be a competitive advantage	7-Eleven; Co-op
Limited line	Narrow and deep	Traditional = avoids price competition; new kinds = low prices	Vary by type	Bicycle stores; sports stores
Specialty	Very narrow and deep	Avoids price competition	Standard; extensive in some	Bridal boutiques; athletics shops
Category killer	Narrow and very deep	Low prices	Few to moderate	Ikea; Officeworks; Media Market
Supermarket	Broad and deep	Some = low price; others = avoid price disadvantages	Few and self-service	Carrefour; Tesco; Ahold Delhaize; Auchan
Superstores	Very broad and very deep	Low prices	Few and self-service	Tesco Extra; Walmart

clothing, hardware, music, groceries, and dairy products to soft furnishings. Operating with minimum customer service and centralized register and transactional terminals, supermarkets provide the benefits of a wide product assortment in a single location, offering convenience and variety. Today, supermarkets are the dominant institution for food retailing.

- *Convenience stores*, or 'corner shops', offer a range of grocery and household items that cater for convenience and last-minute purchase needs. Key characteristics include long opening times (e.g. 24 hours a day, seven days a week, or 24/7), being family-run, and belonging to a trading group. The 7-Eleven, Spar, and Co-op are all examples. Increasingly, we are seeing smaller convenience stores threatened by large supermarket chains such as Asda and Tesco, especially as laws for longer opening times for larger stores are relaxed (such as Sunday trading hours in the UK).

Visit the **online resources** and complete Internet Activity 9.2 to learn more about the variety of Internet retailing sites and the importance of delivery information for the music sector.

Market Insight 9.4 **Programmatic Commerce**

Gone are the days when having a website with an online shopping facility was considered the height of innovation for retailers. Nowadays, most leading companies are aware that they need to aim for a consistent service delivery across a multiplicity of channels, both online and off. This trend is often called 'omnichannel' retailing. But as companies adjust to managing the complexity of multiple retailing formats, the next revolution is already taking shape. Some call it 'programmatic commerce' and it is essentially based on the seamless integration of the Internet of things—the idea that devices can increasingly communicate with each other through the Internet—into existing retailing systems.

With more than thirty billion devices connected to the Internet in 2020, it is now possible to let technology make purchase decisions for us on the basis of pre-programmed consumer needs and learned preferences. Today, it can take seconds for you to review the option and confirm the purchase. In fact, you could even completely automate the decision to buy a certain product when it runs out, so that you save time making decisions. For example, in 2019, Amazon released the Dash Smart Shelf for businesses. The fully connected device can automatically send low-inventory notifications and reorder supplies without human intervention.

This new model of retailing requires the widespread availability of interconnected devices, as well as consumers feeling comfortable with sharing more of their personal data with organizations they trust. The advantage is an increase in the ease of choice: many decisions that customers need to make every time they buy a product, especially in the FMCG area, will become automatic. Some online retailers such as Amazon are already experimenting with this paradigm, offering discounts for subscriptions to products that consumers routinely purchase.

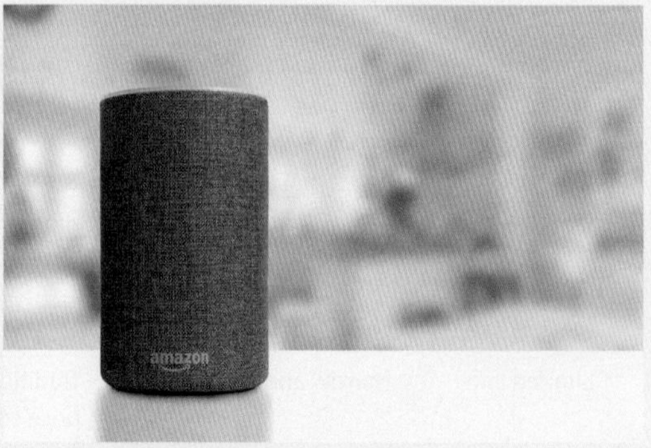

Smart speakers like the Amazon Alexa respond to vocal commands and can directly place orders.
Source: © seewhatmitchsee/Shutterstock.

Programmatic commerce also has far-reaching implications. It improves efficiencies, because consumption patterns are easier to predict and stocks can be minimized. It also creates important marketing implications, because it leads to an increase in switching costs. Once a brand of coffee becomes a customer's default choice, competitors will find it increasingly difficult to enter into that customer's evoked set (i.e. the list of coffee brands that comes to mind before purchase). Marketers should pay close attention to this accelerating trend and should keep experimenting to find potential solutions for the challenges that this new environment poses.

1. **What are the advantages for customers of programmatic commerce?**
2. **How does programmatic commerce affect the relationship between retailers and manufacturers? What are the advantages and disadvantages of this innovation for manufacturers?**
3. **How could we use programmatic commerce to collect useful customer data? What are the ethical implications of the data collection that this form of commerce can generate?**

Sources: Arthur (2016); Temple (2016); Etherington (2019).

Chapter Summary

To consolidate your learning, the key points from this chapter are summarized below.

- **Describe the nature and characteristics of a marketing channel.**

Marketing channels are chains of organizations that are concerned with the management of the processes and activities involved in creating and moving particular offerings from producers and manufacturers to end-user customers. Marketing channels enable different types of uncertainty to be lowered by reducing the complexity, increasing value and competitive advantage, offering routinization, and/or providing specialization.

- **Explain the different types of intermediary and their roles in the marketing channel.**

An intermediary is an independent organization that operates as a link between producers and end-user consumers or industrial users. There are several different types of intermediary, including agents, merchants, distributors, franchises, wholesalers, and retailers. The main role of intermediaries is to reduce uncertainty experienced by producers and manufacturers, and they promote efficiency. The key difference between the various intermediaries is that not all of them take legal title or physical possession of a product.

- **Understand the different marketing channel structures and their core characteristics.**

There are three main marketing channel structures: a direct channel involves selling directly to end-user customers; an indirect channel involves using intermediaries; and a multichannel involves both. At the simplest level, direct channels offer maximum control, but do not always reach all of the target market. Indirect channels can maximize coverage, but often at the expense of control. This is because intermediaries start adapting the marketing mix and demand a share of the profits in return for their involvement. Multichannel strategies often result in greater channel conflict because intermediaries perceive the manufacturer to be a competitor.

- **Explain the factors that influence the design and structure of marketing channels.**

When establishing or adapting marketing channels, it is necessary to consider the type of market coverage that is required, the number and type of intermediaries to use, and how the relationships between channel members are to be managed. These choices are important because they can affect the value that is ultimately provided to customers.

- **Describe the main elements that constitute supply chain management.**

SCM concerns the various suppliers involved in providing raw materials (upstream), those that assemble and manufacture products, and those who distribute finished products to end-user customers (downstream). It embraces four main activities—fulfilment, transportation, stock management, and warehousing—which also subsume other important activities, such as order processing and purchasing. Although these are not traditionally marketing management decisions, it is important to understand that they require a marketing focus and marketing insight.

- **Consider the role and function of retailers in the marketing channel.**

Retailing concerns all activities directly related to the sale of goods and services to consumers for personal and non-business use. Retailers provide consumers with access to products and help to reduce the uncertainty experienced by other intermediaries in the channel, such as wholesalers and manufacturers. This is achieved by taking small quantities of stock on a regular basis, promoting cash flows, and providing demand for their products and services. The different types of retailing establishment can be classified according to two key characteristics: the marketing strategy (i.e. product, price, and service) and the store presence (i.e. store or non-store retailing).

Review Questions

1 **What do we mean by 'marketing channel management'?**
2 **Why do organizations use intermediaries?**
3 **What are the key elements of a channel strategy?**
4 **What are the advantages and disadvantages of the three different marketing channel structures?**
5 **What are the advantages of using an exclusive, rather than an intensive, marketing channel strategy?**
6 **Why is SCM of increasing importance to marketers?**
7 **What are some of the reasons for channel conflict?**
8 **Identify six types of retailer.**
9 **What does the term 'non-store retailing' mean? Identify the main types.**
10 **Write brief notes on how the role of intermediaries in marketing channels has changed as a result of the introduction of electronic technologies.**

Worksheet Summary

To apply the knowledge you have gained from this chapter, and to test your understanding of implementing the marketing mix, visit the **online resources** and complete Worksheet 9.1.

Discussion Questions

1 Having read Case Insight 9.1, what do you see as the main challenges for Pepsi Cola in managing the requests of its supply chain? How would you advise Pepsi Cola?

2 You are an independent craft seller specializing in home décor in Budapest, Hungary. There are three main outlets for your products: a direct link from your Instagram account to a PayPal page where customers can purchase products advertised on your feed, a shop on the e-commerce platform Etsy, and due to your recent success, a seasonal contract to supply a large department store with hundreds of your Christmas wreaths.

   A What types of intermediaries are involved in bringing your products to end users?
   B What are the advantages and disadvantages associated with each marketing channel?

3 The possible ways in which physical and digital goods are dispatched from producers to end consumers are evolving quickly. Research and list the main innovations that could disrupt marketing channels and supply chains in the next few years.

4 Convenience has become a critical issue in marketing channel decisions. Assess the arguments for and against focusing on convenience from a customer's perspective.

Visit the **online resources** and complete the multiple-choice questions to assess your knowledge of the chapter.

Glossary

blockchain an open and decentralized database system which does not require trust between the parties using it.

direct channel structure marketing channel whereby the product is delivered directly from the producer to the final customer.

distribution centres facilities designed to move goods, rather than only to store them.

distribution channel *see* **marketing channel**

exclusive distribution where intermediaries are given exclusive rights to market the good or service within a defined 'territory', and thus a limited number of intermediaries are used.

fulfilment activities associated with locating and picking stock, packing, and shipping the selected items to the next channel member.

horizontal conflict one that may arise between members of a channel on the same level of distribution.

indirect channel structure marketing channel whereby the product moves from the producer, through an intermediary or series of intermediaries, such as a wholesaler, retailer, franchisee, agent, or broker, before being delivered to the final customer.

information utility the provision of information about the product offering before and after sales. It can also provide organizations with information about those purchasing their offerings.

intensive distribution where an organization places its product or service in as many outlets or locations as possible to maximize the opportunity for customers to find it.

marketing channel an organized network of agencies and organizations that, together, perform all of the activities required to link producers and manufacturers with consumers, purchasers, and users to distribute product offerings.

multichannel structure marketing channel whereby multiple sales channels provide a variety of customer touchpoints.

omnichannel marketing where all sales channels are designed to provide a seamless and integrated customer experience.

ownership utility the immediate availability of goods from the intermediaries' stocks, allowing ownership to pass to the purchaser.

place utility the relocation of an offering to enable more convenient purchase and consumption.

retailing also known as the 'retail trade', all of the activities directly related to the sale of goods and services to the end consumer for personal and non-business use.

selective distribution where some, but not all, available outlets for the good or service are used.

stock management activity involving achieving a balance between the anticipated number of finished goods required by customers and a sufficient store of unfinished goods that can be assembled at a later date or when the stock of finished goods runs low.

storage warehouses facilities that store goods for moderate-to-long periods.

supply chain management (SCM) an activity formed when organizations link their individual value chains.

time utility the gap bridged when manufacture, purchase, and consumption might occur at differing points in time.

transportation the physical movement of products using, for example, road, rail, air, pipeline, and shipping.

vertical conflict arises between sequential members in a distribution network, such as producers, distributor, and retailers, over such matters as carrying a particular range or price increases.

vertical integration a strategy in which a company acquires control of stages of its supply chain or distribution channels.

warehousing facilities used to store tangible goods for the periods between production, transportation, and purchase/consumption.

References

Arthur, R. (2016) 'The next big thing in retail: Programmatic commerce', *Forbes*, 24 February. Retrieve from: https://www.forbes.com/sites/rachelarthur/2016/02/24/the-next-big-thing-in-retail-programmatic-commerce/ (accessed 30 October 2020).

Brewer, P. C., and Speh, T. W. (2000) 'Using the balanced scorecard to measure supply chain performance', *Journal of Business Logistics*, 21(1), 75–95.

Bustos, C. A., and Moors, E. H. (2018) 'Reducing post-harvest food losses through innovative collaboration: Insights from the Colombian and Mexican avocado supply chains', *Journal of Cleaner Production*, 199, 1020–34.

ConsenSys (2019) 'LVMH, ConsenSys and Microsoft announce AURA, a consortium to power the luxury industry with blockchain technology'. 16 May. Retrieve from: https://content.consensys.net/wp-content/uploads/AURA_ConsenSys_Press-Release_May-16-2019-2.pdf (accessed 30 October 2020).

Etherington, D. (2019) 'Amazon launches a Dash Smart Shelf for businesses that automatically restock supplies', *TechCrunch*, 21 November. Retrieve from: https://techcrunch.com/2019/11/21/amazon-launches-a-dash-smart-shelf-for-businesses-that-automatically-restocks-supplies/ (accessed 30 October 2020).

Fehrenbacher, K. (2016) '7 reasons why Tesla insists on selling its own cars', *Fortune*, 19 January. Retrieve from: https://fortune.com/2016/01/19/why-tesla-sells-directly/ (accessed 30 October 2020).

Fill, C., and McKee, S. (2012) *Business Marketing*, Oxford: Goodfellow.

Gaski, J. F. (1984) 'The theory of power and conflict in channels of distribution', *Journal of Marketing*, 48(3): 9–29.

Katz, D., and Kahn, R. L. (1978) *The Social Psychology of Organisation* (2nd edn), New York: Wiley.

Kolodny, L. (2019) 'Tesla has a secret lab trying to build its own battery cells to reduce dependence on Panasonic'. CNBC, 26 June. Retrieve from: https://www.cnbc.com/2019/06/26/tesla-secret-lab-building-battery-cells-to-reduce-panasonic-dependency.html (accessed 30 October 2020).

Kotler, P., and Keller, K. (2009) *Marketing Management*, Englewood Cliffs, NJ: Prentice Hall.

Larsen, G. (2017) 'What Disney and IBM can teach omnichannel marketers'. *Chief Marketer*, 11 September. Retrieve from: https://www.chiefmarketer.com/what-disney-ibm-can-teach-omnichannel-marketers/ (accessed 21 December 2019).

Melnyk, S. A., Lummus, R. R., Vokurka, R. J., Burns, L. J., and Sandor, J. (2009) 'Mapping the future of supply chain management: A Delphi study', *International Journal of Production Research*, 47(16), 4629–53.

OECD (2019) 'Trade in fake goods is now 3.3 % of world trade and rising', *OECD*. Retrieve from: https://www.oecd.org/newsroom/trade-in-fake-goods-is-now-33-of-world-trade-and-rising.htm (accessed 21 December 2019).

Park, S. Y., and Keh, H. T. (2003) 'Modelling hybrid distribution channels: A game theory analysis', *Journal of Retailing and Consumer Services*, 10(3): 155–67.

Parker, M., Bridson, K., and Evans, J. (2006) 'Motivations for developing direct trade relationships', *International Journal of Retail and Distribution Management*, 34(2), 121–34.

Rosenbloom, B. (2007) 'Multichannel strategy in business-to-business markets: Prospects and problems', *Industrial Marketing Management*, 36(1), 4–9.

Seiders, K., Berry, L. L., and Gresham, L. G. (2000) 'Attention retailers! How convenient is your convenience strategy?', *Sloan Management Review*, 41(3), 79–89.

Shipley, D., and Egan, C. (1992) 'Power, conflict and co-operation in brewer–tenant distribution channels', *International Journal of Service Industry Management*, 3(4)44–62.

Temple, J. (2016) 'Programmatic commerce: The next big thing'. Retrieve from: https://www.salmon.com/en/resources/blogs/programmatic-commerce (accessed 30 October 2020).

Part 4

Managing Marketing Relationships

Chapter 10 Digital and Social Media Marketing

Learning Outcomes

After studying this chapter, you will be able to:

- define 'digital marketing' and 'social media marketing';
- explain how digitization is transforming marketing practice;
- discuss key techniques in digital marketing and social media marketing;
- review how practitioners measure the effectiveness of social media marketing; and
- discuss crowdsourcing and explain how it can be harnessed for marketing.

Case Insight 10.1
Spotify

Market Insight 10.1
Fighting Fake Online Reviews

Market Insight 10.2
Digital Marketing Games

Market Insight 10.3
Searching the Amazon

Market Insight 10.4
Native Advertising on YouTube

Case Insight 10.1 **Spotify**

What role do social media play and how should organizations incorporate them into their communication campaigns? We talk to Chug Abramowitz (pictured), vice president of global customer service and social media at Spotify, to find out more.

Spotify's dream is to make all of the world's music available instantly to everyone.

Our streaming service launched in Sweden in 2008 and, as of 2020, we're available in ninety-two markets, with more than 299 million active users. Of these, more than 138 million are paid users. Today, Spotify brings you the right music for every moment—on computers, mobiles, tablets, home entertainment systems, cars, gaming consoles, and more.

Social media have been an important part of Spotify's growth in two ways: the marketing team has worked with agencies to create social media campaigns that engage customers and attract them to the Spotify brand, while the customer support team has monitored social media channels and used them as tools to help dissatisfied customers.

Lately, we've noticed that the customer support social media team is more effective than our agencies at customer engagement. The agencies are typically less in tune with what Spotify actually stands for and our tone. And while customer service is primarily about reacting to customers' concerns and praise, our reactions help to build the Spotify brand. For example, after solving someone's issue, our customer support social team regularly replies by drafting a message in the form of a playlist. Jelena Woehr, a satisfied customer, shared her experience online of a playlist in which the titles of the songs spelled out the message 'Jelena/You Are Awesome/ Thanks a Lot/For These Words/It Helps Me/Impress/ The Management'. The list quickly went viral.

We call these 'RAKs', which stands for 'random acts of kindness'. This is our way of doing something special for our customers that highlights music and our product in a very Spotify way. Our internal support advisers came up with RAKs, which is why I think they nail our tone of voice so well.

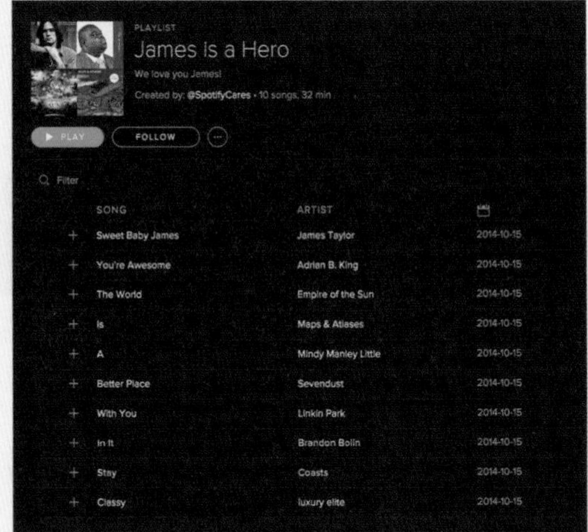

Another example of Spotify's use of playlists as random acts of kindness.
Source: Courtesy of Spotify.

My focus now is to devise a strategy that incorporates the spot-on tone our social media support team has in our marketing campaigns. Most likely, campaigns will continue to be agency-created, but they will have to be filtered through the lens of our in-house social media crew. We also need to be better at using what we already have internally, in terms of both our content and our people. At Spotify, we create tons of content and we're not maximizing its value. Why have an agency make content when internal teams are developing materials that espouse Spotify's brand at its core? On top of that, Spotify's employees love music and go to gigs every week. We're missing an engagement opportunity with tremendous potential to show who we are and our entire company's love of music.

It's clear that social media offer so many possibilities, especially to a brand like Spotify that's centred on music, an integral part of most people's life. Social media offer the potential to show a company's passion for what it does and nobody is fully taking advantage of that yet. There are many brands out there doing interesting things here and there, but no one has been able to put it all together on a consistent basis. We're going to be the ones who do it.

To move forward, Spotify needs to answer the question: how can it combine customer support's great engagement with the type of advance planning and scale needed for marketing campaigns?

See also Griner (2013).

Introduction

Consider for a moment your own personal use of digital technology and **social media**. How often do you go online? Which websites do you visit the most? What device do you use? It is most likely that you will notice that your behaviours have changed rather dramatically in the past five years. Devices such as the Amazon Echo and the Apple Watch, now an integral part of many people's everyday lives, were first introduced to the market as recently as 2014 and 2015, respectively. The same is true for many of the services and apps that we use. Spotify (founded in 2006), Airbnb (founded in 2008) and Uber (founded in 2009), which have used digital technology to transform where we stay when we travel, how we listen to music, and how we move around cities, all began their international expansions in the 2010s. In the last ten years, Netflix established itself as a global media streaming platform by successfully transforming its offering from DVD subscriptions to online streaming (Usborne, 2018).

In 2019, 57 per cent of the total world population used the Internet, with a 9.1 per cent increase since 2018, spending on average more than six hours online every day. Moreover, 45 per cent of the world population are active social media users and own multiple online accounts on a range of platforms including Facebook, WeChat, Instagram, and QQ (Kemp, 2019). With increasing broadband penetration (largely via mobile devices), the adoption of digital and social media marketing techniques is vital. Social network platforms, apps, blogs, personal websites, online video channels and other multimedia sharing services have become commonplace.

The technological development is rapidly changing the way in which consumers behave and marketers need to adapt accordingly. For example, when Instagram launched 'Stories' in 2016 (copying Snapchat's similar feature) to allow users to share short-lived images and videos with their followers, it took less than six months for the platform to integrate seamless ads (Constine, 2017).

As people change how they communicate, the marketing profession has turned to digital and social media marketing to complement, and sometimes replace, traditional marketing channels and activities. However, digitization is not only altering consumers' expectations of their interaction with organizations online, but also changing marketing in all forms.

In this chapter, we will focus on **digital marketing** and social media marketing as a tool with which to communicate and interact with consumers. First, we define digital and social media marketing, and track their evolution. We will then move on to discuss key areas of digital marketing communications, Internet advertising, search marketing, email marketing, social media marketing, content marketing, and **mobile marketing**. We then define 'crowdsourcing' and explain how it is used in marketing. Finally, we review some wider considerations in the development of digital marketing strategy.

Digital Marketing

Digital marketing is the management and execution of marketing using digital electronic technologies and channels (for example web, email, digital television, wireless media) and digital data about user/customer characteristics and behaviour. It is an established, and increasingly important, subfield of marketing brought about by advancements in digital media technologies and digital media environments. Digital marketing extends beyond Internet marketing, which is one form of digital marketing specific to the use of Internet-only technologies (such as web, email, intranet, extranets), in that it makes use of a range of different electronic technologies and channels, such as mobile telephony, digital display advertising, and the Internet of things.

A variety of terms are used in relation to digital marketing, including 'e-marketing', 'Internet marketing', 'direct marketing', 'interactive marketing', 'mobile marketing', and 'social media marketing', among many others. While these terms are sometimes incorrectly used interchangeably, they each have their own specific meaning (see Table 10.1). Sometimes, 'social marketing' is used as a synonym for 'social media marketing'. This is incorrect, however, because social marketing is an established term referring to the use of marketing to influence the behaviour of a target audience in which the benefits of that behaviour are intended by the marketer to accrue primarily to the audience, or to the society in general (hence are social), and not to the marketer. Social media marketing, meanwhile, is a tool increasingly being used by, for example, non-profits and public organizations to achieve such social benefits.

Before looking more closely at different types of digital marketing activity, we will briefly review the evolution of digital and social media marketing.

Evolution of the Internet

Since the early 1990s, the Internet has evolved and, with it, digital marketing. The rise of social media has led marketing to evolve away from a hierarchical, one-sided mass communication model towards more participatory technologies (such as social channels and online communities). These technologies facilitated the practice of user-generated, co-created, and user-shared content with a focus on the active (not passive) user/participant. By facilitating user participation, they

Table 10.1 Defining digital marketing terms

Term	Definition
Digital marketing	Management and execution of marketing using digital electronic technologies and channels (e.g. Internet, email, digital television, wireless media) and digital data about user/customer characteristics and behaviour.
Direct marketing	'A specific form of marketing that attempts to send its communications direct to consumers using addressable media such as post, Internet, email, and telephone and text messaging' (Harris, 2009).
E-marketing	Process of marketing accomplished or facilitated through the use of electronic devices, applications, tools, technologies, platforms, and/or systems. Not limited to one specific type or category of electronic technology (e.g. Internet, television), but includes both older analogue and developing digital electronic technologies.
Interactive marketing	Marketing that moves away from a transaction-based effort to a conversation (i.e. two-way dialogue) and can be described as a situation or mechanism through which marketers and a customer (e.g. stakeholders) interact, usually in real time. Not all interactive marketing is electronic (e.g. face-to-face sales).
Internet marketing	Process of marketing accomplished or facilitated via the use of Internet technologies (e.g. web, email, intranet, extranets).
Mobile marketing	'Mobile marketing is any advertising activity that promotes products and services via mobile devices, such as tablets and smartphones. Mobile marketing makes use of features of modern mobile technology, including location services, to tailor marketing campaigns based on an individual's location' (Kenton, 2020).
Social marketing	'The application of marketing to persuade the citizen to modify their actions and behaviour in particular circumstances and situations to benefit themselves and society' (Harris, 2009).
Social media marketing	A form of digital marketing that describes the use of the social web and social media (e.g. social networks, online communities, blogs, wikis) or any online collaborative technology for marketing activities.

contributed to a digital development away from a one-way model of information being 'pushed' through to target audiences towards a multichannel and multi-user approach in which web users were empowered to 'pull' down information, and/or to interact with the organization and content, as well as with each other (that is, consumer-to-consumer, or peer-to-peer).

This development means that consumers are increasingly relying on digital tools to guide their behaviours. It also means that consumers are becoming increasingly used to determining what information they want, when they want it, and how they want it. The web enables consumer pull (rather than organization push), ever-greater customer participation, co-creation of offerings (not only mass production), dialogue, and shared control over the form and content of a brand. This, in turn, is changing how marketers communicate, share information, interact, and create (or produce) an offering. The implications for digital marketing will be discussed further later in the chapter.

Evolution of Social Media

Social media have had a significant impact on marketing since the early 2000s. 'Social media' refers to a wide range of social network, video sharing, blogging and microblogging platforms developed to encourage users to generate their own content and share it with other users (boyd, 2014). Social media enable individuals and organizations to connect to each other by means of digital devices such as laptops, tablets, smartphones, and smartwatches. Whereas social interactions have always been central to human, and thus consumer, behaviour, social media enable those interactions to expand in time and place. They also enable consumers to be made visible to more people, marketers included.

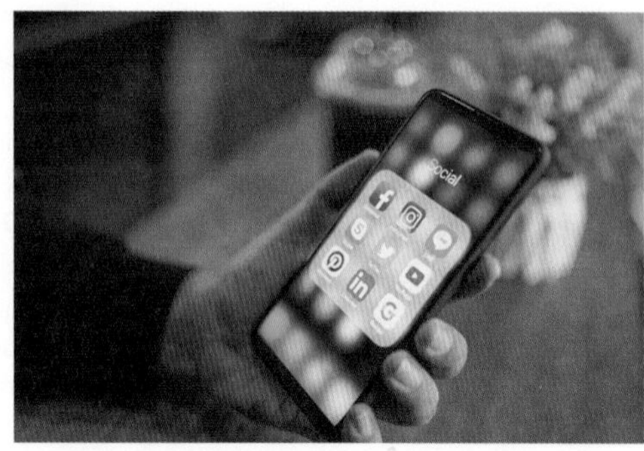

Consumers often have accounts on multiple social media, all accessible from one device.
Source: © Nopparat Khokthong/Shutterstock.

In 2019, the global average social media penetration was 45 per cent, with North America having the highest penetration, at 70 per cent. In Europe, about half of the population has at least one social network account (in Western Europe, 53 per cent; in Eastern Europe, 48 per cent). Social networking sites especially have seen massive growth since their inception. In Europe, Malta (88 per cent) and Cyprus (84 per cent) had the largest share of active social media users, followed by Iceland (83 per cent), Sweden (72 per cent), Norway and Denmark (both 71 per cent). In 2019, 67 per cent of the UK population had a social media profile, and users spent on average 110 minutes on social media per day, across seven social media accounts (Kemp, 2019). Facebook is the world's largest social network, with more than 2,271 million users globally, followed by YouTube (1,900 million users) and Instagram (1,000 million users). For an overview of the top ten largest social media networks in 2019, see Table 10.2.

Social media have had a major impact on marketing. In fact, many argue that they have turned marketing practice upside down. Former beliefs no longer hold and marketers are working on adjusting to these changes, of which two are particularly noteworthy.

The first major change has to do with *power*. Social media enable users to generate, share, and comment on content at their own discretion (van den Bulte and Wuyts, 2007). Content in social media is co-created by consumers rather than (as in traditional offline media) primarily created by media companies and marketers. The proliferation of **user-generated content (UGC)**—that is, content made available over the Internet, which reflects creative effort, and is created outside professional routine and practices (Wunsch-Vincent and Vickery, 2007)—such as review sites (for example, Tripadvisor, Amazon, and Trustpilot) and widely shared first-hand feedback about consumer experiences (for example through a picture and comment on Instagram) means that consumers have become increasingly influential (see also Market Insight 10.1). Social media allow consumers to share their experiences with each other at their own discretion, making

Table 10.2 Top ten social media platforms in 2019

Social platform	Type	Users (millions)
Facebook	Social network	2,271
YouTube	Social network	1,900
WhatsApp	Messenger/VoIP	1,500
Facebook Messenger	Messenger/VoIP	1,300
Weixin/WeChat	Messenger/VoIP	1,083
Instagram	Social network	1,000
QQ	Messenger/VoIP	803
Qzone	Social network	531
Douyin/TikTok	Social network	500
Sina Weibo	Social network	446

Source: Kemp (2019).

service and product quality assessments widely available, thereby shifting power from marketers to consumers (Kim and Johnson, 2016).

The second shift has to do with *control*. Whereas marketers have traditionally been in charge of the messages they communicate, this is no longer the case. In a computer-mediated environment, consumers not only are able to create and modify content to suit their needs, then share this content with consumers, companies, or third parties, but also have a voice in reacting to product offers and marketing that they do or do not like. As an example, the choice of (very thin or objectified) models used by fashion retailers in their advertisements is frequently debated and questioned in social media (recent examples include H&M and American Apparel), forcing the retailers to rethink the way in which they cast models in all of their marketing

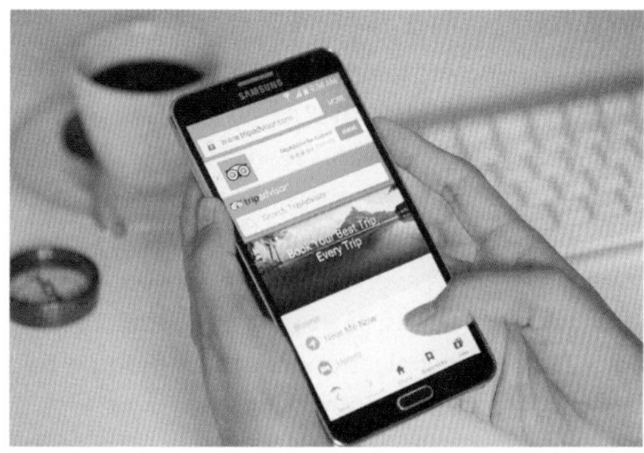

Tripadvisor is only one among a myriad of review sites that are a critical source of information for consumers.
Source: © zaozaa19/Shutterstock.

communications. With social media come higher transparency and less control for marketers in terms of how their communication is received and passed on.

 Visit the **online resources** and complete Internet Activity 10.1 to learn more about how EY uses Twitter to maintain an ongoing real dialogue with its followers.

How Digitization Is Transforming Marketing

Digital technology has the potential to transform marketing (see also Market Insight 10.2). According to a study by McKinsey and Co., companies that are integrating digital technology into their businesses perform significantly better financially than those who are not (Alldredge et al., 2015). According to the same study, the key characteristics for such digitally advanced companies are as follows.

- *Strategy*—Some 90 per cent of online leaders have digital initiatives fully integrated into their strategic planning process, not as a bolt-on.
- *Culture*—While 84 per cent of companies indicate their culture to be risk-averse, companies such as Amazon and Google embrace a different mentality. Instead of waiting for perfection, digital leaders adopt a fail–fast-forward mindset.
- *Organization*—Leading companies use non-traditional organizational structures, digital talent acquisition, and management to execute their digital vision. Some 65 per cent of digital leaders have an aggregated digital budget and sufficient budget allocation to scale their digital initiatives.

Market Insight 10.1 **Fighting Fake Online Reviews**

Online reviews have become increasingly important for consumers to gather information from peers before making a decision on a purchase, e.g. choosing a local restaurant for an evening out. A survey conducted in the USA in 2018 shows that 86 per cent of respondents read reviews of local businesses and that 57 per cent of them do not use a business that has fewer than four out of five stars. This trend is even more pronounced with younger generations, as 91 per cent of the 18–34 age category trust electronic word-of-mouth just as much as personal recommendations.

Companies advertising on online platforms which heavily rely on customers' reviews (such as Amazon, Facebook, or eBay) have also become aware of the importance of these reviews. This has led to the multiplication of fake '5-star' customer reviews that boost businesses and their products to the top listings in their categories. These reviews can be from unscrupulous sellers themselves (via a different pseudonym) or written by third-party consumers in exchange for a reward.

The techniques used by scammers often make use of the technical limitations of online platforms. For example, identical reviews posted for slightly different versions of a products are not always directly detected. Specialized Facebook groups also incentivize their members to write positive reviews after their purchase and then get reimbursed.

Because online reviews have become crucial to the development of e-commerce, several organizations now solely focus on building more trust between online companies and their potential customers. For example, the Danish platform Trustpilot directly gathers customers' reviews of online businesses. These reviewers can be verified, attesting that

Market Insight 10.1 (continued)

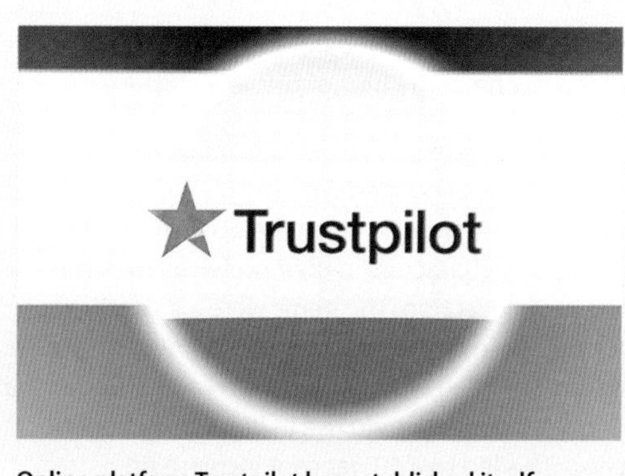

Online platform Trustpilot has established itself as a way for consumers to trust online businesses.

Source: © Il.studio/Shutterstock.

they actually bought products. Businesses are also encouraged to reply to individual reviews to show that they are aware of their customers' feedback, and to address it when it is negative.

1 **Why do you think young generations trust electronic word-of-mouth?**

2 **What are the long-term consequences for businesses generating fake positive reviews for their products?**

3 **Visit the Trustpilot website. What measures has Trustpilot put in place to combat fake reviews on its platform?**

Sources: Murphy (2018); Walsh (2019); https://uk.trustpilot.com/trust/combating-fake-reviews.

Research Insight 10.1

To take your learning further, you might wish to read this influential paper.

Kozinets, R. V., de Valck, K., Wojnicki, A. C., and Wilner, S. J. S. (2010) 'Networked narratives: Understanding word-of-mouth marketing in online communities', ***Journal of Marketing*****, 74(2), 71–89.**

This paper develops a theoretical framework for understanding conversations around brands in social media. By means of a qualitative study of social media marketing using bloggers and an extensive review of extant word-of-mouth theory, the article gives insights into how marketers employing social media marketing should plan, target, and leverage social media conversations.

 **Visit the online resources to read the abstract and access the full paper.**

- *Capabilities*—Digital leaders make decisions based on data, and build capabilities that connect people, processes, and technology across all channels that engage with consumers. Some 80 per cent of digital leaders effectively invest in their digital IT infrastructure to support growth. That means moving beyond model building into implementing processes that can bring relevant internal and external resources to take action quickly.

Market Insight 10.2 Digital Marketing Games

The digital landscape is said to offer unlimited possibilities for companies to connect and influence their audiences. Social, digital, and mobile are transforming marketing communications. However, clouds are gathering on this clear digital sky as consumer exposure to communications in these channels increases. How can companies succeed in the digital landscape without getting stuck in ad-blockers or fading away in a cluttered environment?

Underwear brand Björn Borg was more than aware of these challenges when launching a new sportswear collection targeted at a young audience. How could it make an underwear campaign that was attention-grabbing, fun, and relevant? And could this campaign merge market communications with e-commerce? Meet 'First Person Lover'—a free online computer game in which players, dressed in their favourite underwear, battle evil forces with kisses and love grenades. To maximize the connection with the audience and to stimulate publicity, the game was filled with Internet jokes and political references. The audience loved it.

International media picked up on the game and, a few days after its launch, YouTube star PewDiePie (with more than 107 million subscribers) praised the game as one of the best of the year.

The results were instant: 512,000 players from 190 countries engaged with the game. Before playing, they were all given the opportunity to dress their characters in their preferred look from the new collection. The items were also available for purchase directly in the game. Moreover, the game was filled with hidden promotional codes that engaged players could use in Björn Borg's online shop. This led to a 40 per cent increase on online sales.

The digital landscape is filled with new opportunities if new technology is merged with relevant and entertaining communication.

1. **What would you say were the key success factors in the development of Björn Borg's game?**
2. **What benefits and drawbacks can you see of using a game to launch new products?**

Sources: Björn Borg (2015); Wisterberg (2015).

This market insight was kindly contributed by Dr Erik Modig, Stockholm School of Economics, Sweden.

First Person Lover is a free online video game that joins the ability to communicate effectively with an e-commerce environment.

Source: Courtesy of BJÖRN BORG.

Digital Marketing Communications

Investments in digital marketing communications are growing rapidly. Focus is primarily on communication using Internet-only technologies (such as web, email, intranet, extranet), which are accessed using desktops, laptops, mobile devices, and/or tablets, but different types of digital display and tracking device are also increasingly being used to market products and brands.

Whereas traditional media are easily divided into formats based on the logic underlying them, this is not the case for digital marketing communications. The borders between paid ('advertising') media, earned ('publicity' and 'word-of-mouth'), and owned media (for example websites, profiles on social media, emails) are blurry and hard to establish.

In the following sections, we will discuss some of the most frequently used digital marketing communication activities in more detail.

Internet Advertising

'Internet advertising' refers to a form of marketing communication that uses the Internet for the purpose of advertising regardless of what device is being used to access it. Typically, it involves marketers paying media owners to carry their messages on their websites. Payment is either impression-based (for example cost per thousand, or CPM, pricing), performance-based (for example cost per click, sale, lead, acquisition, or application), or straight revenue share (for example percentage commission paid on sale). The aim of Internet advertising is to increase website traffic and/or encourage product trial, purchase, and repeat purchase activity (Cheng et al., 2009), and advertising format and payment should be adapted accordingly.

Internet advertising in the UK totalled £13.44 billion in 2018, after a 15 per cent increase from the previous year and with more than 90 per cent of the growth being driven by smartphones (IAB and PwC, 2018a). Table 10.3 offers a list of different Internet advertising formats and their definitions.

Table 10.3 Types of Internet advertising format

Ad format	Description
Banner advertising	Advertiser pays an online company for space on one or more of the online company's pages to display a static or linked banner or logo.
Sponsorship	Advertiser pays for custom content and/or experiences, which may or may not include ad elements such as display advertising, brand logos, advertorial, or pre-roll video.
Search	Fees advertisers pay online companies to list and/or link their company site domain names to a specific search word or phrase (includes paid search revenues). Search categories include paid listings, contextual search, **paid inclusion**, and site optimization.

Table 10.3 Types of Internet advertising format (continued)

Ad format	Description
Lead generation	Fees paid by advertisers to online companies that refer qualified potential customers (e.g. auto dealers that pay a fee in exchange for receiving a qualified purchase inquiry online) or provide consumer information (demographic, contact, and behavioural) whereby the consumer opts in to being contacted by a marketer (email, postal, telephone, fax). These processes are priced on a performance basis (e.g. cost per action, lead or inquiry), and can include user applications (e.g. for a credit card), surveys, contests (e.g. sweepstakes), or registrations.
Classifieds and auctions	Fees paid to advertisers by online companies to list specific products or services (e.g. online job boards and employment listings, real estate listings, automotive listings, auction-based listings, Yellow Pages).
Rich media	Display-related ads that integrate some component of streaming interactivity. Ads often include Flash or JavaScript, but not content, and can allow users to view and interact with products or services (e.g. scrolling or clicking within the ad opens a multimedia product description, expansion, animation, video or a 'virtual test-drive').
Digital video advertising	Advertising that appears before, during, or after digital video content in a video player (i.e. pre-roll, mid-roll, post-roll video ads). Includes television commercials online and can appear in streaming content or in downloadable video. Display-related ads on a page (that are not in a player) that contains video are categorized as rich media ads.
Mobile advertising	Advertising tailored to and delivered through wireless mobile devices such as smartphones, feature phones (e.g. lower-end mobile phones capable of accessing mobile content), and media tablets. Typically taking the form of static or rich media display ads, text messaging ads, search ads, or audio/video spots, such advertising generally appears within mobile websites (e.g. websites optimized for viewing on mobile devices), mobile apps, text messaging services (i.e. SMS, MMS) or within mobile search results (i.e. 411 listings, directories, mobile-optimized search engines). Mobile advertising formats include search, display (banner ads, digital video, digital audio, sponsorships, and rich media), and other advertising served to mobile devices.
Digital audio	Refers to partially or entirely advertising-supported audio programming available to consumers on a streaming basis, delivered via the wired and mobile Internet.

Source: IAB and PwC (2018b).

Major considerations arising when using Internet advertising include the following.

- *Cost*—Internet adverts are still relatively cheap compared with traditional advertising.
- *Timeliness*—Internet adverts can be updated at any time, with minimal cost.
- *Format*—Internet adverts are richer, using text, audio, graphics, and animation. In addition, games, entertainment, and promotions can be incorporated.

- *Personalization*—Internet adverts can be interactive and targeted towards specific interest groups and/or individuals.
- *Location*—Using wireless technology and geo-location technology (a global positioning system, or GPS), Internet advertising can be targeted towards consumers wherever they are (for example near a restaurant or theatre).
- *Intrusiveness*—Some Internet advertising formats (such as pop-ups) are seen as intrusive and suffer more consumer complaints than other formats.

Search Marketing

The growth in digital content available through the web has given rise to a number of interactive decision aids used to help web users to locate data, information, and/or an organization's digital objects (for example pictures, videos). The main two types of decision aid are a **search directory** (web directory) and a **search engine**.

A *search directory* is a human-edited database of information. It lists websites by category and subcategory, with categorization usually based on the whole website rather than one page or a set of keywords. Search directories often allow site owners to submit a site directly for inclusion and editors review submissions for fitness. Given its large scope, Amazon could also be considered to offer a search directory for shopping.

In contrast, a *search engine* operates algorithmically, or uses a mixture of algorithmic and human input, to collect, index, store, and retrieve information on the web (for example webpages, images, information, and other types of file), making this information available to users in a manageable and meaningful way in response to a search query. Information is retrieved by a web crawler (also known as a 'spider'), which is an automated web browser that follows every link on the site, analysing how it should be indexed, using words extracted from page and file titles, headings, or special fields called 'meta-tags'. The indexed data are then stored in an index database for use in later queries. When a user enters a query into a search engine (typically using keywords), the engine examines its index and provides a search engine result page (SERP)—that is, a listing of webpages ordered according to best match with the input criteria (see also Market Insight 10.3). There are only a few dominant search engines in the market, with Google leading the global market share (88.6 per cent), followed by Bing (5.0 per cent), Yahoo! (2.7 per cent), and Chinese Baidu (0.7 per cent) (Statista, 2019).

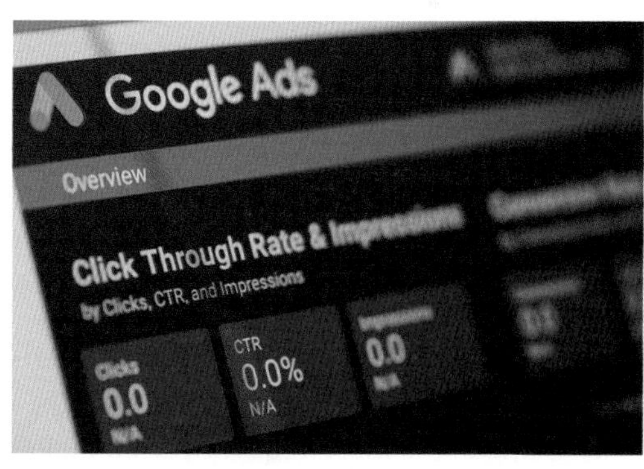

Google makes most of its revenues through Google Ads, where advertisers bid on keywords relevant to their target market.

Source: © PixieMe/Shutterstock.

Search engines have evolved significantly over the years. Whereas, in the early years of the Internet, searches focused on keywords used, today, semantic analysis ensures that they also take into account previous search behaviour and knowledge about the context in which the search is being made (for example when, where, how, and by whom). An example of contextual adaption is local searches whereby search results are adapted to the location where the search is undertaken.

Given the central role of search in consumer online behaviour, it is not surprising that search is central to most digital marketing strategies. In 2018, 45 per cent of all Internet advertising investments were in search (IAB and PwC, 2018b). Search, often referred to as 'search engine marketing' (SEM), is one of the main forms of Internet advertising, with a UK spend of £6.66 billion in 2018 (IAB and PwC, 2018a). Its aim is to promote websites by increasing their visibility in SERPs. Search engine marketing methods include the following.

- *Paid listings*—Payments are made for clicks on text links that appear at the top or side of search results for specific keywords. The more a marketer pays, the higher the position the link gets. Marketers pay only when a user clicks on the text link. Paid listings, or **pay per click (PPC)**, typically mean that the advertisers bid on keywords or phrases relevant to their target market, with sponsored or paid search engine listings aiming to drive traffic to the advertiser's own website. The search engine ranks adverts based on a competitive auction and other related criteria (for example popularity, quality). Google Ads, Verizon Media Native, and Microsoft Advertising are the three largest ad-network operators, with all three operating under a bid-based model.
- *Contextual search*—This is a form of targeted advertising, with adverts (for example banners, pop-ups) appearing on websites, the adverts themselves being selected and served by automated systems based on the content displayed to the user. A **contextual advertising** system scans the text of a website for keywords and returns adverts to the webpage based on what the user is viewing. Google AdSense was the first major contextual advertising programme. Payments are typically made only for clicks (PPC) on text links that appear in an article based on the context of the content rather than a user-submitted keyword.
- *Paid inclusion*—This occurs when a search engine company charges fees related to inclusion of websites in its search index. Some organizations mix paid inclusion with organic listings (for example DuckDuckGo), whereas others do not allow paid inclusion to be listed with organic lists (for example Google). Payments are made to guarantee that a marketer's URL is indexed by a search engine (that is, it is not paid only for clicks, as in paid listings).
- *Search engine optimization (SEO)*—This refers to a process whereby a website's structure and content are improved to maximize its listing in organic SERPs using relevant keywords or search phrases. Payments may also be made to optimize a site to improve the site's ranking in SERPs.

Email Marketing

Email is one of the most frequently used digital marketing tools. Email marketing includes 'opt-in' and 'opt-out' mailing lists, email newsletters, and discussion list subscriptions. Importantly, with email marketing, the communicator sends the message only to those who have agreed to receive messages. Such **permission-based email marketing** is a highly cost-effective form of digital marketing (Waring and Martinez, 2002; Cheng et al., 2009). As a marketing tool, it is easy to use and costs little to send. Still, cost can be higher when personalizing messages and when a database must be developed or purchased. Nevertheless, email can reach millions of willing prospects in minutes. Unsolicited emails, which clog email servers and use up much-needed Internet bandwidth, are referred to as **spam**.

Market Insight 10.3 **Searching the Amazon**

Search is a key behaviour online and Google is the go-to place for search—or is it? In 2015, 44 per cent of US consumers stated that they head directly to Amazon when searching for products, up from 30 per cent in 2012. In comparison, 34 per cent go straight to a search engine such as Google, Yahoo! (now Verizon Media Native), or Bing.

Whereas Google has done its part in making product discovery and search intuitive, convenient, and seamless, Amazon now seems ready to step in and take over. Almost half of US consumers bypass search engines and other websites in favour of Amazon when on a shopping mission. This means that the search bar is increasingly becoming a key asset in Amazon's user experience.

Enabling search not only allows consumers to find the products for which they are looking, but also enables Amazon to collect valuable data on consumer searches and to relate them to actual sales. On-site search queries are clear expressions of user intent. Coupled with reviews from the millions of Amazon customers who have left appraisals on the website, the data are invaluable and Amazon continually leverages those data to intelligently promote products across its website.

Amazon's advanced algorithmic recommendation capability accurately predicts intent and suggests products better than any other website. Now, Amazon is also using its shopping pattern data to derive advantages offline. In November 2015, Amazon opened its first brick-and-mortar bookstore in Seattle, WA. Seattle was chosen for the first physical bookstore because it is close to Amazon's headquarters and because Seattle is a top market for readers.

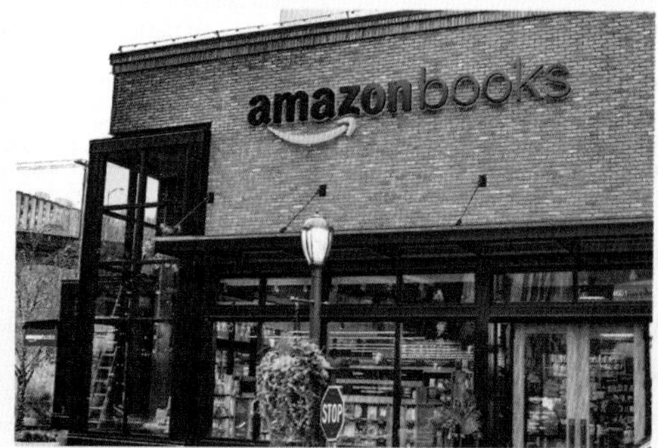

The assortment in Amazon's physical store has been selected using data on online shopping patterns.
Source: © SEA STOCK/Shutterstock.

In opening a bookstore, Amazon is betting that the troves of data it generates from shopping patterns on its website will give it advantages in its retail location that other bookstores cannot match and that using these data to pick titles that will most appeal to Seattle shoppers will allow Amazon to succeed where others have not.

Visit Amazon's website and search for a product in which you are interested.

1 **What options for finding the product do you have? How useful is the directory? How useful is the search engine?**

2 **What type of contextual information does Amazon seem to use to guide the results that are presented?**

3 **How do the search results you get on Amazon differ from what you would get if you were to use Google or Bing?**

Sources: Greene (2015); Leggatt (2015); Johnson (2015).

In designing a successful email campaign, marketers need to think carefully about the target audience and its willingness to receive emails. This means that they should provide a mechanism for list members to opt in or opt out and to choose what type of email offerings they are interested in receiving (for example newsletter, discount offers, and specific updates). As far as possible, emails should be personalized. Using an email system that allows tracking and reporting on all elements of the campaign (including opens, clicks, pass-alongs, unsubscribes, and bounce-backs) allows marketers to closely test and monitor different email marketing strategies in terms of when to send them and how often, as well as what to offer, write, and highlight. The insights gained from such data-mining exercises can be invaluable. For example, one large-scale study of more than one billion emails over a two-year period shows that people are 38 per cent more likely to click—and 47 per cent more likely to convert—when they are presented with a percentage-off rather than a money-off offer (O'Brien, 2015). According to the same study, short subject lines (of between six and ten words), visual and personalized messages, and clear calls to action are key to a successful email.

Social Media Marketing

'Social media marketing' describes the use of the social web and social media (for example social networks, online communities, blogs, wikis) or any online collaborative technology for marketing activities (such as sales, public relations (PR), research, distribution, customer service). Social media marketing includes both the creation and curation of corporate and/or brand profiles and content on social media and advertising. 'Social media advertising' (SMA) refers to advertising delivered on social platforms, including social networking and social gaming websites and apps, across all device types.

Marketers are increasingly investing in social networks (for example Facebook, LinkedIn, and QQ in China), video-sharing sites (for example YouTube), image-sharing sites (such as Instagram and Pinterest), blogging platforms (such as WordPress), and microblogs (for example Twitter) for marketing purposes. According to the 2019 survey of chief marketing officers (CMOs), 11.9 per cent of marketing budgets were invested in social media in 2019 and this share is expected to grow to 22.5 in the following five years (Moorman, 2019). The social web does not make conversations happen; it only supports them. Mangold and Faulds (2009) offer the following examples of marketing activities aiming to stimulate conversations:

- networking platforms (for example Sephora's beauty insiders, Nike+);
- blogs and social media tools to engage customers—because customers like to give feedback on a broad range of issues (see 'Content marketing');
- both Internet and traditional promotional tools to engage customers;
- information on, for example, correct or alternative product usage;
- exclusivity—because people like to feel special;
- offerings that are designed from the perspective of consumers' desired self-images and with talking points to make advocacy easier, for example JetBlue, the US budget airline, making leather seats and televisions available to its customers;
- support for causes that people value; and
- memorable stories.

An example of creating memorable stories is UK food and beverage company innocent which outlines the story of its founding on its website. Innocent has it that three friends set up a stall to sell smoothies at a London music festival. A sign above the stall read 'Should we give up our jobs to make these smoothies?' and people were asked to throw their empties into one of two bins marked either 'Yes' or 'No'. Needless to say, 'Yes' won.

The options available for social media advertising differ between different social media platforms. Moreover, they are constantly subject to change. Visit the **online resources** and complete Internet Activity 10.2 around advertising options on different social media platforms.

Evaluating Social Media

Although marketers agree that social media marketing is key to success in the contemporary marketplace, many marketers are still struggling to identify how to evaluate these activities. In 2019, only 24.1 per cent of CMOs had been able to prove the impact of those investments quantitatively, while 44.6 per cent had a good qualitative sense of the impact and 31.6 per cent had not been able to demonstrate the impact (Moorman, 2019). This clearly shows that engaging in social communities provides opportunities for marketers, but it can also be a challenge.

However, it is possible to measure the effectiveness of social media by following the Social Media Marketing Evaluation Framework developed by Keegan and Rowley (2017):

1. Start by setting specific evaluation objectives of a company's advertising campaign. This first step can be challenging as the marketing capabilities on social media are often not well understood.
2. Identify key performance indicators (KPIs) in line with the evaluation objectives previously set.
3. Identify the metrics to collect for evaluating the selected KPIs. Table 10.4 provides a detailed list of the most frequently used social media measures and how their use has evolved.
4. Collect and analyse the identified metrics from the relevant social media channels. This step can be done in real time by using tools such as Google Analytics and Facebook Audience Insights.
5. Generate reports to communicate the results of the data analysis to clients. This should be succinct and done in a timely manner (for example, weekly).
6. Make a decision based on the insights generated. The conclusions drawn from the previous steps should be used to adjust the current communication campaign and influence the planning of the upcoming ones.

Content Marketing

Content marketing is an approach to marketing communication in which brands create and disseminate content to consumers with the intention that the content will generate interest, engage consumers, and influence behaviour (Stephen et al., 2015). Although branded content has been around for more than one hundred years, this marketing activity has accelerated in the digital space. Table 10.5 lists the top five types of content that were first used or developed by business-to-consumer (B2C) companies in 2018.

Marketers are therefore paying increasing attention to creating online content that can benefit their target audiences by adapting traditional journalism and publisher techniques. These activities are often referred to as 'content marketing'.

Table 10.4	Common social media measures used by marketers

Rank	Measure	% of total respondents, 2010	% of total respondents, 2014
1	Hits/visits/page views	48	60
2	No. of followers and friends	24	45
3	Repeat visits	35	39
4	Conversion rates (from visitor to buyer)	25	31
5	Buzz indicators (mentions, shares)	16	24
6	Sales levels	18	17
7	Online products/service ratings	8	14
8	Customer acquisition costs	12	14
9	Net promoter score	8	13
10	Revenue per customer	17	13
11	Text analysis ratings	7	12
12	Customer retention costs	8	6
13	Abandoned shopping carts	4	6
14	Profits per customer	9	6

Source: Moorman (2014).

The aim of content marketing is to create content that has value for the receiver (for example by being useful, educational, or entertaining in and of itself), thereby pulling the consumer toward the brand. Content marketing is common in both consumer and business-to-business (B2B) marketing. For example, Red Bull has transformed its content operations into a fully fledged media house (Red Bull Media House) specializing in high-quality coverage of extreme sports. There is thus plenty of opportunity to provide value in a way that can be mutually beneficial for the brand and the receiver. **Native advertising** is a different form of social media marketing in which non-disruptive ads are seamlessly integrated with videos, posts, and articles. (See Market Insight 10.4 for an example of native advertising on YouTube.)

Table 10.5 Top B2C types of content in 2018

Rank	Tactic	Use (% of B2C businesses)
1	Social media stories	68
2	Long-form content (e.g. in-depth articles)	57
3	Video snippets	52
4	Branded apps	26
5	Films	20

Source: Murton Beets and Handley (2019).

Mobile Marketing

Mobile marketing is the set of practices that enables organizations to communicate and engage interactively with their audiences through any mobile device or network (MMA, 2009). With the added benefits of store-and-send technology giving the option of message storage, mobile marketing is quick, inexpensive, and reaches markets wherever they are, despite limitations in message content.

Investments in mobile are both through paid (mobile advertising) media and the development of owned media, such as apps. In 2019, in the United States, mobile advertising revenues cumulated to US$69.9 billion (IAB and PwC, 2018b). The associated spending budget had more than tripled since 2017 and is predicted to grow by another 71 per cent in the next five years (Moorman, 2019).

Current changes in behaviours clearly show that mobile marketing is taking over more consumer online searches. Marketers need to consider this to ensure their communications remain relevant and accessible at different stages in the consumer decision process. Increasingly, the use of smartphone apps is becoming the default mechanism for such searches. These apps use a combination of barcode scanning and location-based services to provide relevant information, for example showing only stores near to a consumer carrying out a price comparison. These apps are thus suited to deliver context-specific, and hence more relevant, information to consumers.

Location-based marketing has long been expected to be the next big innovation in mobile advertising. Even if the adoption has been slow, in 2018, companies in the United States spent US$21.4 billion on location-targeted mobile advertising. Location-based marketing is not limited to mobile phones but also covers connected TVs and smart speakers as well as digital out-of-home and automotive (Factual, 2019).

Consumers are increasingly searching for information about products through various digital platforms and devices, but is this the case for all products? Visit the **online resources** and complete Internet Activity 10.3 to find out more about online and offline search.

Research Insight 10.2

To take your learning further, you might wish to read this influential paper.

Rosengren, S., and Dahlén, M. (2015) 'Exploring advertising equity: How a brand's past advertising may affect consumer willingness to approach its future ads', *Journal of Advertising*, 44(1), 1–13.

This paper investigates what drives consumers' willingness to pay attention to advertising. Based on empirical studies of more than 1,700 consumers and one hundred brands in more than twelve different product categories, it shows how adding value in advertising is vital to succeed in a digital environment in which consumers are increasingly in charge of their own media consumption.

Visit the online resources to read the abstract and access the full paper.

Market Insight 10.4 **Native Advertising on YouTube**

The increasing number of content creators uploading videos on YouTube can be attributed to the unmediated and authentic messages that they communicate to their viewers. As some of the most famous YouTube channels gather millions of followers, marketers have seized this new opportunity to promote their offerings to a growing audience. However, most online ads are akin to traditional television advertising: online video ads can usually be skipped and are only displayed for a limited duration. Moreover, most modern Internet browsers feature ad blockers to filter out intrusive adverts.

To overcome these issues, native advertising has become increasingly popular on YouTube. Instead of being played before the videos, ads are directly integrated within the videos and are delivered, with varying degrees of autonomy, by the content creators. Native advertising includes explicit sponsorship, inclusion of links and promotional codes to the brand's products, and free products sent to YouTubers in the hope that they get featured in their videos. In all cases, content creators are rewarded directly by the endorsing brands, bypassing YouTube's own monetization scheme.

With more than 11.5 million subscribers as of 2020, Casey Neistat is one of the most popular American YouTubers. In his video blogs (vlogs), Neistat regularly reviews tech gadgets (e.g. drones, smartphones, and electric skateboards) sent to him from a range of brands. In 2017, he released a video of him spending a day in France. In the last seconds of the video, Neistat reveals that the entire footage was recorded by Samsung's latest smartphone at the time. This provoked strong reactions from his followers who felt that they had been tricked into thinking that the vlog was authentic, but turned out to be a cover-up for a commercial. Neistat argues that including sponsored content in his videos is acceptable, providing he is transparent and honest with his followers.

As this trend has made it increasingly difficult for viewers to differentiate sponsored content from unmediated videos, YouTube allows creators to mark their videos as promotional. If they decide to select this option, a small banner will appear

Market Insight 10.4 (continued)

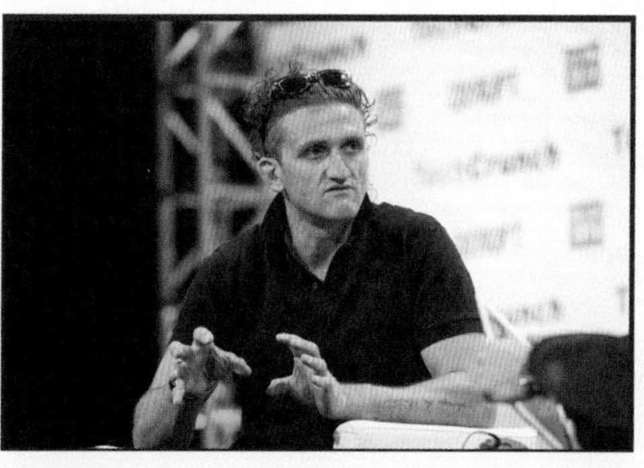

YouTuber Casey Neistat is well known for his regular tech reviews.
Source: © TechCrunch/Flickr.

during the first few seconds on their videos to inform viewers that what they are about to watch contains ads.

1. **What are the advantages for content creators of integrating native advertising into their videos?**
2. **Do you agree with Casey Neistat's view that YouTubers should explicitly announce that their content is sponsored?**
3. **What other social media platforms allow brands to publish seamless ads?**

Sources: Wu (2016); Alvarez (2017); Schwemmer and Ziewiecki (2018); Youtube (2019); https://www.youtube.com/user/caseyneistat

Research Insight 10.3

To take your learning further, you might wish to read this influential paper.

Edelman, D. C., and Singer, M. (2015) 'Competing on customer journeys', *Harvard Business Review*, 9(11), 88–100.

This article discusses how digital and mobile technology has changed how consumers research and buy products, and how companies need to come up with new tools, processes, and organizational structures to proactively lead digital customers from consideration to purchase and beyond. In particular, the authors discuss the characteristics of companies succeeding at building effective customer 'journeys': automation, proactive personalization, contextual interaction, and journey innovation.

 Visit the **online resources** to read the abstract and access the full paper.

Crowdsourcing

This may be defined as:

> engaging a large group of people to come up with an idea or solve a problem. Some companies use the process to draw on the knowledge and opinions of a wide body of Internet users to create better products and marketing plans, or solve other problems.
>
> (Vallone, 2011: 5)

Table 10.6 Forms of crowdsourcing (CS)

Consideration	CS of routine activities	CS of content	CS of creative activities	CS of funds
Role of the crowd	Provision of time; ability to process information	Provision of content (especially information)	Provision of solutions, ideas, knowledge	Provision of monetary recourses
Goal	Division of labour (integrative)	Division of labour (integrative)	Winner takes all (selective)	Raising money
Remuneration	Micro-payments	Micro-payments or voluntary	Micro- to high payments	Equity/loan/reward
Size of the crowd	Very important	Very important	Of little importance	Very important
Diversity of the crowd	Not important	Very important	Very important	Not important
Commercial examples	reCAPTCHA	iStock OpenStreetMap	InnoCentive Wilogo	FundedByMe

Source: Adapted from Burger-Helmchen and Pénin (2011).

Crowdsourcing in marketing is used most commonly in four main categories: routine activities, content, creative activities, and funding (see Table 10.6).

- One example of the crowdsourcing of *routine activities* was reCAPTCHA (which stands for Completely Automated Public Turing test to tell Computers and Humans Apart), the initiative aiming to digitize books by supplying websites with CAPTCHA protection from bots attempting to access restricted sites. The test requires users to retype images of words not recognized by optical character recognition (OCR) machines and, in so doing, helped to digitize the Internet archive and the archives of the *New York Times*.
- iStock and OpenStreetMap are good examples of companies that crowdsource *content*.
- Companies that have used crowdsourcing for *creative activities* include InnoCentive and Wilogo, which use crowdsourcing mechanisms for research and development (R&D) projects and to produce logo designs, respectively.
- When it comes to crowdsourced *funding*, there are several different websites offering this possibility to companies. According to a report from one of them, the success of crowdfunding campaigns is highly contingent on social media sharing, as well as accuracy and reliability of market assessments and financial forecasts (Lundquist and Gromek, 2015).

Crowdsourcing is increasingly ubiquitous in marketing as organizations seek to use it to reduce their marketing costs, to reduce the time taken to undertake a particular task, to find and use resources (skills, labour, money) that do not exist in-house, to obtain information and market intelligence, to design new products and services, and to design promotional material. One of the key considerations when setting up a crowdsourcing task is how to motivate the crowd to take part. One common rule of thumb suggests that 90 per cent of visitors to the site will consume the content (that is, see the task), 9 per cent will partially engage (that is, read the task and consider taking part or request further information), and 1 per cent will fully engage (that is, provide a submission).

Legal and Ethical Considerations

With the rise in digital resources and their increasing use for marketing activities come complications and changes to legislation and regulated business practices. The types of legal, ethical, and regulatory issue that marketers need to consider include the following.

- *Jurisdiction*—Where does digital marketing activity take place? Commercial law is based on transactions within national boundaries, but digital marketing exposes both individual organizations and the community to information, transactions, and social activity outside these boundaries.
- *Ownership*—Who owns the content that we create and share? Copyright law is a national issue and copyright laws (that is, what can and cannot be used without the originator's permission) differ from one country to another. The value of copyright is also being questioned with the increase in UGC and **co-created content (CCC)**, and the rise of the Creative Commons (CC) free licence system.
- *Permissions*—Do we have the right permissions to upload and share content? Privacy legislation is also national or regional and the right of an individual or organization to use information is subject to this legislation.
- *Security*—How secure are the data and information we share? Information and transaction security, and protection from fraud and identity theft, are other areas of increasing change.
- *Accessibility*—Does everyone who wants access have access? Disability and discrimination legislation also require consideration in this regard. As more services and marketing information are shared digitally, the right to access and usability for all becomes an important agenda item for the dissemination of information and services.

Visit the **online resources** and complete Internet Activity 10.4 to learn more about consumer privacy concerns.

Chapter Summary

To consolidate your learning, the key points from this chapter are summarized below.

- **Define 'digital marketing' and 'social media marketing'.**

  'Digital marketing' is the management and execution of marketing using digital technologies and channels (e.g. web, email, digital television, Internet) to reach markets in a timely, relevant, personal, interactive, and cost-efficient manner. It is related to, but distinct from, e-marketing, direct marketing, and interactive marketing. 'Social media marketing' is a form of digital marketing, which uses social networking sites to produce content that users will share, which will, in turn, create exposure of the brand to customers and thereby increase or reinforce its customer base.

- **Explain how digitization is transforming marketing practice.**

  The growth of digital technologies is not only changing consumer behaviours, but also changing business. Digital marketing must therefore be considered and adapted more widely than only as a new communication or distribution channel. It can help organizations to create new business opportunities, and enable new relationships with and between (and thereby insights into) consumers.

- **Discuss key techniques in digital marketing and social media marketing.**

  Key techniques in digital marketing include Internet advertising, search marketing, email marketing, social media marketing, content marketing, and mobile marketing. Characteristic of digital marketing, especially that through social media, is that marketers need to give up some control and power to consumers.

- **Review how practitioners measure the effectiveness of social media marketing.**

  To measure the effectiveness of a social media campaign, marketers should follow a seven-step process, which includes: identifying a set of appropriate social media metrics; reviewing the social media campaign objectives; mapping the campaign by highlighting links to brand-generated content, consumer-generated content, consumer-fortified content, and exposure to content(ed) consumers; choosing the criteria and tools of measurement; establishing a benchmark; undertaking the campaign; and measuring it frequently.

- **Discuss crowdsourcing and explain how it can be harnessed for marketing purposes.**

  Crowdsourcing is the process of outsourcing a task or group of tasks to a generally large community ('crowd') of people. It can be used in marketing to outsource routine activities, to obtain content, or to obtain creative input. It can also be used as a way in which to gain access to financial resources.

Review Questions

1. **Describe how digital marketing differs from interactive and Internet marketing.**
2. **How is digitization transforming marketing practice?**
3. **Compare and contrast the difference between 'pull' and 'push' approaches to digital marketing.**
4. **What are the main features of search marketing? In what contexts is search marketing most effective?**
5. **What are social media and how have they changed marketing?**

6 What is social media marketing and why do marketers use it?

7 How can you measure the effectiveness of social media marketing?

8 What is content marketing and why do marketers use it?

9 How is the growth of mobile devices (e.g. smartphones) impacting on marketing?

10 What marketing activities can crowdsourcing support?

Worksheet Summary

To apply the knowledge you have gained from this chapter, and to test your understanding of digital and social media marketing, visit the **online resources** and complete Worksheet 10.1.

Discussion Questions

1 Having read Case Insight 10.1, how might Spotify use social media to support its service and build customer loyalty?

2 Why are many marketers having difficulties adapting to a situation in which they have to share control and power over a brand with consumers?

3 Having read Market Insight 10.4, select three social media on which you have an account and list the different types of advertising present on these platforms. What do you think are the most effective types of ads to promote brands' offerings?

4 Privacy and ownership of digital information is increasingly challenged. When participating on Facebook, for example, we think that we control our own data and information—but do we? Discuss.

Visit the **online resources** and complete the multiple-choice questions to assess your knowledge of the chapter.

Glossary

co-created content (CCC) content or applications created by at least two parties, potentially the organization and the consumer.

contextual advertising a form of targeted advertising, on websites, whereby adverts are selected and served by automated systems based on the content displayed to the user.

digital marketing the process of marketing accomplished or facilitated through the application of electronic devices, appliances, tools, techniques, technologies, and/or systems.

mobile marketing the set of practices that enables organizations to communicate and engage with their audiences in an interactive and relevant manner through any mobile device or network.

native advertising type of social media marketing in which non-disruptive ads are seamlessly integrated with the rest of the media on which they are displayed.

paid inclusion can provide a guarantee that the website is included in a search engine's natural listings.

pay per click (PPC) advertising that uses sponsored search engine listings to drive traffic to a website, whereby the advertiser bids for search terms and the search engine ranks results based on a competitive auction, as well as other factors.

permission-based email marketing also known as 'opt-in email marketing', a method of advertising by email that the recipient has consented to receive.

search directory a database of information maintained by human editors, which lists websites by category and subcategory, usually based on the whole website rather than one page or a set of keywords.

search engine operates algorithmically, or using a mixture of algorithmic and human input, to collect, index, store, and retrieve information on the web, then make it available to users in a manageable and meaningful way in response to a search query.

spam unsolicited email—that is, the junk mail of the twenty-first century—which clogs email servers and uses up much-needed Internet bandwidth.

user-generated content (UGC) content made publicly available over the Internet that reflects creative effort by users, not professionals.

References

Alldredge, K., Newaskar, P., and Ungerman, K. (2015) 'The digital future of consumer-packaged-goods companies', *McKinsey Insights*, 1 October. Retrieve from: https://www.mckinsey.com/industries/consumer-packaged-goods/our-insights/the-digital-future-of-consumer-packaged-goods-companies (accessed 30 October 2020).

Alvarez, E. (2017) 'YouTube stars are blurring the lines between content and ads', *Engadget*, 25 July. Retrieve from: https://www.engadget.com/2017-07-25-youtube-influencers-sponsored-videos.html (accessed 30 October 2020).

Björn Borg (2015) 'An online fashion game experience: First person lover'. Retrieve from: http://webcollection.se/cannes/2015/fpl/#/(accessed 30 October 2020).

boyd, d. (2014) *It's Complicated: The Social Lives of Networked Teens*, New Haven, CT: Yale University Press.

Burger-Helmchen, T., and Pénin, J. (2011) 'Crowdsourcing: définition, enjeux, typologie' [Crowdsourcing: definition, stakes, typology]. *Revue Management et Avenir*, 41(1), 254–69.

Cheng, J. M.-S., Blankson, C., Wang, E. S.-T., and Chen, L. S.-L. (2009) 'Consumer attitudes and interactive digital advertising', *International Journal of Advertising*, 28(3), 501–25.

Constine, J. (2017) 'Instagram Stories hits 150M daily users, launches skippable adds', *TechCrunch*, 11 January. Retrieve from: https://techcrunch.com/2017/01/11/instagram-stories-hits-150m-daily-users-launches-skippable-ads/ (accessed 9 November 2019).

Edelman, D. C., and Singer, M. (2015) 'Competing on customer journeys', *Harvard Business Review*, 9(11), 88–100.

Factual (2019) *Location-Based Marketing Report*. Retrieve from: https://s3.amazonaws.com/factual-content/marketing/downloads/Factual-2019-Location-Based-Market-Report.pdf (accessed 10 November 2019).

Greene, J. (2015) 'Amazon opening its first real bookstore—at U-Village', *Seattle Times*, 2 November. Retrieve from: https://www.seattletimes.com/business/amazon/amazon-opens-first-bricks-and-mortar-bookstore-at-u-village/ (accessed 30 October 2020).

Griner, D. (2013) 'Spotify thanks customer with custom playlist featuring a secret message', *AdWeek*, 12 July. Retrieve from: https://www.adweek.com/creativity/spotifys-customer-service-looks-and-sounds-just-about-perfect-151157/ (accessed 30 October 2020).

Harris, P. (2009) *Penguin Dictionary of Marketing*, London: Penguin.

Internet Advertising Bureau (IAB) and PricewaterhouseCoopers (PwC) (2018a) *Digital Adspend Study: Measuring the Size of the UK Digital*

Advertising Market. Retrieve from: https://www.iabuk.com/sites/default/files/public_files/123IAB%20UK%20%26%20PwC%20Digital%20Adspend%20Study%202018%20Full%20Report_compressed%20%281%29.pdf (accessed 10 November 2019).

Internet Advertising Bureau (IAB) and PricewaterhouseCoopers (PwC) (2018b) *IAB Internet Advertising Revenue Report, 2018 Full Year Results*. Retrieve from: https://www.iab.com/wp-content/uploads/2019/05/Full-Year-2018-IAB-Internet-Advertising-Revenue-Report.pdf (accessed 10 November 2019).

Johnson, B. (2015) 'The evolution of search on Amazon', *Digital Commerce 360*, 11 June. Retrieve from: https://www.digitalcommerce360.com/2015/06/11/evolution-search-amazon/ (accessed 30 October 2020).

Keegan, B. J. and Rowley, J. (2017) 'Evaluation and decision making in social media marketing', *Management Decision*, 55(1), 15–31.

Kemp, S. (2019) *Digital 2019 Essential Insights into How People around the World Use the Internet, Mobile Devices, Social Media, and E-Commerce*. Retrieve from: https://wearesocial.com/global-digital-report-2019 (accessed 9 November 2019).

Kenton, W. (2020). 'Mobile marketing', *Investopedia*, 27 January. Retrieve from: https://www.investopedia.com/terms/m/mobile-marketing.asp (accessed 30 October 2020).

Kim, A. J., and Johnson, K. K. P. (2016) 'Power of consumers using social media: Examining the influence of brand-related user-generated content on Facebook', *Computers in Human Behavior*, 58, 99–108.

Leggatt, H. (2015) 'Amazon the go-to place for consumers to search for products', *BizReport*, 9 October. Retrieve from: http://www.bizreport.com/2015/10/amazon-the-go-to-place-for-consumers-to-search-for-products.html (accessed 30 October 2020).

Lundquist, A., and Gromek, M. (2015) 'Successful equity crowdfunding campaigns: A Nordic review'. Retrieve from: https://www.slideshare.net/MichalGromek/successful-equity-crowdfunding-campaigns3?qid=8f264dcb-bd76-497a-9fc7-4f30e89ec599&v=&b=&from_search=3 (accessed 30 October 2020).

Mangold, W. G., and Faulds, D. J. (2009) 'Social media: The new hybrid element of the promotion mix', *Business Horizons*, 52(4), 357–65.

Moorman, C. (2014) CMO *Survey Report: Highlights and Insights*, August. Retrieve from: http://slideshare.net/christinemoorman/the-cmo-survey-report (accessed 30 October 2020).

Moorman, C. (2019) *CMO Survey Report: Highlights and Insights*, August. Retrieve from: https://cmosurvey.org/wp-content/uploads/sites/15/2019/02/The_CMO_Survey-Highlights-and_Insights_Report-Feb-2019.pdf (accessed 30 October 2020).

Murphy, R. (2018) 'Local consumer review survey, online reviews statistics & trends'. Retrieve from: https://www.brightlocal.com/research/local-consumer-review-survey/ (accessed 30 October 2020).

Murton Beets, L. and Handley, A. (2019) *B2C Content Marketing 2019: Benchmarks, Budgets, and Trends*. Retrieve from: https://contentmarketinginstitute.com/wp-content/uploads/2018/12/2019_B2C_Research-FINAL-PDF-12_10_18.pdf (accessed 30 October 2020).

O'Brien, M. (2015) 'How to construct the perfect marketing email', *ClickZ*, 22 October. Retrieve from: https://www.clickz.com/how-to-construct-the-perfect-marketing-email/24006/ (accessed 30 October 2020).

Rosengren, S., and Dahlén, M. (2015) 'Exploring advertising equity: How a brand's past advertising may affect consumer willingness to approach its future ads', *Journal of Advertising*, 44(1), 1–13.

Statista (2019) 'Worldwide desktop market share of leading search engines from January 2010 to July 2019', *Statista*. Retrieve from: https://www.statista.com/statistics/216573/worldwide-market-share-of-search-engines/ (accessed 30 October 2020).

Stephen, A. T., Sciandra, M. R., and Inman, J. J. (2015) 'The effects of content characteristics on consumer engagement with branded social media content on Facebook'. Marketing Science Institute Working Paper No. 15–110.

Schwemmer, C. and Ziewiecki, S. (2018) 'Social media sellout: The increasing role of product promotion on YouTube', *Social Media + Society*, 4(3), 1–20.

Usborne, S, (2018) 'Netflix's "new world order": A streaming giant on the brink of global domination', *The Guardian*, 17 April. Retrieve from: https://www.theguardian.com/media/2018/apr/17/netflixs-new-world-order-a-streaming-giant-on-the-brink-of-global-domination (accessed 30 October 2020).

Vallone, J. (2011) 'Crowdsourcing could predict terror strikes, gasoline prices', *Investors' Business Daily*, 29 August, 5.

van den Bulte, C., and Wuyts, S. (2007) *Social Networks and Marketing*, Boston, MA: Marketing Science Institute.

Walsh, H. (2019) 'Exposed: The tricks sellers use to post fake reviews on Amazon', *Which?*, 5 July. Retrieve from: https://www.which.co.uk/news/2019/07/exposed-the-tricks-sellers-use-to-post-fake-reviews-on-amazon/ (accessed 24 November 2019).

Waring, T., and Martinez, A. (2002) 'Ethical customer relationships: A comparative analysis of US and French organisations using permission-based email marketing', *Journal of Database Marketing*, 10(1), 53–70.

Wisterberg, E. (2015) 'Pewdiepie-effekten lyfter Björn Borgs FPS-spel' [Pewdiepie effect raises Bjorn Borg's FPS-games]. *Dagens Media*, 6 December. Retrieve from: https://www.dagensmedia.se/marknadsforing/kampanjer/pewdiepie-effekten-lyfter-bjorn-borgs-fps-spel-6090265 (accessed 30 October 2020).

Wu, K. (2016) 'YouTube Marketing: Legality of sponsorship and endorsement in advertising', *Journal of Law, Business, and Ethics*, 22, 59–91.

Wunsch-Vincent, S., and Vickery, G. (2007) 'Participative web: User-created content', Organization for Economic Co-operation and Development (OECD), DSTI/ICCP/IE(2006)7/FINAL, 12 April. Retrieve from: http://www.oecd.org/internet/interneteconomy/38393115.pdf (accessed 30 October 2020).

YouTube (2019) 'Add paid product placements and endorsements'. *YouTube Help*. Retrieve from: https://support.google.com/youtube/answer/154235?hl=en-GB (accessed 30 October 2020).

Chapter 11
Services Marketing and Customer Experience Management

Learning Outcomes

After studying this chapter, you will be able to:

- explain the nature and characteristics of services;
- describe what is meant by the term 'service encounters';
- outline the principles of relationship marketing and the relationships between trust, commitment, and customer satisfaction; and
- define the term 'customer experiences' and explain its dimensions, how it has evolved, and how it might be measured.

Case Insight 11.1
Novartis Pharmaceuticals

Market Insight 11.1
Purely Products and Purely Services

Market Insight 11.2
Revolutionizing the Shopping Encounter with Digital Mirrors

Market Insight 11.3
Co-creating the Future of Logistics at DHL

Case Insight 11.1 **Novartis Pharmaceuticals**

Employing approximately 108,000 people across the globe, Novartis's treatments reach more than 750 million people and are available in approximately 155 countries. We speak to Mark Chakravarty, global head, communications and patient advocacy, Novartis Pharmaceuticals, to find out how this Swiss multinational communicates about its offerings in such a tightly regulated market.

Novartis is a global medicines company based in Switzerland dedicated to creating medicines that improve and extend people's lives. The company uses innovative science and digital technologies to create transformative treatments in areas of great medical need. Benefiting from a continued focus on innovation, it has one of the industry's leading product pipelines, with more than 200 products in clinical development. We are committed to ensuring that medicines are accessible to as many patients as possible. The pharmaceutical industry is highly regulated worldwide and marketing and advertising protocols vary between countries. While Novartis strives to deliver global strategies for the consistency and persistency of brand messages and the associated **creative**, local launches and programme implementations can differ significantly depending on the region in which the team operates.

Within Novartis, there are multiple teams, each responsible for liaison with a specific group of customers. This spans from medical teams working with scientific investigators on data development, health policy experts interacting with local government officials through to marketing and sales representatives liaising with healthcare professionals. We partner with patient communities around the world to discover new ways to improve and extend people's lives. At the core of these partnerships is the Novartis Commitment to Patients and Caregivers. The Novartis Communications and Patient Advocacy team is front and centre in ensuring the patient voice and authentic experience is reflected in the company's external programmes and activities. We serve to infuse patient insights, beliefs, and values into cross-functional internal decisions and business activities. While this part of the Novartis business works closely with commercial operations in the company, much of our work is not promotional and features only the Novartis corporate branding, without any mention of specific treatment names.

Our team utilizes a broad range of traditional and digital media channels to inform the public and target audiences (e.g. business and trade media), with relevant developments on Novartis and by sharing balanced and medically accurate information regarding disease areas to equip patients with the knowledge and tools to manage their health condition in the best way possible. At the heart of the work in patient advocacy is the identification and understanding of patient insights, which ensure that all information and materials produced are of value to the intended audiences, and address an unmet need. These insights are gathered through patient advisory councils, social media listening, and ongoing partnerships with advocacy groups. These partnerships with advocacy groups can often involve identifying a mutual challenge or opportunity, then working together to develop and launch a programme which meets this.

Case Insight 11.1 (continued)

Our stakeholders value Novartis as a trusted partner. In 2018, independent research conducted by PatientView demonstrated that Novartis globally ranked as having the top corporate reputation of all pharmaceutical companies in dermatology. PatientView surveyed patient groups **specializing in skin conditions** and analysed the reputation of fifteen pharmaceutical companies **within the sector**. The research focused on twelve indicators such as patient-centred strategy, information, safety, quality of products, pricing policies, transparency, integrity, patient partnerships, and patient engagement. We achieved the highest scores across all companies in nine of the indicators. This result was attributed to investment in expanding **access to skin health medicines,** and continued investment in patient care and support tools.

In psoriasis, for example, the company is investing in more than one hundred scientific studies to drive the scientific understanding of this disease. More than 125 million individuals are affected by psoriasis worldwide and one out of three has a family member with the condition. Up to 30 per cent of people with psoriasis will develop a form of arthritis called psoriatic arthritis (PsA). If left untreated, PsA can cause permanent severe joint damage. Both psoriasis and psoriatic arthritis are part of a family of conditions called psoriatic disease, and both cause inflammation. In psoriasis, this inflammation happens on the skin, with red, itchy, and scaly patches (known as plaques) appearing most commonly on the elbows, knees, scalp, chest, and lower back. In PsA, however, this inflammation is not as obvious to the eye; it results in swollen and painful joints and tendons, occurring in any part of the body.

In a number of countries, the science around the links between skin and joint health was generally well established among specialized physicians like dermatologists and rheumatologists who manage these diseases. However, it became apparent that this was not yet the standard in all healthcare settings nor was the connection well understood among the general public and those living with psoriasis. The broad lack of understanding of the link between psoriasis and PsA was attributed to a number of factors. For example, when we went deep into understanding these factors in a country like Canada, we found through survey data that many people were unaware of PsA as a condition, so did not understand the importance of monitoring for joint symptoms. In instances where patients were aware of PsA, they did not necessarily understand the link to psoriasis or recognize that identifying the links between skin and joint health is critical to preventing the joint damage that can come with PsA. More often than not, joint pain and stiffness are wrongly attributed to ageing or trauma due to injury or some strenuous activity. This core insight about the gap between skin and joints was observed by the Canadian Association of Psoriasis Patients—a leading Canadian patient organization dedicated to improving patient care and quality of life—who noticed little to no information existed for patients. Meeting this need for in-depth information regarding PsA became the mutual focus and shared objective for a national collaboration.

Ultimately, the challenge was how to ensure that Canadians living with or at risk of psoriasis were thinking about 'more than their skin' and proactively looking out for any changes in their joint health. To achieve this, a market category shift was required which put patient outcomes at the centre. By raising awareness about the connection and encouraging meaningful discussions, the goal was to shift from 'skin' as the most significant aspect of psoriasis towards a more comprehensive approach where both skin and joints are valued and addressed.

The question for us was how should we go about designing and branding a disease-awareness campaign of this type?

Introduction

Services and products are different. One of the distinguishing dimensions of products is that they have a physical presence. Services do not have a physical presence and they cannot be touched. This is because their distinguishing characteristic is that they are an act or a performance (Berry, 1980). A service cannot be put in a bag, taken home, stored in a cupboard, and used at a later date. A service is consumed at the point at which it is produced. For example, watching a play at a theatre, learning maths at school, or taking a holiday all involve the simultaneous production and consumption of the play, new knowledge, and leisure.

The service industry sector forms a substantial part of most developed economies. Not surprisingly, the range of services is enormous, and we consume services in nearly all areas of our work, business, home, and leisure activities. In fact, services represent two-thirds of the EU's economy and 90 per cent of new jobs (European Commission, 2017). Table 11.1 indicates the variety of sectors and some of the areas in which we consume different types of service.

The sheer number of services that are available has grown, partly because it is not always easy to differentiate products based only on feature, benefit, quality, or price. Competition can be very intense and most product innovations or developments are copied quickly. Services provide an opportunity to add value, yet not be copied, because each service is a unique experience.

Most products contain an element of service: there is a product–service combination designed to provide a means of adding value, differentiation, and earning a higher return. The extent to which a service envelops a product varies according to a number of factors—that is, the level of tangibility associated with the type of product, the way in which the service is delivered, variations in supply and demand, the level of customization, the type of relationship between service providers and customers, and the degree of involvement with the service that people experience (Lovelock et al., 1999).

Many grocery products have few supporting services—only shelf stocking and checkout operators. The purchase of new fitted bedroom furniture involves the cupboards, dressers, and wardrobes, plus the professional installation service necessary to make the furniture usable. At the other end of the spectrum, a visit to the dentist or an evening class entails little physical product-based support, because the personal service is delivered by the service deliverer in the form of the dentist or tutor.

Table 11.1 Service sectors

Sector	Examples
Business	Financial, airlines, hotels, solicitors, lawyers
Manufacturing	Finance and accountants, computer operators, administrators, trainers
Retail	Sales personnel, cashiers, customer support advisers
Institutions	Hospitals, education, museums, charities, churches
Government	Legal system, prisons, military, customs and excise, police

The Nature of Services

In view of these comments about the range and variety of services, and before moving on, it is necessary to define what a 'service' is. As with many topics, there is no firm agreement, but, for our purposes, the following definition, derived from a number of authors, will be used:

> A service is any act or performance offered by one party to another that is essentially intangible. Consumption of the service does not result in any transfer of ownership even though the **service process** may be attached to a physical product.

Much of this definition is derived from the work of Grönroos (1990), who considered a range of definitions and interpretations. What this definition provides is an indication of the various characteristics and properties that set services apart from products (see also Market Insight 11.1).

Research Insight 11.1

To take your learning further, you might wish to read this influential paper.

Shostack, G. L. (1977) 'Breaking free from product marketing', *Journal of Marketing*, 41(2), 73–80.

This passionately written paper seeks to draw a clear and distinct line between the requirements for marketing products and services. The author states that a marketing mix that is appropriate for products is not suitable for services. A key thrust of the paper is the need for an understanding of the difference between image (for products) and evidence (for services).

 Visit the **online resources** to read the abstract and access the full paper.

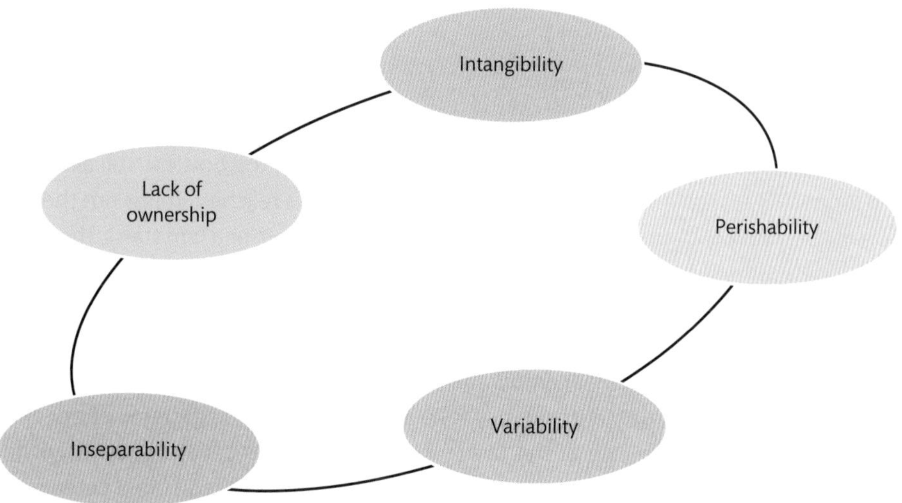

Figure 11.1 The five core characteristics of services

Distinguishing Characteristics

Services are characterized by five distinct characteristics: **intangibility**, **perishability**, **variability**, **inseparability**, and a lack of **ownership** (see Figure 11.1). These are important aspects that shape the way in which marketers design, deliver, and evaluate the marketing of services.

Intangibility

The purchase of products involves the use of most of our senses. We can touch, see, smell, hear, or even taste products before we buy them, let alone use them. When purchasing a tablet or smartphone, for example, it is possible to see the physical product and its various attributes such as size and colour, to test its functionality, to feel its weight and touch it. These are important purchasing decision cues, and even if the equipment fails to work properly, it is possible to take it back for a replacement.

If a decision is made to buy additional insurance or support, however, this will be itemized on the receipt, but it is not possible to touch, taste, see, hear, or smell it. Services are intangible, and they are delivered and experienced only post-purchase.

Intangibility does not mean that customers buy services without using their senses. What it does mean is that they use substitute cues to help them to make these purchasing decisions and to reduce the uncertainty, because they cannot touch, see, smell, or hear the service. People make judgements based on a range of quality-related cues. These cues serve to make tangible the intangible service. Two types of cue can be identified: intrinsic and extrinsic (Olson and Jacoby, 1972). *Intrinsic* cues are drawn directly from the 'service product' itself, and are regarded as difficult to change. *Extrinsic* cues, on the other hand, are said to surround the 'service product' and can be changed relatively easily. Brady et al. (2005) found that different types of service brand need different types of cue. Financial and investment-based brands prosper from the use of intrinsic cues, which stress objective information sources, such as a strong reputation, industry rankings, and favourable media reviews. The reverse is true for services that have a more tangible element, such as hotels and transport services. In these circumstances, more subjective communication, such as advertising and referrals through word-of-mouth, are more influential.

Perishability

A bottle of shampoo on a supermarket shelf attracts a number of opportunities to be sold and consumed. When the store closes and opens again the following day, the bottle is still available to be sold, and it remains available until purchased or the expiry date is reached. This is not the case with services. Once a train pulls out of a station, or an aeroplane takes off, or a film starts, those seats are lost and can never be sold. This is referred to as 'perishability' and is an important aspect of services marketing. Services are manufactured and consumed simultaneously; they cannot be stored either prior to or after the **service encounter**.

The reason why these seats remain empty reflects variations in demand. This may be the result of changes in the wider environment and may follow easily predictable patterns of behaviour, for example family holiday travel. One of the tasks of service marketers is to ensure that the number of empty seats and lost-forever revenue is minimized. In cases of predictable demand, service managers can vary the level of service capacity—a longer train, a bigger aircraft, or extra screenings of a film (multiplex facilities), for example. However, demand may vary unpredictably, in which case service managers are challenged to provide varying levels of service capacity at short notice.

One of the main ways in which demand patterns can be influenced is by means of differential pricing. By lowering prices to attract custom during quieter times and raising prices when demand is at its highest, demand can be levelled and marginal revenues increased. Hotel and transport reservation systems have become very sophisticated, making it easier to manage demand and improve efficiency, and, of course, customer service. Some football clubs categorize matches according to the prestige or ranking of the opposition and adjust prices to fill the stadium. In addition to differential pricing, extra services can be introduced to divert demand. Hotels offer specialist weekend breaks, such as golfing or fishing and mini vacations, to attract retired people outside of the holiday season. Leisure parks offer family discounts and bundle free rides into prices to stimulate demand.

Variability

As already noted, an important characteristic of services is that they are produced and consumed by people, simultaneously, as a single event. One of the outcomes of this unique process is that it is exceedingly difficult to standardize the delivery of services. It is also difficult to deliver services so that they always meet the brand promise, especially because these promises often serve to frame customer service expectations. If demand increases unexpectedly and there is insufficient capacity

It is difficult to standardize the delivery of services, because each 'event' is unique. This variability of service delivery can be observed in theatre performances.

Source: © Pavel L. Photo and Video/Shutterstock.

to deal with the excess number of customers, service breakdown may occur. A flood of customers at a restaurant may extend the arrival of meals for customers already seated and who have ordered their meals; too many train passengers may mean that there are not enough seats: in both of these cases, it is not possible to provide a service level that can be consistently reproduced.

A different way of looking at variability is to consider a theatre. The show may be doing well and the lead actors performing to critical acclaim. However, the actual performance that each actor delivers each night will be slightly different. This change may be subtle, such as a change in the tone of voice or an inflexion, and will pass by relatively unnoticed. At the other extreme, some actors go out of their way to make their performances very different. It is alleged that English actor Jane Horrocks once remarked that, during the performance of a certain theatre play, she deliberately changed each evening's show to relieve her boredom.

There has been substantial criticism of some organizations that, in an effort to lower costs, have relocated some or all of their call-centre operations offshore. These strategies sometimes fail because the new provider has insufficient training and local or product knowledge, or, in some cases, simply cannot be understood. This type of service experience will vary among customers and by each customer. The resulting fall in customer satisfaction can lead to increased numbers of customers defecting to competitors.

The variability of services does not mean that planning is a worthless activity. By anticipating situations in which service breakdown might occur, service managers can provide facilities. For example, entertainment can be provided for queues at cinemas or theme parks, to change the perception of the length of the time it takes to experience the service (film or ride).

Inseparability

As established earlier, products can be built, distributed, stored, and eventually consumed at a time specified by the ultimate end-user customer. Services, on the other hand, are consumed at the point at which they are produced. In other words, **service delivery** cannot be separated from or split out of service provision or service consumption.

This event in which delivery coincides with consumption means that not only do customers come into contact with the service providers, but also there must be interaction between the two parties. This interaction is of particular importance not only to the quality of service production, but also to the experience enjoyed by the customer. So, to continue the earlier example of a theatre play, the show itself may provide suitable entertainment, but the experience may be considerably enhanced if the lead actor—Jane Horrocks, Carole Bouquet, or Carey Mulligan—actually performs, rather than has the night off because she is unwell. Alternatively, a personal trainer may develop a strong reputation and, should there be an increase in demand beyond manageable levels, pricing can be used to reduce or reschedule demand for their coaching services.

These examples of service experiences highlight service delivery as a mass service experience (the play) and as a solo experience (the personal trainer). The differences impact on the nature of the interaction process. In the mass service experience, the other members of the audience have the opportunity to influence the perceived quality of the experience. Audiences create atmosphere and this may be positively or negatively charged. A good production can involve audiences in a play and keep them focused for the entire performance. However, a poor performance can frustrate audiences, leading to some members walking out, and hence influencing the perception others have of the performance and experience of the play.

Interaction within the solo experience (personal trainer–client) allows for greater control by the service provider, if only because it can manage the immediate context within which the interaction occurs and not be unduly influenced by wider environmental issues. Opportunities exist for flexibility and adaptation as the service delivery unfolds. For example, a check-out assistant in H&M operates within a particular context, is not influenced by other major events during the interaction, and can adapt tone of voice, body language, and overall approach to meet the needs of particular customers.

Market Insight 11.1 **Purely Products and Purely Services**

Sweden's Tetra Pak revolutionized the food packaging industry; Finland's Huhtamäki Oyj is one of the world's leading manufacturers of paper cups and plates; Danish company Schur Technology is a leading North European total supplier of packaging solutions; and Norwegian company Elopak is a leading global supplier of cartons for liquid food products. London-based DS Smith is one of the world's leading packaging groups and an expert in recycling operations to supply environmentally friendly solutions.

What is common to all of these organizations? Their skill and core competence is in packaging. They make tangible products to which, traditionally, there are few service additions. Their role has become essential given that product packaging not only protects the product in transit from the manufacturer to the end user but also performs marketing functions (e.g. product differentiation).

Packaging is an example of a 'pure product' that cannot be enhanced through extra services.
Source: © Getty/Amy Sussman/Stringer.

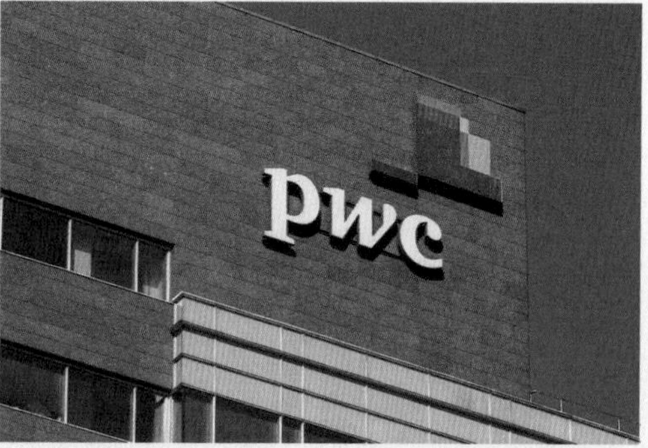

Multinational professional services networks such as PwC offer an extensive range of technical services based on knowledge and intangible expertise.
Source: © Konektus Photo/Shutterstock.

Alternatively, Ernst & Young, Deloitte, KPMG, and PricewaterhouseCoopers (PwC) are the four largest accounting and auditing firms in the world. These global organizations are professional service networks and provide a wide range of services to their clients, including audits of public and private firms. These organizations do not make or sell any products; they provide knowledge and skills—that is, pure services.

1 **Identify ways in which packaging might influence consumers.**

2 **What different activities might a marketing consultant working for PwC undertake?**

3 **Draw the product–service spectrum and place on it various product–service combinations.**

Sources: https://www.elopak.com; https://www.huhtamaki.com; https://www.schur.com; https://www.tetrapak.com; https://www.dssmith.com; https://www.pwc.com.

One final aspect of variability concerns the influence arising from the mixture of customers present during the service delivery. If there is a broad mix of customers, service delivery may be affected because the service provider has to attend to the needs of different groups. Such a mixture may dilute the impact of the service actually delivered.

Lack of Ownership

The final characteristic associated with services marketing arises naturally from the other features: services cannot be owned because nothing is transferred during the interaction or delivery experience. Although a legal transaction often occurs with a service, there is no physical transfer of ownership as there is when a product is purchased. The seat in a theatre, or on a train, plane, or ferry is rented on a temporary basis in exchange for a fee. The terms associated with the rental of the seat determine the time and use or experience to which the seat can be put. However, the seat remains the property of the theatre owner, rail operator, airline, or ferry company, respectively, because it needs to be available for renting to other people for further experiences.

One last point concerns **loyalty** schemes, such as frequent-flyer programmes and membership clubs, whereby the service provider actively promotes a sense of ownership. By creating customer involvement and participation, even though there is nothing to actually own, customers can develop an attitude based around their perceived right to be a part of the service provider.

Visit the **online resources** and complete Internet Activity 11.1 to learn more about the role of marketing in the Professional Marketing Services Group.

Service Encounters

The development of service marketing strategies involves understanding the frequency with and the ways in which customers contact service providers. Once this is understood, strategies can be developed that maintain required levels of service, but the processes and linkages that bring the elements of the services marketing mix and associated systems together can be reformulated. Service marketing strategy should therefore be based on insight into the ways in which customers interact or contact a service. The form and nature of the customer encounter is of fundamental importance.

A service encounter is best understood as a period of time during which a customer interacts directly with a service (Shostack, 1985). These interactions may be short and encompass all of the actions necessary to complete the service experience. Alternatively, they may be protracted, involve several encounters and several representatives of the service provider, and indeed several locations, so that the service experience can be completed. Whatever their length, the quality of a service encounter impacts on perceived service value, which, in turn, influences customer satisfaction (Gil et al., 2008).

Originally, the term 'encounter' was used to describe the personal interaction between a service provider and customers. A more contemporary interpretation needs to include all interactions that occur through people and their equipment and machines with the people and equipment belonging to the service provider (Glyn and Lehtinen, 1995), as set out in Market Insight 11.2. As a result, three levels of customer contact can be observed: high-contact services, medium-contact services, and low-contact services (see Table 11.2).

Market Insight 11.2 Revolutionizing the Shopping Encounter with Digital Mirrors

Digital technologies are increasingly being used to innovate and improve service encounters. The shopping industry is seeing the rapid adoption of new technologies such as artificial intelligence (AI) and augmented reality (AR) that allow customers to virtually try out a wide range of products before purchase. Moreover, these technologies enable products to be personally advertised to customers based on their own characteristics and the preferences of other similar shoppers.

Although these technologies are often used to improve online shopping, they can also be used to enhance the service encounter in-store. For example, in-store interactive digital mirrors allow customers to see themselves wearing the item of interest. Virtual changing rooms, wearable devices, and personal shopping assistants are other examples of technologies that allow for a deeper level of in-store interaction between shoppers and brands. Manufacturers are also interested in these technologies because it can generate useful information on which items are attracting consumers' attention.

Beauty products retailer Sephora has developed its 'Virtual Artist' interactive digital mirror to allow in-store customers to try cosmetics before purchase. As this tool does not require customers to physically apply lipstick or blusher, customers can try a greater number of products in a short amount of time. The 'Virtual Artist' also recommends shades of make-up based on the customer's skin tone. Sephora also provides these services as a smartphone app to allow potential consumers to try beauty products at home, thus offering a seamless and consistent experience from digital and mobile platforms to physical stores.

Interactive digital mirrors are revolutionizing the service encounter for in-store shoppers.
Source: © David Pereiras/Shutterstock.

However, the use of modern technologies such as digital mirrors in retail stores should not be considered the only way to enhance customers' in-store experience. As brick-and-mortar stores are no longer only physical locations for transactions but spaces of interaction between brands and their consumers, customer service should be enhanced through the use of new technology rather than being replaced by it.

1 **How would you classify Sephora's 'Virtual Artist' as a form of service encounter?**

2 **How might business-to-business (B2B) marketers use the information generated by in-store digital mirrors?**

3 **How might in-store digital mirrors impact on the relationships between retailers and their customers?**

Sources: DeNisco Rayome (2018); Alexander and Cano (2019).

One of the interesting developments in recent years is the decision by some organizations to move their customers away from high-contact services into low-contact services. Clear examples of this are to be found in the banking sector, with first automatic teller machines, then telephone and now Internet and app banking, all of which either lower or remove personal contact with bank employees. Further examples include vending machines, self-service or rapid checkout facilities in hotels, and online ticket purchases.

Table 11.2	Levels of customer contact
Contact level	**Explanation**
High-contact services	Customers visit the service facility, so they are personally involved throughout the service delivery process, e.g. retail branch banking and higher education.
Medium-contact services	Customers visit the service facility, but do not remain for the duration of the service delivery, e.g. consulting services, and delivering and collecting items to be repaired.
Low-contact services	Little or no personal contact between customer and service provider, with service delivered from a remote location, often through electronic means, e.g. software repairs, and television and radio entertainment.

Sirianni et al. suggest that, by actively branding service encounters, organizations can reinforce brand meaning and positioning, whilst influencing customers' responses to brands; they define 'branded service encounters' as:

> service interactions in which employee behaviour is strategically aligned with the brand positioning. This strategic alignment may be evident in various elements of the employee's presented behaviour, appearance, and manner that can reinforce brand meaning during service interactions with customers.
>
> (2013: 108)

This suggests that branded service encounters should be an integral element of any integrated marketing communication activity.

Key Dimensions of Services Marketing

The marketing of services can be improved by understanding how customers evaluate service performance. This begs the question: how do customers judge the quality of a bank's services, or those of an airline? This is potentially very difficult because complex services such as surgery or stockbroking have few tangible clues upon which to base a judgement about whether the service was extremely good, good, satisfactory, poor, or a disgrace. Customers purchasing physical goods can make judgements about the features, style, and colour, prior to purchase, during purchase, and even post-purchase, returning faulty or otherwise unwanted goods. This is not possible with some types of service—especially people-processing services.

Service performance is regarded as an important contributor to a firm's financial outcomes. Heskett et al. (1994) show that superior customer service, within a consumer context, leads to increased financial performance. The notion of service time as an indicator of service performance (Lund and Marinova, 2014) has also gained increasing attention as service providers in general, and retailers in particular, look to gain competitive advantage.

Zeithaml (1981) determined a framework that categorizes different services, which, in turn, influences the degree to which market offerings can be evaluated, identifying three main properties, as follows.

- *Search* properties are those elements that help customers to evaluate an offering prior to purchase. As mentioned above, physical products tend to have high search attributes that serve to reduce customer risk and increase purchase confidence.
- *Experience* properties do not enable evaluation prior to purchase. Sporting events, holidays, and live entertainment can be imagined, explained, and illustrated, but only by experiencing the performance or sitting in an audience of 100,000 people can a customer evaluate the service experience.
- *Credence* properties relate to those service characteristics that, even after purchase and consumption, customers find difficult to evaluate. Zeithaml (1981) refers to complex surgery and legal services to demonstrate the point.

As demonstrated earlier, most physical goods are high in search properties. Services, however, reflect the strength of experience and credence characteristics that, in turn, highlight their intangibility and their variability.

Garry and Broderick (2007), however, challenge this classification on the basis that it does not entirely reflect contemporary service markets. Whereas the original classification vested expertise in the service provider, emerging research recognizes customer expertise and sophistication. With more information, customers have increasing skills and abilities to make judgements about the quality of service offerings, prior to purchase. According to Garry and Broderick (2007), this increased focus on customer attributes should also be matched with a consideration of the attributes that we associate with service encounters. Here, they consider issues relating to information accessibility, time and interactivity, and the level of customer-centricity present within a customer experience.

Many organizations recognize the importance and complexities associated with the marketing of services. As a result, they often develop and plan their marketing activities in such a way that they help and reassure their customers prior, during, and after purchase. This is achieved through the provision of varying levels of information to reduce **perceived risk** and to enhance the service experience. Two techniques, branding and internal marketing, are instrumental in delivering these goals in services marketing.

Understanding service encounters, customer satisfaction, and associated service measurement techniques, however, fails to lead to an understanding beyond the moment of truth—that is, the point at which the service is actioned. Understanding and measuring the experience that customers take away as a result of an interaction is much more pertinent and insightful.

Principles of Relationship Marketing

Our attention now turns to ideas about **relationship marketing**. First, we look at founding ideas about the exchanges that occur between a pair of buyers and sellers, two main types of which can be identified: **market (or discrete) exchanges** and **collaborative exchanges**.

Market exchanges occur where there is no prior history of exchange, and no future exchanges are expected between a buyer and seller. In these transactions, the primary focus is on the product and price. Often referred to as 'transactional marketing', the 4Ps approach to the marketing mix variables (the 'marketing management' school of thought) is used to guide and construct transaction behaviour. Buyers were considered to be passive and sellers, active, in these short-term exchanges.

The assumption, however, that buyers are passive was soon challenged by the notion that, in reality, buyers are active problem-solvers, seeking solutions that are both efficient and effective. Research into business markets identified that, in practice, purchasing is not about a single discrete event; rather, it is about a stream of activities between two organizations. These activities are sometimes referred to as 'episodes'. Typically, these may be price negotiations, meetings at exhibitions, or a buying decision, but these all take place within the overall context of a relationship. This framed the 'relationship marketing' school of thought—one in which the buyer–seller relationship was the central element of analysis. This meant that the focus was no longer the product, or even the individual buying or the firm selling, but rather the relationship and its particular characteristics over time.

Relationship marketing is therefore based on the principle that there is a history of exchanges and an expectation that there will be exchanges in the future. Furthermore, the perspective is long-term, envisioning a form of loyalty or continued attachment by the buyer to the seller. Price, as the key controlling mechanism, is replaced by customer service and quality of interaction between the two organizations. The exchange is termed 'collaborative' because the focus is on both organizations seeking to achieve their goals in a mutually rewarding way and not at the expense of one another. Table 11.3 offers a more comprehensive list of fundamental differences between transactional and collaborative-based marketing exchanges.

Table 11.3 Characteristics of market and collaborative exchanges

Attribute	Market exchange	Collaborative exchange
Length of relationship	Short-term	Long-term
	Ends abruptly	Continuous process
Relational expectations	Conflicts of goals	Conflicts of interest
	Immediate payment	Deferred payment
	No future problems (there is no future)	Future problems expected to be overcome by joint commitment
Communication	Low frequency of communication	Frequent communication
	Formal communication predominates	Informal communication predominates
Cooperation	No joint cooperation	Joint cooperative projects
Responsibilities	Distinct responsibilities	Shared responsibilities
	Defined obligations	Shared obligations

Although market exchanges focus on products and prices, there is nonetheless a relational component, if only because interaction requires a basic relationship between parties for the transaction to be completed (Macneil, 1980).

Dwyer et al. (1987) refer to relationship marketing as an approach that encompasses a wide range of relationships, not only those with customers, but also those that organizations develop with suppliers, regulators, government, competitors, employees, and others. From this, relationship marketing might be regarded as all marketing activities associated with the management of successful relational exchanges.

Theron et al. (2013), among others, recognize that the role of collaboration in relationship marketing is important. Many organizations, however, maintain a variety of relationships with their different customers and suppliers—some highly collaborative and some market-oriented, or, as Spekman and Carroway (2005: 1) suggest, 'where they make sense'.

Relationship Trust, Commitment, and Satisfaction

Trust is a key feature of personal, intra-organizational, and inter-organizational relationships, and is necessary for their continuation. Gambetta (1988) argues that trust is a means of reducing uncertainty so that effective relationships can develop.

Cousins and Stanwix (2001) also suggest that although 'trust' is a term used to explain how relationships work, it often actually refers to ideas concerning risk, power, and dependency, and these propositions are used interchangeably. From their research of vehicle manufacturers, it emerges that B2B relationships are about the creation of mutual business advantage and the degree of confidence that one organization has in another.

Trust involves judgements about reliability and integrity, and is concerned with the degree of confidence that one party to a relationship has that another will fulfil its obligations and responsibilities. It has been claimed that the three major outcomes from the development of relationship trust are satisfaction, reduced perceived risk, and continuity (Pavlou, 2002).

- Satisfaction is determined by the extent to which customer expectations are met, which is a consequence of the buyer–seller relationship. The presence of trust in a relationship is important because it reduces the possibility of conflict, which, in turn, increases the probability of buyer satisfaction.
- Perceived risk is concerned with the expectation of loss and is therefore tied closely with organizational performance. Trust that a seller will not take advantage of the imbalance of information between buyer and seller effectively reduces risk.
- Continuity is related to business volumes, necessary in online B2B marketplaces, and the development of both online and real-world enduring relationships. Trust is associated with continuity and, when present, is consequently indicative of long-term relationships.

Trust within a consumer context is important because it can reduce uncertainty. Customers of American financial services company Wells Fargo lost trust in the brand after millions of fake bank accounts were discovered in 2016. The organization worked towards regaining their trust by offering services to mitigate potentially negative consequences for their customers. For example, they refunded incurred fees and developed their complaints programme (Wadley, 2017). Strong brands provide sufficient information for consumers to make calculated purchase decisions in the absence of full knowledge. In a sense, consumers transfer their responsibility for brand decision-making, and hence brand performance, to the brand itself. Through regular brand purchases, habits, or 'routinized response behaviour', develop. This is important not only because complex decision-making is simplified, but also because the amount of communication necessary to assist and provoke purchase is considerably reduced.

The presence of trust within a relationship is influenced by four main factors: the duration of the relationship; the relative power of the participants; the presence of cooperation; and various environmental factors that may be present at any one moment (Young and Wilkinson, 1989). Although pertinent, these are quite general factors, and it is Morgan and Hunt (1994) who established what are regarded today as the key underlying dimensions of relationship marketing. In their seminal paper, they argued that it is the presence of both **commitment** and trust that leads to cooperative behaviour, customer satisfaction, and, ultimately, successful relationship marketing.

Commitment is important because it implies a desire that a relationship continues and is strengthened because it is of value. Morgan and Hunt (1994) proposed that commitment and trust are the **key mediating variables (KMV)** between five antecedents and five outcomes (see Figure 11.2).

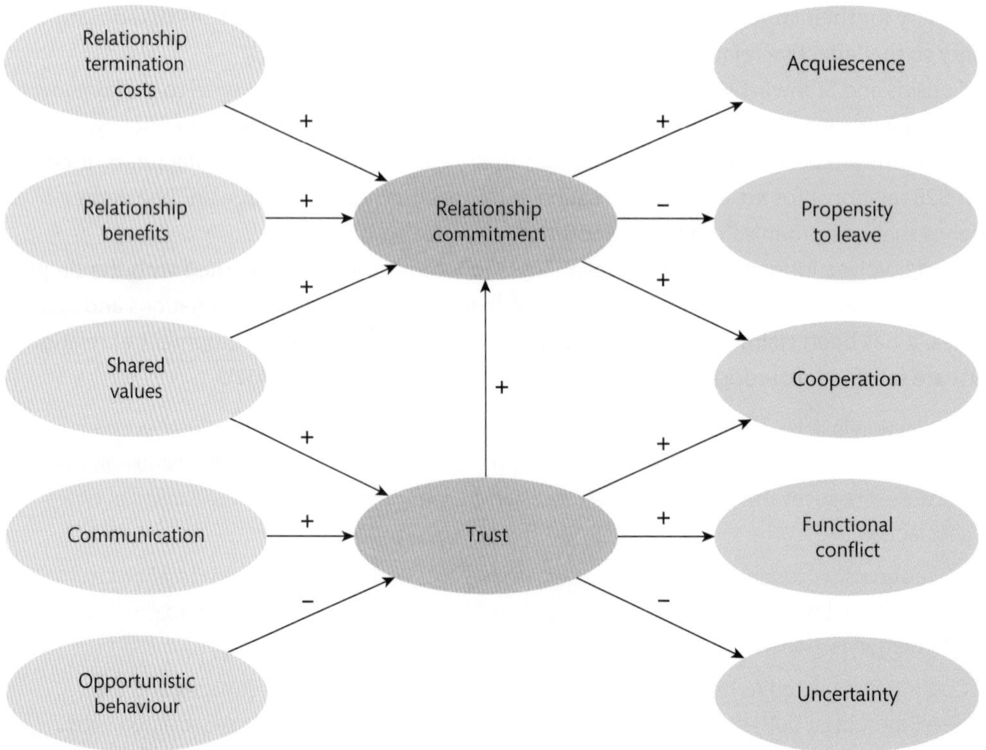

Figure 11.2 The KMV model of relationship marketing

Source: Reprinted with permission from R. M. Morgan and S. D. Hunt (1994). The commitment–trust theory of relationship marketing. *Journal of Marketing*, 58(July), 20–38, published by the American Marketing Association.

Research Insight 11.2

To take your learning further, you might wish to read this influential paper.

Morgan, R. M., and Hunt, S. D. (1994) 'The commitment–trust theory of relationship marketing', *Journal of Marketing*, 58(3), 20–38.

This well-known paper examines the role of trust and commitment in buyer–supplier relationships. The authors present the KMV model to explain various behavioural and cognitive aspects associated with exchange partnerships. Using social exchange theory, it is argued that, through mutually beneficial exchanges, trust and commitment develop, which, in turn, lead to longer lasting relationships.

 **Visit the online resources to read the abstract and access the full paper.**

According to the KMV model, the greater the losses anticipated through the termination of a relationship, the greater the commitment expressed by the exchange partners. When relationship partners share similar values, commitment increases. Morgan and Hunt (1994) proposed that building a relationship based on trust and commitment can give rise to a number of benefits, including developing a set of shared values, reducing costs when the relationship finishes, and increasing profitability because a greater number of end-user customers are retained as a consequence of the inherent value and satisfaction they experience. Cooperation arises from a relationship driven by high levels of both trust and commitment (Morgan and Hunt, 1994).

Ryssel et al. (2004: 203) recognize that trust (and commitment) has a 'significant impact on the creation of value and conclude that value creation is a function of the atmosphere of a relationship rather than the technology employed'. Trust and commitment are concepts that are central to relationship marketing.

Customer Satisfaction

A natural outcome from building trust and developing commitment is the establishment of customer satisfaction. This is seen as important because satisfaction is thought to be positively related to **customer retention**, which, in turn, leads to an improved return on investment (ROI) and hence profitability. Unsurprisingly, many organizations seek to improve levels of customer satisfaction, with the intention of strengthening customer relationships and driving higher levels of retention and loyalty (Ravald and Grönroos, 1996). The simple equation is: build trust, drive satisfaction, improve retention, and increase profits.

Customer satisfaction is not driven by trust alone, however; customer expectations also play an important role and help to shape a customer's perception of product or service performance. Customers compare performance against their expectations and, through this process, feel a sense of customer satisfaction or dissatisfaction. More recent ideas suggest that the **perceived value** of a relationship can be more important than trust when building customer satisfaction (Ulaga and Eggert, 2005).

If expectations are met, then customer satisfaction is achieved. In Spain for example, B2B IT providers Everis and DXC Technology boast the highest levels of customer satisfaction among firms with the highest IT expenditures, topping Amazon Web Services (AWS) and Accenture (Whitelane Research, 2019). If expectations are not met, then customers will be said to be dissatisfied. This simplistic interpretation can be misleading, because satisfaction does not always imply loyalty (Mittal and Lassar, 1998): what may be seen as loyalty may be nothing more than convenience, or even inertia—and this means too that dissatisfaction need not result in brand desertion (O'Malley, 1998).

Cumby and Barnes (1998) provide a useful insight into what contributes to customer satisfaction, citing:

- *core product/service*—the bundle of attributes, features, and benefits that must reach competitive levels if a relationship is to develop;
- *support services and systems*—the quality of services and systems used to support the core product/service;
- *technical performance*—the synchronization of the core product/services with the support infrastructure to deliver on the promise;
- *elements of customer interaction*—the quality of customer care demonstrated through face-to-face and technology-mediated communications; and
- *affective dimensions of services*—the subtle and non-core interactions that say something about how the organization feels about the customer.

This is a more useful insight into what it is that drives customer satisfaction, because it incorporates a wide range of factors and recognizes the importance of personal contact. Customer satisfaction and the quality of customer relationships are related, in differing ways, among differing people and contexts. However, one factor that is common to both is the perceived value of the interaction between parties.

Measuring Service Quality and Performance

Measuring the quality of a service encounter is an important factor in managing service-based organizations. Service quality is based on the idea that customer expectations of the service they will receive shape their perception of the actual service encounter. Customers therefore compare perceived service with expected service.

If the perceived service meets or even exceeds expectations, customers are satisfied and much more likely to return in future. However, if the perceived service falls below that expected, they may feel disappointed and not return.

Various models have been proposed to help organizations achieve consistent levels of service, including asking customers to rate the performance of a service encounter, asking customers what is expected from a service against what is delivered and comparing the performance of the different elements that make up a service with the customer's perception of the importance of these elements. Each approach has strengths and weaknesses but the approach that has received most attention is **SERVQUAL** developed by Parasuraman et al. (1988). For some, it represents the benchmark approach to managing service quality.

SERVQUAL is based on the difference between the expected level of service and the actual perceived level of service. This approach assumes that there is a service quality gap overall which breaks down into five sub-variants as follows.

- GAP 1—the gap between the customer's expectations and management perception. By not understanding customer needs correctly, management directs resources into inappropriate areas. For example, train service operators may think that customers want places to store bags, whereas they actually want a seat in a comfortable, safe environment.
- GAP 2—the gap between management perception and service quality specification. In this case, management perceives customer wants correctly but fails to set a performance standard, fails to clarify it, or sets one that is unrealistic and unachievable. For example, the train operator understands customer desire for a comfortable seat but fails to specify how many should be provided relative to the anticipated number of passengers on each route.
- GAP 3—the gap between service quality specifications and service delivery. In this situation, the service delivery does not match the service specification. This may be due to human error, poor training, or a failure in the technology necessary to deliver parts of a service. For example, the trolley buffet service on a train may be perceived as poor because the trolley operator was impolite because he/she had not received suitable training, or because the supplier had not delivered the sandwiches on time.
- GAP 4—the gap between service delivery and external communications. The service promise presented in advertisements, on the website, and in sales literature helps set customer expectations. If these promises are not realized in service delivery practice, customers become dissatisfied. For example, if an advertisement shows the interior of a train with comfortable seats and plenty of space, yet a customer boards a train only to find a lack of space and hard seating, the external communications have misled customers and distorted their view of what might be realistically expected.
- GAP 5—the gap between perceived service and expected service. This gap arises because customers misunderstand the service quality relative to what they expect. This may be due to one or more of the previous gaps. For example, a customer might assume that the lack of information when a train comes to a standstill for an unexpectedly long period of time is due to ignorance or a 'they never tell us anything' attitude. In reality, this silence may be due to a failure of the internal communication system.

Using this GAPS approach, five different dimensions of service quality have been established.

1. Reliability—the accuracy and dependability of repeated performances of service delivery.
2. Responsiveness—the helpfulness and willingness of staff to provide prompt service.
3. Assurance—the courtesy, confidence, and competence of employees.
4. Empathy—the ease and individualized care shown towards customers.
5. Tangibles—the appearance of employees, the physical location and any facilities and equipment, and the communication materials.

The SERVQUAL model consists of a questionnaire containing twenty-two items based around these five dimensions. When completed by customers it provides management with opportunities to correct areas where service performance is perceived to be less than satisfactory and learn from and congratulate people about the successful components. Although SERVQUAL has been used extensively, it is not without perceived problems. Difficulties concern the different dimensions customers use to assess quality, which varies according to each situation. In addition, there are statistical inconsistencies associated with measuring differences and the scoring techniques plus reliability issues associated with asking customers about their expectations after they have consumed a service (Gabbott and Hogg, 1998). Finally, ideas about measuring satisfaction are being overtaken as understanding about customer experience becomes more widely known. This is explored in the next section.

Customer Experiences

The path of this chapter began with an exploration of the evolution of marketing practices related to services marketing, then moved on to consider ideas about customer relationships. This chapter closes with an exploration of customer experiences (Maklan and Klaus, 2011).

The idea that providing a superior customer service might help in the (repeat) purchase decision process is something that several organizations now appreciate. For a long time, it was assumed that product quality and pricing were sufficient differentiators. However, product quality is no longer a viable means of establishing competitive advantage, simply because of shortening life cycles and evolving technologies. Service, although difficult to deliver in a consistent way, is very difficult to replicate and has become an important aspect of customer management.

Although generating customer satisfaction is important, it provides an incomplete picture. Of greater interest is 'customer experience'. As Prahalad and Ramaswamy (2004: 137, cited by Iyanna et al., 2012) suggest, the literature on value is no longer embedded in goods and services, or indeed relationships, but 'is now centred in the experiences of consumers'. Customer value is regarded by an increasing number of academics and practitioners as the central marketing activity (Iyanna et al., 2012) and that value is now central to customers' experiences. The implications for marketing are clearly asserted by Meyer and Schwager (2007: 118) when they say that 'customer experience encompasses every aspect of a company's offering—the quality of customer care, of course, but also advertising, packaging, product and service features, ease of use, and reliability' (see also Market Insight 11.3). (For a deeper understanding of the issues arising from the adoption of a customer experience perspective, see Research Insight 11.3.)

For the Hard Rock Cafe, the iconic brand and associations with music are also part of the customer experience.
Source: © Marcin Supinski/Unsplash.

The importance and significance of customer experience to both individuals and society was first established by Pine and Gilmore (1998) when they referred to the 'experience economy', a term that is used frequently by authors and researchers in this area. Chang and Horng (2010) suggest that themed restaurants, such as Starbucks and Hard Rock Cafe, are prime examples of customer experience. These brands are not only about the consumption of coffee and food, but also a situation or environment in which the consumption of services occurs and relationships are developed, and in total provide a meaningful or valuable customer experience. Ismail et al. (2011) refer to the trend towards creating unique experiences for customers with a view to developing a competitive advantage—something that is sustainable particularly for those in the service sector, because replication is very difficult.

Before exploring the characteristics and issues associated with customer experience, it is helpful to consider how the concept is defined, in which regard there has been little consensus. Some of the more notable attempts are set out in Table 11.4.

There are some similarities across many of these definitions. Customer experience is seen to be an individual event, and as concerning emotional reactions following direct and indirect interaction with an organization. It is also related to events prior to, during, or post consumption. Perhaps one crucial point is that it is not possible for two people to have or to share the same experience (Pine and Gilmore, 1998). As a result, the task of managing and measuring customer experiences is inherently complex.

To help us to disentangle some of this complexity, Pine and Gilmore (1998) derive four distinct realms of experience, based on two dimensions. These dimensions concern a customer's participation in an experience (weak/passive or active/strong) and an individual's connection with the environment of the experience or environmental relationship (from absorption/weak to immersion/strong).

The four realms of experience that emerge from these dimensions are as follows.

- *Educational realm*—This arises when individuals learn and enhance their skills and knowledge as a result of the events unfolding before them (Pine and Gilmore, 1999; Oh et al., 2007).
- *Entertainment realm*—This arises when an individual views a performance, listens to music, or reads for pleasure, during which the experience is absorbed passively (Pine and Gilmore, 1999).

Research Insight 11.3

To take your learning further, you might wish to read this influential paper.

Meyer, C., and Schwager, A. (2007) 'Understanding customer experience', *Harvard Business Review*, 85(2), 116–26.

This paper looks at how firms can benefit from adopting a customer experience perspective. It provides a clear understanding of what customer experience is practically and discusses the managerial issues that can be avoided by utilizing an experience-based view, rather than a relationship-based view. It also contains a useful table showing how customer relationship management (CRM) differs from customer experience management.

 **Visit the online resources to read the abstract and access the full paper.**

Table 11.4 Definitions of experience

Source	Definitions
Csikszentmihalyi (1977: 36)	The individual is experiencing flow when they have: a unified flowing from one moment to the next, in which he is in control of his actions and in which there is little distinction between self and environment, between stimulus and response, between past, present and future.
Holbrook and Hirschman (1982), cited in Carù and Cova (2003)	Experience is defined as a personal occurrence, often with important emotional significance, founded on the interaction with stimuli that are the products or services consumed.
Carbone and Haeckel (1994: 8)	The take-away impression formed by people's encounters with products, services, and businesses, a perception produced when humans consolidate sensory information.
Schmitt (1999: 60)	From a customer perspective: Experiences involve the entire living being. They often result from direct observation and/or participating in the event—whether they are real, dreamlike or virtual.
Shaw and Ivens (2002: 6)	an interaction between an organization and a customer. It is a blend of an organization's physical performance, the senses stimulated and emotions evoked, each intuitively measured against customer experience across all moments of contact.
Gentile et al. (2007: 397)	The customer experience originates from a set of interactions between a customer and a product, a company, or part of its organization, which provoke a reaction. This experience is strictly individual and implies the customer's involvement at different levels (rational, emotional, sensorial, physical and spiritual). Its evaluation depends on the comparison between a customer's expectations and the stimuli coming from the interaction with the company and its offering in correspondence of the different moments of contacts or touch-points.
Brakus et al. (2009: 53)	Subjective, internal consumer responses (sensations, feelings, and cognitions) and behavioural responses evoked by brand related stimuli that are part of a brand's design and identity, packaging, communications, and environments.
Ismail et al. (2011)	Emotions provoked, sensations felt, knowledge gained, and skills acquired through active involvement with the firm before, during, and after consumption.

Source: Adapted from Ismail et al. (2011).

Market Insight 11.3 **Co-creating the Future of Logistics at DHL**

Founded in 1969, DHL is one of the international leaders in logistics as the company delivers more than 1.6 billion parcels a year in over 220 countries. To maintain its leadership and conquer new markets, DHL positions itself as an innovative company, listening to the ideas of its 380,000 employees and the needs of its customers.

To achieve this, DHL has heavily invested in co-creation processes, fostering close collaborations with its customers to create value by offering them direct input in the design of new service solutions. In doing so, DHL can gain in-depth understanding of the true needs of its customers and develop successful new services in response to this. Although DHL now relies on its customers to design new services, it took the company several years and a lot of effort to gain the trust of sceptical customers and employees.

Two DHL 'Innovation Centres', located near the company's headquarters in Bonn, Germany and in Singapore, have been developed to stimulate cooperation with customers and business partners. By looking into the future of logistics as far as 2050, DHL offers workshops with experts and annual innovation days to discuss, explore and leverage technological, economic, and cultural trends and apply them to the domain of global logistics.

Over the years, DHL and its partners have successfully managed to create truly innovative services. For example, SmartSensors are designed to remotely monitor the environment and shipping conditions of sensitive life sciences and healthcare parcels in near real-time while in transit. 'Vision Picking', designed with DHL's customer Ricoh, a multinational imaging and electronics company, is a solution based on AR technology. Its goal is to increase the productivity of warehouse workers by 15 per cent by equipping them with smart glasses.

By constantly engaging with its customers, DHL develops modern and innovative logistics services.
Source: © Ilya Platonov/Shutterstock.

The autonomous DHL Parcelcopter was also developed in collaboration with German agencies and drone manufacturer Wingcopter. The goal of the project is to disrupt the delivery industry by dispatching small parcels to remote locations in a short amount of time. In 2018, the Parcelcopter successfully delivered medicines to an island in Lake Victoria in Africa over a six-month period, without requiring major infrastructure changes.

1. **What recent innovations in the parcel delivery industry have changed the way consumers order goods?**
2. **What are the advantages for DHL of launching its own innovation centres?**
3. **How can companies gain the trust of customers and partners that they are willing to co-create with?**

Sources: Bodine (2013); Crandell (2016); https://www.logistics.dhl.

- *Aesthetic realm*—This arises when an individual passively appreciates an event or environment, but leaves without affecting or altering the nature of the environment (Pine and Gilmore, 1999; Oh et al., 2007).
- *Escapist realm*—This arises when individuals become completely immersed in their environment and actively participate, so that they affect actual performances or occurrences in the environment (Pine and Gilmore, 1999; Oh et al., 2007).

This approach has subsequently led to research that focuses on the ways in which experiences are produced, narrated, and mediated (Lofgren, 2008).

Various authors have contributed to what might be the key dimensions of customer experience. Of these, Nysveen and Pedersen (2014) used the dimensions highlighted by Brakus et al. (2009)—namely, sensory, affective, intellectual, and behavioural—and added a further relational dimension, as determined by Nysveen et al. (2013).

- The *sensory* dimension refers to the extent to which a brand appeals to, and makes impressions on, consumers' senses.
- The *affective* dimension refers to how strongly a brand induces consumer feelings and emotions.
- The *intellectual* (or *cognitive*) dimension refers to how much a brand stimulates a consumer's curiosity, thinking, and problem-solving.
- The *behavioural* dimension refers to how strongly a brand engages consumers in physical activities.
- The *relational* dimension refers to how well an experience creates value for customers by driving social engagement, and providing a social identity and a sense of belonging.

From their research, Nysveen and Pedersen (2014) validated the importance of all of these dimensions. They stressed, however, the significance of the relational dimension, and its strong positive influence on both brand satisfaction and brand loyalty.

Visit the **online resources** and complete Internet Activity 11.2 to learn more about the Customer Experience Professionals Association (CXPA) and how companies manage customers' experiences.

Chapter Summary

To consolidate your learning, the key points from this chapter are summarized below.

- **Explain the nature and characteristics of services.**

  Unlike products, services are considered to be processes, and products and services have different distinguishing characteristics. These are based around their intangibility (you can touch a product, but not a service), perishability (products can be stored, but you cannot store a service), variability (each time a service is delivered, it is different, but products can be identical), inseparability (services are produced and consumed simultaneously), and a lack of ownership (you cannot take legal possession of a service). These are important because they shape the way in which marketers design, develop, deliver, and evaluate the marketing of services.

- **Describe what is meant by the term 'service encounters'.**

  A 'service encounter' is best understood as a period of time during which a customer interacts directly with a service (Shostack, 1985). There are three levels of customer contact: high-contact services, medium-contact services, and low-contact services.

- **Outline the principles of relationship marketing and the relationships between trust, commitment, and customer satisfaction.**

  Relationship marketing is based on the premise that retained customers are more profitable than transactional marketing-based customers. There are several key concepts associated with the management of customer relationships, the main ones being trust, commitment, and satisfaction. These are interrelated, and the management of customer relationships should be based on the principles of reducing the influence of power and the incidence of conflict to build customer trust, gain customer commitment, and, through loyalty and retention, generate customer satisfaction. This approach should increase the perceived value of the relationship for all parties.

- **Define the term 'customer experiences', and explain its dimensions, how it has evolved, and how it might be measured.**

  Customers' experience an emotional transition and response through interactions with an organization and its offerings. This individuality of experience implies that there are different types or levels of experience, such as rational, emotional, sensorial, physical, and spiritual. The development of customer experience marketing has been built on evolving ideas concerning service encounters, perceived value, relationship marketing, and customer satisfaction.

Review Questions

1. **Identify the essential characteristics of services and make brief notes explaining how these characteristics affect the marketing of services.**
2. **What are the main types of service process? Identify their key characteristics.**
3. **Explain the term 'service encounter'.**
4. **How does an understanding of the relevant search, experience, and credence properties of a service influence the way in which they are marketed?**
5. **What are the key differences between transaction marketing and relationship marketing?**
6. **Why is trust an important aspect of relationship marketing?**
7. **Describe the key mediating variables (KMV) model and the relationships between its components.**
8. **To what extent does the concept of 'relationship intensity' assist our understanding of relationship marketing?**
9. **Make notes for a short presentation in which you explain the term 'customer experience' and track its evolution.**
10. **Compare and contrast three of the different definitions of customer experience offered in Table 11.4.**

Worksheet Summary

To apply the knowledge you have gained from this chapter, and to test your understanding of services marketing and customer experience management, visit the **online resources** and complete Worksheet 11.1.

Discussion Questions

1 Having read Case Insight 11.1, how would you advise Novartis on how best to evaluate the quality of its service offering?

2 To what extent is the traditional marketing mix a useful basis for developing marketing strategies for service organizations?

3 Westcliffe and Sons makes a range of fruit juice drinks. The business falls into two main segments, consumer and business user, such as local councils and catering companies. Recent sales figures suggest that orders from some catering companies are down on previous years and that some have stopped buying from them altogether. The marketing director of Westcliffe has reported that he cannot understand the reason for the decline in business, because product quality and prices are very competitive. Advise the marketing director about the key issues he should consider and discuss how the company should re-establish itself with the catering companies.

4 A new electric scooter hire company has launched in Cologne, Germany, loaning out 5,000 scooters throughout the city via a smartphone app. There are already more established companies with a similar concept, yet they aim to attract loyal customers as well as one-off users such as tourists to the city.

A How important are trust, commitment, and satisfaction in the relationships the company seeks to build with its customers?

B How might the company secure the loyalty of existing electric scooter users in the city and convert non-users of electric scooters?

C How might the company measure its service quality and performance?

Visit the **online resources** and complete the multiple-choice questions to assess your knowledge of the chapter.

Glossary

collaborative exchanges a series of transactions between a buyer and seller in which the relationship is the main focus.

commitment a desire that a relationship should continue.

creative the content developed by art directors, copywriters and other creative personnel, for use in adverts.

customer experience the individual feelings and emotions felt during interactions with an organization and its offerings.

customer retention a stage in a buyer–seller relationship that is stable, and at which levels of trust and commitment are strongest.

inseparability a characteristic of a service, referring to its instantaneous production and consumption.

intangibility a characteristic of a service, referring to its lack of physical attributes, which means that it cannot be perceived by the senses—that is, tasted, seen, touched, smelled, or possessed.

key mediating variables (KMV) the dimensions of commitment and trust used within the Morgan and Hunt (1994) model of relationship marketing.

loyalty the extent to which a customer supports, possibly through repeat purchases, a particular brand.

market (or discrete) exchanges a type of transaction between a buyer and seller in which the main focus is on the product and price.

perceived risk the real and imagined uncertainties that customers consider when purchasing products and services.

ownership possession of and control over goods.

perceived value the 'net satisfaction' derived from consuming and using a product, not only the costs involved in obtaining it.

perishability a characteristic of a service, referring to the fact that any spare or unused capacity cannot be stored for use at some point in the future.

relationship marketing those marketing activities associated with the management of successful relational (collaborative) exchanges.

service delivery the means through which services are experienced by customers.

service encounter an event that occurs when a customer interacts directly with a service.

service process a series of sequential actions that lead to the delivery of a predetermined service.

service quality the extent to which customer expectations of a service are met through an actual service encounter.

SERVQUAL a model which measures the difference between the expected service and the actual perceived service.

trust a judgement about the reliability, integrity, and degree of confidence that one party to a relationship has that another will fulfil its obligations and responsibilities.

variability a characteristic of a service, referring to the amount of diversity allowed at each step of service provision.

References

Alexander, B., and Cano, M. B. (2019) 'Futurising the physical store in the omnichannel retail environment', in W. Piotrowicz and R. Cuthbertson (eds), *Exploring Omnichannel Retailing*, New York: Springer, 197–24.

Berry, L. L. (1980) 'Services marketing is different', *Business*, 30(3), 24–30.

Bodine, K. (2013) 'Why should you co-create your customer experience?', *Forrester*, 1 February. Retrieve from: https://go.forrester.com/blogs/13-02-01-why_should_you_co_create_your_customer_experience/ (accessed 5 January 2020).

Brady, M. K., Bourdeau, B. L., and Heskel, J. (2005) 'The importance of brand cues in intangible service industries: An application to investment services', *Journal of Services Marketing*, 19(6), 401–10.

Brakus, J. J., Schmitt, B. H., and Zarantonello, L. (2009) 'Brand experience: What is it? How is it measured? Does it affect loyalty?', *Journal of Marketing*, 73(3), 52–68.

Carbone, L. P., and Haeckel, S. H. (1994) 'Engineering customer experiences', *Marketing Management*, 3(3), 8–19.

Carù, A., and Cova, B. (2003) 'Revisiting consumption experience: A more humble but complete view of the concept', *Marketing Theory*, 3(2), 267–86.

Chang, T.-C., and Horng, S.-C. (2010) 'Conceptualizing and measuring experience quality: The customer's perspective', *Service Industries Journal*, 30(14), 2401–19.

Cousins, P. D., and Stanwix, E. (2001) 'It's only a matter of confidence! A comparison of relationship management between Japanese and UK non-owned vehicle manufacturers', *International Journal of Operations and Production Management*, 21(9), 1160–80.

Crandell, C. (2016) 'Customer co-creation is the secret sauce to success', *Forbes*, 10 June. Retrieve from: https://www.forbes.com/sites/christinecrandell/2016/06/10/customer_cocreation_secret_sauce (accessed 3 January 2020).

Csikszentmihalyi, M. (1977) *Beyond Boredom and Anxiety*, San Francisco, CA: Jossey-Bass.

Cumby, J. A., and Barnes, J. (1998) 'How customers are made to feel: The role of affective reactions in driving customer satisfaction', *Customer Relationship Management*, 1(1), 54–63.

DeNisco Rayome, A. (2018) 'How Sephora is leveraging AR and AI to transform retail and help customers buy cosmetic', *TechRepublic*, 15 February. Retrieve from: https://www.techrepublic.com/article/how-sephora-is-leveraging-ar-and-ai-to-transform-retail-and-help-customers-buy-cosmetics/ (accessed 1 January 2020).

Dwyer, R. F., Schurr, P. H., and Oh, S. (1987) 'Developing buyer–seller relationships', *Journal of Marketing*, 51(2), 11–27.

European Commission (2017) *A Services Economy that Works for Europeans*, 10 January. Retrieve from: https://ec.europa.eu/growth/content/services-economyworks-europeans-0_en (accessed 30 October 2020).

Gabbott, M., and Hogg, G. (1998) *Consumers and Services*, Chichester: Wiley.

Gambetta, D. (1988) *Trust: Making and Breaking Co-operative Relations*, New York: Blackwell.

Garry, T., and Broderick, A. (2007) 'Customer attributes or service attributes? Rethinking the search, experience and credence classification basis of services'. Paper presented at the 21st Service Workshop of the Academy of Marketing, 15–17 November, University of Westminster.

Gentile, C., Spiller, N., and Noci, G. (2007) 'How to sustain the customer experience: An overview of experience components that co-create value with the customer', *European Management Journal*, 25(5), 395–10.

Gil, I., Berenguer, G., and Cervera, A. (2008) 'The roles of service encounters, service value, and job satisfaction in business relationships', *Industrial Marketing Management*, 37(8), 921–39.

Glyn, W. J., and Lehtinen, U. (1995) 'The concept of exchange: Interactive approaches in services marketing', in W. J. Glyn and J. G. Barnes (eds), *Understanding Services Management*, Chichester: Wiley, 89–118.

Grönroos, C. (1990) *Service Management and Marketing: Managing the Moment of Truth in Service Competition*, Lexington, MA: Lexington Books.

Heskett, J. L., Jones, T. O., Loveman, G. W., Sasser, S. E., Jr., and Schlesinger, L. A. (1994) 'Putting the service-profit chain to work', *Harvard Business Review*, 72(2), 164–7.

Holbrook, M. B., and Hirschman, E. C. (1982) 'The experiential aspects of consumption: Consumer fantasies, feelings and fun', *Journal of Consumer Research*, 9(2), 132–40.

Ismail, A. R., Melewar, T. C., Lim, L., and Woodside, A. (2011) 'Customer experiences with brands: Literature review and research directions', *Marketing Review*, 11(3), 205–25.

Iyanna, S., Bosangit, C., and Mohd-Any, A. A. (2012) 'Value evaluation of customer experience using consumer-generated content', *International Journal of Management and Marketing Research*, 5(2), 89–102.

Lofgren, O. (2008) 'The secret lives of tourists: Delays, disappointments and daydreams', *Scandinavian Journal of Hospitality and Tourism*, 8(1), 85–101.

Lovelock, C., Vandermerwe, S., and Lewis, B. (1999) *Services Marketing: A European Perspective*, Harlow: FT/Prentice Hall.

Lund, D. J., and Marinova, D. (2014) 'Managing revenue across retail channels: The interplay of service performance and direct marketing', *Journal of Marketing*, 78(5), 99–118.

Macneil, I. R. (1980) *The New Social Contract*, New Haven, CT: Yale University Press.

Maklan, S., and Klaus, P. (2011) 'Customer experience: Are we measuring the right things?', *International Journal of Market Research*, 53(6), 771–92.

Meyer, C., and Schwager, A. (2007) 'Understanding customer experience', *Harvard Business Review*, 85(2), 116–26.

Mittal, B., and Lassar, W. M. (1998) 'Why do consumers switch? The dynamics of satisfaction versus loyalty', *Journal of Services Marketing*, 12(3), 177–94.

Morgan, R. M., and Hunt, S. D. (1994) 'The commitment–trust theory of relationship marketing', *Journal of Marketing*, 58(3), 20–38.

Nysveen, H., and Pedersen, P. I. (2014) 'Influences of co-creation on brand experience', *International Journal of Market Research*, 56(6), 807–32.

Nysveen, H., Pedersen, E. E., and Skard, S. (2013) 'Brand experiences in service organizations: Exploring the individual effects of brand experience dimensions', *Journal of Brand Management*, 20(5), 404–23.

Oh, H., Fiorie, A. M., and Jeoung, M. (2007) 'Measuring experience economy concepts: Tourism applications', *Journal of Travel Research*, 46(2), 119–32.

Olson, J. C., and Jacoby, J. (1972) 'Cue utilization in the quality perception process', in M. Venkatesan (ed.), *Proceedings of the Third Annual Conference of the Association for Consumer Research*, Toronto, ON: Association for Consumer Research, 167–79.

O'Malley, L. (1998) 'Can loyalty schemes really build loyalty? ', *Marketing Intelligence and Planning*, 16(1), 47–55.

Parasuraman, A., Zeithaml, V., and Berry, L. L. (1988) 'SERVQUAL: A multiple-item scale for measuring consumer perceptions of service quality', *Journal of Retailing*, 64(1), 5–37.

Pavlou, P. A. (2002) 'Institution-based trust in interorganisational exchange relationships: The role of online B2B marketplaces on trust formation', *Journal of Strategic Information Systems*, 11(3–4), 215–43.

Pine, B. J., and Gilmore, J. H. (1998) 'Welcome to the experience economy', *Harvard Business Review*, 76(4), 97–105.

Pine, B. J., and Gilmore, J. H. (1999) *The Experience Economy: Work Is Theatre and Every Business a Stage*, Boston, MA: Harvard Business School Press.

Prahalad, C. K., and Ramaswamy, V. (2004) *The Future of Competition: Co-creating Unique Value with Customers*, Boston, MA: Harvard Business School Press.

Ravald, A., and Grönroos, C. (1996) 'The value concept and relationship marketing', *European Journal of Marketing*, 30(2), 19–33.

Ryssel, R., Ritter, T., and Gemunden, H. G. (2004) 'The impact of information technology deployment on trust, commitment and value creation in business relationships', *Journal of Business and Industrial Marketing*, 19(3), 197–07.

Schmitt, B. H. (1999) *Experiential Marketing*, New York: Free Press.

Shaw, C., and Ivens, J. (2002) *Building Great Customer Experiences*, New York: Palgrave Macmillan.

Shostack, G. L. (1977) 'Breaking free from product marketing', *Journal of Marketing*, 41(2), 73–80.

Shostack, G. L. (1985) 'Planning the service encounter', in J. A. Czepiel, M. R. Solomon, and C. F. Surprenant (eds), *The Service Encounter*, Lexington, MA: Lexington Books, 243–54.

Sirianni, N. J., Bitner, M. J., Brown, S. W., and Vlandel, N. (2013) 'Branded service encounters: Strategically aligning employee behavior with the brand positioning', *Journal of Marketing*, 77(6), 108–23.

Spekman, R. E., and Carroway, R. (2005) 'Making the transition to collaborative buyer–seller relationships: An emerging framework', *Industrial Marketing Management*, 35(1), 10–19.

Theron, E., Terblanche, N. S., and Boshoff, C. (2013) 'Building long-term marketing relationships: New perspectives on B2B financial services', *South African Journal of Business Management*, 44(4), 33–45.

Ulaga, W., and Eggert, A. (2005) 'Relationship value in business markets: The construct and its dimensions', *Journal of Business-to-Business Marketing*, 12(1), 73–99.

Wadley, M. (2017) 'Wells Fargo's progress on making things right and rebuilding trust', *Wells Fargo Stories*, 24 March. Retrieve from: https://stories.wf.com/wells-fargos-progress-making-things-right-rebuilding-trust/ (accessed 5 January 2020).

Whitelane Research (2019) '2019 Spanish IT outsourcing study results published'. 14 November. Retrieve from: https://whitelane.com/spain-2019/ (accessed 30 October 2020).

Young, L. C., and Wilkinson, I. F. (1989) 'The role of trust and co-operation in marketing channels: A preliminary study', *European Journal of Marketing*, 23(2), 109–22.

Zeithaml, V. A. (1981) 'How consumer evaluation processes differ between goods and services', in J. H. Donnelly and W. R. George (eds), *Marketing of Services*, Chicago: American Marketing Association, 186–90.

Chapter 12
Marketing, Society, Sustainability, and Ethics

Learning Outcomes

After studying this chapter, you will be able to:

- assess the negative impact that marketing can have on society;
- define sustainable marketing and its implications for marketing practice;
- understand corporate social responsibility and define stakeholder marketing;
- define marketing ethics; and
- understand how ethical breaches occur in marketing mix programmes.

Case Insight 12.1
Tarkett

Market Insight 12.1
The 'Green Gap'

Market Insight 12.2
Patagonia's Commitment to Sustainability

Market Insight 12.3
Tony's Chocolonely Slave-Free Chocolate

Market Insight 12.4
The Cambridge Analytica/ Facebook Scandal

Case Insight 12.1 **Tarkett**

With a history stretching back more than 140 years, Tarkett is a world leader in innovative flooring and sports surface solutions. We spoke to Fabrice Barthélemy, CEO of Tarkett, to find out how this multinational flooring company, with headquarters based in France, innovates in a rapidly changing and increasingly sustainability-centric marketplace.

We offer a wide range of products including vinyl, linoleum, carpet, rubber, wood, laminate, artificial turf, and athletic tracks, and we serve customers in more than one hundred countries worldwide. With 12,500 employees across the globe and thirty-three industrial sites, we sell 1.3 million square metres of flooring every day, to hospitals, schools, housing, hotels, offices, stores, and sports fields.

In 2019, we launched our new strategic plan 'Change to Win', positioning the circular economy at the heart of our strategy. We are convinced we have a role to play in changing the game in our industry by embracing the circular economy—a virtuous model to address resource scarcity and the climate emergency. We are particularly proud of the breakthrough we achieved in 2019 by fully closing the loop on the life cycle of commercial carpet tiles in Europe with our partner, Aquafil. The circular economy is a key challenge for us and the entire building industry, notably in the development of eco-designed products and circular services.

We are convinced that getting all stakeholders involved will contribute to accelerating the transition to a circular economy. The recent Covid-19 crisis is a painful but necessary wake-up call on the need for a more inclusive economy, more respectful of natural resources, climate, and biodiversity.

We need to move away from a linear economy, based on production, use and disposal of a product to a circular economy model, where waste can be a resource for our manufacturing, and where our products can be recycled to create new resources after use. That is why we have set a target of tripling to 30 per cent the share of recycled materials in our purchased raw materials by 2030.

At Tarkett, we have been pioneers in many areas of sustainability, leading the industry in developing flooring with a Cradle to Cradle® approach and a special focus on healthy materials and the indoor air quality of our products (i.e. plasticizers without phthalate, very low levels of volatile organic compounds, full materials health transparency), and implementing take-back and recycling programmes such as Restart® for our products. We also follow UN Global Compact principles, align with UN Sustainable Development Goals, contributing to discussions inside platforms such as the CE 100 (Circular Economy) of the Ellen Mac Arthur Foundation.

Globally, compared to ten years ago, there is a significantly increased demand from stakeholder groups (employees, customers, scientific institutes, universities, standardization bodies, public authorities, and professional trade associations) for organizations to adopt and implement responsible management practices. Our stakeholders expect Tarkett to take an active role in addressing social and environmental challenges.

They also expect transparency and clarity about how our corporate social and environmental responsibility has become an integral part of our

Case Insight 12.1 (continued)

strategy and our day-to-day operations. Over the last few years, many customers have asked us if we can develop flooring solutions that combine technical performance (resistance, easy maintenance, hygiene, acoustics), design (colours, patterns, shapes), and sustainability in terms of healthy spaces and recycling. However, they also do not want us to make any trade-offs between these components and they seek flooring certified by recognized labels, such as Cradle to Cradle®.

The challenge for us is: how can we develop constantly new products that both meet customers' high standards in terms of sustainability while simultaneously delivering high performance and aesthetic design?

Introduction

Should companies focus on satisfying customer requirements or maximizing profits? Why should marketers assess the effects of their activities on the environment and society as a whole? To what extent should ethics and morality influence marketing practices? These are some of the questions that we consider in this chapter.

We first consider the need for a critical marketing approach. This is necessary to rethink marketing practices and the negative impact that they can sometimes have on society. We emphasize that marketing ought to be sustainable, given increasing numbers of more mindful consumers and the need to conserve scarce resources on planet earth. Organizations are increasingly recognizing the need to consider their environmental impacts. Consequently, we highlight organizations' responsibilities to consider societal issues while conducting their business. Finally, we look into ethical decision-making and describe what marketers should consider to be unethical actions when implementing the marketing mix.

In the next section, we consider unsustainable marketing, as a foil to the more positive impacts on marketing in society that we explored in Chapter 1 and return to later in this chapter.

Unsustainable Marketing: the Critical 'Turn'

Marketing can fail to serve the common good. It is frequently criticized for being unethical in nature, manipulative, and creating wants and needs where none previously existed (Packard, 1960). We agree that not all of marketing's contributions to society are positive; consequently, there is a need to develop a critical approach to understanding marketing practice. To truly understand the discipline, we need to study both mainstream and critical marketing (Shankar, 2009).

Critical marketing analysis helps in 'problematizing hitherto uncontentious marketing areas to reveal underlying institutional and theoretical dysfunctionalities' (Saren, 2011: 95). A critical approach to marketing suggests that we consider.

- the need to (re-)evaluate marketing activities, categories, and frameworks, and to improve them so that marketing operates in a desirable manner within society;
- the extent to which marketing knowledge is developed based on our contemporary social world—for example much current marketing knowledge encompasses American (and Western) practice only;
- how the historical and cultural conditions in which we operate, as consumers and as students of marketing, impact on how we perceive marketing as a discipline; and
- how marketing can benefit from other intellectual perspectives such as social anthropology, social psychology, linguistics, philosophy, and sociology (Burton, 2001).

Some key topics in critical marketing include notions of marketing as manipulation, **commodity fetishism**, and the nature of need versus choice (see Tadajewski, 2010). We consider each of these topics next, starting with the idea that marketing is inherently manipulative.

Marketing as Manipulation

Packard (1960) levelled the charge that marketing beguiles its target audiences, often covertly, and frequently without people understanding that they are being manipulated. It is true that marketers and public relations officers 'frame' their communications to make them more persuasive. **Framing** is the action of presenting persuasive communication and the action of audiences in interpreting that communication to assimilate it into their existing understanding (Scheufele and Tewksbury, 2007). Framing takes place via the framing of situations (such as by highlighting sales promotions available for a fixed time only), attributes (such as by highlighting usage features of, say, a smartphone), choices (such as by showing a potential car buyer options across the range), actions (such as 'buy now, pay later' schemes), political issues (e.g. Starbucks explaining it would hire 10,000 refugees as US President Trump instigated a travel ban from Muslim countries in 2017; see Vaughan and Rushe, 2017), responsibilities (e.g. Save the Children explaining why African children need help to elicit donations), and news (e.g. Volkswagen explaining why its chief executive was replaced after the emissions scandal).

The problem arises when framing becomes 'spin', because 'marketing promotion' becomes corporate propaganda. For example, photographic tricks are often used to make food offerings look great in print adverts including using motor oil as syrup or honey, or glue or shampoo as milk in cereals. For hotels and resorts, photos are frequently doctored to remove unwanted elements or wide-angle lenses are used to make scenes look expansive (Anon., 2014). In the next section, we look at the idea that consumers can place too much regard in objects for their material value rather than for their inherent worth, based on the labour put into them.

Visit the **online resources** and complete Internet Activity 12.1 to learn more about manipulative practices in marketing.

Commodity Fetishism

'Commodity fetishism' is a critical perspective, derived from Marxist economic theory (Marx, 1867 [1990]). It proposes that society is overly dominated by consumption, and that it places supreme value on it (i.e. it fetishizes it). Marx suggested that, prior to industrialization, goods were produced for their use value. A producer manufactured a product for a user and exchanged it with the customer. After industrialization, the social relationship between producer and user changed. The idea was put forward that workers were exploited for their labour, because they became removed from the product they produced and were paid a piece rate rather than a share of the financial return generated by their labour. In the process, the commodity produced acquired exchange value, becoming tradable with other commodities within the capitalist market system, benefiting the capitalist (i.e. the investor). This means that the price generated for an item sold substantially exceeds the cost of producing that item. Marx felt that this was bad because it disempowered the worker. Thus, he would 'turn in his grave' at the price people are prepared to pay now for Hermès handbags, Rolex watches, or Lamborghini cars, for example, which are classic examples of fetishized products. This idea that we worship consumption raises the question of whether marketers meet consumer wants or needs, or neither—a topic we consider next.

Need and Choice

Most people believe marketing works to meet customers' and consumers' needs. However, Alvesson (1994), coming from outside the marketing discipline, rejects this notion. He argues that people in affluent societies seek more without gaining any further long-term satisfaction from such consumption, because much consumption is superficial anyway, and because appealing to people's fantasies and highlighting their imperfections (to encourage them to reduce these feelings of inadequacy by buying a particular offering) leads to narcissistic tendencies. The notion is therefore that more choice is good—but is it so, when more choice can lead to customer confusion and a decline in trust? (Newman, 2001). Some customers are persuaded and manipulated into purchasing offerings they do not want or which are unfit for their requirements: for example, UK financial services companies were charged with mis-selling payment protection insurance (PPI) between 1990 and 2010. By August 2019, British banks had put aside £48.5 billion to settle millions of customers' compensation claims and cover the extra administration costs (Jones, 2019).

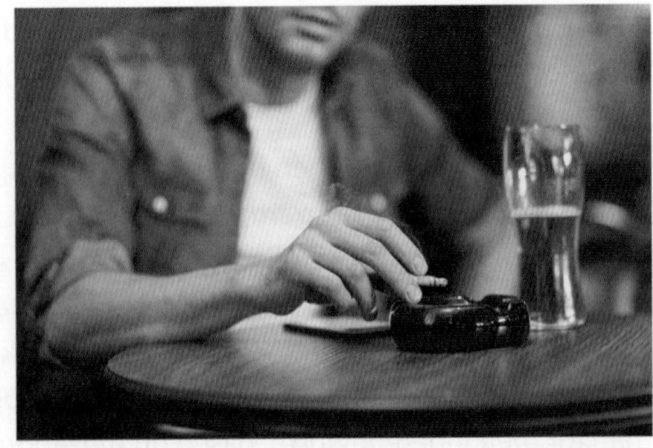

The aggregate marketing system can provide consumers with choices which are not in their long-term interests. What are the implications for marketers?
Source: © Syda Productions/Shutterstock.

Although the marketer, or what Wilkie and Moore (1999) term the **aggregate marketing system**, distributes life-saving medicines, food, and important utilities (such as heat and light), it also distributes alcohol, tobacco, gambling products, and cannabis (in those parts of the world where it has been decriminalized or legalized), among other things (see Chapter 1). Most would regard these latter offerings as dangerous to our health and well-being. Similarly, while in many cultures, people enjoy drinking, smoking, and gambling, if these are used to excess, all can cause harms because of their addictive properties.

Furthermore, if guns and hard drugs, such as heroin, were to be made legal, the aggregate marketing system would distribute them. Soft drugs such as cannabis are already distributed in many countries including the Netherlands, Canada, and Uruguay, for instance. The aggregate marketing system is amoral—that is, not *im*moral (designed to harm), but designed without any care as to whether it harms or not. The system is made moral by the decisions taken by government and other institutional actors regulating the aggregate marketing system. But it is also up to marketers to make moral decisions of their own volition. We tackle such positive action by marketers in the next section.

Sustainable Marketing

Supporters of **sustainable marketing** accept the limitations of marketing philosophy and acknowledge the need to impose regulatory constraints on marketing (van Dam and Apeldoorn, 1996), particularly concerning its environmental impacts. Sustainable economic development—that is, development that meets current generational needs without imposing constraints on future generations' needs—was first proposed at a United Nations Conference in Stockholm in 1972 (WCED, 1987). To understand why a sustainable development policy is necessary, consider the following two examples of companies causing catastrophic environmental impacts.

- *BP, 2010*—More than 200 million gallons of oil were spilled into the Gulf of Mexico after an oil rig explosion killed eleven people. The oil spill affected 1,000 miles of shoreline, killing thousands of birds, around 153 dolphins, and other local wildlife. The disaster caused BP to initially lose half its share value and total costs (including fines, compensations, legal fees, and other costs) for the disaster were US$53.8 billion in 2015 (Bryant, 2011; Anon., 2015). BP's contractor, Transocean, shared some blame for the incident, receiving a fine of US$1.4 billion from the US authorities (BBC News, 2013). Another contractor, Halliburton, was also found to be partly liable for some of the damage caused by the incident and reached a US$1.1 billion settlement in 2014 (Rushe, 2014).
- *Tokyo Electric Power (Tepco), 2011*—Three former executives at Tepco were charged with professional negligence contributing to death and injury from the meltdown in 2011 at the Fukushima Daiichi nuclear plant (McCurry, 2016). The meltdown was caused after a magnitude-9 earthquake caused a massive tsunami, flooding the nuclear reactors. The men were charged with failing to take measures to defend the plant, despite knowing the risks of a tsunami. More than 300,000 people were made homeless and 20,000 killed as a result of the earthquake and the tsunami across Japan (Conca, 2015). In Fukushima Prefecture alone, a further 1,656 people died as a result of post-disaster health conditions occurring after the government-enforced evacuation of everyone living within 20 km of the site—that is, as a result of stress from the evacuation, transfer trauma in relation to the infirm, and those with chronic illnesses unable to access medical treatments (World Nuclear Association, 2020).

Sustainable marketers attempt to broaden sustainable development to the practice of marketing, beyond simple economic development. They introduce the following maxims, known as the 'three Es of sustainability'.

- *Ecological*—Marketing should not negatively impact upon the environment.
- *Equitable*—Marketing should not allow or promote inequitable social practices.
- *Economic*—Marketing should encourage long-term economic development as opposed to short-term economic development.

Sustainable marketing has been coined the 'third age' of green marketing (Peattie, 2001). In the 'first age', ecological green marketing (*c*.1960s–1970s) concerned itself with automobile, oil, and agrichemical companies encountering environmental problems in the production process. In the 'second age', environmental green marketing (*c*.1980s), the **green consumer** emerged—that is, someone who purchased offerings to avoid negative environmental impacts (e.g. reusable straws made from glass and metal instead of plastic). But green marketing was too heavily focused on the purchasing element of consumption (Peattie and Crane, 2005), perhaps because the sustainability debate did not consider the business-to-business (B2B) dimension sufficiently.

The 'third age' of green marketing is sustainable green marketing. Sustainable marketers should focus on positioning and demand stimulation for recycled/remanufactured products and build-to-order offerings, as well as considering supply chain management issues, such as enabling materials recovery from end-consumers, designing offerings to enable their dismantlement, enabling **reverse logistics** for recycling and remanufactured offerings, and reducing supply by build-to-order options (Sharma et al., 2010). In the third age, companies need to lengthen the time horizons within which they achieve investment returns, requiring emphasis on the full costs of purchase rather than simply the price paid. In the following sections, we consider the characteristics of the green consumer and collaborative consumption before discussing what constitutes a sustainable marketing strategy.

The Green Consumer

In 2019, 50 per cent of consumers reported a willingness to pay more for sustainable products (Accenture, 2019). Notably, in separate studies, 59 per cent of consumers claimed they would pay a premium for sustainable fashion items (Mintel, 2019) while 39 per cent of consumers stated they would pay more to support sustainable initiatives in the travel industry (Mintel, 2020). Moreover, consumers under the age of 20 (Generation Z) and millennials reported a greater willingness to spend more on sustainable offerings compared to previous generations (Nielsen, 2015). The recent rise in the number of green consumers is evidenced by the increasing global consumption of **fair trade** products; a market worth €9.8 billion in 2018 (Fairtrade International, 2019).

These consumers are conscious of the impact of their consumption habits and draw on additional criteria during their decision-making. These additional criteria can be internal, where the individual focuses on the offering's perceived personal benefits, or external criteria, where the wider implications of the purchase on the environment and society are considered (Harrison et al., 2005: 2). In practice, consumers draw on both internal and external criteria when making a sustainable purchase. For example, young professionals may purchase organic produce because of the perceived superior taste and health benefits as well as environmental concerns around pesticide use (Shaw Hughner et al., 2007).

Belgian company Ecover produces ecological cleaning products from clean ingredients and recycled plastic.
Source: © oleasea vetrial/Shutterstock.

Consumers frequently compromise when making green purchases because they usually come at a higher cost, a **green premium**, compared with their conventional equivalents. The higher price can result from higher development costs and smaller production scales. For example, a bottle of the washing-up liquid Ecover is pricier than standard alternatives because of its sustainable design and ecological ingredients. However, the perceived compromise made by green consumers is not always of a financial nature as sustainable products may perform less well than conventional counterparts or may be less convenient to use or purchase. That said, this may not be considered as a trade-off by green consumers, depending on their values and knowledge in relation to sustainability (Young et al., 2010). For example, an energy-saving dishwasher will probably have a higher cost at the time of purchase but will incur savings in energy bills in the long run.

Although consumers say that they are ready to pay more for sustainable products, their motivation does not always result in concrete purchases. The **attitude–behaviour gap** is defined as the difference between intention to purchase a sustainable product and the actual purchase itself (see Market Insight 12.1 on the 'green gap').

Market Insight 12.1 **The 'Green Gap'**

Why do consumers say they will act on climate change but then don't? Scotland is a northern European country with 5.4 million inhabitants making up 30 per cent of the landmass of the United Kingdom. It has the third largest oil and gas reserves in Europe and 25 per cent of its offshore wind energy capacity.

In response to the unequivocal evidence showing that human activities are changing our climate at a growing and dangerous rate, the Scottish government has adopted some of the most stringent legislation in the world designed to tackle this problem. It is now committed to ensuring Scotland's carbon pollution is reduced to net zero levels, will ban the sale of new diesel and petrol cars by 2042, and set up a deposit return scheme where you get 20p back for every eligible plastic bottle returned and all retailers must now charge 5p for every plastic bag they give out.

These measures give business and organizations in Scotland a clear indication of government priorities from which to manage their products and services strategically. It also sends a clear message to consumers that our lifestyles need to change so we can live within the boundaries set by our planet. Encouragingly, most people in Scotland agree, with 70 per cent saying they want greater action on climate change.

Unfortunately, as set out in the Ethical Consumption report and supported by statistics from other sources, what consumers say they will do is not matched by the steps they actually take. This means sustainable brands typically only capture small market shares. For example, the entire ethical and sustainable food and

Market Insight 12.1 (continued)

drink markets was worth less than 10 per cent of the overall market (i.e. £13.9 billion). It also means that the rates of people undertaking pro-environmental behaviours such as driving less show little sign of improving. In fact, people are driving more.

The gap between what people state are their intentions and what they do has been studied widely, through lenses such as the theory of planned behaviour. This theory argues that intentions to act, for example intending to cycle more, are influenced by factors such as attitudes and whether you want to comply with social pressures. Despite containing a comprehensive set of influences, studies using this approach are not able to explain fully why in many instances intentions are not acted on.

1 **Produce a list of three times you intended to take an action that would have helped the environment but did not actually perform it. What were the reasons you did not do what you said you would?**

2 **Using your answers to question 1, produce a comprehensive list of barriers stopping people doing what they say they will do.**

3 **How can the barriers identified in question 2 be overcome?**

Sources: Ethical Consumer Research Association (2018); IPCC (2018); ONS (2018); Scottish Government (2016; 2018); Stop Climate Chaos (2019).

This market insight is kindly contributed by Professor Iain Black, University of Stirling, Scotland.

Collaborative Consumption

The success of online social platforms coupled with the growing awareness for sustainability has led to the development of **collaborative consumption**. This alternative mode of consumption, based on peer-to-peer sharing and exchange of goods, is usually orchestrated via online community platforms (Hamari et al., 2016). In the **sharing economy**, consumers can use others' possessions instead of purchasing new ones limited to personal use.

Collaborative consumption includes both the access to others' belongings as well as transfers of ownership (Hamari et al., 2016). For example, Airbnb enables homeowners to advertise and rent their spare rooms to guests looking for authentic and unique travel experiences. As of 2019, Airbnb hosts had earned more than US$80 billion sharing their spare rooms (Airbnb, 2019). Alternatively, smartphone apps such as Too Good to Go enable restaurants to sell surplus food about to be wasted, and which can be collected by consumers for a fraction of the original price (Ferguson, 2019).

Sustainable Marketing Strategy

Contrary to a short-term profit-based approach, sustainable marketing strategies aim to provide long-term market advantage over competitors. To achieve this, organizations must adapt to the needs of their customers and other stakeholders with regard to economic, environmental, and social issues (Hult, 2011), often by involving the other members of the whole supply chain.

Proposition development activities should fully consider, equitably, inputs and cooperation from all members of the supply chain. In 2019, 85 per cent of European retailers reported a significant

Research Insight 12.1

To take your learning further, you might wish to read this influential paper:

Hamari, J., Sjöklint, M., and Ukkonen, A. (2016) 'The sharing economy: Why people participate in collaborative consumption', *Journal of the Association for Information Science and Technology*, 67(9), 2047–9.

In this article, the authors describe the concept of collaborative consumption and explain its development prompted by the rise of interactive online platforms. Based on a survey of 168 members of collaborative consumption platforms, their results indicate that the motivations of consumers to participate in the sharing economy include a desire to consume more sustainably, for economic reasons such as reducing costs of consumption, and for the enjoyment of meeting like-minded people.

 Visit the **online resources** to read the abstract and access the full paper.

sales increase in sustainable products sales which resulted in 76 per cent of them moving towards sustainable supply chains and imposing codes of conduct on their suppliers (International Trade Centre, 2019).

Companies need to adopt environmental auditing methods (such as including costs for disposal, as well as development, delivery, and consumption) and organizations may actually discourage consumption in certain cases (Bridges and Wilhelm, 2008)—or at least encourage more mindful consumption and temperance, rather than acquisitive, repetitive, or overly consumptive behaviour (Sheth et al., 2011). For example, in 2013, Coca-Cola launched a worldwide campaign on obesity, partnering in the UK until 2015 with StreetGames, a sport participation charity, by introducing smaller bottles (375 ml) and by displaying detailed calorie content on packs (Mintel, 2013). But Coca-Cola has not always been consistent: in 2012, the company was said to have used more water than had a quarter of the world's population—that is, 79 billion gallons to dilute its syrup and an extra 8 trillion gallons in other elements of production (Gwyther, 2015). In 2014, the Body Shop—to maintain its own strict policy against animal testing—removed all products from duty-free shelves in airports in China after consumer watchdog, Choice, revealed that the Chinese government conducted post-market testing of Body Shop products on animals (Davidson, 2014).

There are varying motivations behind the adoption of a sustainable marketing strategy. First, companies may adopt sustainable practices to obtain a large market share and increase long-term profits. Simultaneously, such an approach can contribute to better reputation and enhanced brand image. The origins of these motivations can also be found within the company, its leadership team, and its employees (Dangelico and Pujari, 2010). When Microsoft announced its commitment in 2020 to offset all the carbon the company has emitted since its creation by 2050, the company developed a key competitive advantage over other cloud-computing competitors such as Amazon and Google (Greene, 2020).

A sustainable marketing approach can also be driven by wider political factors and legislation that can shape the way companies develop and market new offerings. For example, in 2020, the French government banned the use of several single-use plastic products, which will eventually influence how take-away restaurants package and deliver their orders (France 24, 2019).

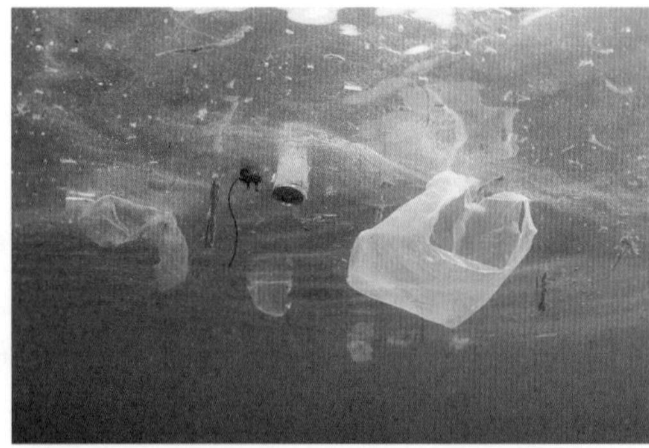

In 2020, France banned the use of single-use plastic products such as cups and cotton buds to avoid waste and pollution.
Source: © Rich Carey/Shutterstock.

Based on the characteristics of their target consumers and their differentiation via sustainable products against those of competitors, companies may adopt one of the following green marketing strategies (Ginsberg and Bloom, 2004):

- 'lean green': developing sustainable initiatives to reduce production waste and costs, without emphasizing those efforts to their target segment;
- 'defensive green': adopting temporary sustainable behaviours to improve their reputation (e.g., in response to an environmental scandal);
- 'shaded green': putting in place long-term measures for sustainability while only communicating it as a secondary feature; and
- 'extreme green': embracing core sustainable values that are integral to the organization and its processes (see also Market Insight 12.2).

Via annual sustainability reports, companies are increasingly making use of transparency to communicate their operational practices with their stakeholders. Labels are also crucial to convey the legitimacy of a product's sustainability and attest to its certification (e.g., the European Union's green organic logo or the UK Soil Association's organic symbol). Moreover, product packaging is often designed to minimize waste while also helping communicate a consistent brand image and to educate consumers on the benefits of sustainable products.

While in this section, we have discussed what organizations do to secure their own futures and the future of the planet, usually achieved via operational supply chain and marketing process re-engineering, in the next section, we discuss how organizations communicate what they have achieved to their stakeholders via corporate social responsibility initiatives.

The European Union logo helps consumers identify certified organic products.
Source: © Dusan Milenkovic/Wikimedia Commons.

Market Insight 12.2 Patagonia's Commitment to Sustainability

Companies are also adopting the logic of customer experience in the promotion of environmental and/or social causes consistent with their overall positioning. In the past, environmental concerns of consumers translated into the development and promotion of more environmentally sustainable, or 'green', alternatives. From this focus on discrete 'green' exchanges, companies are shifting towards relational practices aimed at the promotion of sustainability. Consequently, they are increasingly introducing long-term initiatives that engage consumers over time and are not simply associated with a single purchase.

Some of Patagonia's sustainable practices focus on the reuse of old materials for new clothing items.
Source: © LMWH/Shutterstock.

Patagonia is an American brand of premium outdoor clothing. As a company strongly committed to environmental protection, Patagonia has been able to leverage its support to environmental movements and grassroots campaigners to reinforce its customer experience and its core brand values. The company has also published a manual, *Patagonia Tools for Grassroots Activists: Best Practices for Success in the Environmental Movement*, aimed at supporting grassroots organizations.

The company donates 1 per cent of its annual revenues to non-profit environmental organizations—once giving away the entirety of its 2016 Black Friday sales. However, Patagonia's impact is not limited to financial contributions to environmental initiatives. In 2018, the new online platform, Patagonia Action Works, was launched to help customers fund and join local committed communities and events on biodiversity, climate, and land issues.

Patagonia is also committed to designing high-quality clothing and gear using recycled and responsibly sourced materials while limiting the impact of its operations. As such, in 2018, 52 per cent of the fabrics used to manufacture Patagonia's jackets, T-shirts, and fleeces came from recycled or renewable sources. The company also operates 72 repair centres around the world and runs the Worn Wear programme to help prolong the life of sold items. Finally, as an employer, Patagonia provides health insurance and parental leave, and fosters a diverse culture.

These activities are not instrumental; they are motivated primarily by the brand's concern for the environment and long-standing commitment to positive change. Nonetheless, they reinforce customers' experience of the brand, and represent an extension to the sustainability arena of the concept of 'experience economy' popularized by Pine and Gilmore (1999).

1 **Which of the four green marketing strategies described earlier has Patagonia adopted?**

2 **Who is Patagonia's target market and why do you think the brand's core sustainable values appeal to them?**

3 **Choose a brand you are familiar with and list the different ways it might benefit from being more sustainable.**

Source: Patagonia (2018).

Corporate Social Responsibility

Corporate social responsibility (CSR) refers to the set of business practices an organization undertakes to adopt a sustainable approach while considering its impact on stakeholders, typically via its corporate or marketing communications team. From that perspective, CSR initiatives look back on what a company has achieved in making a contribution to society. They are increasingly common and many companies publish annual CSR reports.

Governments and supranational organizations such as the United Nations' Global Compact project actively encourage CSR initiatives, and CSR practitioners and academics try to demonstrate the commercial effectiveness of such programmes to explain why being 'good' translates into being profitable.

Porter and Kramer (2006) emphasize that CSR and economical goals are not mutually exclusive and that business decisions can be profitable while also benefiting society if common objectives are identified and prioritized correctly. Moreover, Carroll (1991) explains that philanthropic (i.e. promoting welfare and contributing resources to society) and ethical (i.e. doing what is right and avoiding harm to others) responsibilities rely on the company being economically profitable and respectful of laws and regulations.

Despite any obvious return, business people and companies have given to charity for centuries. Famous cases include the John Paul Getty Foundation in the United States (built on oil industry profits), which funds art and social projects, and Anglo American, the mining conglomerate that provides welfare support for its employees living with HIV/AIDS in Africa. Similarly, Apple iPhones have been made available in the colour red when the company partnered with (PRODUCT)RED to redistribute some of the profit made on these models to fund HIV/AIDS programmes in sub-Saharan countries.

The rationale for developing CSR initiatives, irrespective of their financial contribution, is based around the following ideas (Buchholz, 1991: 19).

- Corporations have responsibilities beyond profit-making.
- These responsibilities involve helping to solve important social problems—especially those that they have helped to create.
- Corporations have a broader constituency of stakeholders than shareholders alone.
- The impacts of corporations go beyond simple marketplace transactions.
- Corporations serve a wider range of human values, not captured solely by a focus on economic values.

A portion of the profit made by Apple when selling the iPhone 11 (PRODUCT)RED helped fund HIV programmes.
Source: © Sergey Eremin/Shutterstock.

Marketers have echoed the need for a focus on CSR and some have called for the need to introduce the concept of **stakeholder marketing**. Stakeholder marketing explicitly recognizes the important role played by a multiplicity of stakeholders (e.g. employees, suppliers, government, media, publics) in generating positive outcomes for the organization and for society at large (Hult et al., 2011). From this point of view, therefore, CSR is necessary for a firm's success because it nurtures the organization's ability to act in harmony with its stakeholders.

There are two aspects to the implementation of stakeholder marketing. The first is recognizing marketing's important role in engaging with stakeholders meaningfully to define suitable CSR programmes. The second relates to the importance of managing stakeholders' relationships to achieve superior performance. In other words, actively managing relationships with many stakeholders is a specific capability of the firm, since these relationships are strategic resources to be leveraged to achieve a competitive advantage (Kull et al., 2016). Think of a pharmaceutical company developing a new drug treatment. Success here depends on a large network of stakeholders: regulators need to approve the drug; doctors will recommend it; insurance companies might need to be involved and offer coverage; and nurses might teach patients how to use the new drug. Advocacy groups or the media might also play important roles in covering the launch and supporting the adoption of the new medicine.

In particular, **authenticity** has become increasingly important for companies to gain the trust of their stakeholders when implementing CSR practices. To maximize their impact, organizations should communicate their purpose and their own stories transparently and take humans into consideration for each decision (Deloitte, 2019). See, for example, Market Insight 12.3 for an example from the **chocolate countline** market. So far, we've assumed that organizations make either ethical or unethical decisions but how do they differentiate between the two approaches? We consider this in the next section.

Research Insight 12.2

To take your learning further, you might wish to read this influential paper.

Mason, C., and Simmons, J. (2014) 'Embedding corporate social responsibility in corporate governance: A stakeholder systems approach', *Journal of Business Ethics*, 119(1), 77–86.

In this article, the authors highlight the need to assess the impact of CSR. They argue that investors, customers and suppliers, employees and the wider community play a crucial role in shaping CSR strategy. The authors propose a model which can be used by organizations to consider these stakeholders' views to inform their CSR policy, practice, and outcomes.

 Visit the **online resources** to read the abstract and access the full paper.

Market Insight 12.3 **Tony's Chocolonely Slave-Free Chocolate**

Tony's Chocolonely is a successful challenger chocolate brand in the Netherlands, launched to raise awareness of slavery and child labour in the cocoa industry. Founded in 2003, Tony's is now the leading chocolate brand in the Netherlands, and this success has come without using a single piece of paid advertising. How is that possible?

First, Tony's changed consumers' choice criteria. While conventional chocolate brands often competed on price, quality, taste, or cocoa levels, Tony's unique selling point (USP) introduces the option of 'slave-free' chocolate. In 2007, competitors claiming that there is no such thing as 'slave-free' chocolate famously sued Tony's. However, a court ruling in Amsterdam officially acknowledged that Tony's Chocolonely chocolate was produced in a 100 per cent slave-free manner, reinforcing its USP and providing the company with much press coverage.

With an overwhelming number of consumers willing to recommend a brand supporting a good cause over one that does not, Tony's relies on word-of-mouth (WoM) to spread brand awareness and its mission. However, pushing a social/ethical unique selling point can turn some consumers off. Hence, Tony's second most important strategy is to make any first impression a memorable one, via its packaging. Tony's does not look like any other chocolate brand. The wrapping paper is uncoated, the colours are garish and bright, and each individual chocolate flavour has its own unique colour, making identification among its own and competitors' varieties easy.

Tony's Chocolonely uses bright colours to draw attention to their slave-free chocolate.
Source: © emka74/Shutterstock.

Its mission to tackle slavery and child labour in chocolate production is addressed once the wrapper is opened. Inside, one can read about what drives the company. Hence the second, unpaid communication strategy is to get the product noticed in the saturated chocolate market, and then create awareness about the ethical issue it seeks to tackle.

On the product itself: Tony's makes its chocolate bar something to talk about. When you unwrap Tony's Chocolonely, you discover it is not divided into neat equal chocolate squares. Instead, each bar divides into unequal chunks, making it slightly more difficult to break it up than conventional chocolate. Making it harder for the consumer to break up the chocolate is Tony's way of drawing attention to the unfair and unequal cocoa industry, where the big chocolate companies make millions, while children and slaves in Ghana and the Ivory Coast work without rights and, often, for free. The chocolate bar itself acts as a talking point and a clever tool for WoM and referral.

Lately, Tony's provides consumers with the ability to create their own chocolate bars in its flagship store in Amsterdam. One can customize both the flavour of the chocolate bar, and the wrapper. Based on the success in the Netherlands, Tony's has now expanded into Belgium, Germany, Sweden, and the United Kingdom.

1. **When expanding abroad, can Tony's rely on its successful communication strategy, or will it need to change that to be able to enter foreign markets successfully?**
2. **What communication strategies would Tony's need to implement in the various countries into which it has expanded?**
3. **Is Tony's mission sufficiently strong to allow the brand to become an international market leader?**

Sources: Bliss (2018); Brown (2019) www.tonyschocolonely.com.

This market insight is kindly contributed by Dr Frauke Mattison Thompson at Universiteit van Amsterdam, the Netherlands.

Ethics and the Marketing Mix

Ethics, as a subdiscipline of philosophy, can be defined as 'moral principles that govern a person's behaviour or the conducting of an activity' and 'the branch of knowledge that deals with moral principles' (Lexico, 2020). Marketing, like any other area of business, is affected by **normative ethics**, the branch of ethics which relates to how we *ought to* behave (see Market Insight 12.4). For example, most professional marketing organizations have a code of professional practice requiring members to behave and act in certain ways, as of course do many companies and organizations. For example, the AMA requires the following of its members (AMA, 2020):

1. **Do no harm.** This means consciously avoiding harmful actions or omissions by embodying high ethical standards and adhering to all applicable laws and regulations in the choices we make.
2. **Foster trust in the marketing system.** This means striving for good faith and fair dealing so as to contribute toward the efficacy of the exchange process as well as avoiding deception in product design, pricing, communication, and delivery of distribution.
3. **Embrace ethical values.** This means building relationships and enhancing consumer confidence in the integrity of marketing by affirming these core values: honesty, responsibility, fairness, respect, transparency, and citizenship.

How one ought to behave, normative ethics, typically comprises three general approaches in business ethics:

1. **Deontological ethics, often known as duty-based ethics,** proposes that the rightness of an action depends on the action itself, based on a set of criteria and rules (Alexander and Moore, 2016). For example, the ICC/ESOMAR International Code describes a set of principles and responsibilities for businesses conducting market research. The code includes guidelines on transparency while carrying out market research, as well as respect for research participants (ICC/ESOMAR, 2016).
2. **Teleological ethics** suggest that whether or not an action is ethical depends on the consequences of that action (Hunt and Vitell, 1986). Within this view, **ethical egoism** proposes that an action is considered ethical if its consequences are favourable to the person (or organization) performing that action (Hunt and Vitell, 1986). **Universal consequentialism,** however, considers an action ethical if, for all members of society, the positive consequences of that action exceed the negative ones (Sinnott-Armstrong, 2019).
3. Finally, **virtue ethics** do not focus on the action or its consequences but stress the development of virtuous principles of the individual or organization at the origin of that action (Hursthouse and Pettigrove, 2016).

Market Insight 12.4 **The Cambridge Analytica/Facebook Scandal**

Cambridge Analytica was a political consulting company based in London which specialized in data mining and analysis. It ceased operations in 2018, shortly after its unethical practices were publicly exposed.

The firm developed an application that required Facebook users to answer more than one hundred questions for a personality survey. For their patience and effort, respondents were rewarded with a small cash prize. After completing the survey, respondents were asked to log in via their Facebook profile to collect their reward. However, the application was designed to collect as much data as possible not only from the respondents' profiles but also from all their contacts on the social media platform without their consent. Cambridge Analytica was then able to directly associate the responses to the personality test with individuals and their social connections.

Cambridge Analytica created a colossal data set which, when analysed with advanced data science techniques, generated hundreds of fine-grained insights about the respondents. From the models produced, the firm could predict the personalities and political affiliations of individuals for any Facebook user based on the pages and posts they liked on social media and the profiles they followed.

Cambridge Analytica collected personal data of Facebook users for political advertising targeting.
Source: © AlexandraPopova/Shutterstock.

From these extremely personal inferences, advertising firms, including those working for political parties, were able to target people on an individual level. For example, a certain political message could be tailored differently depending on whether the targeted voter was introverted, conscientious, with a small social network or extroverted, neurotic, with a large number of Facebook contacts. This targeted approach makes voters feel closer to political parties which appear more relatable to their audience. This can sway the electorate to the desired outcome.

Ultimately, eighty-seven million Facebook profiles were used by Cambridge Analytica to build these models. Moreover, following the scandal, Facebook's CEO, Mark Zuckerberg, was forced to apologize publicly and promise that users' personal data would be kept private on the platform in future.

1. **What, if anything, was unethical about Cambridge Analytica's approach to individual targeting?**
2. **According to a teleological ethics perspective, did Facebook act appropriately? (Hint: look on the Internet at the consequences for Facebook.)**
3. **How can social media companies protect users against these practices? (Hint: apply a deontological perspective.)**

Sources: Hern (2018); Bradshaw and Howard (2019); Wong (2019).

Research Insight 12.3

To take your learning further, you might wish to read this influential paper:

Hunt, S. D., and Vitell, S. (2006) 'The general theory of marketing ethics: A revision and three questions', *Journal of Macromarketing*, 26(2), 143–53.

This article builds upon the authors' 1986 paper—one of the most highly cited in marketing ethics—which defined the study of marketing ethics (Hunt and Vitell, 1986). This 2006 article suggests that the original 1986 theory required revision because the model was applicable in any ethical decision-making situation, not only in business and management contexts, and required empirical testing. The authors argue that ethical judgements lead to intentions and hence to behaviour. Our intentions to act ethically, however, can be based on two different types of motivation, based on deontological and teleological ethics. Which of these two is preferred will depend on contextual and personal factors.

 **Visit the online resources to read the abstract and access the full paper.**

Products and Ethics

The American Marketing Association suggests that marketers should honestly and transparently communicate the features of products they sell (AMA, 2020). Indeed, misleading or ambiguous marketing communication could dupe customers into buying products based on false information. Where consumers have concerns about a particular company's product quality, they can inform a government body, which will be charged with looking into it on behalf of the consumer. For example, to standardize the laws on misleading and comparative advertising, the European Union (2006) published a directive to standardize laws across countries.

However, despite governmental efforts, cases of misleading advertising remain common. In 2015, the US Environmental Protection Agency found out that the German car manufacturer Volkswagen lied about the eco-friendliness of its diesel vehicles by cheating emission tests. The scandal affected eleven million cars worldwide as the company lost the trust of many of its customers (Atiyeh, 2019).

In spite of companies' best efforts to design safe products and marketers' honest advertising campaigns, it is possible for products to malfunction in customers' hands. In this case, companies should respond quickly to customers' complaints and refund or replace products regardless of the reputational damage and the additional cost incurred. For example, in 2019, Whirlpool recalled more than 500,000 washing machines in the UK due to fire risks. This followed past criticism of Whirlpool after the company was forced by regulators to recall five million dryers (Smithers, 2019).

Pricing and Ethics

The principal ethical concern in pricing is fairness—the perception from all involved in a financial transaction that the cost of their participation is equal to their returns. In particular, aspects of fair prices include distribution (i.e. that one party's profit causes loss to another), reliability (i.e. that the prices remain stable over time), and honesty (i.e. that pricing is transparently communicated to other parties) (Diller, 2008). Key considerations relate to:

- **Price gouging** which happens when sellers set the price of their products or services beyond a level that is considered reasonable. Price gouging occurs when companies operate a demand-pricing formula where demand is very high, leading the companies to charge customers high prices. For example, pharmaceutical company Questcor Pharmaceuticals (now Mallinckrodt) raised the price of the H.P. Acthar Gel (a drug aimed at curing infant seizure disorder) from US$40 to US$39,000 between 2000 and 2019. The increase resulted in annual sales of over US$1 billion for the company while the cost was covered by US national health insurance scheme, Medicare (Drash, 2019). During the Covid-19 pandemic in 2020, face mask prices went up by 166 per cent on Amazon at one point in the US (Tyko, 2020).
- Price discrimination occurs when companies price the same product or service differently based on who purchases it. Although price discrimination is considered unethical when systemically practised on certain groups of consumers, price variations are not always considered as such (Elegido, 2011). For example, **dynamic pricing** is often used by electricity companies to cater for fluctuating demand and production. Time-of-use tariffs enable an increasing number of individual customers to pay more or less depending on the time of the day (Hussain and Torres, n.d.).
- Price collusion occurs when competitors work together to set prices to the detriment of consumers and competitors. It is unethical because it results in unfair, and higher, charges to customers and it stifles innovation because competitors do not need to develop better offerings. In 2016, four major truck manufacturers were fined £3.4 billion by the European Union after fixing their prices for fourteen years and delaying the release of fuel-efficient vehicles (RHA, 2018).

Distribution and Ethics

Companies should maintain high ethical standards in their relationships with competitors, suppliers, and distributors. With regard to suppliers, this includes following a code of ethics, transparency, and respect for confidentiality (Bendixen and Abratt, 2007). Ethical breaches in supply chain management occur when, for example, companies collude over production quotas, abuse their monopoly status, or overcharge or exploit supply chain partners. The following are some examples of companies and situations in which ethical breaches have occurred:

- *Collusion*—The best-known and most tolerated global example of production **collusion** is that which takes place in the oil industry, through the Organization of Petroleum-Exporting Countries (OPEC), to co-manage oil production quotas in countries such as Nigeria, Saudi Arabia, Iran, and Venezuela.
- *Abuse of monopoly status*—In 2018, Google was fined €4.3 billion by EU regulators for taking advantage of market dominance with its Android phones. The company forced manufacturers to install other Google products (Google Chrome, Google Search app) and restricted the use of alternative versions ('forks') of its operating system (Warren, 2018).

- *Exploitation of supply chain partners*—In France, the Châtel Act stops supermarkets selling at below-cost prices (which damage supply chain partners' margins) and is aimed at increasing competition in the sector. All discounts and services provided by the distributor to the supplier now require stipulation upfront in an annual agreement (Boutin and Guerrero, 2008).

Promotion and Ethics

Many issues relating to marketing communications prompt ethical consideration, for example shock and sex appeal in advertising, the labelling of consumer products, the use of propaganda and advertising in political campaigns, and marketing to children, each of which is considered next.

This ad featuring Evan Rachel Wood and Chris Evans required both actors to model naked on Gucci's campaign shoot.
Source:

The Use of Sexual and Shock Appeals

Advertisers use emotional appeals to capture attention. We are persuaded because we are less likely to consider objections about why we might not agree with the message. For Baudrillard (2005), all advertising has an erotic element to it, because it seduces us into buying something. But the ethical question arises where sexual themes are used explicitly (e.g. naked or semi-naked models) and depending on the circumstances. Italian fashion brand Diesel famously used sexual appeal, advertising on dating apps Tinder and Grindr, and adult website Pornhub (Allwood, 2016). Pornhub even became its top referral website (Maytom, 2016).

Critics argue that sex appeals exploit women, and sometimes men, as sex objects. The fashion industry has decided not to use models aged 16 years or under, but it does use—and encourages them to become—painfully thin models. Israel was the world's first country to ban the use of female models whose body mass index (BMI) was less than 18.5 in 2013 (Bannerman, 2015). Others argue that sexual advertising appeals can be appropriate, depending on the fit of the appeal to the offering: for example, it is more appropriate for perfume.

Shock advertising appeals can also create controversy. Charities often use hard-hitting guilt appeal messages to raise funds for sick children in Africa, for example.

Product Labelling

Product labelling can raise ethical issues when it is perceived as misleading the public. It is important in the food, pharmaceutical, and cosmetic industries because we consume and absorb these offerings into our bodies. Food products—and particularly meat products in Europe and elsewhere—are required to demonstrate their country of origin. If products are deliberately mislabelled, this is usually considered a criminal offence. This occurred in 2013, when Irish authorities first identified that horsemeat had been used in what was supposed to be 'pure beef' products, imported from French company, Spanghero, and exported to around thirteen countries (Willsher, 2019). Several men received prison sentences in France as a result (Anon., 2019).

Political Advertising

Another area ripe with arguably unethical marketing communications is political advertising. In many countries, political advertising is often exempt from the rules and regulations associated with traditional advertising. As a consequence, it can be highly negative, by using vitriolic statements to damage the credibility of other candidates and parties. In the UK, political advertising on billboards, in cinemas, and in magazines is exempt from the rules set by the Advertising Standards Authority (ASA). Political parties are not expected to be truthful, unlike their commercial counterparts. For example, the 'No' campaign during the Scottish independence referendum was criticized for an overly negative message, labelled 'Project Fear' (Pike, 2015), but others argue that the political context often justifies a negative campaign stance when the risks posed to society are great (Morris, 2008).

Marketing to Children

Scholars have debated whether or not children should be targeted by advertising, given their immature views of time, money, and identity. This is especially the case given that researchers have found evidence that children are explicitly targeted in promotional campaigns. As Daniels and Holmes (2005) relate, both parents and marketers are concerned by this because:

- Children are more exposed to marketing than before and parents increasingly feel that they are losing control of the marketing directed at their children.
- Parents are particularly concerned about the marketing channels used (e.g. Internet, mobile phone, social media, and advergames) to target children directly.
- Inappropriate marketing to children damages the brand, making it less likely that marketers will get past the parent as gatekeeper.
- More appropriate marketing methods are informative and help parents to feel more in control.
- Consumers are willing to support companies that communicate with children in a responsible way.

An example of a company under pressure for its promotion to children is McDonald's, whose offerings appeal particularly to children via the use of licensed characters and celebrity endorsement. Child obesity is regarded as a major problem in many countries (e.g. Australia, the United States, and the UK, along with the European Union generally). The problem is partly caused by advertising food to children, although inactive lifestyles and lack of exercise also play a part. Fast-food retailers are consequently coming under increasing pressure to make their menus healthier.

All of these issues lead us back to the discussion of the moral principles that should guide how marketers behave, presented earlier in this chapter. In the configuration of their marketing communications mix, therefore, marketers should consider the potential harm caused by their campaigns and they should strive to act responsibly to foster trust in the marketing system.

Chapter Summary

To consolidate your learning, the key points from this chapter are summarized below.

- **Assess the negative impact that marketing can have on society.**

  The critical marketing perspective suggests that marketing can impact negatively on society. The perspective calls for the (re-)evaluation of marketing activities, categories, and frameworks to improve them, so that marketing can operate in a more desirable manner within society.

- **Define sustainable marketing and its implications for marketing practice.**

  Sustainable marketing has been termed the 'third age' of green marketing, and is concerned with the ecological, equitable, and economic impacts of marketing practice. Sustainable marketers seek to meet the needs of existing generations while not compromising those of future generations. This is particularly important given the increasing number of conscious consumers who are keen to pay more for sustainable goods and ready to challenge traditional consumption practice.

- **Understand corporate social responsibility and define stakeholder marketing.**

  Organizations have responsibilities with regard to society that go beyond developing offerings solely for generating profit for shareholders. These social responsibilities do not have to compromise the economic goals of organizations. Stakeholder marketing is important for an organization's ability to develop successful CSR programmes that demonstrate a concern for social and/or environmental issues.

- **Define marketing ethics.**

  Marketing ethics is concerned with how marketers go about the marketing process. In particular, it is the application of moral principles to decision-making in marketing and the consideration of the outcomes of those decisions. Normative ethics, the branch of ethics related to how we should behave, is particularly important for marketing. Three types of normative ethics should be considered: deontological ethics (doing the right thing), teleological ethics (doing what has the best consequences), and virtue ethics (doing what a good person would do).

- **Understand how ethical breaches occur in marketing mix programmes.**

  Ethical breaches occur in all aspects of an organization's marketing activity, including pricing, promotion, product, and place (distribution) policies. Ethical breaches usually occur when companies abuse their power over other stakeholders and fail to follow existing regulations and codes of conduct.

Review Questions

1. **Name the key concepts in critical marketing.**
2. **What are the three ages of green marketing?**
3. **What are the characteristics of green consumers?**
4. **What is collaborative consumption?**
5. **How can organizations adopt sustainable marketing strategies?**
6. **What are the motivations for adopting sustainable marketing strategies?**

7 **What is corporate social responsibility?**

8 **What is stakeholder marketing?**

9 **What types of normative ethics should marketers consider?**

10 **What are the key ethical concerns when implementing the marketing mix?**

Worksheet Summary

To apply the knowledge you have gained from this chapter, and to test your understanding of sustainable marketing and market ethics, visit the **online resources** and complete Worksheet 12.1.

Discussion Questions

1 Having read Case Insight 12.1, what would you advise Tarkett to do when faced with the question of how to develop a new product that meets customers' high sustainability requirements while also delivering high performance and aesthetic design?

2 Go online to find examples of companies with a strong stance on sustainable marketing. Are there any common characteristics across these companies? (**Hint**: take a look at any of the following companies' websites and search for their sustainability credentials: Unilever (Anglo-Dutch); Sweden's SCA; France's Danone; and Germany's BASF.)

3 You are chief customer officer of a manufacturer of hand sanitizer during the 2020 Covid-19 crisis. The crisis has created unprecedented global demand for your product. You simply cannot produce enough to keep up with demand. Your sales director suggests increasing the price of your product by 500 per cent to ensure that you meet all demand and maximize profits. Discuss this ethical problem using the following approaches:

A Ethical egoism—that is, the principle of self-interest.

B Universal consequentialism—that is, the principle of the greater good for the greatest number of people.

C Deontological ethics—that is, the principle of duty-based ethics.

Glossary

aggregate marketing system is the system of considering *en masse* all the individual market exchanges that take place in the world as people and companies buy and sell products and services everywhere.

attitude–behaviour gap the difference between a consumer's point of view and their actions.

authenticity the quality of being true to oneself.

chocolate countline a term for chocolate bars sold at the shop counter or near the supermarket till, usually to stimulate impulse purchase.

circular economy an alternative to a traditional linear economy (make—use—dispose) in which we keep resources in use for as long as possible, extract the maximum value from them while in use, and then recover and regenerate products and materials at the end of each service life.

collaborative consumption the trend towards the sharing, swapping, and renting of possessions.

collusion when a group of competitor companies conspires to control the market, often at the expense of the consumer or customer and typically in relation to price fixing.

commodity fetishism a Marxian notion that material objects are seen too much from an economic, market exchange perspective and too little from the result of the social and labour processes that went into the making of them.

corporate social responsibility (CSR) typically, a programme of social and/or environmental activities undertaken by a company on behalf of one or more of its stakeholders to develop sustainable business operations, foster goodwill, and develop the company's corporate reputation.

deontological ethics a form of ethical approach whereby the rightness or wrongness of an action or decision is not judged to be exclusively based on the consequences of that action or decision.

dynamic pricing a pricing strategy in which the price of products or services is set depending on real-time fluctuating demand.

ethical egoism the consequentialist view in which an action is considered good if it is profitable to the individual performing that action.

fair trade an agreement whereby developed countries equitably pay producers from developing countries.

framing the dual action by which communicators present ideas and concepts, and members of an audience interpret those concepts by assimilating them into their pre-existing cognitive schema.

green consumer a consumer who is sensitive to negative environmental impacts when considering various offerings.

green premium the additional cost associated with environment-friendly products.

normative ethics the branch of ethics that questions how individuals should act.

price gouging occurs when a seller sets the price of a good or service at a level far higher than is considered reasonable.

reverse logistics the process of returning goods in a physical distribution channel, which might be a flow from customer to manufacturer via a retailer (e.g. for repair or replacement).

sharing economy an economic model based on peer-to-peer exchanges.

stakeholder marketing activities undertaken in a system of interaction with different stakeholders and aimed at generating value for all stakeholders involved, both internal and external to the organization.

sustainable marketing activities undertaken to meet the wants or needs of present customers without compromising the wants or needs of future customers, particularly in relation to negative environmental impacts on society.

teleological ethics a form of ethical approach whereby the rightness or wrongness of an action or decision is judged primarily based on the intentions of the decision-maker.

universal consequentialism the consequentialist view in which an action is considered good if it is profitable for society as a whole.

virtue ethics a branch of ethics that stresses the importance of developing virtuous principles, with right character, and the pursuit of a virtuous life.

References

Accenture (2019) 'More than half of consumers would pay more for sustainable products designed to be reused or recycled, Accenture survey finds'. 4 June. Retrieve from: https://newsroom.accenture.com/news/more-than-half-of-consumers-would-pay-more-for-sustainable-products-designed-to-be-reused-or-recycled-accenture-survey-finds.htm (accessed 30 October 2020).

Airbnb (2019) 'Update on the Airbnb community'. 18 September. Retrieve from: https://news.airbnb.com/update-on-the-airbnb-community/ (accessed 3 February 2020).

Alexander, L., and Moore, M. (2016) 'Deontological ethics'. Retrieve from: https://plato.stanford.edu/entries/ethics-deontological/ (accessed 3 February 2020).

Allwood, E. H. (2016) 'Why Diesel is about to start advertising on Pornhub', *Dazed*, January. Retrieve from: http://www.dazeddigital.com/fashion/article/29089/1/why-diesel-is-about-to-startadvertising-on-pornhub (accessed 3 February 2020).

Alvesson, M. (1994) 'Critical theory and consumer marketing', *Scandinavian Journal of Marketing*, 10(3), 291–313.

American Marketing Association (AMA) (2020) 'Statement of ethics'. Retrieve from: https://www.ama.org/codes-of-conduct/ (accessed 3 February 2020).

Anon. (2014) 'The art of deceptive advertising: From brown shoe polish on burgers to hairspray for brighter ingredients, how commercials trick us into buying their products', *Mail Online*, 11 June. Retrieve from: http://www.dailymail.co.uk/femail/article-2655351/The-art-deceptive-advertising-From-brown-shoe-polish-burgers-hairspray-brighter-ingredients-commercials-trick-buying-products.html (accessed 3 February 2020).

Anon. (2015) 'BP and Deepwater Horizon: A costly mistake', *The Economist*, 2 July. Retrieve from: http://www.economist.com/news/business-and-finance/21656847-costly-mistake (accessed 3 February 2020).

Anon. (2019) 'Horse meat trial: Judgements made after six years, but another scandal is possible', *Foodwatch*, 30 April. Retrieve from: https://www.foodwatch.org/en/news/2019/horse-meat-trial-judgements-made-after-six-years-but-another-scandal-is-possible/ (accessed 30 October 2020).

Atiyeh, C. (2019) 'Everything you need to know about the VW diesel-emissions scandal', *Car and Driver*, 4 December. Retrieve from: https://www.caranddriver.com/news/a15339250/everything-you-need-to-know-about-the-vw-diesel-emissions-scandal/ (accessed 3 February 2020).

Bannerman, L. (2015) 'I won't lose weight, says angry model', *The Times*, 16 October. Retrieve from: https://www.thetimes.co.uk/article/i-wont-lose-weight-says-angry-model-csbtczmrtkp (accessed 3 February 2020).

Baudrillard, J. (2005) *The System of Objects* (trans. J. Benedict), London: Verso.

BBC News (2013) 'Transocean agrees to pay $1.4bn oil spill fine'. 3 January. Retrieve from: http://www.bbc.co.uk/news/business-20905472 (accessed 3 February 2020).

Bendixen, M., and Abratt, R. (2007) 'Corporate identity, ethics and reputation in supplier–buyer relationships', *Journal of Business Ethics*, 76, 69–82.

Bliss, J. (2018) 'How this Dutch company made €44.9m in sales without advertising', Challenger Project. Retrieve from: https://thechallengerproject.com/blog/2018/how-this-dutch-company-made-49m-in-sales-without-advertising (accessed 30 October 2020).

Boutin, X., and Guerrero, G. (2008) 'The "loi galland" and French consumer prices. Conjoncture in France'. June. Retrieve from: https://www.insee.fr/en/indicateurs/analys_conj/archives/june2008_d1.pdf (accessed 7 April 2020).

Bradshaw S., and Howard, P. N. (2019) *The Global Disinformation Order 2019: Global Inventory of Organised Social Media Manipulation*. Retrieve from: https://comprop.oii.ox.ac.uk/wp-content/uploads/sites/93/2019/09/CyberTroop-Report19.pdf (accessed 7 April 2020).

Bridges, C. M., and Wilhelm, W. B. (2008) 'Going beyond green: The "why" and "how" of integrating sustainability into the marketing curriculum', *Journal of Marketing Education*, 30(1), 33–46.

Brown, J. (2019). How Tony's Chocolonely chocolate brand plans to end slavery. *Independent*, 10 May. https://www.independent.co.uk/life-style/food-and-drink/tonys-chocolonely-chocolate-brand-plans-end-slavery-netherlands-teun-van-de-keuken-a8874801.html (accessed 30 October 2020).

Bryant, B. (2011) 'Deepwater Horizon and the Gulf oil spill: The key questions answered', *The Guardian*, 20 April. Retrieve from: https://www.theguardian.com/environment/2011/apr/20/deepwater-horizon-key-questions-answered (accessed 30 October 2020).

Buchholz, R. A. (1991) 'Corporate responsibility and the good society: From economics to ecology—Factors which influence corporate policy decisions', *Business Horizons*, 34(4), 19–31.

Burton, D. (2001) 'Critical marketing theory: The blueprint?', *European Journal of Marketing*, 35(5–6), 722–43.

Carroll, A. B. (1991) 'The pyramid of corporate social responsibility: Toward the moral management of organization stakeholders', *Business Horizons*, 34(4), 39–48.

Conca, J. (2015) 'The Fukushima disaster wasn't disastrous because of the radiation', *Forbes*, 16 March. Retrieve from: https://www.forbes.com/sites/jamesconca/2015/03/16/the-fukushima-disaster-wasnt-very-disastrous/ (accessed 30 October 2020).

Dangelico, R. M., and Pujari, D. (2010) 'Mainstream green product innovation: Why and how companies integrate environmental sustainability', *Journal of Business Ethics*, 95(3), 471–86.

Daniels, J., and Holmes, C. (2005) *Responsible Marketing to Children: Exploring the Impact on Adults' Attitudes and Behaviour*, London: Business in the Community.

Davidson, H. (2014) 'Body Shop removes all its products from Chinese duty free stores', *The Guardian*, 12 March. Retrieve from: https://www.theguardian.com/

world/2014/mar/12/body-shop-removes-products-from-chinese-duty-free-stores (accessed 30 October 2020).

Deloitte (2019) '2020 global marketing trends: Bringing authenticity to our digital age'. Retrieve from: https://www2.deloitte.com/content/dam/Deloitte/uk/Documents/consultancy/deloitte-uk-consulting-global-marketing-trends.pdf (accessed 30 October 2020).

Diller, H. (2008) 'Price fairness', *Journal of Product & Brand Management*, 17(5), 353–55.

Drash, W. (2019) 'Whistleblowers: Company at heart of 97,000 % drug price hike bribed doctors to boost sales', *CNN*, 30 April. Retrieve from: https://edition.cnn.com/2019/04/30/health/mallinckrodt-whistleblower-lawsuit-acthar/index.html (accessed 30 October 2020).

Elegido, J. M. (2011) 'The ethics of price discrimination', *Business Ethics Quarterly*, 21(4), 633–60.

Ethical Consumer Research Association (2018) 'Ethical consumer markets report 2018'. Retrieve from: https://www.ethicalconsumer.org/research-hub/uk-ethical-consumer-markets-report (accessed 7 April 2020).

European Union (2006) Directive 2006/114/EC of the European Parliament and of the Council of 12 December 2006 concerning misleading and comparative advertising. Retrieve from: https://eur-lex.europa.eu/legal-content/EN/TXT/PDF/?uri=CELEX:32006L0114&from=EN (accessed 3 February 2020).

Fairtrade International (2019) '2018–2019 annual report: choosing a fairer future through trade'. 15 November. Retrieve from: https://www.fairtrade.net/library/2018-19-annual-report-choosing-a-fairer-future-through-trade (accessed 3 February 2020).

Ferguson, D. (2019) 'Food waste: How to get cheap grub and help save the planet', *The Guardian*, 6 July. Retrieve from: https://www.theguardian.com/environment/2019/jul/06/food-waste-how-to-get-cheap-grub-and-help-save-the-planet (accessed 30 October 2020).

France 24 (2019) 'France to phase out single-use plastics starting January 1'. 31 December. Retrieve from: https://www.france24.com/en/20191231-france-begins-phasing-out-single-use-plastics (accessed 3 February 2020).

Ginsberg, J. M., and Bloom, P. N. (2004) 'Choosing the right green marketing strategy', *MIT Sloan Management Review*, 46(1), 79–84.

Greene, J. (2020) 'Microsoft pledges to remove more carbon than it produces by 2030', *Washington Post*, 16 January. Retrieve from: https://www.washingtonpost.com/technology/2020/01/16/microsoft-climate-change-pledge/ (accessed 3 February 2020).

Gwyther, M. (2015) 'The real thing: Ain't what it used to be', *Management Today*, 42(3), 45–6.

Hamari, J., Sjöklint, M., and Ukkonen, A. (2016) 'The sharing economy: Why people participate in collaborative consumption', *Journal of the Association for Information Science and Technology*, 67(9), 2047–59.

Harrison, R., Newholm, T., and Shaw, D. (2005) *The Ethical Consumer*, London: SAGE Publications.

Hern, A. (2018) 'Cambridge Analytica: How did it turn clicks into votes?', *The Guardian*, 6 May. Retrieve from: https://www.theguardian.com/news/2018/may/06/cambridge-analytica-how-turn-clicks-into-votes-christopher-wylie (accessed 30 October 2020).

Hult, G. T. M. (2011) 'Market-focused sustainability: Market orientation plus!', *Journal of Academic Marketing Science*, 39, 1–6.

Hult, G. T. M., Mena, J. A., Ferrell, O. C., and Ferrell, L. (2011) 'Stakeholder marketing: A definition and conceptual framework', *AMS Review*, 1(1), 44–65.

Hunt, S. D., and Vitell, S. (1986) 'A general theory of marketing ethics', *Journal of Macromarketing*, 6(1), 5–16.

Hunt, S. D., and Vitell, S. J. (2006) 'The general theory of marketing ethics: A revision and three questions', *Journal of Macromarketing*, 26(2), 143–53.

Hursthouse, R., and Pettigrove, G. (2016) 'Virtue ethics'. Retrieve from: https://plato.stanford.edu/entries/ethics-virtue/ (accessed 3 February 2020).

Hussain, A., and Torres, M. P. (n.d.) 'Time to pick up pace of dynamic electricity pricing', *Frontier Economics*. Retrieve from: http://www.frontier-economics.com/uk/en/news-and-articles/articles/article-i6106-time-to-pick-up-pace-of-dynamic-electricity-pricing/ (accessed 3 February 2020).

ICC/ESOMAR (2016) *International Code on Market, Opinion and Social Research and Data Analytics*. Retrieve from: https://www.esomar.org/uploads/pdf/professional-standards/ICCESOMAR_Code_English_.pdf (accessed 30 October 2020).

Intergovernmental Panel on Climate Change (IPCC) (2018) *Summary for Policymakers of IPCC Special Report on Global Warming of 1.5°C Approved by Governments*. Retrieve from: https://www.ipcc.ch/2018/10/08/summary-for-policymakers-of-ipcc-special-report-on-global-warming-of-1-5c-approved-by-governments/ (accessed 30 October 2020).

International Trade Centre (2019) 'The European Union market for sustainable products'. Retrieve from: http://www.intracen.org/uploadedFiles/intracenorg/Content/Publications/EU%20Market%20for%20Sustainable%20Products_Report_final_low_res.pdf (accessed 3 February 2020).

Jones, R. (2019) 'The end of a scandal: Banks near a final release from their PPI liabilities', *The Guardian*, 24 August. Retrieve from: https://www.theguardian.com/money/2019/aug/23/ppi-end-of-a-scandal-banks-final-release-liabilities-deadline (accessed 30 October 2020).

Kull, A. J., Mena, J. A., and Korschun, D. (2016) 'A resource-based view of stakeholder marketing', *Journal of Business Research*, 69(12), 5553–60.

Lexico (2020) 'Ethics'. Retrieve from: https://www.lexico.com/definition/ethics (accessed 3 February 2020).

McCurry, J. (2016) 'Former Tepco bosses charges over Fukushima meltdown', *The Guardian*, 29 February. Retrieve from: https://www.theguardian.com/environment/2016/feb/29/former-tepco-bosses-charged-fukushima (accessed 3 February 2020).

Mason, C, and Simmons, J. (2014) 'Embedding corporate social responsibility in corporate governance: A stakeholder systems approach', *Journal of Business Ethics*, 119(1), 77–86.

Marx, K. ([1867] 1990) *Capital: Critique of Political Economy, Vol. 1*, London: Penguin.

Maytom, T. (2016) 'Pornhub becomes Diesel's top referral website following ad deal', *Mobile Marketing*, 21 March. Retrieve from: https://mobilemarketingmagazine.com/pornhub-becomes-diesels-top-referral-site-following-ad-deal (accessed 30 October 2020).

Mintel (2013) 'Coca-Cola brings anti-obesity push to the UK'. 11 April. Retrieve from: https://reports.mintel.com/display/590204/ (accessed 30 October 2020).

Mintel (2019) 'Fashion & sustainability—UK, August'. Retrieve from: https://reports.mintel.com/display/972478/ (accessed 30 October 2020).

Mintel (2020) 'The ethical traveller—UK, February'. Retrieve from: https://reports.mintel.com/display/1003782/ (accessed 30 October 2020).

Morris, D. (2008) 'Negative campaigning is good for America', *US News & World Report*, 6 October. Retrieve from: https://www.usnews.com/opinion/articles/2008/10/06/dick-morris-negative-campaigning-is-good-for-america (accessed 31 October 2020).

Newman, K. (2001) 'The sorcerer's apprentice? Alchemy, seduction and confusion in modern marketing', *International Journal of Advertising*, 20(4), 409–29.

Nielsen (2015) 'The sustainability imperative: New insights on consumer expectations'. 15 October. Retrieve from: https://www.nielsen.com/wp-content/uploads/sites/3/2019/04/Global20Sustainability20Report_October202015.pdf (accessed 31 October 2020).

ONS (2018) *Spending Patterns of UK Households, with Findings taken from the Living Costs and Food Survey (LCF)*, London: Office for National Statistics.

Packard, V. O. (1960) *The Hidden Persuaders*, Harmondsworth: Penguin.

Patagonia (2018) *Annual Benefit Corporation Report*. Ventura, CA.: Patagonia.

Peattie, K. (2001) 'Towards sustainability: The third age of green marketing', *Marketing Review*, 2(2), 129–46.

Peattie, K., and Crane, A. (2005) 'Green marketing: Legend, myth, farce or prophesy?', *Qualitative Market Research*, 8(4), 357–70.

Pine, B. J., and Gilmore, J. H. (1999) *The Experience Economy: Work is Theatre and Every Business a Stage*, Boston, MA: Harvard Business School Press.

Pike, J. (2015) *Project Fear: How an Unlikely Alliance Left a Kingdom United But a Country Divided*, London: Biteback.

Porter, M. E., and Kramer, M. R. (2006) 'The link between competitive advantage and corporate social responsibility', *Harvard Business Review*, 84(12), 78–92.

RHA (2018) 'Truck cartel claim'. Retrieve from: https://cdn2.hubspot.net/hubfs/3387682/documents/RHA_Truck_Cartel_Booklet_2018.pdf (accessed 3 February 2020).

Rushe, D. (2014) 'Halliburton reaches $1.1bn settlement over Deepwater Horizon spill', *The Guardian*, 2 September. Retrieve from: https://www.theguardian.com/environment/2014/sep/02/halliburton-11bn-settlement-deepwater-horizon-spill (accessed 31 October 2020).

Saren, M. (2011) 'Critical marketing: Theoretical underpinnings', in G. Hastings, K. Angus, and C. Bryant (eds), *The Sage Handbook of Social Marketing*, London: Sage, 95–107.

Scheufele, D. A., and Tewksbury, D. (2007) 'Framing, agenda setting and priming: The evolution of three media effects models', *Journal of Communication*, 57(1), 9–20.

Scottish Government (2018) 'Policy: Food and drink'. Retrieve from: https://www.gov.scot/policies/food-and-drink/ (accessed 24 September 2019).

Scottish Government (2016) 'Summary transport statistics'. Retrieve from: https://www.transport.gov.scot/publication/scottish-transport-statisticsno-35-2016-edition/sct01171871341-03/ (accessed 31 October 2020).

Shankar, A. (2009) 'Reframing critical marketing', *Journal of Marketing Management*, 25(7–8), 681–96.

Sharma, A., Gopalkrishnan, I. R., Mehotra, A., and Krishnan, R. (2010) 'Sustainability and business-to-business marketing: A framework and implications', *Industrial Marketing Management*, 39(2), 330–41.

Shaw Hughner, R., McDonagh, P., Prothero, A., Shultz II, C. J., and Stanton, J. (2007) 'Who are organic food consumers? A compilation and review of why people purchase organic food', *Journal of Consumer Behaviour*, 6(2–3), 1–17.

Sheth, J. N., Sethia, N. K., and Srinivas, S. (2011) 'Mindful consumption: A customer-centric approach to sustainability', *Journal of the Academy of Marketing Science*, 39(2), 21–39.

Sinnott-Armstrong, W. (2019) 'Consequentialism'. Retrieve from: https://plato.stanford.edu/entries/consequentialism/ (accessed 3 February 2020).

Smithers, R. (2019) 'Whirlpool recalls more than 500,000 washing machines over fire risk', *The Guardian*, 17 December. Retrieve from: https://www.theguardian.com/business/2019/dec/17/whirlpool-washing-machines-to-be-recalled-over-fire-hazards-in-uk (accessed 31 October 2020).

Stop Climate Chaos (2019) '70% of people in Scotland support further action on climate change amid surging levels of concern, poll shows'. 1 April. Retrieve from: https://www.stopclimatechaos.scot/70-of-people-in-scotland-support-further-action-on-climate-change-amid-surging-levels-of-concern-poll-shows/ (accessed 24 September 2019).

Tadajewski, M. (2010) 'Towards a history of critical marketing studies', *Journal of Marketing Management*, 26(9–10), 773–24.

Tyko, K. (2020) 'Coronavirus price gouging: Face masks prices increased 166% on Amazon, report finds', *USA Today*, 11 March. Retrieve from: https://eu.usatoday.com/story/money/2020/03/11/amazon-price-gouging-report-coronavirus-face-masks/5007990002/ (accessed 7 April 2020).

van Dam, Y. K., and Apeldoorn, P. A. C. (1996) 'Sustainable marketing', *Journal of Macromarketing*, 16(2), 45–56.

Vaughan, A. and Rushe, D. (2017) 'Starbucks vows to hire 10,000 refugees as US companies condemn US travel ban', *The Guardian*, 30 January. Retrieve from: https://www.theguardian.com/business/2017/jan/30/trump-travel-ban-starbucks-hire-10000-refugees (accessed 31 October 2020).

Warren, T. (2018) 'Google fined a record $5 billion by the EU for Android antitrust violations', *The Verge*, 18 July. Retrieve from: https://www.theverge.com/2018/7/18/17580694/google-android-eu-fine-antitrust (accessed 3 February 2020).

Wilkie, W. L., and Moore, E. S. (1999) 'Marketing's contributions to society', *Journal of Marketing*, 63(3–4), 198–218.

Willsher, K. (2019) 'Horsemeat scandal: Four on trial in Paris accused of fraud', *The Guardian*, 21 January. Retrieve from: https://www.theguardian.com/uk-news/2019/jan/21/horsemeat-scandal-paris-fraud-trial (accessed 31 October 2020).

Wong, J. C. (2019) 'The Cambridge Analytica scandal changed the world—But it didn't change Facebook', *The Guardian*, 18 March. Retrieve from: https://www.theguardian.com/technology/2019/mar/17/the-cambridge-analytica-scandal-changed-the-world-but-it-didnt-change-facebook (accessed 31 October 2020).

World Commission on Environment and Development (WCED) (1987) *Our Common Future: The Brundtland Report*, Oxford: Oxford University Press.

World Nuclear Association (2020) 'Fukushima Daiichi Accident'. Retrieve from: https://world-nuclear.org/information-library/safety-and-security/safety-of-plants/fukushima-daiichi-accident.aspx (accessed 31 October 2020).

Young, W., Hwang, K., McDonald, S., and Oates, C. J. (2010) 'Sustainable consumption: Green consumer behaviour when purchasing products', *Sustainable Development*, 18(1), 20–31.

Index

D

E